Applications
of
Secondary School Mathematics
Readings from the *MATHEMATICS TEACHER*

edited by

Joe Dan Austin

Rice University
Houston, Texas

NATIONAL COUNCIL OF TEACHERS OF MATHEMATICS
1991

Library of Congress Cataloging-in-Publication Data:

Applications of secondary school mathematics: readings from the
Mathematics teacher / edited by Joe Dan Austin.
    p. cm.
    Includes bibliographical references and indexes.
    ISBN 0-87353-336-4
    1. Mathematics—Study and teaching (Secondary)   I. Austin, Joe
Dan.
QA12.A67 1991   91-5044
510′.71′2—dc20   CIP

Printed in the United States of America

CONTENTS

INTRODUCTION

THE NCTM *Curriculum and Evaluation Standards for School Mathematics* (1989) recommends an increased use of real-world applications in teaching mathematics in grades 5–8 and in grades 9–12 (pp. 70, 126). Applications should be used both to motivate students and to apply the mathematical theory. Publications that suggest how applications can be used in instruction and indicate some applications teachers might use include *Applications in School Mathematics* (NCTM 1979) and *A Sourcebook of Applications of School Mathematics* (NCTM 1980). This book is intended to supplement these publications with additional applications in mathematics to use with secondary school mathematics students. The articles in this volume were selected from the *Mathematics Teacher* issues of the past fifteen years. These articles often use mathematics from several courses. Such is often the nature of applications—the necessary mathematics is not always neatly enclosed within curriculum boundaries.

The articles are grouped into chapters that reflect the main secondary school mathematics courses. An article is placed at the highest level of mathematics needed for understanding its contents. Often, though, the material in an article may be used in several courses by selecting the appropriate parts.

Each chapter begins with a short introduction outlining some early historical applications of the topic and containing a brief overview of the articles in the chapter. References are given for readers desiring additional information. Although the historical origin of a mathematical field is not always needed to meet instructional goals, some understanding of the origin should be part of a teacher's knowledge. Not *all* mathematics was developed as a direct response to real-world problems, but this text will make a case that much of what is currently taught in secondary school mathematics classes has such origins.

Two cautions merit mention when applications become a major focus of curriculum or instruction. The first is that usefulness must not become the sole justification for inclusion in the curriculum. Such a narrow view was seen when applications were stressed in the 1930s. For example, in 1939 Charles Prosser claimed that because of usefulness, "business arithmetic is superior to plane or solid geometry; . . . learning the techniques of selecting an occupation, to the study of algebra; simple science of everyday life to geology; simple business English to Elizabethan Classics" (Hofstadter 1962, p. 346). The second caution is that the structural aspect of mathematics is necessary for mathematics to develop and advance. Without an understanding of the structure, mathematics would seem to consist of hundreds of isolated problems, each requiring a special trick to solve. Hardy (1940) argues that "what is useful above all is *technique*, and mathematical technique is taught mainly through pure mathematics" (p. 74). This position seems extreme for precollege mathematics instruction. However, it illustrates that although applications may have a fundamental role in mathematical instruction, one cannot ignore the value of the mathematical structure.

REFERENCES

Hardy, Godfrey H. *A Mathematician's Apology.* Cambridge: At the University Press, 1940.

Hofstadter, Richard. *Anti-Intellectualism in American Life.* New York: Random House, 1962.

Joint Committee of the Mathematical Association of America and the National Council of Teachers of Mathematics. *A Sourcebook of Applications of School Mathematics*. Reston, Va.: The Council, 1980.

National Council of Teachers of Mathematics. *Applications in School Mathematics*. 1979 Yearbook of the National Council of Teachers of Mathematics, edited by Sidney Sharron. Reston, Va.: The Council, 1979.

_____ . *Curriculum and Evaluation Standards for School Mathematics*. Reston, Va.: The Council, 1989.

_____ . *Historical Topics for the Mathematics Classroom*. Thirty-first Yearbook of the National Council of Teachers of Mathematics. 2d ed. Reston, Va.: The Council, 1989.

1

USING APPLICATIONS IN TEACHING

You can read the articles in this book for your own enjoyment and professional enrichment, but it is hoped that you will use the text more directly in your teaching. Here are two questions for reflection: What is an application? and How can applications be used in teaching mathematics?

To answer the first question, consider the following problems:

● The area of a 2 × 2 square is 4. How does one change each side to make a new square with twice the original area?

● In the town of Konigsberg in the eighteenth century, seven bridges crossed the river Pregel. They connected the two islands in the river with each other and with the opposite banks. Is is possible to cross the seven bridges in a continuous walk without recrossing any of them? (See fig. 1.1.)

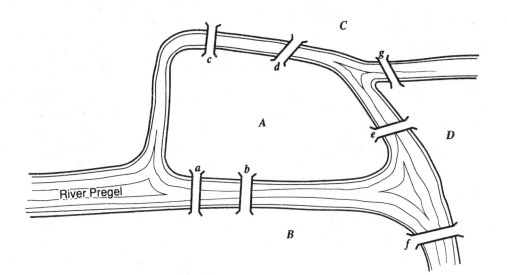

Fig. 1.1. Königsberg bridges

● A loaf of bread is divided among four people. How much bread does each receive if the ratios of the amount each receives are

$$\frac{2}{3} : \frac{1}{2} : \frac{1}{3} : \frac{1}{4} ?$$

● God granted him to be a boy for the sixth part of his life, and adding a twelfth part to this, He clothed his cheeks with down. He lit him the light of wedlock after a seventh part, and five years after his marriage He granted him a son. Alas! late-born wretched child; after attaining the measure of half his father's life, chill Fate took him. After consoling his grief by this science of number for four years he ended his life. [Find how long he lived.]

Socrates (469–399 B.C.) posed the first problem in *Meno* (Plato 1956). It is the example used in his illustration of the Socratic teaching method. The second problem was solved by

Euler in 1735. His solution began the mathematical field of graph theory. (See Newman, [1953] for Euler's solution and Chartrand [1977] for an introduction to graph theory.) The third problem is from the Rhind Mathematical Papyrus, one of the oldest collections of mathematical problems, written in ancient Egypt no later than the nineteenth century B.C. (Chance [1979] discusses the mathematical content of the Rhind Papyrus.) The fourth example is from a mathematics book called the *Greek Anthology*, published in the fourth century A.D. (Paton 1918).

Which problems are applications? The first problem is an application because it solves a physical problem, although it was used in a philosophical discussion to illustrate a teaching method. The second is an application to a physical problem that is intriguing, though perhaps appearing frivolous if one is unaware of the mathematical consequences of Euler's solution. The third application may solve a physical problem, but it is more likely that it was made up for students to apply or practice previously learned techniques. This is an application in the sense of the "Application" items in National Assessment of Educational Progress reports or International Studies of Mathematical Achievement. The fourth problem is clearly designed to practice mathematics, since we would not expect to need to solve a problem to find a person's age. The answer came first, and then the problem was created. Ironically, this problem is the only surviving evidence of the age of the Greek mathematician Diophantus when he died [84]!

These four applications, however, may not be appropriate for your students. Applications for classroom instruction must be appropriate for the course curriculum and for the students' backgrounds and interests. A student's background is not just mathematical background; it may also include other knowledge necessary to understand the application. Such background, especially if technical, must be taught with the application or must be a prerequisite for the application.

In this book the focus is on real-world problems and not on problems invented to practice the mathematics taught. This does not mean that you cannot use applications to practice and improve mathematical skills. Rather, it means the focus is on problems where it is natural to use the mathematics to better understand something in the real world or something about the problem.

The second question for reflection is how applications can be used in teaching. There are three main ways applications have been used in teaching mathematics. The most common method seems to be to teach some mathematical content and then introduce some problems or applications at the end of the unit. This approach seems designed to achieve the following goals:

- Students learn new mathematical content.
- Students apply or practice the mathematics they have learned.
- Students see applications of what they have learned.

This approach focuses on the mathematics and not on any initial understanding needed to understand the applications. However, when applications are at the end of a unit, students often consider them the most difficult part of mathematics and not essential to the content. Also, when applications are at the end of the unit, they are easily skipped. If the applications are skipped, students will not understand why mathematics is useful and will probably not be empowered to use mathematics to solve problems in the physical world.

A second method of using applications in teaching is to present them at the beginning of a unit. Discovery teaching often uses this procedure. In the development of much of mathematics, applications come first. A problem arises that cannot be easily solved, and the mathematics is developed to solve the problem. Science classes usually introduce the applications first; then the mathematics becomes a tool to better understand the physical world. When the teacher introduces applications at the beginning of a mathematics lesson, the goals include the following:

- Students learn that mathematics applies to real problems.
- Students learn that applications are an essential introduction for the problem-solving process because they often suggest mathematical questions.
- Students learn the mathematics necessary to understand the solution to the application.

A third way to use applications in mathematics teaching is to use them throughout the unit. Applications can introduce the unit and form the focus of group or individual projects in the unit to extend or synthesize ideas. Simple applications review skills and concepts previously learned. This interweaving of applications can show many situations where the mathematics is useful.

Although you may have to experiment to see which approach is preferable in your classes, applications should be used more regularly than they were in textbooks written before the publication of the *Curriculum and Evaluation Standards*.

The articles in this book give a sampling of the many possible applications that can be used in teaching precollege mathematics. There are two indexes—one by application area and one by mathematical area—to help locate articles to use in your classes. Use an entire article or only parts of it, but it is important to incorporate applications to increase the students' understanding of the usefulness of mathematics and of the mathematical content itself. Applications can also provide a useful context for problem solving, and you may find that applications help answer the perennial student question, "Why do we need to know this?"

For additional suggestions on using applications in teaching school mathematics, the articles in *Applications in School Mathematics* (NCTM 1979) are especially recommended.

In the readings in this section, Kennedy discusses the nature and origins of real-world applications in mathematics. Hilton, an eminent mathematician, reflects on applied and theoretical mathematics and on how each relates to the mathematics curriculum. Perham and Perham describe a precollege course on mathematical decision theory, stressing applications from areas other than science and technology. Swetz discusses the critical role of mathematical modeling in linking mathematical applications and problem solving.

REFERENCES

Chace, A. B. *The Rhind Mathematical Papyrus.* 2 vols., 1927–29. Reprint (2 vols. in 1). Reston, Va.: National Council of Teachers of Mathematics, 1979.

Chartrand, Gary. *Introductory Graph Theory.* New York: Dover Publications, 1977.

National Council of Teachers of Mathematics. *Applications in School Mathematics.* 1979 Yearbook of the National Council of Teachers of Mathematics. Reston, Va.: The Council, 1979.

Newman, James R. "Leonhard Euler and the Königsberg Bridges." *Scientific American* (July 1953), pp. 66–70. Reprinted in *Mathematics: An Introduction to Its Spirit and Use*, edited by Morris Kline, pp. 121–24. San Francisco: W. H. Freeman & Co., 1979.

Paton, W. R., ed. *The Greek Anthology.* New York: G. P. Putnam's Sons, 1918.

Plato. *Meno.* In *Great Dialogues of Plato*, edited by Eric H. Warmington and Philip G. Rouse. New York: New American Library, 1956.

Mathematics in the Real World, Really

By DAN KENNEDY, Baylor School, Chattanooga, TN 37401

Just in case the title of this article is not a sufficient warning to the reader that the contents fall short of being profound, let me assure all who have read this far that you are not likely to learn much mathematics in these pages. Indeed, it is the very triviality of these applications that prompted me to write this paper.

I have found that mathematicians in general, and mathematics teachers in particular, tend to refer rather blithely to the Real World when pointing out a known application of a given morsel of mathematics when, in fact, the world they speak of might be fairly remote from their own acquaintance with reality. The unreal qualities of some of our classic Real World problems have been widely discussed by more capable pundits than I, so let me simply capture the essence of their case with a favorite rhetorical question from Zalman Usiskin: "Where *is* this guy who rows *upstream* at a *constant rate* for *two hours?*" The rhetorical answer, of course, is that he is in the Real World. Sure he is.

Once one begins to question the reality of these Real World applications, however, it is difficult to stop. Mixing three pounds of nuts at $2.00 a pound with x pounds of nuts at $4.50 a pound to make a mixture worth $3.00 a pound, for example, seems like a perfectly reasonable task for a nut vendor, but I will confess to never having done it. Indeed, I have solved scores of mixture problems in the classroom (presumably, the Unreal World), yet never once have I had the occasion to solve such a problem for real. Neither have I cut squares from the corners of a rectangular piece of cardboard and folded up the sides to contain a maximum volume, nor launched a rocket straight up with velocity v_0, nor slid a ladder down a vertical wall by pulling the

bottom away at a constant rate—even though, as a mathematics teacher, I can tell you what to expect when I do any of these things.

Frankly, most of the mathematical applications that crop up in my Real World are rather pedestrian, especially when compared to the challenges confronted daily by the folks in the exercises in textbooks. The same is probably true of a great many mathematics teachers and even of a great many research mathematicians outside their areas of research. Yet I would wager that each of us, at one time or another, has experienced that "Magic Moment" when the Real World has presented, directly in our path, an unanticipated locked door for which our training has serendipitously supplied us with the key. Since I am old enough to have acquired some interesting examples of this phenomenon, and young enough to remember them, I shall offer a few here as one mathematician's view of the Real World.

The Magic Retail Numbers

This example is so simple that I feel it must happen all the time. If it has not happened to you, I hope it does someday, under circumstances as favorable as these.

The father of one of my former students owns a retail store that sells wine, et cetera, and one afternoon I happened to be purchasing a fifth of et cetera. Realizing that I taught mathematics and concluding incorrectly that I would be interested in a discourse on the travails of retail pricing, the proprietor began telling me how difficult it was to compute the discounted shelf price of a bottle on the basis of the wholesale cost. To make his point, he demonstrated the problem with a case of wine that cost him $37.50. Dividing by 12, he arrived at a price of $3.125 for each bottle. He computed that the 20 percent markup would be $.625, which he added to the base price to get $3.75. He then computed the state tax and added it on, the local tax and added it on, and a 10 percent discount and subtracted it, finally arriving at a shelf price for this particular wine. Oh, he lamented, what he would not give for a magic formula that would enable him to do this in one step!

You see what I mean by the "Magic Moment."

Praying that I could demonstrate this formula without making it appear too easy, I stroked my chin thoughtfully and said that, yes, I thought I could help him. Was this always the procedure for wines? Yes, he said. Same numbers but different wholesale costs. And for other beverages? Almost the same, but the markup was a different fixed percentage. Stroking my chin a few more times for effect, I savored the moment, much as a poker player must savor a royal flush, and then unsheathed my calculator. Now then, I said, trying to look serious, what were those percentages again?

When the calculator had multiplied two products of the form

$$(1 + p_1)(1 + p_2)(1 + p_3)(1 - p_4)$$

for the percentages corresponding to the various markups, taxes, and discounts, I presented the wide-eyed merchant with two numbers written on a paper bag, assuring him that multiplication by these numbers would do the trick in the dreamed-of single step. When he tried the wine number on his $3.125 burgundy and discovered that it worked to the penny, I thought the man was going to cry. I was unaccustomed to seeing high school algebra bring this much joy to anyone, and I was rather unprepared for the reverence that I had suddenly earned from this man, but since I had no intention of charging him for my services, I rationalized that allowing him to regard me as the second coming of Isaac Newton would be fair compensation.

There was no charge for my order that day, and I still cannot walk into that store within a month of Christmas without being forced to accept a free bottle of champagne. The paper bag on which I had written the magic numbers is still displayed on the wall of the office.

The Bypass

Some bits of mathematical knowledge are so uninteresting in themselves that one feels obliged to embellish reality to find an application that is worth talking about. Such is the case with the relatively trivial observation that the circumference of a circle varies directly as the radius, that is,

$$\Delta r = \left(\frac{1}{2\pi}\right)\Delta C$$

for a circle of any size. Many puzzle fans are probably familiar with the classic application of this principle to the case of a steel band wrapped tightly around the equator of the earth. First you hypothesize the existence of such a band; then you hypothesize the addition of an extra ten feet, after which the enlarged band is spaced evenly above ground level all the way around the earth. The problem, then, is to decide whether you could crawl under it. If you have heard this problem before, then you can probably recall your initial disbelief on discovering that, yes, you could crawl under it, and that, in fact, you could do so while a person with a sixty-inch waistline heaved through right beside you. This no-longer-quite-so-uninteresting formula shows the clearance (Δr) to be a roomy $10/2\pi$ feet.

Obviously, nobody is about to suggest that this classic problem is from the Real World, but, of course, that is precisely its charm. Once you know the answer you must still perform a small leap of faith just to accept it, and performing the experiment on a grapefruit will do little to ease your incredulity. However, when the same principle unlocks one of those doors in your Real World, the solution takes on a different level of significance.

I was driving along an interstate highway one day, approaching a major city. As with most major cities, a circular bypass went around the center of town, with signs inviting drivers to save time by going around the city. The alternative, as usual, was to follow the interstate through town along a diameter, proceeding at a slower pace because of increased traffic, and thus losing time despite the shorter distance. I usually do what is expected of me in these instances and take the bypass, but this time the signs gave me sufficient advanced warning to ask myself, Just how much slower would the traffic need to move along the diameter to make the bypass a time-saver? I thought about the problem for a moment, decided that I needed to know the diameter of the city, concluded that I would surely crash if I tried to extract that information from the road map while cruising along a crowded interstate, and almost abandoned the problem—when the Magic Moment suddenly intervened: the radius was irrelevant to the problem! Since the ratio of distances involved (a semiperimeter and a diameter) was $\pi/2$, the traveling times would be the same if the ratio of average speeds were $\pi/2$, regardless of the size of the circle.

Rounding 55 mph to 60 mph for computational convenience (an excuse that is unlikely to stand up in traffic court), I concluded that I would save time going through town if I could average $(2/\pi)(60)$ mph—a little less than 40 mph, which I figured I could beat with ease. With the smug confidence of a mathematician who knows he has beaten the Real World, I sneered at the bypass exit and went barreling along the diameter.

Ten miles later I encountered a forty-five-minute delay on the downtown expressway while a fleet of wreckers removed a stalled truck from the main bridge. Nobody ever said that the Real World plays fair.

The Elliptical Table

The following events actually happened to a friend of mine, Bryce Harris, and the story is one of my favorites about the Real World.

Before he retired from teaching mathematics and acquired more time to pursue his craft, Bryce had already become a skilled woodworker, turning out some very beautiful pieces: clocks, cabinets, hobbyhorses, and all varieties of furniture. He had a fairly well equipped woodworking shop behind his home, near Gatlinburg, but apparently he did not have a router that would perform all the tricks he needed. Figuring it was worth a try, he stopped by one of the professional furniture-making establishments in Gatlinburg and asked if they would allow him to use their router during slow periods. The man in charge was quick to reply that this would be impossible, for reasons that Bryce accepted. A conversation about their craft ensued, during the course of which Bryce happened to comment on a particularly fine elliptical table that was in the latter stages of production. The man agreed that he was proud of that particular piece, but he assured Bryce that he would never have chosen that shape if it had not been specifically commissioned, due to the enormous difficulty of getting it to come out right. Bryce asked the man how he went about making an ellipse, and the man explained his method: First you fold a paper into quarters, and then you very carefully cut a smooth arc that starts and finishes at right angles to the fold. If it looks good when you unfold it, you have your pattern; otherwise, you must try again. It usually takes several tries to get a smooth arc.

Bryce nodded sagely. After all those years of teaching conic sections, he was experiencing a Magic Moment. He asked the furniture maker if he had some string and a couple of thumbtacks. Sure, said the man. Well then, said Bryce, in his best poker face, let me show you a little trick.

Not many of us get the opportunity to walk into the jungle on the day of a total eclipse and have a little fun with the natives, but the sensation is probably not unlike the one you experience when you fix two ends of a loose string to a board, pull it taut with a pencil, and twirl off a perfect ellipse in front of a skilled artisan who has wasted whole afternoons trying to luck into one using paper and scissors.

From that moment on, Bryce was extended full use of any machine in that Real World shop, any time he wanted.

The Senior-Trip Schedule

Sometimes a Magic Moment occurs when you solve the problem at hand, but it can also occur when you save everyone the trouble of trying, by explaining that it cannot be solved. Part of the satisfaction one derives from this situation is that it is so rare in the Real World. Most of us, for example, go through life armed with the knowledge that you cannot trisect an angle with a compass and an unmarked straight-edge, but then nobody in the Real World ever asks us to do it.

Once they determine that we are mathematicians, however, people do ask us to do all kinds of things, especially to solve scheduling problems. Some of these are straightforward, and some are clearly impossible (seven teams, each team plays every other team twice, three games a day for ten days), but the solution of the solvable and the declaration of the impossible in these instances are rarely satisfying enough to qualify as Magic Moments. I would not have considered a scheduling problem capable of such stature until the time they tried to reschedule the senior trip.

For the past ten years, our seniors have closed out their high school days with a six-day outdoor experience known as the "senior trip." The format that has evolved over the years calls for the class to be divided into twelve heterogeneous groups, each with a faculty participant whose instinct for survival is somewhat deficient. Six different activities are scheduled for the six days, and each group is paired with a companion group for the duration of the trip.

Six pairs, six days, six activities: what we veteran schedulers refer to as a "piece of cake." Indeed, this scheduling problem (called a Latin square) has so many different solutions that one can impose such additional niceties as the separation of any two river activities with a day on land. A typical schedule appears in table 1.

The schedule in table 1 was considered to be ideal until someone suggested that it would be better if we could encourage more interaction between classmates without sacrificing the special chemistry of the groups. The obvious solution was to pair the groups differently each day. Thus was born the Senior Trip Scheduling Problem, a child of the Real World, and it did not waste much time finding its way to "someone who knows math," in this case, me. Since the director of the senior trip is also the chairman of our English department, I clearly had no way to refuse the challenge.

While he was still explaining the particulars of the desired schedule, with the attention to irrelevance that so characterizes the Real World, I had already redefined the problem in my own mind: two different Latin squares with rows and columns labeled as in table 1, one for groups A, C, E, G, I, and K, the other for groups B, D, F, H, J, and L. When superimposed, no two *pairs* of overlapping groups could be the same.

By the time he finished issuing the challenge, I had arrived at the Magic Moment. I told him it could not be done.

That I was able to reach this conclusion so suddenly was a definite shock to my colleague and, indeed, it even amazed me. Somewhere in the course of my mathematical studies I had encountered a Real World

TABLE 1					
Day	Ropes Course	Rafting I	Rock Climbing	Rafting II	Nature Hike	Canoe Trip
1	A–B	C–D	E–F	G–H	I–J	K–L
2	C–D	E–F	G–H	I–J	K–L	A–B
3	E–F	G–H	I–J	K–L	A–B	C–D
4	G–H	I–J	K–L	A–B	C–D	E–F
5	I–J	K–L	A–B	C–D	E–F	G–H
6	K–L	A–B	C–D	E–F	G–H	I–J

problem concerning military officers marching in a 6 × 6 formation, a problem that was allegedly posed to Leonhard Euler, who could not solve it, but that was finally resolved more than a century after his death. The solution called for two 6 × 6 Latin squares satisfying the same independence condition (called orthogonality) as the one required for the senior trip schedules. Euler, unable to find such a pair, conjectured that the problem was impossible because 6 was twice an odd integer. He was unable to prove that conjecture, which was understandable, since it was eventually shown to be false. The 6 × 6 problem, however, did turn out to be impossible, and it is now known to be the *only* case (larger than 2 × 2) for which these orthogonal Latin squares fail to exist (Liu 1968, 369–70).

In some ways, this kind of deflating response to a Real World problem is more impressive to a champion of the liberal arts than the anticipated cranking out of the solution. My colleague could hardly believe I was serious. One *more* day or one *fewer* day on the senior trip and we could have had our schedule, but just because we happened to have *six* days, we were doomed? This was the stuff of classical tragedy, not algebra. The beautiful irony seemed to mitigate the disappointment of being unable to schedule the mixed groups, and it obviously amused the director to learn that a number could be so capricious; but a total defeat at

the hands of the number 6 is Real World mathematics at its dramatic best, and such a performance could not pass before an English teacher unappreciated. I acquired a new mystique simply for having known of this sorcery, whereas I might have gotten a wink and a handshake for solving the problem if it had been solvable. For my own part, naturally I was grateful that my training in the Unreal World had prepared me for this particular Magic Moment; otherwise I might be on my sixth ream of paper trying to schedule an impossible dream.

These anecdotes are surely not unique, but I hope they were worth relating in these pages. If they only serve to remind you of your own Magic Moments, when mathematics gave you the opportunity to open unexpected doors in your Real World and step proudly through, then they will have served a valuable purpose. As mathematicians we must cherish those moments, and as teachers we must communicate their excitement to those who would learn mathematics from us.

You can only vicariously row upstream at a constant rate for so long before you become very, very tired.

REFERENCE

Liu, Chung L. *Introduction to Applied Combinatorial Mathematics*. New York: McGraw-Hill Book Co., 1968. ●

Cryptanalysis in World War II —and Mathematics Education

By PETER HILTON, State University of New York, Binghamton, NY 13901

One tragic aspect of the First World War (1914–18), so far as Britain was concerned, was that no effective use was made of the skills and talents of young British scientists, mathematicians, engineers, and experts in other relevant areas. Such people simply entered the armed services, usually the army, and fought in the infantry and other combat battalions. I am not arguing that the lives of such specialists are inherently more valuable than those of other mortals and that they should therefore be kept safe, but it is surely obvious that such people should be using their skill and expertise in the war effort, rather than doing a job that could be done equally well by somebody else. (Indeed, one may lament the death in two world wars of some of England's finest young poets: Rupert Brooke in World War I and Sidney Keyes in World War II. It is hard to argue that they should have been excused from conscription, but their loss was a heavy one.)

Fortunately, by the time of the Second World War, this lesson had been learned, and those with skills relevant to the effective conduct of the war were employed, broadly speaking, where they could be most useful. Thus it came about that a somewhat motley collection of young (and, in a few cases, not so young) mathematicians were gathered together in Bletchley Park in Buckinghamshire, England, to participate in the astonishing enterprise of trying to decipher German (and Japanese) codes. The intention was nothing less than the daily reading of the secret signals passing between the German High Command, its ships at sea (including U-boats), air force, and army groups, and this goal was successfully

This article is based on an invited lecture at the NCTM Banquet, Detroit, April 1983.

achieved! No wonder that Churchill described this effort as "Britain's secret weapon," a weapon far more effective than the buzz bombs and the rockets that Werner von Braun designed for a German victory, a weapon absolutely decisive, in the judgment of many, in winning the war for the Allies.

It was my good fortune to be a member of that team of cryptanalysts whose work proved to be so extraordinarily successful. I was recruited early in January 1942 and remained until the end of the war. I have chosen to recall these events now for two reasons. I want to pay tribute to the person whose contribution to our success far exceeded that of any other individual, Alan Turing, and I want to draw attention to certain implications of that success for the teaching of mathematics, implications that I regard as of great importance as we continue the ongoing process of reconsidering the curriculum at all levels.

Alan Turing and the Computer

It is a rare experience to meet an authentic genius. Those of us privileged to inhabit the world of scholarship are familiar with the intellectual stimulation furnished by talented colleagues. We can admire the ideas they share with us and are usually able to understand their source; we may even often believe that we ourselves could have created such concepts and originated such thoughts. However, the experience of sharing the intellectual life of a genius is entirely different; one realizes that one is in the presence of an intelligence, a sensitivity of such profundity and originality that one is filled with wonder and excitement.

Alan Turing was such a genius, and those, like myself, who had the astonishing and unexpected opportunity, created by the strange exigencies of the Second World War, to be able to count Turing as colleague and friend will never forget that experience, nor can we ever lose its immense benefit to us.

Alan Turing

Turing was a mathematician, a logician, a scientist, a philosopher—in short, a thinker. It is not possible to convey the full, rich flavor of his thought in all these varied domains, but the skilled expositor can, with care, explain the nature of the ideas without stooping to vulgarization. Such a comprehensive exposition is now available to us in the fine biography by Andrew Hodges (1983). Nevertheless, the phase of Turing's creative life that will most appeal to the reader's curiosity must be that in which he was making a unique and absolutely fundamental contribution to the winning of World War II by developing and establishing the basic methods of deciphering enemy codes.

Much has been written in recent years of the astonishing success of "Britain's secret weapon," but Hodges's is the first book to do justice to Turing's part in that great story. Others of us shared the excitement of successful achievement; some, like the mathematician Max Newman, deserved great credit for providing the organizational framework—not to be confused with its antithesis of bureaucratic structure—essential to the full exploitation of that success; but Turing stood alone in his total comprehension of the nature of the problem and in devising its solution—essentially by

inventing the computer. (Of course, the process of invention was also occurring independently elsewhere; one must cite the pioneering work of John von Neumann in the U.S.A.)

Naturally, these ideas did not arrive suddenly and fully formed in Turing's head in 1940. Before the war, in 1935, he had done fundamental work in mathematical logic and had invented a *concept* that has come to be known as a Turing machine. His purpose was to make precise the notion of a computable mathematical function, but he had in fact provided a blueprint for the most basic principles of computer design and for the foundations of computer science.

Essentially, a Turing machine is a machine that can receive a tape on which is printed a finite sequence of symbols drawn from a finite alphabet. The machine can scan any place on the tape and erase or change the symbol it finds. It must be understood that this machine was, to Turing

Turing made precise the notion of a computable mathematical function.

in 1935, a "thought experiment"; it was, in fact, a brilliant conceptual innovation, bringing precision to the hitherto rather vague notion of a mathematical procedure. However, during the war, it became essential to build machines that could contribute to the decoding of secret messages. Thus prototypes of the Turing machine were actually built (they were called, rather colorfully, "Bombes" and "Colossi") to decipher the German signals encoded on the Enigma and similar machines.

After the war, Turing continued his work on the development of a computer, first at the National Physical Laboratory (NPL) and then at Manchester University. Max Newman had gone from Bletchley Park to be head of the department of mathematics at Manchester University, and he invited Turing to take a readership in the department and to work with him on the design of a computer to be built by Ferranti. (I was also fortunate to be invited by Newman to take a junior position in the department in 1948.) Turing, who had been frustrated by bureaucratic obstructions at the NPL, was happy to accept, and the collaboration with Newman was crowned with success.

Unfortunately, the story of Turing's life is more the stuff of tragedy than of triumph. Turing was a homosexual. He was, characteristically, wholly honest about this and not ashamed, though he was never ostentatious about his preference. But after the war, the law against the expression of male homosexuality was upheld with rigorous fervor in Britain, and in January 1952, Turing, then a reader at Manchester University and a Fellow of the Royal Society, was arrested and charged with committing "an act of gross indecency" with his friend, Arnold Murray. Of course, he didn't deny the charge, but he did not agree that he had done anything wrong. He was bound over on condition that he submit to hormonal treatment designed to diminish his libido; the only obvious effect was that he developed breasts. He was placed on probation till April 1953; as a byproduct of his plea of guilty, he was no longer permitted to work as a consultant to Government Communications Headquarters (GCHQ), Cheltenham, where the codebreakers worked, nor to visit the United States. It is a tragic irony that British security services should have been mobilized to exclude Turing, whose contribution to the work of GCHQ was of such inestimable value during the war, but should have failed so conspicuously to detect the activities of the mole Geoffrey Prime. I. J. Good, a wartime colleague and friend, has so aptly remarked that it is fortunate that the authorities did not know during the war that Turing was a homosexual; otherwise, the Allies might have lost the war.

On 7 June 1954, just short of his forty-second birthday, Turing committed suicide by swallowing cyanide. He left no note, and it is generally supposed that, in the words of his friend and executor, Nick Furlong, "he planned for the possibility, but in the end acted impulsively." Hodges (1983) has told the story of Turing's life and death with honesty and candor and a fine sense of balance. We are in his debt for bringing us closer to a marvelous person and for chastening our intolerant society.

Pure and Applied Mathematics

I now want to turn my attention from the poignant story of Alan Turing to a very different matter. What inferences can we draw from the success of that group of mathematicians during the Second World War? Let us remember that the German Intelligence (*Abwehr*) believed right up to the end of the war that their ciphers were absolutely secure, so that our success was truly remarkable and, thus, requires explaining. I believe that in considering this question, we will make some important discoveries highly relevant to our task as teachers of mathematics.

The relevant facts are these. Gathered together at Bletchley Park was a group of mathematicians, each of whom would be described as quintessentially "pure." Each of them occupied a position in the academic world or aspired to such a position after the war. None of them had any experience in industry or in applying mathematics to problems in the real world, although all had, as undergraduates, taken courses in the classical areas of applied mathematics—statics, dynamics, and continuous mechanics. Each of them (modesty compels me to admit the possibility of an exception) was a good mathematician, but none was a specialist in statistics or probability theory. All were strongly motivated by a determination to do everything possible to win the war as quickly as possible. Remember that World War II was perceived as the last "good" war, in which right was unquestionably on one side and wrong on the other, without qualification. This fact would not have been held by my colleagues to justify the use of any means (for example, nuclear weapons) to win the war, but fortunately, our success would contribute significantly to victory without increasing human suffering. Finally, we *were* amazingly successful; despite Turing's enormous contribution, this effort was no "one man show," and it is impossible to imagine how we could have been more successful.

Given these facts, then, what are the hypotheses that might explain them? So far as I am concerned, they are these. To get people effectively to apply mathematics, the essential ingredients are (1) a strong education in mathematics; (2) the ability to think mathematically, to understand how to formulate a problem in precise mathematical terms (what Speiser called "Mathematische Denkweise," or "mathematical way of thinking"), and (3) a strong motivation to solve a given problem or problems. That these ingredients are necessary would, I believe, be denied by only few. That they are sufficient is less obvious and would be denied by many. For it is claimed that to create an appetite and an ability for applied mathematics, it is also necessary to train an individual in the actual practice of applying mathematics and to teach that individual some science to such a depth of understanding that he or she really understands what is involved in making progress in a scientific or engineering discipline by the use of mathematical methods. Moreover, those who put forward this point of view usually rate these two requirements so highly that they advocate curricula in which exigencies of time, if not inclination, and often both, compel them to reduce the mathematical content and to pay very limited attention to the need to develop understanding rather than mere skill. Thus, in effect, by apportioning priorities to take account of limited resources of time, these advocates actually recommend programs that pay insufficient respect to the first two ingredients listed earlier.

The facts might appear at first sight to support the idea that courses in "applied mathematics" are necessary to subsequent success in applying mathematics. Certainly I would not deny that such courses, *properly designed,* are highly desirable, but the evidence from our wartime experience does not suggest that they are necessary. In my judgment, the traditional courses to which we had been exposed had not been properly designed—they tended to be cookbook courses in which certain mechanical principles (e.g., laws of conservation or conditions of equilibrium) were mechanically applied to create standard mathematical problems of no particular interest. I am convinced that not one of us at Bletchley Park would have attributed our success to such courses. Moreover, I would argue, and have indeed argued elsewhere (Hilton and Young [1982]), that so-called pure mathematics offers many opportunities to develop a familiarity with the procedures of mathematical modeling, including numerical analysis and experimentation with special cases, which have often been regarded as the exclusive preserve of the applied mathematician.

If we now assume the truth of our hypotheses, what conclusions can we draw about the mathematical curriculum at the undergraduate and precollege levels? In the main, these conclusions are obvious. Our

> Successful mathematicians do not recognize barriers between different branches of mathematics.

mathematics courses must be rich in content; we must teach them so that understanding will result—this approach does not deny the importance of skill but views it more as a by-product than as the purpose of the major educational thrust; and we must inculcate an appetite for solving real-world problems. The second and third objectives do, perhaps, need elaboration if we wish to translate them into actual curricular recommendations. Mathematical understanding requires a recognition of the nature of mathematics as a unified field of human activity. This means that artificial barriers between mathematical disciplines must be broken down. A prime example of an area needing such reform is the current separation in our curriculum of geometry and algebra. Geometry on its own results in lots of questions with no systematic method of answering them; algebra, however, when taught in isolation, provides a whole gamut of answers to questions no student would ever think of posing or have any reason to pose. Thus, geometry without algebra is frustrating, and algebra without geometry is pointless, unmotivated, and boring. But the true relation of geometry to algebra is only one example, though a supremely important one, of the connections between various mathematical disciplines, whose artificial separation makes the acquisition of real mathematical understanding unnecessarily difficult.

The question of how to inculcate a desire to use mathematics in the solution of real-world problems is a profound one, not to be treated blandly in a relatively short article such as this. Suffice it to say that, plainly, a love of mathematics, an understanding of mathematics, and a curiosity about the real world are necessary to such a development. Beyond this, I wish to express the view that it is simply not realistic to expect many students to acquire, prior to their graduate studies, a sufficient grasp both of mathematics and of some science, say physics, to be able meaningfully to apply the one to the study of the other. (I emphasize that my remarks on the mathematical curriculum are not to be regarded as applying to graduate studies in applied mathematics.) I believe that it is perfectly reasonable to provide the students in a mathematics course, on an ad hoc basis, with the necessary concepts and scientific models to enable them to see how mathematics can be applied and what steps are essential in a genuine piece of applied mathematics. One advantage of this approach is that one runs a serious risk of discouraging students if one insists that they study a particular science in which they have no special interest. By varying the domain of the applications, one may hope to keep the students' interest alive.

Finally, I should like to deal with the possible objection that the experience of a group of mathematicians is scarcely relevant to the consideration of what, and how, we should be teaching our students at the precollege level. Even if it is generally conceded that for those destined to become mathematicians, their early education must affect their destinies, many would argue—do, in fact—that it is positively misleading to consider the needs of future mathematicians in designing the curriculum and teaching strategies. I contest this view strongly; but here I have only to argue that the particular kind of activity in which my colleagues were so successful renders this example relevant to the consideration of the features of a mathematics education that should help *all* students. In the Second World War we were not using our particular expertise as topologists, algebraists, or geometers; we were simply using a mathematical approach to a new problem. We faced that problem confidently and skillfully because we had confidence in the efficacy and universality of mathematical methods. The *degree* of our success was certainly a function of our competence as mathematicians, but the *fact* of our success was a reflection of the nature of mathematics itself. (Before World War II, military cryptanalysis had mostly been in the hands of linguists; but such experts were largely powerless in the face of the high-grade ciphers encountered in that war. Subsequent developments have further emphasized the importance of mathematics in cryptanalysis. Indeed, it is now regarded as a branch of applied mathematics.) If we believe that education in mathematics is an essential part of a preparation for intelligent living, and especially for quantitative reasoning, then we must conclude that cryptanalysis in World War II was a test case for mathematics and that the relevance of the arguments *adduced* in this article is thereby established.

REFERENCES

Hilton, Peter J., and G. S. Young, eds. *New Directions in Applied Mathematics*. New York: Springer Publishing Co., 1982.

Hodges, Andrew. *Alan Turing: The Enigma*. New York: Simon & Schuster, 1983. ◗

APPLICATIONS REVISITED

*A report of a one-semester course in applications drawn
from the management sciences.*

By ARNOLD E. PERHAM
St. Viator High School
Arlington Heights, IL 60004

and BERNADETTE H. PERHAM
Ball State University
Muncie, IN 47306

Mathematics teachers are sensitive to the benefits derived from relating the abstract notions developed in the mathematics classroom to the use of these notions outside the classroom. Applications have the potential to build interest and to offer direction in career options. Although students know very little about specific applications of mathematics in related fields, they nevertheless can identify the areas in which mathematics is used.

The teacher interested in implementing an applications approach to teaching mathematics is confronted with several well-known barriers. Although existing texts indicate areas of applications, frequently what is offered merely hints at the application and does not involve the student in it. Moreover, the search for serviceable, ready-made materials that fit easily into the topics currently being covered oftentimes proves fruitless. Then, too, if the teacher is to give more than a cursory look at applications, the inevitable conflict between the existing syllabus and the time allotment for new topics will need to be resolved. The resolution of the conflict will probably be made in favor of the "nuts and bolts" rather than the "frosting on the cake."

One approach to applications that deserves serious consideration is the introduction of applications courses into the mathematics curriculum. Moreover, we believe that a course in the mathematics of decision making in the management sciences should be given priority.

In recent years there has been a growing interest among our college-bound students in the applications of mathematics in fields other than science and technology. To meet their interests we have written materials for an applications course that draws students into an elementary consideration of how decisions are made in the management sciences. The one-semester course has been taught for the past five years at St. Viator High School, a school of 900 enrollment in north suburban Chicago. The results indicate that the course contains ideas that are not too sophisticated, that a sufficient number of students elect to take the course and find it both interesting and stimulating, and that the course is supported by administrators, teachers, and parents. At the times we have presented the course at mathematics conferences, many teachers have expressed interest in using the materials.

At this point, it is appropriate to look at the type of student who takes such a course and how the course fits into the curriculum. College-bound students enroll in the course, many of whom enroll at the same time in another course in the mainstream of the mathematics curriculum, for example, algebra 2-trigonometry, precalculus, or calculus. Others enrolled in the course have had algebra 2-trigonometry as juniors, but feel that they do not, at this point in their mathematics study, want to take precalculus. As an alternative to dropping mathematics or taking an available mathematics course for which they are overprepared, they enroll in the applications course in their senior year. The result is a class with a spectrum of abilities together with a junior/senior mix of population. This mix has not deterred the effectiveness of the course. In fact, the opposite is true. College-bound students with less ability in mathematics, or those with a high anxiety level, have enjoyed working with those who feel more comfortable in mathematics.

Currently, the course has four topics: game theory, linear programming, network theory, and Markov chains. Another topic, queuing theory, is in preparation. The topics are taught sequentially with each new topic introduced with a problem. For example, when game theory is introduced, it is done in terms of a popular finger-matching game played by adolescents. In game literature it is called two-finger Morra. The game is played by a pair of students who simultaneously display one or two fingers. Before the start of the game, one of the players agrees to win a point if the sum of the displayed fingers is odd; the other wins if the sum is even.

Students with high mathematics anxiety enjoy the course.

A number of questions are initially asked: is the game fair? does it make a difference whether a student chooses to be an even or odd player? The general student response is that it is a fair game and it is immaterial whether a student chooses to play even rather than odd. After the introduction of the game, the students study the kinds of mathematics needed to analyze the two-finger game. This leads to the basic types of games, namely, strictly determined and undetermined games and how one determines the strategies for optimizing the play for each partner. In the process, the students discover that the finger-matching game is an unfair game and it does make a difference whether they play even or odd.

The students are eventually led to see that game theory has the possibility of being employed in those situations that have *game* characteristics, for example, when one newspaper competes against another to capture a greater degree of circula-

tion, when submarines are hunted by aircraft, or in similar situations.

The other topics are introduced through a similar strategy: introducing a relatively simple problem that cannot be solved with their current mathematical skills, building new skills needed to solve this problem and similar ones, and theorizing on other possible applications of this kind of mathematics.

The problem used to introduce linear programming arises out of an imaginary toy factory. To date, this factory has produced only one model. Unfortunately, the demand for this toy has leveled off. The time has come to think about adding a luxury model to the line. The outlet stores indicate that they can sell all the luxury models made and keep the same level of sales among the standard cars. The profit would be higher on the luxury model and would use the same amount of material in production. However, it would take longer to make the luxury model.

At this point in time, the factory does not want to expand: it is becoming difficult to obtain plastics because of the oil crisis. Given the shortage of plastics, a fixed staff, and limited production facilities, what should the company do? The first impression of many students is that the company should produce only one model, namely, the luxury model. After some discussion it becomes clear that this is not the best decision. Linear programming gives them a tool whereby they can calculate the quantity of each model to make in order to optimize profits.

In the course of their exposure to this topic, the students are additionally motivated by some of the real-world applications of linear programming. An example they rarely forget is that one of the earliest applications of linear programming was in the Berlin airlift after World War II.

The automobile is again used to introduce the study of the Markov chain theory. In a mythical town, there are three automobile dealers: Ford, Chevrolet, and Buick. On a yearly basis each dealer tends to keep a certain percentage of his former business but loses the remainder to his competitors. If the trend continues what will the market look like for each of the companies after two years? three years? many years?

At points during the course, the students are asked to make up their own hypothetical problems. This section of the course tends to produce the most interesting examples. Oftentimes these problems are based on fictitious personal habits of students with a view of what their habits will be in some future time. For example,

> M. G. likes to play hockey; he does not like to study. In fact, M. G. has a rule: he never studies two nights in succession. If M. G. does not study tonight, the probability of his studying tomorrow night is 1/3. Since it is Tuesday, the probability of M. G. studying tonight is 0.7. If that is the case, what is the probability of M. G. studying Thursday night? In the long run, what percentage of the time does M. G. study?

The fact that some companies have used Markov chain theory to study personnel shifts between management positions and then predict what the distribution of office personnel will look like in the future also adds considerable interest to the study of the subject.

The final section of the course contains a collection of topics that can be loosely grouped under the topic, network theory. The topic is introduced by presenting the students with a complicated network and then asking how they would get from one point to another using the shortest distance path. The students are then asked if the shortest distance path is necessarily the shortest time path for the network at hand.

A study of this and similar problem situations leads to a consideration of how airlines save fuel in crossing the Atlantic and how Admiral Rickover used network theory to schedule the diverse assembly jobs in bringing the first atomic submarine to launching.

Students are frequently concerned about whether they possess the mathematics background necessary to profit from this course. After teaching the course for five years, we find that the students who benefit most are those who have the mathematical maturity associated with second-year algebra; that is, students should feel comfortable with variables and the techniques for the manipulation of variables.

Below is an outline of the four topics currently included in the course and the prerequisite topics from algebra and geometry.

I. Game theory
   A. Two-by-two games
      1. Saddle-point games
      2. Non-saddle-point games
      3. Mathematical expectation
      4. Methods for playing non-saddle-point games
   B. Games that can be reduced to two rows and two columns
      1. Row or column dominance
      2. Games with two rows and more than two columns
      3. Games with two columns and more than two rows
   Prerequisites: operations with signed numbers, definition of probability, solutions of linear equations in one variable

II. Linear programming
   A. Convex polygonal regions
   B. Proof that the objective function takes on its maximum value at a vertex
   C. Geometric solutions (limited to two variables)
   D. Simplex method
   E. Concept of duality
   F. Identifying from final tableaux the coordinates of the point where a maximum occurs and the coordinates where a minimum occurs
   Prerequisites: slope of a line, linear inequalities, graphing of equations in two variables, solution of simultaneous equations in two variables, concave and convex polygons

III. Network theory
  A. Concept of a graph
  B. Connected and disconnected graphs
  C. Definition of a network
  D. Minimal spanning trees
  E. Kruskal's algorithm for determining a minimal spanning tree
  F. The square of a directed network and its interpretation
  G. Applications
    1. Königsberg bridges—Euler's network.
    2. Why are there only five regular polyhedra?
  H. Connecting storage bins to assembly areas
  I. Critical path analysis
  J. Shortest path through a network
  Prerequisites: multiplication of polynomials, solution of linear equations in one variable, definition and characteristics of regular polyhedra.
IV. Markov chains
  A. Kemeny trees
  B. Stochastic processes
  C. Definition of a Markov chain
  D. Transition diagram and its corresponding transition matrix
  E. Powers of the transition matrix and their significance
  F. Fixed-point probability vector
  G. Markov chains with absorptive states
  H. Monte Carlo method
  I. Comparison of the Monte Carlo method and the Markov chain method
  Prerequisites: operations with signed numbers, definition of probability, solution of equations in one variable

Matrix theory is applied throughout the course. However, few incoming students would have experience in this area. To fill in this deficiency, the first three weeks of the course are spent in developing the elementary concepts of matrix theory. Mastery of the necessary skills is achieved through classroom instruction combined with a programmed learning package. The items covered are listed below.

  A. Definition and characteristics of a matrix
  B. Operations with matrices
  C. Identity matrices for addition and multiplication
  D. Determinant of a square matrix
  E. Matrix of cofactors
  F. Adjoint of a matrix
  G. Inverse of a matrix

One of the unexpected benefits of the course is that it has provided students who have a knowledge of computer programming with an opportunity to use their skill. Over the years these students have created a library of programs, which all students taking the course have found valuable. The course, then, not only gives students an opportunity to see how mathematics is used in a decision-making process but also to see that the computer is an efficient and useful tool in that process.

BIBLIOGRAPHY

Gardner, Martin. "Mathematical Games." *Scientific American* 234 (April 1976):126–30.

Graham, Ronald L. "The Combinatorial Mathematics of Scheduling." *Scientific American* 238 (April 1978):124–32.

Hoffman, Nathan. "The Weather as a Markov Process." *Mathematics Teacher* 69 (November 1976):542–45.

Mathers, Jolly. "The Barber Queue." *Mathematics Teacher* 69 (December 1976):680–84.

Nadler, Maurice. "A Geometric Interpretation of the SIMPLEX Method of Linear Programming." *Mathematics Teacher* 66 (March 1973):257–64.

Recommendations for the Preparation of High School Students for College Mathematics Courses. The Mathematical Association of America, 1225 Connecticut Avenue N.W., Washington, DC 20036.

Reeves, Charles A. "Network Theory—an Enrichment Topic." *Mathematics Teacher* 67 (February 1974):175–78.

Spaulding, Raymond E. "Recreation: Traceable Houses." *Mathematics Teacher* 67 (May 1974):423–25.

Willcutt, Robert. "Paths on a Grid." *Mathematics Teacher* 66 (April 1973):303–7.

When and How Can We Use Modeling?

By FRANK SWETZ

Increasingly over the past ten years, national conferences and committees investigating the state of North American mathematics education have urged an increased instructional emphasis on problem solving and mathematical applications (CBMS 1975; NCTM 1989). But despite these repeated recommendations and exhortations, in general, little progress has been made on the introduction and use of mathematical-modeling techniques in the secondary school classroom. In part, teachers are unsure about just what mathematical modeling is and why and how it should be incorporated into the curriculum. Let's examine each one of these issues separately.

Kinds of Modeling

Intuitively, the word *model* conjures up the image of a physical entity. A model in the usual sense of the word is a replica, frequently scaled down, of some object. Children and some hobbyists make model boats and airplanes. Their toylike models display many, if not all, the physical features of the real object in question. Some models actually function in a manner similar to the object they are imitating. Such models are said to be good if they emulate most of the properties and characteristics of the object they are portraying.

But the making of models is not limited to the recreational pursuits of children and hobbyists alone. A sculptor intent on producing a large statue in stone may first create a miniature design in a more easily workable medium, such as clay or plaster, and when he or she is satisfied with the design, will transfer and enlarge it through the use of measuring instruments to the block of stone to be cut. Automobile designers use a familiar process in fashioning new body prototypes. Easily manipulated and changed when necessary, models offer their users a certain degree of freedom for experimentation and control of expenses. In many industrial and technological situations, the design and use of models in planning and production processes is imperative.

Not all modeling is physical in nature. Theoretical models are collections of principles or rules that accurately describe the behavior of a phenomenon in the mind of an observer. Economists speak of "economic models," population planners employ "demographic models," and so on. When the principles of a theoretical model are mathematically based, then a mathematical model has been created. Thus, a mathematical model is a mathematical structure that approximates the features of a phenomenon of concern. The active process of devising a mathematical model is called *mathematical modeling*.

Mathematical Models

Mathematical models can take many forms. Some basic mathematical structures of the secondary school curriculum that readily lend themselves to modeling situations are numerical tables of data, graphs, equations (formulas), systems of equations or inequalities, and algorithms, including some contained in computer programs.

Consider the situation of an engineer working for a swimming-pool-accessory company who is given the task of determin-

Frank Swetz is a professor of mathematics and education at Pennsylvania State University at Harrisburg, Middletown, PA 17057, where among his duties he coordinates and supervises mathematics teacher-training programs. His pedagogical focus has centered on the humanization of the instructional process. This interest has taken him on excursions into ethnomathematics, the history of mathematics, and mathematical applications.

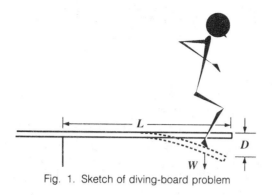

Fig. 1. Sketch of diving-board problem

ing the safety of a diving board constructed from a new synthetic material. One of her safety concerns is the amount of deflection a board experiences when a person stands on its free end. She analyzes the situation and determines that the principle factors affecting deflection, D, are the weight of the person in question, W; the length of the board, L; the cross-sectional shape of the board; and the material from which the board is made. See figure 1.

The length of the board is standard and is thus fixed, and the material of the board and its cross-sectional area are predetermined. This situation involves two variables, weight and deflection. The dependence of deflection on weight can easily be determined by applying different weights to the end of the board and recording the resulting deflection. The numerical table of values thus obtained serves as a model of the board's deflection under different weight loads. If the values are plotted on a graph, the graph itself can serve as a model. The numerical data can also yield a functional relationship, based on simple proportionality between weight and deflection, namely

$$D = \frac{W}{K}.$$

For convenience, since the engineer does not want to build a board and load it with weights, this last model, a simple equation, is the most useful. Seeking to refine her model, the engineer uses more advanced analytic methods to determine

$$K = \frac{3EI}{L^3}$$

and

$$D = \frac{WL^3}{3EI},$$

where E is the modulus of elasticity that depends on the material used and I is the moment of inertia of the board's cross-sectional area.

Next let us examine the steps inherent in this modeling process:

1. Determine the problem, in this instance, the effects of weight on diving-board deflection.

2. Isolate the factors of concern (W, E, I, D, L).
   a) Which are parameters? (E, I, L)
   b) Which are variables? (D, W)

3. Determine the mathematical relationships that exist between relevant factors and that are useful in solving the problem ($D = f(W)$).

4. Establish the relationship and form a model ($D = W/K$).

5. Test the model—determine values for known situations and examine accuracy.

6. Refine the model as required to obtain more useful or accurate information ($D = WL^3/3EI$).

In the refining of this model, the engineer may ask herself several questions. For example, "Will this relationship hold for all values of W?" "Does it have to?" The answer to both questions is, of course, no. The functional relationship between W and D will be linear only within a finite domain consisting of those values of W that do not strain the board to exceed its elastic limits. Since the diving board in question is a high board, ten feet above the water, it is usually not used by small children or large adults; therefore, using her experience, the engineer can safely fix the domain $80 \le W \le 300$.

Consider another modeling situation, one easily within the mathematical capabilities and interest of secondary school students (Sloyer 1986):

A freight-hauling company is initiating a helicopter service for short distance express hauls, that is, deliveries of less than 1000 miles. There are two ways freight can be hauled by a helicopter: internally or externally, slung beneath the body of the helicopter. There are advantages and disadvantages to both methods: external loading and unloading is quicker, but during flight, the external load produces a drag, slowing down the helicopter and extending delivery time. Assume the cargos carried are protected from the weather by coverings. When should the different methods be used?

A load master must determine the most economical method of loading to be used for deliveries within 1000 miles of the helicopter's base. He assumes that incurred cost is directly proportional to delivery time; therefore, he seeks a relationship between time, T, and delivery distance, D. He identifies the problem and determines the variables. To proceed further, he needs some actual data, so he makes test runs using a standard load. The results of the test are summarized in table 1.

From the data in table 1 we can find that the time required for an internally loaded helicopter, T_i, is given by

$$T_i = \frac{30}{60} + \frac{D}{144} + \frac{20}{60} = \frac{120 + D}{144}$$

and that the delivery time for an externally loaded helicopter, T_e, is

$$T_e = \frac{15}{60} + \frac{D}{120} + \frac{10}{60} = \frac{50 + D}{120}.$$

Next the load master decides to determine the values of D for which $T_e < T_i$; thus his mathematical model becomes

$$\frac{50 + D}{120} < \frac{120 + D}{144}$$

or

$$600 + 12D < 1200 + 10D,$$

so

$$D < 300 \text{ miles.}$$

Thus for deliveries under 300 miles, external loading is preferred, whereas internal loading should be used for deliveries that exceed 300 miles. What about deliveries of exactly 300 miles? He refines his model by testing the situation of 300 miles in the expression for T_i and T_e:

$$T_i = \frac{120 + 300}{144} = 2.9\text{h}$$

$$T_e = \frac{50 + 300}{120} = 2.9\text{h}$$

$T_i = T_e$ when $D = 300$ miles, but since external loading and unloading is quicker, the load master decides to use external loading for deliveries involving exactly 300 miles. On the basis of these modeling results the loading scheme is set as follows:

$0 < D \leq 300$—use external loading to reduce delivery expenses

$300 < D \leq 1000$—use internal loading to reduce delivery expenses

Why Modeling in the Curriculum?

An ultimate goal of mathematics teaching is to prepare young people to function knowledgeably and confidently in real-world problem-solving situations. Mathematical modeling is a paramount form of real-world problem solving. It brings into play a variety of mathematical skills and forces attention on the problem as a whole rather than on just a solution. The problem solver is compelled to define and clarify the problem with care. In understanding the problem the solution method is revealed.

Modeling is an especially perceptive form of problem solving. Usually, a model does not supply a specific answer but rather a range of answers that describe the behavior of some phenomenon. Understanding is of a dynamic, active nature rather than a static, passive one. The modeler experiences a sense of participation and control in the so-

TABLE 1
Internal-External Loading Comparisons

Loading Method	Average Speed (mph)	Time (min)	
		Loading	Unloading
Internal	144	30	20
External	120	15	10

lution process. Models can be mathematically manipulated by changing variables and parameters. For example, in the diving-board problem, an investigation of behavior can be made with weight, W, fixed and board length, L, varied; or the effect of different construction materials on the board's performance can be determined by varying E. The use of a mathematical model helps to achieve an understanding of how a diving board works.

Modeling helps expose the dynamics inherent in many problem situations. Consider the following problem:

> A lawn-service contractor wishes to establish his business in a new development of 400 homes. His lawn maintenance services cost \$275 a year for each customer. He knows from experience that in such a situation he can obtain about 100 customers but seeks more. To attract more customers, he makes an offer that for each "bonus customer" in excess of 100, he will give a \$1.50 discount to all customers in the development. Under this policy, how many customers will yield the greatest revenues for the contractor?

Assume that first-year algebra students have been given this problem. They have not learned about maximizing a function. How can they be guided to solve this problem? Just what is the problem? The problem is to *see* how revenues behave in relation to the number of acquired customers beyond 100. So the behavior of revenues had to be modeled. Using a calculator, some values can be obtained computationally and tabulated and a pattern of behavior sought. See table 2.

The data from table 2 indicate that for additional customers beyond 100, revenues increase, then revenues begin to fall. A more careful search pattern is warranted around $C = 150$. See table 3. Maximum revenues are found with 142 customers, allowing individual customers in the development a discount of \$63.00. The table of values serves as a model by showing that revenues increase for $100 < C \leq 142$ and decrease for $142 < C \leq 400$. A more succinct model would be

TABLE 2
Discounted-Customer Effect on Revenues

Number of Customers (C)	Charges to Each Customer (\$)	Total Revenues (R)
100	275	27 500
101	275 − (1.50)	27 623.50
102	275 − (1.50 × 2)	27 744
. . .	. . .	. . .
110	275 − (1.50 × 10)	28 600
. . .	. . .	. . .
150	275 − (1.50 × 50)	30 000
200	275 − (1.50 × 100)	25 000

the graph of the relationship $R = f(C)$ or the derivation of an actual revenue function for the situation,

$$R = 275C$$

for $1 \leq C \leq 100$ and

$$R = (C)(425 - 1.50C)$$

for $100 < C \leq 400$. Therefore, in advertising his special offer, the contractor should include the phrase "for a limited time only" so that he can discontinue the offer when he has acquired 142 customers.

After such a modeling experience, students can better appreciate such concepts as limit of a process and maximum. In the context of the modeling situation, the table of values and the graph obtained are more than just a collection of numbers or a picture. They have special meanings in their designation of mathematical behavior associated with a problem. Modeling allows for a better appreciation of the power of mathematics.

In modeling exercises, the mathematics

TABLE 3
Refined Customer-Revenue Search

Number of Customers (C)	Charges to Each Customer (\$)	Total Revenues (R)
160	275 − (1.50 × 60)	29 600
155	275 − (1.50 × 55)	29 837.50
151	275 − (1.50 × 51)	29 973.50
140	275 − (1.50 × 40)	30 100
145	275 − (1.50 × 45)	30 087

flows from the problem. Students recognize this fact. Mathematical modeling situations can also serve as a vehicle for introducing new concepts: investigations of population growth and natural-resource depletion lead to the use of exponential functions; interaction analysis and food-chain models employ matrix algorithms; and computer programs can generate simulation models of varied phenomena, such as the flight of a projectile.

How to Incorporate Mathematical Modeling?

The answer to this question, of course, depends on the knowledge, interests, and personality of the teachers involved and the ability of the classes to be taught. Although no hard-and-fast answer can be given, some observations and reflections can be offered. A modeling approach to problem solving should be incorporated gradually and in a low-key manner into all existing mathematics curricula. Words like *model* and *modeling* can be employed in appropriate situations. Steps in the modeling process can be followed and designated. When models are established, they should be identified—for example, "Here we have a model for the salesperson's commission"—explored, and manipulated (MMSC Project 1988). The separation and isolation of mathematical modeling or problem solving from the rest of the mathematics curriculum tends to raise suspicions in the minds of students that they are being exposed to something exotic or difficult. Hence, no need arises for separate courses or sections of a course devoted exclusively to mathematical modeling.

REFERENCES

Conference Board of the Mathematical Sciences (CBMS). *Overview and Analysis of School Mathematics Grades K–12*. Washington, D.C.: CBMS, 1975.

MMSC Project. *Mathematical Modeling in the School Curriculum: A Resource Guide of Classroom Exercises*. Middletown, Penn.: Pennsylvania State University at Harrisburg, 1988.

National Council of Teachers of Mathematics, Commission on Standards for School Mathematics. *Curriculum and Evaluation Standards for School Mathematics*. Reston, Va.: The Council, 1989.

Sloyer, Cliff. *Fantastiks of Mathematiks: Applications of Secondary Mathematics*. Providence, R.I.: Janson Publications, 1986.

2

ARITHMETIC

Arithmetic, derived from the Greek *arithmetike*, meaning "number science," is the oldest branch of mathematics. Surviving evidence of the antiquity of arithmetic includes a wolf's bone found in 1937 in Czechoslovakia. The bone is over 30 000 years old and has fifty-five deep notches. The first twenty-five notches are arranged in groups of five, with double notches separating these from the remaining thirty notches (Bunt, Jones, and Bedient 1976, p. 2). What the notches represent on this prehistoric bone is unknown, as is who made them. (It would be another 25 000 years before writing was finally developed in Sumeria around 3500 B.C.) However, the notches seem designed to match a number of objects being counted. There is a clear attempt to record the notches in an organized, concise way so that they may be easily recounted. The quest for a simpler representation for numbers was continued by the Babylonians, the Egyptians, the Greeks, and the Romans, to name only a few. The quest finally ended around A.D. 1000 when the Arabs developed the Arabic numerals used today. Amazingly, the notation

$$0, 1, 2, 3, 4, 5, 6, 7, 8, 9, 10, 11, \ldots$$

is today understood the world over, though the symbols are read in many different ways.

All early societies found arithmetic computations difficult. For example, the Rhind Papyrus contains school mathematics problems from early Egypt. The scribe Ahmes copied the text about 1650 B.C. from an earlier source dated about 1850 B.C. Problem 79 is the multiplication problem 2801 × 7. The solution of 19 607 is obtained as follows (the Egyptian notation is given in fig. 2.1):

	1	2 801
	2	5 602
	4	11 204
Total	7	19 607

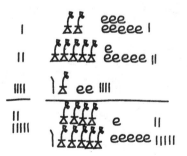

Fig. 2.1. Egyptian numerals

Aside from the first and last lines, each entry is twice the corresponding entry on the previous line. If the product were 2801 × 11, the fact that 1 + 2 + 8 is 11 would be used to select the numbers in the right-hand column to add. The smaller number is expressed

25

as the sum of powers of two. (Bunt, Phillip, and Bedient [1976] give additional details on computations in ancient Egypt.) Until the Arabic number system was developed, no simple algorithms for performing multiplication or division existed.

Two theoretical results were especially important in the development of arithmetic. The first was Euclid's proof, about 300 B.C. (Book 9, Proposition 20 of *The Elements*), that there are an infinite number of primes (Lott 1989, pp. 62–64). The second was the fundamental theorem of arithmetic, which states that every integer can be written uniquely as a product of primes, except for order. These two results were essential for an understanding of the mathematical structure of numbers. They would prove to be important in extending the number system beyond integers or ratios of integers.

Today the power of arithmetic lies both in its simple representation of numbers and in its computational algorithms. Arithmetic is the foundation of mathematics because of the central role of numbers. The properties and structure of numbers form the base of much that is studied in other mathematical areas, particularly algebra.

Using the Arabic notation for numbers and the computation algorithms, the authors of the articles in this section sample the numerous applications of arithmetic. Some articles evaluate expressions using computation. These are considered arithmetic or prealgebra because the expressions (or equations) are not derived using algebra. The articles by Knill and Fawcett, "This Is Your Life," and by Knill, "Mathematics in Forensic Science," use computations to answer questions about the human body. Human activities can also often be studied using arithmetic. Knill considers financial decisions in "Marketing Records." Gerber considers examples relating to speed in traveling, and Fawcett uses formulas in optics and computation to answer questions about cameras.

Even with computation algorithms, some computations are very tedious and are better done using a calculator. Johnson uses a calculator to consider problems from bank interest, and Vest uses calculators to study the costs of home ownership. (A derivation of the formula used by Vest is given by Soler and Schuster in chapter 4.)

Beyond computations in arithmetic, Knill and Fawcett use graphs to study travel speed in "Skidmarks Estimate Speed." Ewbank uses graphs to analyze patterns in sports records. Sconyers uses prime numbers to explain patterns found in insect populations. Usiskin uses the greatest integer to investigate rounding and a wide range of applications.

REFERENCES

Bunt, Lucas N., S. J. Phillip, and J. D. Bedient. *The Historical Roots of Elementary Mathematics*. Englewood Cliffs, N.J.: Prentice-Hall, 1976.

Lott, Fred W. "The Infinitude of Primes." In *Historical Topics for the Mathematics Classroom*. Thirty-first Yearbook of the National Council of Teachers of Mathematics. 2d ed. Reston, Va.: The Council, 1989.

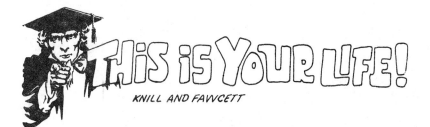

KNILL AND FAWCETT

1. You know how old you are in years, but do you know how old you are in days, hours, minutes, and seconds? When you try to find out, don't forget about the leap years!

The Respiratory System

2. The average person breathes at a rate of seventeen breaths per minute while at rest. Approximately how many breaths have you taken in your life?

3. Every time you breathe, you inhale about 0.6 liters of air.

   a. How much air have you taken in in one year?

   b. If only one-fifth of the air you breathe is oxygen, how much oxygen have you taken into your lungs in one day?

c. The body uses only one-twentieth of all the air that one inhales. How much of the total amount of air you have taken in in your life has been used? What percentage is this?

d. One-fifth of the oxygen you breathe in makes its way to the blood stream. How much oxygen gets into the blood in one day?

The Circulatory System

4. It is a fact that the smaller the size of an individual the faster the heartbeat. The average man's heart pumps at a rate of 70 beats per minute, the woman's is slightly more by 6 to 8 beats per minute, and a child's can be as high as 130 beats per minute. Find your own pulse and record the number of times your heart beats in 15 seconds. What is your heartbeat rate? Using this number as an average, find the approximate number of times your heart has beaten in a day, in a year, and in the last five years?

5. Find out your heartbeat rate after five minutes of vigorous exercise. By what percentage has your rate increased? Smoking also affects the rate. Look up how much it increases or decreases the rate per minute.

6. The human heart is approximately the size of a human fist. Measure your fist to determine the size of your heart. The mass of a man's heart is about 312 grams and a woman's is 255 grams.

7. For every heart-beat, 0.06 liters of blood is passed through the heart. In one week, how much blood goes through your heart?

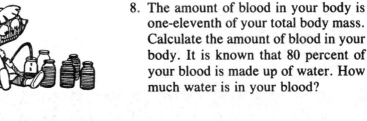

8. The amount of blood in your body is one-eleventh of your total body mass. Calculate the amount of blood in your body. It is known that 80 percent of your blood is made up of water. How much water is in your blood?

The Muscles

9. In a man, 40 percent of his total mass is muscle. However, only 30 percent of a woman's mass is muscle. Calculate the mass of muscle in your body.

The Skeletal System

10. The bones of your body are divided up as follows:

face	14	arm (2 × 3)	6
cranium	8	wrist (2 × 8)	16
ear (2 × 3)	6	palm (2 × 5)	10
throat	1	fingers (2 × 14)	28
spinal cord	26	hip (part of torso)	2
chest	25	legs (2 × 4)	8
collarbone	2	ankles (2 × 7)	14
shoulder (part of torso)	2	foot (2 × 5)	10
		toes (2 × 14)	28

What is the total number of bones in your body? What percentage of the bones are used for walking?

11. Find out the percentage of bones in each of the following: (a) head, (b) torso, (c) arms and hands, (d) legs and feet. Which section has the highest percentage of bones in it? Take your answer to one decimal place.

Answers: 3. (a) 5 361 120 L, (b) 2 937.6 L, (c) 1%, (d) 587.52 L. 10. (a) There are 206 bones in the body, (b) walking → 62/206 × 100 = 30.1%. 11. (a) Head → 28/206 × 100 = 13.6%, (b) torso → 57/206 × 100 = 27.7%, (c) arms and hands 60/206 × 100 = 29.1%, (d) legs and feet 60/206 × 100 = 29.1%.

Interesting Facts

1. The heart is linked by 160 934 km of pipelines to all parts of the body.
2. The length of time to completely digest one meal and discharge the waste is 48 hours. For example:

   6:00 p.m.—dinner eaten
   6:01 p.m.—first food enters stomach
   10:30 p.m.—stomach completely empty
   1:00 a.m.—food passes through the small intestine
   6:00 p.m.—next day, first waste is ready to leave
   6:00 p.m.—third day, last waste is ready to leave

3. The average adult body has 1.67 m² of skin.
4. A newborn baby has 26 billion cells in its body.
5. The average human body has 50 trillion cells.

MARKETING RECORDS

By GEORGE KNILL
Board of Education for the
City of Hamilton
Hamilton, ON L8N 3L1

The record industry provides many interesting applications of percent. In making a record, a company (the publisher) provides a studio, background musicians, a producer, technicians, and recording equipment as well as pays the artist for recording. These initial expenses can be substantial. The record company gets a return on this investment from marketing the record.

Some companies use the following method to determine the retail price of a record.

Transaction	% Mark-up
Publisher (record company) to Wholesaler	20%
Wholesaler to Rackjobber	15%
Rackjobber to Retailer	15%
Retailer to Consumer	40%

The rackjobber services a number of stores in an area providing them with the records they need.

If the initial cost to produce an album is $3.14, then

1. the publisher sells to a wholesaler, after a 20% mark-up, for

$$\$3.14 + \$0.63 = \$3.77$$

2. the wholesaler sells to a rackjobber, after a 15% mark-up, for

$$\$3.77 + \$0.57 = \$4.34$$

3. the rackjobber sells to a retailer, after a 15% mark-up, for

$$\$4.34 + \$0.65 = \$4.99$$

4. the retailer sells to the consumer, after a 40% mark-up, for

$$\$4.99 + \$2.00 = \$6.99.$$

Problems

1. How much would you pay for an album that cost a publisher $4.00 to produce? (Answer: $8.89)

2. If a double record album sells at a record store for $12.98, how much did it cost the publisher to produce? (Answer: $5.84)

Royalties

Every time a song is played on the air the radio station must pay $0.06 to the Royalty Society. From this amount, 15 percent is retained by the society for its expenses. Of the remainder, 75 percent goes to the record company and 25 percent goes to the songwriter.

Problem

On a network of 100 radio stations, each station played a particular song 4 times a day during the first two weeks after its release, 13 times a day during the next two weeks, 22 times a day for the next three weeks, and 9 times a day for the next three weeks. How much money would the royalty society, the record company, and the songwriter receive?

Solution

The number of times the song was played:

$$100(14 \times 4 + 14 \times 13 + 21 \times 22 + 21 \times 9) = 88\ 900$$

The total royalties are:

$$88\ 900 \times \$0.06 = \$5334.00$$

The society keeps:

$$\$5334.00 \times 0.15 = \$800.10$$

The remainder is:

$$\$5334.00 - \$800.10 = \$4533.90$$

The record company receives:

$$\$4533.90 \times 0.75 = \$3400.43$$

The songwriter receives:

$$\$4533.90 - \$3400.43 = \$1133.47$$

MATHEMATICS IN FORENSIC SCIENCE

By **GEORGE KNILL**
Board of Education for the
City of Hamilton
Hamilton, ON L8N 3L1

Knowing the exact physical dimensions of a victim of a crime is extremely useful in identifying the victim. When a skeleton is found, a forensic scientist uses the lengths of certain bones to calculate the height of the living person. The bones that are used are the femur (F), the tibia (T), the humerus (H), and the radius (R). See figure 1. When the length of one of these bones is known, one of the following formulas is used to determine the height. All measurements are in centimeters.

Male
$$h = 69.089 + 2.238\,F$$
$$h = 81.688 + 2.392\,T$$
$$h = 73.570 + 2.970\,H$$
$$h = 80.405 + 3.650\,R$$

Female
$$h = 61.412 + 2.317\,F$$
$$h = 72.572 + 2.533\,T$$
$$h = 64.977 + 3.144\,H$$
$$h = 73.502 + 3.876\,R$$

After the age of thirty, the height of a person begins to decrease at the rate of approximately 0.06 cm per year. This shrinkage must be considered when the age of the victim is known.

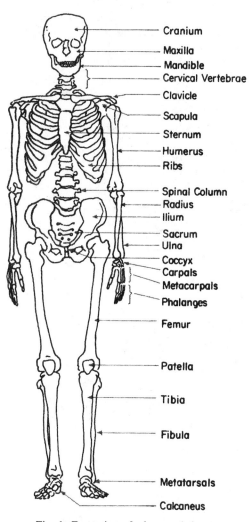

Fig. 1. Front view of a human skeleton

Problems

1. The femur of a 25-year-old male measured 49.7 cm. What was the height of the person?

2. The tibia of a 32-year-old female measured 33.5 cm. What was the height of the person?

3. Have students use the formulas to calculate the lengths of their femur, tibia, humerus, and radius.

4. Have students contact the forensic science branch of the police department to determine how mathematics is used in crime detection.

Answers: 1. 180.3 cm, 2. 157.3 cm.

APPLICATIONS

GEARS, RATIOS, AND THE BICYCLE

By DANIEL TIMOTHY GERBER

Inevitably a teacher will encounter students who see "no reason" to study mathematics beyond the basics. When asked why they are enrolled in a higher mathematics course, students usually mention college requirements. It then becomes the responsibility of the textbook author and the instructor to generate interest in mathematics. Authors generally include applied mathematics problems in their texts; however, students find such problems more interesting when they can directly acquire the information needed for solution. This approach is certainly a teaching advantage if the instructor is willing to bring props into the classroom. In this spirit, I have used a ten-speed bicycle to illustrate gear function because it is familiar to most students.

Understanding the workings of a ten-speed bicycle involves a knowledge of bicycle anatomy and gear function. A ten-speed bicycle has seven gears of interest. The two largest gears, the large and small sprockets, are permanently attached to the pedals. The bicycle chain links these sprockets with five sprockets (cogs) on the back wheel. Cogs vary in size and are used to regulate speed (see fig. 1).

Bicycle gears perform two functions. They increase or decrease the speed of applied motion and magnify or reduce the force that is applied (Bureau of Naval Personnel 1971, 161). The second function is of greatest interest as it applies to bicycles. To determine how gears increase or decrease speed, we must understand the relationship of one gear to another by calculating a ratio between them. To determine the ratios among all gears on a

bicycle, the number of teeth on each gear must be counted. Figure 1 diagrams the gear arrangement and gives measurements taken from a typical ten-speed bicycle. Gear ratios are calculated by comparing the number of teeth on the sprocket to the number of teeth on the cog. The large and small sprockets have fifty-one and thirty-nine teeth, respectively. In figure 1, a ratio was calculated for each sprocket:cog relationship by dividing the number of teeth on the sprocket by the number of teeth on the gear (i.e., the largest sprocket:largest cog ratio is 51/28 ≈ 1.8, or 1:1.8, which means that each time the sprocket makes one revolution, the cog makes 1.8 revolutions).

Two more principles of bicycle anatomy must be explained here. The large and small sprockets are directly fixed to the pedals.

Cog Size	Teeth per Cog	Ratio of Large Sprocket:Cog	Ratio of Small Sprocket:Cog
Largest cog	28	1:1.8	1:1.4
Second cog	24	1:2.1	1:1.6
Third cog	20	1:2.6	1:2.0
Fourth cog	17	1:3.0	1:2.3
Smallest cog	15	1:3.4	1:2.6

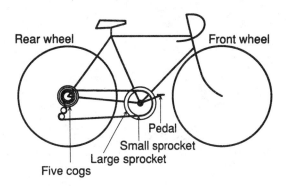

Fig. 1. Bicycle anatomy (1:10 scale) and sprocket:cog ratios

Daniel Gerber teaches chemistry and algebra at Westwood High School, Camilla, GA 31730. He is interested in mathematical applications in science and mechanics.

Thus, for each revolution the pedals make, both sprockets turn one revolution also. Likewise, each time the back wheel completes one revolution, each cog on the wheel turns one revolution also; however, the cyclist must pedal continuously. The sprocket:gear ratio becomes important in distance calculations.

The distance a cyclist travels in one revolution of the pedals is termed *gear* and is calculated using the circumference of the back tire and the sizes of the sprocket and cog (Delong 1974, 278). Gear is calculated in England and America using the general formula

$$\text{gear} = \left(\frac{\text{sprocket teeth}}{\text{cog teeth}}\right) \times \left(\begin{array}{c}\text{rear wheel diameter}\\\text{in inches}\end{array}\right).$$

Its metric equivalent is termed *development*, which is calculated using meters rather than inches. For example, if the chain links the small sprocket and the largest cog, then each time the cyclist pedals one full revolution the small sprocket also turns once. The cog rotates 1.4 times; therefore, the back tire (circumference ≈ 2.20 m) also turns 1.4 times. The development equals (1.4)(2.20 m) = 3.08 m. If the cyclist moves the chain to the second cog, the development equals (1.6)(2.20 m) = 3.52 m. The development increases as the sprocket:cog ratio increases. In table 1 we see an inverse relationship between gear size and development.

At this point we are able to calculate the speed of the bicycle. If the cyclist pedals 90 revolutions per minute (rpm) in the last example, the bicycle moves at (3.52 m)(90 rpm) = 316.80 m/min, or approximately 19 km/h. If the cyclist changes to the third cog, then the speed is (2.0)(2.20 m) = 4.40 m and (4.40 m)(90 rpm) = 396 m/min, or approximately 24 km/h. Table 1 shows an inverse relationship between gear (cog) size and speed. This relationship explains how gears increase or decrease the speed of applied motion. Having discussed gear, development, and speed calculations, we can focus on applied mathematics problems.

In the opening paragraph, I suggested that teachers bring a ten-speed bicycle into the classroom as a prop. Several direct measurements from a bicycle would enable students to perform all the calculations made in this article. Initially, they must count the number of teeth on each cog and sprocket, allowing them to set up their own version of figure 1. After counting teeth, all sprocket: cog ratios can be calculated. Sprocket:cog ratios can also be calculated by directly measuring the diameters for each and calculating circumferences. Note that each diameter is measured from the center of the chain as it sits on the gear and not from the top of the teeth. The ratio is calculated by dividing the sprocket's circumference by the cog's circumference. If the students' measurements are accurate, the new ratios will closely approximate those values already generated using teeth number.

Next, the students should directly measure the rear-wheel diameter (even if they know it is a twenty-seven-inch bicycle) and calculate the circumference. Wrap a string around the outside of the tire and measure

		TABLE 1			
		Distance and Speed Relationships			
Cog	Number of Teeth	Development[1] (Large Sprocket) (m)	Development[2] (Small Sprocket) (m)	Speed[3] (km/h)	Speed[4] (km/h)
Largest	28	4.01	3.06	22	17
Second	24	4.68	3.58	25	19
Third	20	5.61	4.29	30	23
Fourth	17	6.60	5.05	36	27
Smallest	15	7.48	5.72	40	31

[1] Development = (tire circumference)(51)/number of teeth.
[2] Development = (tire circumference)(39)/number of teeth.
[3] Calculates speed using ninety revolutions per minute of large sprocket
[4] Calculates speed using ninety revolutions per minute of small sprocket

its length to see how closely their calculated circumference approximates the "real" value. The students can now set up their own version of table 1. With sprocket:cog ratios and the circumference of a wheel, they can generate development values for their version. To generate speed values, I used ninety pedal revolutions per minute (rpm) (considered a "comfortable" racing speed); however, they may use any or several different values for the rpm. The students will have generated two tables of information from their own direct measurements.

Many interesting questions can be asked of the students on the basis of the information in their tables. (1) Will sprocket:cog ratios change when converting from metric to English units? Ratio values will be the same. (2) What would happen if a third larger or smaller sprocket or different-sized cogs were added? To best illustrate what would occur, the students can calculate additional ratio values (see fig. 1) by increasing or decreasing the number of teeth on a cog or sprocket. For example, if a cog with twelve teeth was added to a bicycle, the ratio of the large sprocket:cog would be 51/12, or 1:4.3, and the ratio of the small sprocket:cog would be 39/12, or 1:3.3. (3) If all gear ratios remained the same but a larger wheel was fitted on the bicycle, what would happen to all the speed and development calculations? Because all speed and development calculations include tire circumference in their formulas, an increase or decrease in tire size affects their values. For example, all speed and development calculations in table 1 were done using a tire circumference of 2.2 m. If a larger tire was used, a larger tire circumference would increase speed and development calculations.

Advanced students can be challenged by asking questions needing trigonometric solutions. Angular velocity (ω) equals displacement (θ) per unit time (t): $\omega = \theta/t$. In speed calculations (see table 1), an angular velocity of ninety revolutions per minute was used. Converted to rad/s, 90 rpm = 540 degrees/s = 3π/s. (4) Is the angular velocity of the sprockets different from that of the cogs? Figure 1 shows the ratios of sprocket revolution to cog

revolutions. For example, if the bicycle chain links the large sprocket to the largest cog, then for each revolution the sprocket makes the cog will rotate 1.8 times. Thus, the angular velocities of the sprocket and cog are different. (5) Is the angular velocity of the cogs the same as that of the rear wheel? Because the cogs and rear wheel rotate the same number of times per unit time, they all have the same angular velocity. (6) A cyclist is pedaling at ninety revolutions per minute. His bicycle chain links the largest sprocket and third cog. Using figure 1 to determine the sprocket:cog ratio, what is the angular velocity of the rear wheel? The rear wheel's angular velocity is (90 rpm)(2.5) = 225 rpm = 7.5π rad/s. (7) Why must we know the sprocket:cog ratio to determine the wheel's angular velocity? The rear wheel has the same angular velocity as the cog.

Linear velocity (v) equals angular velocity (ω) times the radius (r) of a point on a cog or wheel: $v = \omega r$. (8) Does a point on a tooth of the smallest cog have the same linear velocity as one on a tooth of the largest cog or a point on the rear wheel's rim? Even though the rear wheel and all the cogs have the same angular velocities, the different cogs and rear wheel have different radii; therefore, a point on the tooth of one cog has a different linear velocity from a point on a different-sized cog or a point on the wheel. (9) What is the linear velocity of a point on a tooth of the largest sprocket (0.12 m) in the foregoing problem? $v = \omega r = (3\pi$ rad/s) (0.12 m) = 0.36 rad–m/s.

The simple principles learned in this article can be applied to many different machines that employ gears in mechanical function. Common household items from the simple egg beater and electric clock to more complex power tools and motorized vehicles have gears. Having students list or bring to class common items that use gears should increase their interest in gear function, ratios, and applied mathematics.

REFERENCES

Bureau of Naval Personnel. *Basic Machines and How They Work*. New York: Dover Publications, 1971.

Delong, Fred. *Delong's Guide to Bicycles and Bicycling*. Radnor, Penn.: Chilton Book Co., 1974. ▰

applications

SKID MARKS ESTIMATE SPEED

By GEORGE KNILL
Ministry of Education
Willowdale, ON M2J 1W4

and GEORGE FAWCETT
Board of Education for the
City of Hamilton
Hamilton, ON L8N 3L1

It is common knowledge that the faster a vehicle is going, the greater the distance required to stop after the brakes are applied. Conversely, the greater the braking distance, the faster the car must have been going when the brakes were applied. In the case of accidents, it is often important to estimate the speed from the braking distance.

For a given speed the braking distance depends on the force slowing the vehicle down. The braking force depends on many factors, some of which include the following:

1. The condition of the brakes and brake linings
2. Pressure applied to the brake pedal
3. Nature and condition of the tires—snow tires, radial tires, worn, and so on

4. Type of surface—asphalt, concrete, brick, gravel, and so on
5. Air and surface temperature
6. Moisture, snow, ice, and so forth, on the surface
7. Foreign material on the surface—sand, mud, leaves, and so on
8. Traction devices, such as chains or studded tires

In spite of all the variables affecting the braking distance, there are three conditions under which a reasonable estimate of initial speed may be made from the braking distance:

1. All four tires skid for the full braking distance.

2. The car comes to a stop without hitting another object.

3. The coefficient of friction between tires and road surfaces is known.

The coefficient of friction is the force required to drag a car with all four wheels locked divided by the mass of the car. Approximate coefficients for a number of road surfaces have been obtained and are indicated on the left side of the chart.

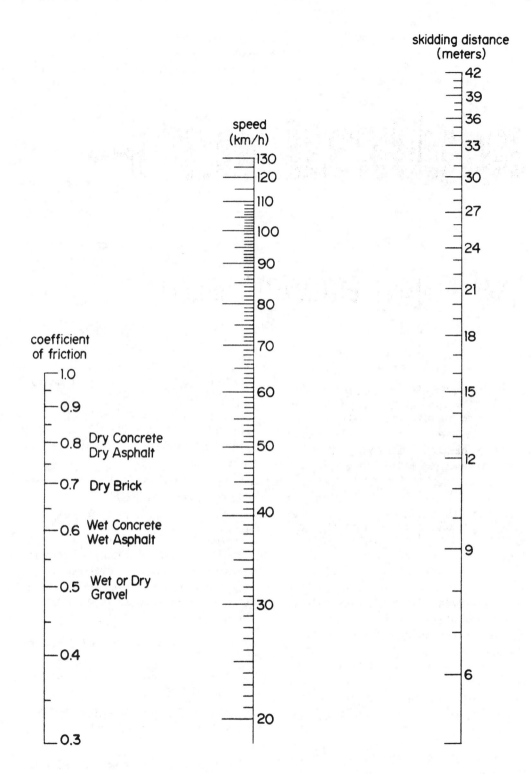

However, if you wish to determine the coefficient of friction for any given set of tires and road conditions and not use the approximate coefficients given on the chart, you may use the formula

$$f = \frac{S^2}{252D},$$

where f is the coefficient of friction, S the speed of the car (km/h), and D the braking or skidding distance in meters.

For example, for a stop in 12 m at a speed of 50 km/h,

$$f = \frac{S^2}{252D}$$

$$= \frac{50^2}{252 \times 12}$$

$$= \frac{2500}{3024}$$

$$= 0.83.$$

A nomogram provides a simple way of determining the speed of an automobile using the skidding distance. For example, if a car skidded 21 m on dry concrete, we draw a line from 0.8 on the left bar in the chart to 21 on the right bar. The line would cross the center bar at 65, indicating the speed of the car at the time the tires started to skid. Of course the car may have been traveling at 80 km/h and slowed down to 65 km/h before the tires started to skid. For this reason a speed determined from the chart is really a minimum speed.

The slope of a road is called its *grade:*

$$\text{GRADE} = \frac{\text{rise}}{\text{run}}$$

It is easier to stop a car when driving uphill than it is when driving downhill. An uphill grade increases the coefficient of friction (makes it easier to stop) by the value of the grade (slope). A downhill grade decreases the coefficient of friction by the value of the grade (slope).

Example

A car is traveling uphill. The grade (slope) of the hill is 0.2. The road surface is wet concrete. The coefficient of friction is then $0.6 + 0.2 = 0.8$. If the same car was traveling downhill on the same road, the coefficient of friction would be $0.6 - 0.2 = 0.4$.

Problems

1. A car skidded 24 m on a level gravel road. What was the speed of the car?

2. A car traveling uphill on a dry concrete road with a grade of 0.1 skidded 27 m. Find the speed of the car.

3. A car traveling downhill on a wet asphalt road with a grade of 0.2 skidded 30 m. Find the speed of the car.

4. If road conditions remain the same, what effect on the skidding distance does doubling the speed have?

Answers: 1. 55 km/h, 2. 78 km/h, 3. 55 km/h, 4. increases by a factor of 4.

PRIME NUMBERS—A LOCUST'S VIEW

By JAMES M. SCONYERS
19 Main Street
Quincy, MA 02169

Why is there a seventeen-year locust? In trying to answer this question, some people have been tempted to conclude that it's purely a matter of arithmetic. Can a case be made for bugs that calculate? Let's look at one explanation.

What is called the seventeen-year locust is actually the periodic cicada *magicicada septendecim*. It remains underground in the nymph stage for a period of seventeen years, emerges as an adult, lays eggs, then dies. The eggs hatch into nymphs and so on. An unanswered question about these periodic insects is the significance of the length of the cycle. Is it simply an accidental number? Or does the length of the cycle contribute in some way to the survival and well-being of the species?

There are both thirteen-year and seventeen-year locusts. There is not a twelve-year, six-year, or twenty-year locust. What possible advantage could there be for these insects to emerge every thirteen or seventeen years instead of some other interval?

The locust is the object of predation and parasitism by other insects, birds, and fungi. Not being particularly well endowed with defensive armor or weaponry, every stratagem of defense must be exploited. Though the evidence is circumstantial, some biologists strongly suspect that the seventeen-year period is an adaptation to avoid predators with periods synchronized to the locust's former period, from which the seventeen-year period evolved. In other words, the seventeen-year cycle itself appears to have an advantage in increasing survival chances for the locust. If the locust's cycle peaks at the same time as its predator's cycle, the prospects for survival are diminished. It would be in the locust's favor for its cycle to have simultaneous peaks with the predator's cycle as seldom as possible. Thus the advantage of the thirteen- or seventeen-year cycle.

Suppose the locust had a six-year cycle and predators had two-, three-, or four-year cycles. The two-year and three-year predators would peak simultaneously with the locust every six years (each locust peak) after an initial matching peak, and the four-year predator would have a peak matching the locust's every twelve years. On the other hand, suppose the locust had a five-year cycle. Then the two-year predator would peak in the same year as the lo-

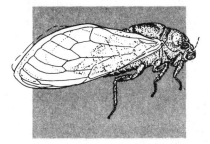

cust every ten years, the three-year predator every fifteen years, and the four-year predator every twenty years. Why do we find longer intervals between common peaks for the five-year locust, even though its cycle is shorter?

The answer is elementary number theory. Five is a prime number, but 6 is not. The incidence of common peak years is itself periodic. If ℓ is the period of the locust cycle and p is the period of the predator cycle, then the interval between common peaks is the least common multiple (LCM) of ℓ and p. Assuming that predators do not have a one-year cycle or a cycle the same as the locust's, the LCM will, in general, be greater when ℓ and p have no common factors. Of course, a prime number has no common factors with any integer other than itself and 1. Here we see the advantage of a prime life cycle. If p is prime, as is the case for the seventeen-year locust, then the LCM of ℓ and p is ℓp. If p were not prime, the LCM of ℓ and p might very well be less than ℓp, depending on the value of ℓ. The prime life cycle guarantees the longest possible predator-free time span for the locust. It will be subject to heavy predation relatively infrequently, able to thrive and multiply over long periods of safety.

Both 13 and 17 are prime numbers. An eleven- or nineteen-year period would have achieved the same happy goal, but number theory cannot begin to explain why there is a seventeen-year locust but not a nineteen-year one! It can, however, show a clear difference between a twelve- and a thirteen-year locust, and between a seventeen- and a sixteen- or eighteen-year locust.

THE GREATEST INTEGER SYMBOL—AN APPLICATIONS APPROACH

A collection of problems for classroom use.

By ZALMAN USISKIN

The University of Chicago
Chicago, IL 60637

This article has two major purposes. One is to demonstrate the surprising number of applications of a topic that is often presented in books but taught without any applications. The second is to demonstrate that real situations can be used to introduce this mathematical topic; this is what is meant by the phrase "applications approach." This use of applications tends to enhance the mathematical skills and theory underlying the symbol [ ].

All elementary school students have experiences with the idea of rounding, both in and out of school. They know that $3.75 can "round up" to $3.80 or $4.00 and can "round down" to $3.70 or $3.00, depending on the question asked. Questions of rounding 5 1/2 to the nearest integer require more rules (the most common being "round halves up" or "round to the even integer"), and even these rules are known by students.

The different types of rounding are easy to calculate when specific numbers are given. But, as often is the case, these rules are a bit harder to describe and handle in their general, or symbolic, forms. These symbolic forms are needed if we wish to understand the operation of computers or calculators, which must round every infinite decimal because they have only finite capacity; or if we want to symbolize the workings of businesses, who round costs or weights or mileage; or if we are interested in mathematically estimating possible errors that might occur because of rounding.

The symbolization of rounding is made easy by using the symbol [ ], commonly called the "greatest integer symbol" and normally defined in the following manner:

$[x]$ = the greatest integer less than or equal to x.

For example, $[\pi] = 3$; $[73] = 73$; $[-\frac{1}{2}] = -1$; $[0] = 0$.

The wording of the customary definition is pedagogically unfortunate, for the phrase "greatest integer less than" confuses many students and disguises the relationship to rounding. In this article, we instead call the greatest integer symbol [ ] the "rounding down" symbol, a name whose appropriateness is illustrated by the examples above.

The "rounding down" (or "greatest integer") function, by which we mean the function with equation $y = [x]$, is a simple example of a *step function*, so called because of its graph (see fig. 1). It is also a

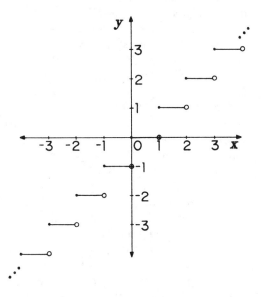

Fig. 1. Graph of rounding down function (Rotate 180° about origin to get graph of rounding up function.)

good example of a function that is not continuous. Thus a study of the symbol [ ] can be interesting even if one is not interested in rounding applications. But here we concentrate on applications and nontrivial problems—aspects not as commonly found in textbooks.

Rounding down is often used in business when someone wants to pay as little as possible.

1. If a kitchen chair can be bought for 5 books of trading stamps, how many such chairs can be bought for n books?

$$\left(\text{Answer: } \left[\frac{n}{5}\right].\right)$$

2. A salesman receives a $100 bonus for each $1000 worth of equipment that he sells over his base requirement. How much bonus will he receive for d dollars in sales over his base requirement? (Answers to this and other questions are at the end of the article.)

It is important to realize a difference in the real-world application of questions 1 and 2, although the mathematics is identical. To answer question 1, the symbol [ ] is probably never used. The consumer divides n by 5 and ignores any fraction that might occur. But commissions on sales are now often calculated by computer. So in question 2, the programmer must instruct the computer to round down, and this is done by an operation equivalent to the use of the symbol [ ].

A natural question arises when rounding down: Is there a symbol for rounding up? It is clear that people round up when they want to receive as much as possible. For example, when a parcel is weighed for mailing, the weight is rounded up, not down, so that the next higher cost is charged. It may surprise students to learn that there is no need for a new symbol; that is, rounding up can be done in terms of the rounding down symbol. But the problem is difficult; as so often happens in problem solving, it is best to consider first a simpler problem.

3. (Original problem.) How can rounding up be done in terms of rounding down?

(a) (Simplified problem.) What would the graph of a rounding up function look like? (This is an easy question to answer by trial and error. Students must learn to look at both integer and noninteger behavior in this function.)

(b) (Comparison with known situation.) How does the graph of the rounding up function compare with that of the rounding down function? (Answer: Rotating the graph of the rounding down function 180° about the origin gives the graph of the rounding up function, see fig. 2).

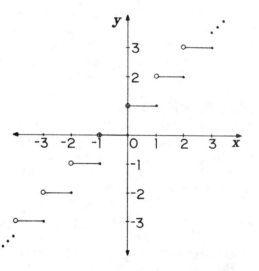

Fig. 2. Graph of rounding up function (Some points on graph are $(\pi, 4)$, $(-1, -1)$, $(1\frac{1}{4}, 2)$, and $(-1\frac{1}{2}, -1)$

(c) (Continuation of this direction.) If we have an equation for a relation, how can we get an equation for an image under a 180° rotation about the origin? (Answer: Replace x by $-x$ and y by $-y$. The answer is best obtained by considering other examples.)

(d) (Application to original problem.) So if we replace x by $-x$ and y by $-y$ in an equation for the rounding down function, we get the desired equation: $-y = [-x]$, or in its more traditional form, $y = -[-x]$.

In other words, $x \to -[-x]$ maps a number onto the smallest integer *greater* than or equal to the number. For example,

$$\pi \to -[-\pi] = -(-4) = 4,$$

$$-7.2 \to -[-(-7.2)] = -[7.2] = -7,$$

and

$$6 \to -[-6] = 6.$$

Notice the use of negative numbers to round up a positive number.

Many real situations require rounding up:

4. First-class mail now (1977) costs 13¢ an ounce to mail. How much postage must be paid for a parcel in this class that weighs w ounces? (This is a reasonable question if a computer is weighing parcels.)

5. If you have a charge account that adds a finance charge of 1 percent each month to each unpaid bill, how much will be added in two months to a bill of $29.95? Here the point to be made is that it is not 0.2995 that is added to the bill the first month, but the next higher cent. Indeed,

$$0.30 = \frac{-[-100(0.2995)]}{100},$$

and in general, if the unpaid balance was B, the amount added would be

$$\frac{-[-100(0.01B)]}{100}.$$

6. Can rounding to the nearest integer be written in terms of rounding down? If so, how can it be done? If not, why not? (To simplify this problem, you might wish to assume that halves are rounded up.)

7. To keep the number of participants down, an interscholastic math contest committee decides to allow each school at most one representative for each 250 students. Suppose a school has n students. How many representatives is it allowed? (Here the phrase "for each

250 students" must be interpreted. Does this mean round up? Round down? Round to the nearest 250? As with many reasonable, practical questions, certain decisions must be made before a mathematical picture of the problem can be generated. The author has no single answer for this question. Each student might decide what is fair and make an appropriate expression based on that judgment.)

8. If a taxi ride costs 40¢ for the first 1/4 mile and 10¢ for each additional 1/4 mile, find an expression relating cost C (in cents) and miles traveled m.

9. Make up a question like question 8 for long-distance telephone rates to the city where someone you know lives.

The problems above are only the most obvious (even though nontrivial) instances that could use the symbol [ ]. Here are some others.

10. (Truncating.) The rounding down symbol lops off the "decimal" part of a number. This process is called truncating the number. Truncating after two decimal places was required in question 5. Any calculator or computer must truncate the decimal expansion of any number after a certain number of places because of its finite storage capacity. It is natural to ask if one could express truncation after four (or some other number of) decimal places, using the symbol [ ]; for example, can you find an expression for a function that would contain the following ordered pairs?

    (log 2, 0.3010), (π, 3.1415), (-5, -5), ($\sqrt{3}$, 1.7320), and (1.98643, 1.9864)

11. If you work with a hand calculator that has square root and squaring keys and if you press 2, the square root key, and the squaring key—in that order—why will some calculators not list 2 as the final result?

12. (A variant of truncating.) Suppose you are dealing with large numbers and wish to instruct a computer to print the

numbers in thousands (as is often done with census figures). For example, 345 678 would be written as 345. What expression indicates the number onto which *n* should be mapped?

A totally different collection of uses for the symbol [ ] is found by examining the intersection of the graphs of $y = [x]$ and $y = x$. As pictured (fig. 3), it is obvious that the set of first coordinates of the points of intersection is the set of integers.

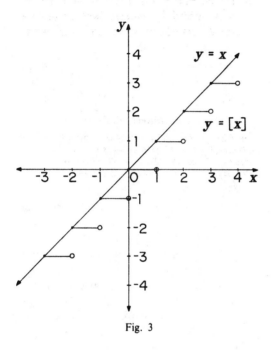

Fig. 3

13. (Rewriting statements.) The English statement "*x* is an integer" can be denoted mathematically as $[x] = x$. What about "*x* is not an integer"?

14. Denote each of these statements by a single equation with the aid of the symbol [ ]. (Answers at end of article.)
    (a) *n* is an even integer.
    (b) *z* is an odd integer.
    (c) *m* is divisible by 3.
    (d) *m* is divisible by *n*.
    (e) $v \equiv 7 \pmod{41}$

15. (Sentences for graph paper (!).) Ordinary, commercial graph paper has all the lines printed for integer values of *x* or *y*. If we think of this as the graph of

a relation, an English sentence for that relation is "*x* is an integer or *y* is an integer." An equation can easily be derived:

$$([x] - x) \cdot ([y] - y) = 0.$$

16. What is a sentence for the lattice of all points having integers for *both* coordinates?

Finally, we come to the granddaddy of all applications of the symbol, which I first found in *A Source Book of Mathematical Applications* (NCTM 1942).

17. (Day of the week.) Number the days of the week with Sunday = 1, Monday = 2, and so on, allowing Sunday = 8, Monday = 9, and so on. Number the months of the year with March = 3, April = 4, . . . , December = 12, January = 13, February = 14. Let *W* = the number of the day in the week, let *D* = the day of the month, let *M* = the number of the month as above, and let *N* = the year. For January and February, replace *N* by *N* − 1. Then

$$W = D + 2M + \left[\frac{3(M+1)}{5}\right] + N$$
$$+ \left[\frac{N}{4}\right] - \left[\frac{N}{100}\right] + \left[\frac{N}{400}\right] + 2.$$

Test this formula by verifying that Pearl Harbor was bombed on a Sunday, 7 December 1941.

18. All parts of the formula above are explainable. The first use of the symbol [ ] is a correction for the differing numbers of days in the months. The last three uses are caused by leap years, which occur every fourth year except at the beginning of the century, unless the century number is 2000, 2400, and so on. Why isn't the formula useful for finding out the day of the week for a date before 1700?

Notes, Answers, and Hints

2. $100 \cdot \left[\dfrac{d}{1000}\right]$. Note that $100 \cdot \left[\dfrac{d}{1000}\right]$
   $\neq \dfrac{d}{10}$.

4. $-13 \cdot [-w]$. Sales tax is a related notion but usually much more difficult to describe mathematically.

6. If halves are rounded up, $[x + \frac{1}{2}]$ rounds x to the nearest integer.

8. Assume that the meter clicks on the quarter-mile. $C = 40 + 10[4\dot{m}]$

9. Car rental or other rates could also be used.

10. $y = \dfrac{[10\ 000x]}{10\ 000}$. You should generalize this.

11. For example, the SR-51A, SR-40, TI-30, and Monroe 99 are calculators that would give 2 as the answer, but the Novus and Omron are calculators in which the operations yield an answer less than 2. The Novus and Omron calculators truncate the decimal expansion of $\sqrt{2}$ and square this approximation.

12. $\left[\dfrac{n}{1000}\right]$. With the use of negative exponents, exercises 10 and 12 are seen to use the same mathematical idea.

13. $[x] \neq x$

14. (a) $\left[\dfrac{n}{2}\right] = \dfrac{n}{2}$ (b) $\left[\dfrac{z+1}{2}\right] = \dfrac{z+1}{2}$

    (c) $\left[\dfrac{m}{3}\right] = \dfrac{m}{3}$ (d) $\left[\dfrac{m}{n}\right] = \dfrac{m}{n}$

    (e) $\left[\dfrac{v-7}{41}\right] = \dfrac{v-7}{41}$

16. $([x] - x)^2 + ([y] - y)^2 = 0$

18. In the eighteenth century, the calendar was moved up eleven days to correct for errors due to too many leap years.

REFERENCES

National Council of Teachers of Mathematics. *A Source Book of Mathematical Applications.* Seventeenth Yearbook. New York: Bureau of Publications, Teachers College, Columbia University, 1942.

applications

CAMERA CALCULATIONS

By **GEORGE FAWCETT**
Board of Education for the
City of Hamilton
Hamilton, ON L8N 3L1

On most single lens reflex (SLR) cameras there is a series of settings on a dial that regulates the amount of light reaching the film. The dial turns a mechanism called a diaphragm, which is a group of thin plates that vary the size of the aperture (the opening for light to enter the camera).

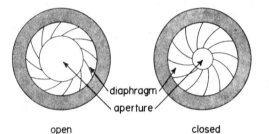

open   closed

The settings of the diaphragm are called f-stops. The value of an f-stop is a ratio of the focal length of the camera lens (the distance that light travels after passing through the lens until it converges to a point) divided by the diameter of the aperture. Each increasing f-stop setting cuts by half the amount of light entering the camera. Since the amount of light entering the camera depends on the area of the aperture, each increasing f-stop halves the area of the previous aperture area. In evaluating f-stops, focal length is taken into account so that the same f-stop setting on all cameras will allow the same amount of light to hit the film.

Area of Aperture of 2d f-stop

$$= \frac{1}{2} \text{ Area of Aperture of 1st f-stop}$$

Since the aperture is approximately a circle, the following would apply:

Area of 1st f-stop aperture $= \pi r_1^2$,

where r_1 is the radius of 1st stop aperture.

Area of 2d f-stop aperture $= \pi r_2^2$,

where r_2 is the radius of 2d stop aperture.

$$\therefore \pi r_2^2 = \frac{1}{2} \pi r_1^2.$$

Thus

$$\frac{r_2^2}{r_1^2} = \frac{1}{2};$$

so

$$\frac{r_2}{r_1} = \frac{1}{\sqrt{2}}.$$

Since the diameter is twice the radius,

$$\frac{2d \text{ diameter}}{1st \text{ diameter}} = \frac{2r_2}{2r_1} = \frac{r_2}{r_1} = \frac{1}{\sqrt{2}}.$$

The ratio of f-stop values

$$= \frac{f_2}{f_1} = \frac{\text{focal length/diameter 2}}{\text{focal length/diameter 1}}$$

$$= \frac{\text{diameter 1}}{\text{diameter 2}} = \frac{1}{(1/\sqrt{2})} = \sqrt{2}.$$

Thus each f-stop setting is $\sqrt{2}$ times the previous one.

We can then set up a geometric sequence

with $t_1 = 1$ and $r = \sqrt{2}$ (and round our answers to two digits of accuracy):

$$t_1 = a = 1$$
$$t_2 = ar = 1 \times \sqrt{2} = 1.4$$
$$t_3 = ar^2 = 1 \times (\sqrt{2})^2 = 2.0$$

and so on. The student should then calculate the next four or five terms and compare them to the existing f-stops: f/1.0, f/1.4, f/2.0, f/2.8, f/4.0, f/5.6, f/8, f/11.

Problems

1. Fill in the missing standard f-stops between f/5.6 and f/64 (to two digits).

(8, 11, 16, 22, 32, 45)

2. Given the following f-stops and focal lengths, calculate the areas of the apertures:

f-stop	Focal Length	Area of Aperture
1.0	50 mm	(625π)
2.0	95 mm	(564π)
1.4	100 mm	(1275π)
5.6	150 mm	(179π)

3. Calculate the f-stops (to two digits) given the following areas of apertures and focal lengths:

Focal Length	Area of Aperture	f-stop
100 mm	319π mm^2	(2.8)
70 mm	306π mm^2	(2.0)
90 mm	17π mm^2	(11)
120 mm	7π mm^2	(22)

Square root is involved in the calculations to determine the f-stop when a flash unit is used with an SLR camera.

A guide number (GN) is published by the flash manufacturer based on the approximate light output of the flash. Then the GN is used to calculate an f-stop (lens opening), because most camera light meters do not work with light from a flash. The f-stop is found by dividing the guide number by the distance, d, from the flash to the object.

$$\text{f-stop} = \frac{GN}{d}$$

Example: If your flash has a GN of 33 m and the subject is 3 m away, find the f-stop setting.

Solution: f-stop = 33/3 = 11. The lens opening should be set at f/11.

A published GN is for one speed of film only. If you use a different film with a different speed, the new GN can be found using the following formula:

New GN

$$= \text{Old } GN \times \sqrt{\frac{\text{New film speed}}{\text{Published film speed}}}$$

Example: If your flash's GN is 20 m for an ASA 25 film but you want to use ASA 200 film, what is the new GN?

Solution: New $GN = 20 \times \sqrt{\dfrac{200}{25}}$

$$= 20 \times \sqrt{8}$$
$$= 20 \times 2.8 = 56.$$

The new GN is 56 m.

Exercise

A flash has guide number $GN = 16$ m for ASA 100. The following chart will be placed on the back of each flash unit sold. In order to complete the chart, two operations must be carried out:

1. Calculate the GN for each new film speed.

2. Use the GN and each distance in the chart to calculate each f-stop.

Distance (m) / ASA	1	1.5	2	2.5	3.5	5
25–32						
50–64						
80–125			f/8			
160–250						
320–400						

Notes

1. Because most cameras have fixed f-

stops of 1.4, 2, 2.8, 4, 5.6, 8, 11, 16, 22, and 32, the number inserted in the chart in each location must be one of these.

2. Because each category in the ASA column gives a range of speed, the student must choose an "average" film speed in the range to use in the calculations.

BIBLIOGRAPHY

Jeffrey, Neil J. "Mathematics in Photography." *Mathematics Teacher* 73 (December 1980):657–62.

The Summer Olympic Games: A Mathematical Opportunity

By WILLIAM A. EWBANK, Taylor University, Upland, IN 46989

"In the Spring a young man's fancy lightly turns to thoughts of love," wrote Tennyson, but this spring other events will claim his attention (and hers)— the summer Olympic Games! The 1984 Olympiad will be held in our own back yard (Los Angeles), and it can offer many interesting topics for investigation by the mathematics class.

One activity can be based on records of performance found in an almanac or book of records. For example, a circle graph can be drawn showing the continents where the Olympics have been held since the modern Olympiads began in 1896 (see table 1). Statistics such as these can lead to nonmathematical but relevant questions—why have the Games been held so often in Europe? Why have they never been held in Africa, and only once each in Asia and Australia? How are the sites chosen? Does holding the Games cost the host nation a great deal of money, or does the country make a profit from them? The references at the end provide many answers, and interested teachers should look at the information published by the U.S. Olympic Committee.

TABLE 1

Sites of the Olympic Games 1896–1980

	Summer Games	Winter Games
Europe	15	14
Asia	1	1
Africa	0	0
Americas	4	4
Australia	1	0

Source: *The World Almanac and Book of Facts, 1983*

The author would like to acknowledge the help of George Glass, a coach at Taylor University, in the preparation of this article.

Gold medals are the most coveted award at the Olympics. Which country has won the most gold medals? Is there any pattern in how they were won in each decade? Such questions will provide opportunities for research and practice in graphs and statistics.

Data on track and field events are a good way to discuss metric measurement. Some Olympic records, and questions that might be asked, are the following:

High jump: Gerd Wessig (East Germany)
1980 2.36 m
How does this record compare with the height of the tallest teacher or the tallest student or the height of a door in your school?

Long jump: Robert Beamon (U.S.A.)
1968 8.90 m
How does this length compare with the length of your classroom?

Pole vault: Wladyslaw Kozakiewicz (Poland)
1980 5.78 m
How does this height compare with the height of your school or its flagpole?

Discus throw: Mac Maurice Wilkins (U.S.A.)
1976 68.28 m
How does this length compare with the length of your school or the length of a football field?

100-m dash: James Ray Hines (U.S.A.)
1968 9.95 s
How does this time compare with the speed limit on the road outside your school? Would Hines get a ticket?

Although the Olympic records themselves provide interesting mathematics for younger students, more advanced students may enjoy studying the rate at which records are broken in different events. Runners run faster, javelins are hurled farther, and so on. The phenomenon of the "super athlete" who broke a record in the early years and whose record has not been bettered does not seem to occur in the Olympics. This fact raises several interesting questions about the causes of this improved performance, but they will not be addressed here. It can be instructive to select various events and graph the records against time, that is, the year the record was broken. Should the points on the graph be joined when the figures are graphed? Strictly speaking, no, because the graph does not describe a continuous function. In this instance, however, as in business statistics (e.g., annual profit graphs), we can make a line graph to clarify the situation. An example of such a graph, showing the improvement in the long jump results from 1896 to 1980, appears in figure 1. Women's

results can be shown on the same graph, as here, or separately. Using information from this graph, forecast the long jump results for 1984. For 2000.

Comparisons with school records can also be made, and these data can be graphed on the same graph as the Olympic results. More concrete comparisons can be made by marking record distances for jumps and throws on lawns or in school hallways.

Some students may become involved in more complex questions, such as whether the record time for a track race is proportional to the distance run. In general, no, but the question is more difficult than it looks. If the Olympic records for the 100-m, 200-m, 400-m, and 800-m runs are graphed (fig. 2), no straight line runs through the

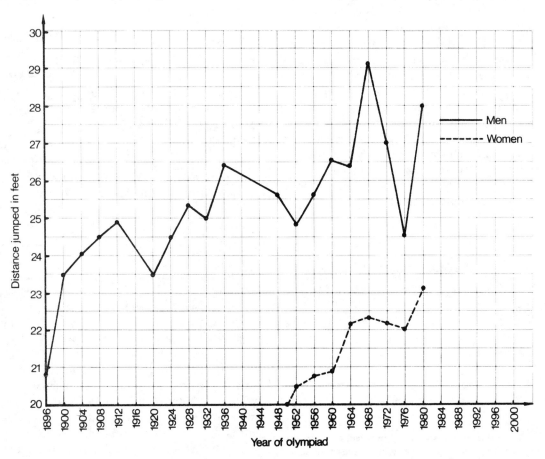

Fig. 1. Distances jumped by Olympic gold medalists in the long jump, 1896–1980.

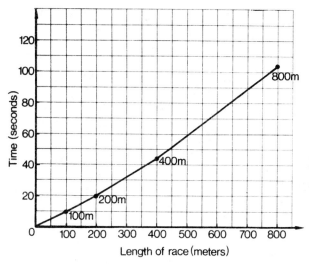

Fig. 2. Olympic records for the men's 100-m, 200-m, 400-m, and 800-m races

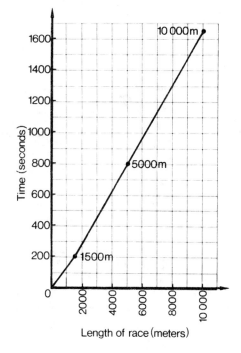

Fig. 3. Olympic records for the 1500-m, 5000-m, and 10 000-m races

origin (the sign of a relationship of direct proportion). The same would be true for the 1500-m, 5000-m, and 10 000-m runs (fig. 3). The times for these events are graphed on separate axes because if only one set of axes is used, the points for the fastest races would be bunched too close together near the origin.

From these graphs we can see that the ratio of time to distance is not the same in each case. Why? The sprinter can only maintain a high speed for a limited distance, say 150–200 m. The long-distance runner would not stay the course if he or she tackled the 800-m at the pace of a runner in the 100-m dash. Curiously, however, the Olympic records for the 100-m and 200-m races exhibit nearly equal ratios: 9.95 s for 100 m and 19.83 s for 200 m. These results suggest that the runners' average speeds (distance divided by time) were almost the same, but it does not mean that the greatest speed achieved by each record-breaking runner was the same. The reason is that in each race the runner has to start from the rest position and then accelerate to maximum speed. The 200-m runner starts the second hundred meters at top speed and probably completes it in shorter time than the first hundred meters.

A study of the ratio of time to distance is complicated by the fact that in the Olympics, the 100-m race is always run on a straight track, whereas the 200-m race is run on a curved track (probably for space reasons). Running on a curved track involves problems of centrifugal force and balance, especially at high speeds. It can be assumed (although statistics cannot be quoted to illustrate it) that the 100-m specialist would not run 100 m on a curved track as fast as on a straight track.

Figure 4 shows a graph of hypothetical 100-m and 200-m races. If the two runners started at the same time, reached the same maximum speed with the same acceleration, and maintained this speed up to the finishing tapes, the 200-m runner would run the race in *less* than twice the time that it took the 100-m runner (dotted line on the graph). It is possible, but unlikely in runners of international caliber, that the 200-m runner decelerates near the end of the race. If not, the conclusion is that the maximum speed achieved by the 200-m runner is slower than that achieved by the 100-m runner. This

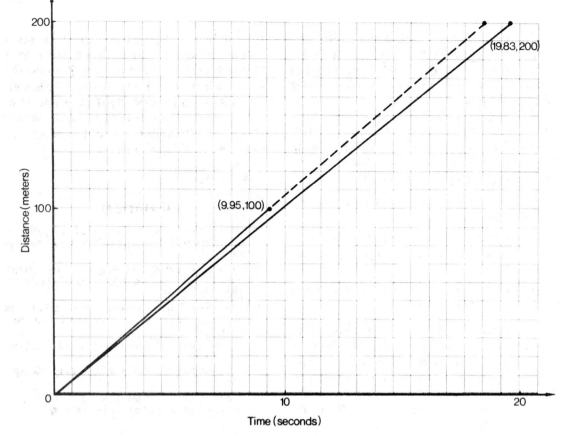

Fig. 4. Hypothetical distance-time graph for Olympic record holders in the men's 100-m and 200-m dashes

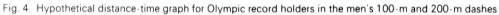

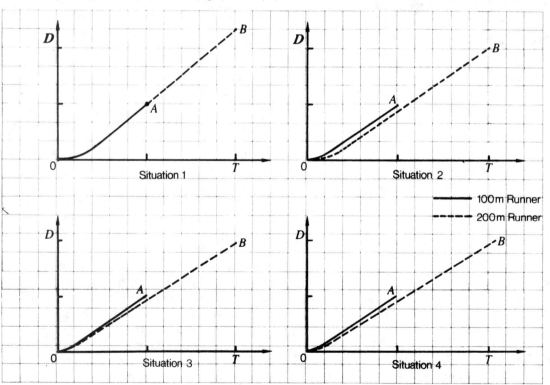

Fig. 5. Graphs showing the relationship between distance (D) and time (T) of two runners running the 100-m and 200-m races under four possible conditions

point can be seen in the slope of the two lines in the graph—in a distance-time graph, speed is proportional to the slope of the line, that is, to the tangent of its angle with the x-axis.

Comparisons of the performance of a 100-m runner (A) with that of a 200-m runner (B) suggest four possibilities (ruling out those in which B decelerates at the end). The 200-m runner runs with—

1. the same acceleration and speed as the 100-m runner,

2. lower acceleration but the same speed,

3. the same acceleration but a slower speed,

4. lower acceleration and a slower speed than the 100-m runner.

The graphs in figure 5 show these possibilities in simplified form. Situation 1 does not fit the facts: B would run the 200-m run in less than twice the time of A for the 100-m, since the slope of the line OA must be less than that of line AB, as we have indicated. Thus, situations 2, 3, and 4 remain, where B has a slower start or a slower maximum speed than A. Perhaps the people involved in track in your mathematics classes can throw light on these matters. These questions and many others make the Olympics a fruitful topic for mathematical investigations.

REFERENCES

McWhirter, Norris, ed. *Guinness Book of Sports Records, Winners & Champions*. New York: Bantam Books, 1981.

Oakley, Cletus, and Justine Baker. "Least Squares and the 3:40-Minute Mile." *Mathematics Teacher* 70 (April 1977): 322–24.

United States Olympic Committee. *The Olympics: An Educational Opportunity*. Colorado Springs: U.S.O.C., 1982.

———. *Enrichment Units K–6*. Colorado Springs: U.S.O.C., 1982.

———. *Enrichment Units 7–9*. Colorado Springs: U.S.O.C., 1982.

The World Almanac and Book of Facts. New York: Newspaper Enterprise Association, 1983. ♥

THE t IN $I = Prt$

By **ALONZO F. JOHNSON**
West Virginia University
Morgantown, WV 26506

A few years ago I was looking for applications in which the calculator would be a useful aid. I decided to take my house payment book to class with me and let the students check the bank's arithmetic. Three lines of my book are included in table 1.

When I took out the $28 000 twenty-year loan the bank told me that my annual interest rate was 7.5 percent. For the December payment, using $I = Prt$, the calculations went nicely:

$$170.96 = 27\ 353.44 \times 0.075 \times \frac{1}{12}.$$

Then for the January payment, the calculation went as follows:

$$170.62 = 27\ 298.83 \times 0.075 \times \frac{1}{12}.$$

But $176.30 was listed for the interest in my payment book. (I should have worked the problems, but I thought I knew how to compute interest!) That day we were not able to verify the bank's figures.

TABLE 1

Date	Interest	Payment	Balance
Nov. 5–73	176.98	225.57	27 353.44
Dec. 5–73	170.96	225.57	27 298.83
Jan. 5–74	176.30	225.57	27 249.56

After class, I called the bank and asked how they obtained the $176.30 interest in my January payment. They quickly let me know that a computer did it. After having my call transferred twice, I found someone who explained that the bank charged interest on a daily basis. Since December has thirty-one days in it, I should expect my interest payment on 5 January to be higher. At last I knew how to compute the interest in the January payment,

$$I = 27\ 298.83 \times 0.075 \times \frac{31}{365}.$$

But when I made this calculation, I came out to be $173.89, not $176.30 as listed in my payment book. After much effort and remembering that I had taught the "6 percent/60-day method" of calculating interest some years ago (this method used 360 days in a year), I finally discovered that

$$176.30 = 27\ 298.83 \times 0.075 \times \frac{31}{360}.$$

So, all the bank was doing was using a 360-day year. But further calculations told me that the bank was charging me interest for 365 days. To make a long story short, I calculated that the excess interest the bank would charge me over twenty years was $999 (see Appendix). After I pointed this out to the bank president and used other persuasive arguments, the bank established a policy of using a 365-day year in its calculations.

Lester H. Lange, in his article "Some Everyday Applications of the Theory of Interest" in NCTM's 1979 Yearbook (p. 100), asks the question, "Do banks use 360 or 365 as the number of days in a year?" Associated questions are "Should the banks use 360 or 365 days in calculating interest?" and "Should we teach interest using 360 days in a year?"

Concerning what method banks should use, I checked with Neal Butler, an attorney in the Consumer Credit Division of the Federal Reserve System. He said that the Federal Reserve System does not tell banks how to charge interest. What they do say is that banks must disclose the correct annual percentage rate (APR) on a loan or round to the nearest 1/4 percent. The APR is based on 365 days.

Using the 360-day method for charging interest, the bank collects interest for five extra days. This increases the interest charged by a factor of approximately $1/72 = 5/360$. For loans with interest rates greater than 9 percent, the 360-day method puts the listed interest rate outside the "nearest 1/4 percent." Thus, banks would violate the Federal Truth in Lending Law if they use 360 days in the banking year and charge interest for 365 days on loans with interest rates greater than 9 percent. As of 1 October 1980, the "nearest 1/4 percent" rule was changed by the Federal Reserve System to the "within 1/8 percent rule." The effect of this ruling is to allow interest rates such as 7.63 percent to be reported as 7.6 percent or 7.7 percent instead of 7.75 percent.

The landmark state court ruling involving the use of 360 days in calculating interest and charging for 365 days is the one by the 1973 Appellate Court of Illinois in the case of *Perlman* v. *The First National Bank of Chicago* (*North Eastern Reporter* 1973). Perlman sued for excess interest charged, claiming that "the phrase 'per annum' or 'per year' as contained in any promissory note . . . means a year of 12 calendar months consisting of 365 days. . ." (p. 240). In the bank's defense it was stated that ". . . according to custom and usage . . . interest on commercial loans was computed by using 360-day years. . ." (p. 237).

The Appellate Court held that ". . . (the) meaning of calendar year within interest statutes could not be varied by customs and usages of banks in connection with commercial loans . . ." (p. 236). Perlman won his case.

It appears that the use of 360 days in calculating interest on a loan is on its way out. Should we quit using the 360-day banking year in our teaching?

The answer is not as simple as it may appear. I believe that my house loan example clearly indicated that the students should not be taught that it is an acceptable way for banks to charge interest on a loan. If calculators are available

(shouldn't they be when studying interest?), the calculations with 365 days are just as easy. For practice in estimating interest, the 360-day year will be around for a long time. (We will keep on using problems that involve $1000 at 12 percent APR for 30 days.) When using it, we should, however, clearly point out that we are *estimating* interest.

APPENDIX

The $999 excess interest charged by using 360 days in the year and charging interest for 365 days was obtained by starting the loan on 1 October. Selected figures from the amortization schedule for 240 months are seen in table 2. Starting the loan at different months gives different amounts owed varying from $1027, starting the loan in March, to $963, starting the loan in February.

TABLE 2

	Outstanding Balance		
Month	Using 360-Day Year	Using 365-Day Year	Difference
1	27 955.26	27 952.79	2.47
2	27 904.41	27 899.53	4.88
12	27 401.74	27 371.86	29.88
24	25 756.35	26 694.92	61.43
36	26 060.15	25 965.45	94.70
48	25 309.14	25 179.34	129.80
60	24 498.97	24 332.19	166.78
72	23 625.00	23 419.28	205.72
84	22 682.19	22 435.50	246.69
96	21 665.16	21 375.34	289.92
108	20 568.03	20 232.88	335.15
120	19 384.51	19 001.74	382.77
132	18 107.80	17 675.01	432.79
144	16 730.54	16 245.30	485.24
156	15 244.83	14 704.58	540.25
168	13 642.12	13 044.27	597.85
180	11 913.21	11 255.04	658.17
192	10 048.14	9 326.91	721.23
204	8 036.20	7 249.11	787.09
216	5 865.81	5 010.00	855.81
228	3 524.52	2 597.04	927.48
240	998.85	−3.22	1002.07

I computed the excess interest charged for a twenty-year loan of $60 000 at 12 percent. At the end of twenty years, making payments that would pay off the loan if interest was charged at 1 percent per month, the borrower still owed $6890 (loan started in January).

All calculations were done on a TI-59.

REFERENCES

Lange, Lester H. "Some Everyday Applications of the Theory of Interest." In *Applications in School Mathematics*, pp. 98–108. 1979 Yearbook of the National Council of Teachers of Mathematics. Reston, Va.: The Council, 1979.

North Eastern Reporter. 2d Series, #305, pp. 236–52. St. Paul, Minn.: West Publishing Co., 1973.

Modeling the Cost of Homeownership

By FLOYD VEST, North Texas State University, Denton, TX 76203

This article presents an investigation of the cost of homeownership by constructing a mathematical model with refinements and illustrates an important type of problem solving with calculators, which falls in line with recommendations found in *An Agenda for Action* (1980, 1, 4).

A recent newspaper article headed "Renters Not Getting Such a Bad Break after All" (Huenneke 1984, 2c) reported that between 1970 and 1980, median rents advanced 74 percent while in the same period the cost of homeownership rose 144 percent. To provide a more specific example, in the region of the country where I live, a modern, previously owned three-bedroom home with central heating and air conditioning, brick exterior, attached garage, carpeting, and so on, can be rented for $400 a month. A new home with these same features would cost at least $55 000. Perhaps before deciding to buy such a house, one should investigate the cost of homeownership. We shall conduct such an investigation by constructing a mathematical scenario, or model.

Mathematical models are based on reasonable assumptions about the situations under consideration. These assumptions, by and large, are stipulated and are not mathematically derived. Nevertheless, assumptions that sometimes appear reasonable do, on occasion, fail to support the empirical evidence. For this reason assumptions must be carefully thought out and acknowledged before one proceeds to derive results based on their presumed validity.

Monthly payments including principal and interest

We shall assume that the house is purchased with a 5-percent down payment and $1500 in closing costs. Closing costs usually include title insurance, legal fees, survey and appraisal fees, taxes, insurance, inspection fees, and a loan-discount fee called "buyer's points." Our problem is to calculate the monthly payments, which usually include principal and interest. We assume a 13-percent interest rate with twenty-five years to pay. To calculate the monthly payments for principal and interest, we use from mathematics of finance the formula (Zill et al. 1982, 386)

$$R = A\left[\frac{i}{1 - (1 + i)^{-n}}\right]$$

with

$A = \$55\,000 - 0.05(\$55\,000) = \$52\,250$ (the amount of the loan),

$i = \dfrac{0.13}{12}$ (the interest rate per month),

$n = 12 \times 25 = 300$ (the total number of monthly payments),

$R =$ monthly payments covering principal and interest.

Using a scientific calculator, we get $R = \$589.30$ a month. (For a derivation of this formula, see Soler and Schuster [1982] or Zill et al. [1982].)

Taxes and insurance

Our model needs to be refined to include taxes and insurance. Let us assume that taxes are $600 a year and insurance is $300 a year. These make the monthly payment $664 = 589.30 + (600 + 300)/12. Since these figures involve estimations, we shall round all subsequent costs to the nearest dollar.

Maintenance and replacement

The landlord who rents a house for $400 a month would use a rule of thumb that the average monthly cost of maintenance and replacement for the house would be 10 percent of the monthly rent. Perhaps the homeowner should include this type of expenditure in the cost of homeownership. Let us make this additional refinement, basing it on the comparable $400 rental:

(1) $664 + $40 = $704 a month

Income-tax deductions

We now consider the effect of federal-income-tax deductions for homeowners. To make this additional refinement in the model we shall assume that the prospective buyer is in a 29-percent income-tax bracket. Since taxes and interest paid are deductible, the individual's tax liability is reduced by 29 percent of these amounts.

To estimate the interest for the first year we calculate

$$0.13(\$52\ 250) = \$6792.$$

The tax break based on interest and $600 taxes will be

$$0.29(\$600 + \$6792) = \$2144 \text{ a year,}$$
$$\text{or } \$179 \text{ a month.}$$

(Assuming that the income-tax brackets are 5510 apart, only a portion of the 600 + 6792 would be taxed at 29% and the rest at the next lower bracket.) Thus, the monthly cost of homeownership becomes

(2) $704 − $179 = $525.

Such a sizeable reduction provides a strong incentive for homeownership.

Principal reduction

Homeowners accumulate what is called equity through the reduction of the principal on the loan. To estimate the principal reduction for the first year, we subtract the estimated interest from the payments for principal and interest to obtain

$$12(\$589.30) - \$6792 = \$280 \text{ for the year,}$$
$$\text{or } \$23 \text{ a month.}$$

It is hoped that these earnings are recovered when the house is sold, but the recovery is not at all certain. We shall proceed by assuming that it can be recovered. But when?

Assuming that the owner waits ten years to sell the home and recapture the principal reduction and that ten-year money is worth 8 percent, we use the following formula (Zill et al. 1982) to calculate the present value of the principal reduction. The present value P is the amount that must be invested to accumulate to the future value S after n years.

$$P = S(1 + i)^{-n},$$

where $S = \$23$ (the future value), $i = 0.08$ (interest rate), and $n = 10$ (number of years), to obtain

$$P = \$23(1 + 0.08)^{-10} = \$11 \text{ a month.}$$

Thus from (2), we estimate a monthly cost of homeownership after principal reduction of

(3) $525 − $11 = $514.

Appreciation

Most homeowners would interject that they not only expect to recover the principal but also anticipate that the home will appreciate. Newspapers report that from 1970 to 1980 the median value of a home rose by 206 percent (Huenneke 1984). Knowing that the years 1970 to 1980 were exceptional, we shall use a more conservative figure of 5 percent compounded annually and calculate the appreciation attributable to the first year to be

$$0.05(\$55\ 000) = \$2750.$$

We assume a waiting period of ten years and no capital-gains taxes and calculate the present value of the appreciation to be

$$\$2750(1 + 0.08)^{-10} = \$1274 \text{ a year,}$$
$$\text{or } \$106 \text{ a month.}$$

This figure yields a monthly cost of homeownership estimated from (3) at $514 − $106 = $408 a month, which looks much better in relation to the cost of renting.

Appreciation after expenses

Certain expenses are involved in selling a home: closing costs, brokerage fees, and perhaps the cost of monthly payments on an unoccupied house. Conducting some rapid calculations with the indicated assumptions, we see that the house sells for

$$(1 + 0.05)^{10}(\$55\ 000) = \$89\ 589,$$

with the following costs:

0.06($89 589) = $5375	6-percent brokerage commission assuming 5-percent appreciation
$1500	Closing costs
3 × $525 = $1575	3 monthly payments while empty, from (2)
$8450	Cost of selling home

To calculate the anticipated earnings from appreciation, we give the following calculations and assumptions:

Selling price	$89589
Selling costs	−$ 8450
	$81139
Acquisition costs	$56500
	$24639

$$\$24\ 639 \div 10 = \$2464$$

Average appreciation a year for 10 years

(4) $$\$2464(1 + 0.08)^{-10} = \$1141$$
Present value of average appreciation for first year, or $95 a month

Using the results from (3), we find that the cost of homeownership is now revalued at

(5) $$\$514 - \$95 = \$419 \text{ a month.}$$

For the first year it may be more economical to rent, especially since the owner has invested $4250 in the down payment and closing costs. How long does it take appreciation to overtake the cost of selling? To estimate this interval, we solve the equation

$$0.06(1 + 0.05)^n(55\ 000) + 1500 + 1575$$
$$= (1 + 0.05)^n(55\ 000) - 55\ 000,$$

where the left side reflects selling costs including, from left to right, brokerage fees, closing costs, and payments while empty and the right side reflects appreciation at 5 percent compounded for n years. Solving the equation gives

$$1500 + 1575 + 55\ 000 = (1 + 0.05)^n$$
$$\cdot (55\ 000)(1 - 0.06)$$
$$1.1233 = (1 + 0.05)^n,$$
$$\frac{\log 1.1233}{\log 1.05} = n,$$
$$2.4 \text{ years} = n.$$

It is estimated that after 2.4 years the homeowner may make money from the sale of the house.

Rate of return on initial investment

The homeowner has invested $4250. What is the anticipated first-year rate of return on this investment if the home is sold in ten years? We make the following calculations:

Present value of first-year principal reduction = $280(1.08)^{-10}		= $ 130
Present value of yearly average share of recovery from appreciation after expenses from (4)		$1141
		$1271

The rate of return on the initial investment is

$$\$1271 \div \$4250 = 30 \text{ percent.}$$

This appears to be a good rate of return.

Forfeited interest earnings

Another way to compare the cost of owning with the cost of renting is to consider the $4250 invested in the house and the loss of earned interest on this money. Assuming $6\frac{1}{2}$-percent return and a 29-percent income-tax bracket, forfeited interest earnings after taxes are

$$\$4250(0.065)(1 - 0.29) = \$196 \text{ a year,}$$
$$\text{or } \$16 \text{ a month.}$$

We add this to the monthly cost of home-ownership from (5) to get

$$\$419 + \$16 = \$435 \text{ a month.}$$

Other refinements in the comparison are apparent. One is the consideration of an increase in the cost of rent. As mentioned earlier, newspapers report that between 1970 and 1980, median rents advanced 74 percent (Huenneke 1984) (equivalent to 5.7 percent compounded annually). Another factor in considering renting is the cost of insurance on the contents of the rented house. This cost should be included in the compared cost of renting, since homeowner's insurance includes coverage for contents. Additionally, one can conduct cost calculations for the second and subsequent years of homeownership.

Conclusion

The costs of homeownership as summarized in table 1 illustrate the different interpretations and the volatility of cost estimates. For individuals in a 29-percent income-tax bracket who are likely to have limited income, any miscalculations, misconceptions, and deceptions could have disastrous consequences, as is emphasized by noticing that the foregoing cost estimates have a range of $296 a month, or $3552 a year. Also the individual faces the prospect of losing the $4250 investment as well as incurring substantial selling expenses. These pitfalls are more likely to be avoided with a knowledge of the mathematics of finance.

It is interesting to note the level of mathematics used in these calculations. Involved are percents, exponents, the solution of equations, the evaluation of formulas, logarithms, concepts of interest, and the use of calculators. Problem solving in finance is a competence that is used very commonly in making business and domestic decisions, yet it is not frequently taught in school mathematics. It should be in the repertoire of many citizens and should be taught in the schools.

TABLE 1

Estimates of Cost of Homeownership

Monthly Cost	Considerations
$589	Monthly payment including only principal and interest
$664	Monthly payment including principal, interest, taxes, and insurance
$704	The monthly cost above plus monthly cost of maintenance and replacement
$525	The monthly cost above less tax break based on taxes and interest
$514	The cost above reduced by present value of first-year principal reduction
$408	The cost above reduced by present value of first-year appreciation
$419	Cost reduced by present value of first-year appreciation after selling expenses
$435	The cost above increased by forfeited interest earning on original investment

BIBLIOGRAPHY

Armstrong, Jan, and Joseph Uhl. "Survey of Consumer Education Programs in the United States." *Journal of Home Economics* 63 (October 1971):524–30.

Bland, Paul, and Betty Given. "An Analysis of Two Car-Buying Strategies." *Mathematics Teacher* 76 (February 1983):124–27.

Brown, Richard G. "The Rule of 72." *Mathematics Teacher* 60 (November 1966):638–39.

Gorman, E. Thomas. *A National Assessment of Consumer Education Literacy of Prospective Teachers from All Disciplines.* Blacksburg, Va.: U. S. Office of Education and Virginia Polytechnic Institute and State University, July 1977.

Huenneke, Steve (business editor). "Renters Not Getting Such a Bad Break after All in Housing Market." *Denton Record Chronical,* Denton, Texas, 4 January 1984.

National Council of Teachers of Mathematics. *An Agenda for Action: Recommendations for School Mathematics of the 1980s.* Reston, Va.: The Council, 1980.

Soler, Francisco deP., and Richard Schuster. "Compound Growth and Related Situations: A Problem-solving Approach." *Mathematics Teacher* 75 (November 1982):640–44.

Zill, Dennis G., Edwin F. Beckenbach, William Wooton, and Irving Drooyan. *College Mathematics for Students of Business, Life Sciences, and Social Sciences.* 2d ed. Belmont, Calif.: Wadsworth Publishing Co., 1982. ❦

3

GEOMETRY

Geometry is from the Greek words meaning "earth" (*geo*) and "measurement" (*metric*). However, pre-Greek Babylonian clay tablets dating from around 2000 B.C. contain geometry applications involving measurements of length, area, and volume. For example, consider the following problem from *Science Awakening* (van der Waerden 1963, p. 76):

A patu (beam?) of length 30 (stands against a wall). The upper end has slipped down a distance of 6. How far did the lower end move?

A diagram, labeled using current notation, is in figure 3.1. The solution uses the Pythagorean theorem or Pythagorean triples, though the problem and solution predate Pythagoras (ca. 580–497 B.C.) by over a thousand years. However, Pythagoras seems to have given the first proof of the theorem.

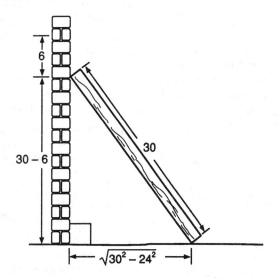

Fig. 3.1. Beam leaning against the wall

The most famous early application of geometry was measuring the circumference of the earth by the Greek Eratosthenes about 230 B.C. Consider figure 3.2. Assume that the earth is spherical and that the sun is far away from the earth. The sun's rays are then parallel and strike two sticks perpendicular to the earth so that the two angles marked θ have equal measures. The radius of the spherical earth is a transversal of the two parallel lines. Eratosthenes had sticks placed in Alexandria and Syene. (Syene is the present-day city of Aswan.) At precisely noon, there was no shadow at Syene, but there was an angle θ of about $2\pi/50$ at Alexandria. The distance from Alexandria to Syene was paced and found to be about 5000 units, where one unit (μ) is about 516.73 feet. Letting C be the circumference of the earth, we find

$$\frac{\theta}{2\pi} = \frac{5000\mu}{C}$$

61

Solving the equation gives that C is approximately 25 000 miles, which is within twenty-five miles of the true value. (A *true* value is an approximation because the earth is not exactly spherical.)

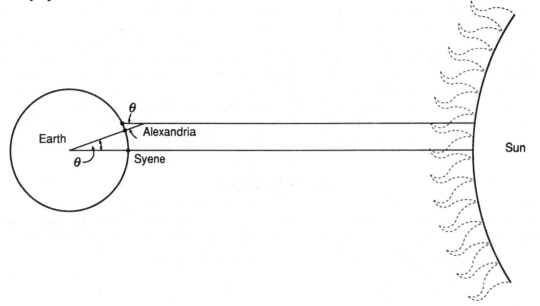

Fig. 3.2. Sun's rays striking the earth

The Greeks developed important theoretical results in geometry. These included the proof by Pythagoras of the theorem bearing his name, the formal verification of the formulas for the area of a circle and the volume of a sphere as well as the bounding of the value of π by Archimedes, and the analysis of the conic sections by Apollonius (ca. 250–200 B.C.). For more mathematical details of these achievements, see *Historical Topics for the Mathematics Classroom* (NCTM 1989).

The most important Greek geometry contribution is *The Elements* by Euclid, dated about 300 B.C. For the first time, a mathematical field was developed from a few basic rules (postulates or axioms), and all the results were established in a logical manner using only these rules. When written, the thirteen books of *The Elements* were a compilation of all mathematical knowledge. The five postulates were the basic rules for geometry, and the five common notions of *The Elements* represented the rules of all mathematics! Although it was the definitive mathematical text for two thousand years, the logical errors in this text were not discovered and rectified until 1900 by David Hilbert in his *Grundlagen der Geometrie* (*Foundations of Geometry* [Hilbert 1980]).

The Elements set the mathematical standard for what it means to understand the mathematical structure of a field and revolutionized the way mathematicians sought to understand their field.

The articles in this section sample a wide range of applications of geometry. As indicated, early empirical work in geometry dealt with measuring land. Steffani uses geoboards to solve surveying problems appropriate for junior high school, senior high school, and college students. In his article "Dirichlet Polygons—an Example of Geometry in Geography," O'Shea considers special polygons and their application in geography.

The analysis of properties of geometric shapes allowed the Greeks to address many applied problems. Roberts considers geometric problems arising from the shape of honeycombs. One problem he considers is covering a plane with regular polygons. This mathematical problem has unexpected artistic applications, as Teeters shows. He extends the discussion of covering the plane by considering the geometry in the work of Escher.

The application of mathematics to other artistic areas was recognized by the early Greeks, who were able to use mathematics to analyze music. Maor discusses in an interview some of the applications of geometry and algebra to music. O'Shea extends this to musical composition by using number theory and geometric transformations in "Geometric Transformations and Musical Composition."

Even sports problems have been considered in geometry. Byrne uses similar triangles to compute angles for pool shots. Backler illustrates some problems with using an appropriate model for physical problems. He uses geometry to show that some pool shots are impossible using the usual models from physics. (Spins, though, can make the shots possible.) Dieffenback uses graphs and matrices to solve sport-team ranking problems.

The formal logic-and-proof aspects of geometry, shown in Euclid's *Elements*, have applications also. Goldberg gives applications of logic to medical diagnoses.

REFERENCES

Euclid. *The Elements*. 2d ed. Edited by Thomas L. Heath. New York: Dover Publications, 1956.

Hilbert, David. *Foundations of Geometry*. Translated by Leo Unger. LaSalle, Ill.: Open Court Publishing Co., 1980.

National Council of Teachers of Mathematics. *Historical Topics for the Mathematics Classroom*. Thirty-first Yearbook of the National Council of Teachers of Mathematics. 2d ed. Reston, Va.: The Council, 1989.

Van der Waerden, B. L. *Science Awakening*. New York: John Wiley & Sons, 1963.

The Bank Shot

By DAN BYRNE, Antelope Valley College, Lancaster, CA 93534

During a game of pool, a player often discovers that no direct shot into a pocket is possible. When confronted with this predicament, the player will often resort to a bank shot. Figure 1 illustrates a typical situation in which the dark object ball is to be banked into the side pocket.

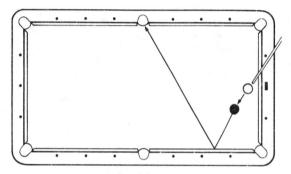

Fig. 1. Where should the black ball hit the side cushion in order to go into the opposite side pocket? (figure not to scale)

Anyone who has ever attempted to bank a ball into a pocket has discovered that this is no simple task. After several misses, one might begin to wonder if there is any method for finding the correct spot on the cushion so the ball will bounce into the desired pocket. We shall investigate two such methods here. Throughout this article, two assumptions will be made: first, that we have a pool table with a perfectly flat surface and whose cushions form a rectangle; and second, that the balls bounce off the cushions in the same way light reflects off a mirror, that is, the angle of incidence is equal to the angle of reflection.

The first technique uses a straightedge and a compass to find the point of contact on the cushion by reflecting the object ball. First, using the center of the object ball as center, draw a circle that intersects the cushion in two points. Then, with the two points as centers, draw two more circles with the same radius as the first one. The

last two circles intersect at two points: the center of the original object ball and the center of its reflected image. Now connect the center of the reflected ball to the side pocket, and the desired point of contact is where the line intersects the cushion (fig. 2).

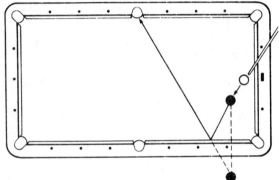

Fig. 2. One approach is to imagine the lines created by the reflected image of the dark ball.

This technique is fine for the mathematician, but it is of little use to the pool player. Another method for making bank shots, which can actually be applied on a pool table, is presented in Martin and Reeves's *The 99 Critical Shots in Pool* (fig. 3): "Drop a line *a* from the object ball to

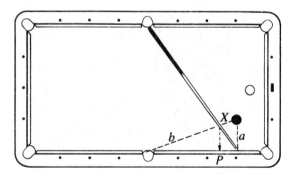

Fig. 3. A more practical approach is to imagine point *P* as the foot of the perpendicular from *X*.

the cushion and another line *b* to the pocket across from the pocket in which you plan to sink your ball.... Lay your cue stick down on the table, reaching from where line *a* touched the cushion to the pocket in which you wish to sink the ball. It crosses line *b* at *X*. Now drop a line in your mind's eye down from *X* to the cushion, and that is the spot to which you shoot the object ball." Let this chosen point be called *P*.

Unlike the first method, this one is clearly applicable on a pool table. But one wonders if *P* is the same point of contact that was found with a straightedge and compass, or if it is just a close approximation good enough for a pool hall. What needs to be demonstrated is that *P* is the same point on the cushion found by using the first method. Assume that *S* is the center of the desired pocket and *T* is the center of the pocket on the opposite side (fig. 4). Suppose the object ball is driven to *P*, rebounds off the cushion, and hits somewhere on the opposite cushion, arbitrarily called *Q*. Let *R* be chosen such that it is directly opposite *Q*, so $\overline{QR}$ is perpendicular to the cushion. If it can be shown that *PR* is equal to *PT*, then *R* must be in the side pocket. Hence, *Q* must be in the opposite side pocket, which shows that *P* was the correct point.

Proof. Since $\angle UVP$ and $\angle QRP$ are both right angles, and $\angle UPV \cong \angle QPR$ by hypothesis, it follows that $\triangle UVP \sim \triangle QRP$

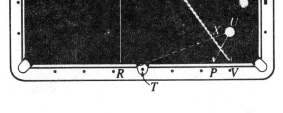

Fig. 4. Similar triangles can be used to show that *P* in this figure is the same point used in the second figure.

from the angle-angle similarity theorem. Therefore,

$$\frac{VP}{UV} = \frac{RP}{QR},$$

so that

(1) $$UV \cdot RP = PV \cdot QR.$$

Since $\triangle STV \sim \triangle XPV$ by the **angle-angle** similarity theorem,

$$\frac{ST}{TV} = \frac{XP}{PV},$$

so that

$$TV \cdot XP = PV \cdot ST,$$

which, after substituting *QR* for *ST*, gives

(2) $$TV \cdot XP = PV \cdot QR.$$

Substituting equation (2) into equation (1) gives

(3) $$UV \cdot PR = TV \cdot XP.$$

And since $\triangle UVT \sim \triangle XPT$ by the angle-angle similarity theorem,

$$\frac{UV}{TV} = \frac{XP}{TP},$$

so that

(4) $$UV \cdot PT = TV \cdot XP.$$

Substituting equation (4) into equation (3) gives

$$UV \cdot PR = UV \cdot PT,$$

and as long as $UV \neq 0$,

$$PR = PT.$$

This result demonstrates that the second method gives the correct point of contact.

Now to the practical considerations involved in making a bank shot. Making the object ball hit point *P* is *not* accomplished by aiming directly at *P*. If one aims directly at *P*, the ball will touch the cushion on the near side of *P*. Hence, the player will have to use some judgment based on experience, even if he or she knows the exact spot where the ball is supposed to strike the cushion.

More judgment is also required when one considers the spin and speed of the ball, because pool balls do not behave the way light rays do, that is, the angle of incidence is equal to the angle of reflection. Hence, there is no guaranteed way of banking the ball. As any good player knows, the way to learn how to bank balls is through practice, practice, and more practice.

BIBLIOGRAPHY

Martin, Ray, and Rosser Reeves. *The 99 Critical Shots in Pool*. New York: New York Times Books, 1977.

May, Beverly A. "Sharing Teaching Ideas: Reflections on Miniature Golf." *Mathematics Teacher* 78 (May 1985): 351–53.

Woodward, Ernest, and Thomas Ray Hamel. "Developing Mathematics on a Pool Table." *Mathematics Teacher* 70 (February 1977):154–63.

A MATHEMATICAL MODEL AND ITS "UNREALISTIC" CONSEQUENCES

A mathematical model of elastic collisions is applied to a shot on a pool table.

By **JORDAN C. BACKLER**

Braintree, Massachusetts

IN USING mathematics to describe a physical process, the physicist often assumes conditions that, though they seem idealized, allow him to gain useful insights from his mathematical model.

A simple mathematical model describes elastic collisions between particles (collisions in which no energy is lost). It provides the interesting result (see, for example, French [1971, pp. 339–44]) that if two particles of equal mass collide elastically, one of them being initially at rest, they will recede along directions at right angles to each other, provided they do not meet head-on (fig. 1). That is, θ and ϕ depend on the impact parameter b ($b > 0$), but $\theta + \phi$ is always 90°.

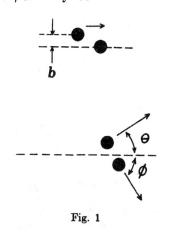

Fig. 1

If we apply this result to a "real life" situation (suggested by George Leung of Southeastern Massachusetts University), we obtain an interesting illustration of the geometry theorem stating that a triangle inscribed in a semicircle must be a right triangle. Theoretically, a ball lying anywhere on the semicircle shown in figure 2 (center at A, radius $w/2$) must "scratch" if one tries to hit it into the pockets at X or Y. (That is, the pool ball will go into one pocket and the cue ball will go into the other.)

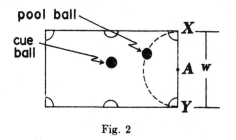

Fig. 2

In reality, of course, there are complications. Sometimes a head-on shot can be made, or "english" (spin) can be put on the cue ball, or the two balls might lie so that the pool ball could be sunk but with friction preventing the cue ball from reaching the other pocket. All these complications violate the assumed conditions of the model, so even though this pool table illustration brings out a geometric point, it is not very "realistic." But the model yields good results if the "pool balls" are, for example, low-energy protons in a particle accelerator. The physicist's model has "realistic" consequences if it is applied to a situation where its assumptions are satisfied.

REFERENCES

French, A. P. *Newtonian Mechanics.* New York: W. W. Norton & Co., 1971.

Lennes, N. J. "On the Motion of a Ball on a Billiard Table." *American Mathematical Monthly* 12 (1905): 152–55.

THE SURVEYOR AND THE GEOBOARD

Polygons, areas, coordinates, determinants,
vectors, surveying, and the geoboard are all tied together.

By RONALD R. STEFFANI
Southern Oregon State College
Ashland, Oregon 97520

DO YOU have a polygonal piece of property? Do you need to know its area? Obviously, you need a surveyor to solve your problem, but did you know that a surveyor will use a geoboard to calculate the extent of your estate? The surveyor's geoboard method presents an applied problem in mathematics that can be studied and analyzed at most any level of school mathematics from grade four to college.

The Problem

The earth, of course, is the geoboard on which a surveyor operates. In order to scale down the activity to classroom size we will consider the problem on an ordinary geoboard. To determine the area of a polygonal figure we need only find the coordinates of the polygon's vertices and then use a bit of arithmetic. For example, consider the pentagon of figure 1.

Using the coordinates, form the "fractions" $\frac{2\ 4\ 4\ 3\ 2\ 2}{1\ 1\ 3\ 4\ 3\ 1}$. Next form the "down" cross products and compute the sum.

$$
\begin{aligned}
2 \times 1 &= 2 \\
4 \times 3 &= 12 \\
4 \times 4 &= 16 \\
3 \times 3 &= 9 \\
2 \times 1 &= \underline{2} \\
\text{Sum} &= \overline{41}
\end{aligned}
$$

This work was completed while the author was on sabbatical leave at the University of Georgia.

Similarly, form the "up" cross products and form the sum.

$$
\begin{aligned}
1 \times 4 &= 4 \\
1 \times 4 &= 4 \\
3 \times 3 &= 9 \\
4 \times 2 &= 8 \\
3 \times 2 &= \underline{6} \\
\text{Sum} &= \overline{31}
\end{aligned}
$$

Finally, find one-half the difference of the two sums, $\frac{1}{2}(41 - 31) = \frac{1}{2}(10) = 5$, which is the area of the polygon in figure 1. Readers are invited to try their skill with other figures to check the validity of this process.

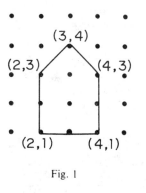

Fig. 1

The General Problem

For students in the primary grades the above examples may be sufficient verification that the process indeed works. However, the problem lends itself nicely to analysis by students from junior high to the college level. Some of the various levels of justification will be explored in the remainder of this article.

Junior high

One of the simplest generalizations of the surveyor's method is to consider a triangle whose base is parallel to one of the axes. (See fig. 2).

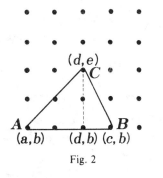

Fig. 2

Using the formula for the area of a triangle we have

$$\text{area } \triangle ABC = \tfrac{1}{2}(c - a)(e - b)$$
$$= \tfrac{1}{2}(ce + ab - ae - bc).$$

The surveyor's method yields
$$\begin{matrix} a & c & d & a \\ b & b & e & b \end{matrix}$$

$$\tfrac{1}{2}((ab + ce + db) - (bc + bd + ea))$$
$$= \tfrac{1}{2}(ce + ab - ae - bc).$$

The next level of difficulty would be to consider any triangle on the geoboard. The analysis of this problem can be found in an article by A. A. Hiatt in the November 1972 *Mathematics Teacher.*

High school

Notice that for those students familiar with determinants, the surveyor's method for triangles is identical to the formula

$$A = \tfrac{1}{2} \begin{vmatrix} 1 & a & b \\ 1 & c & b \\ 1 & d & e \end{vmatrix}.$$

Since any convex polygon can be divided into a finite number of triangles, the method can be generalized to all convex polygons. The reader may enjoy proving the formula for convex *n*-gons and concave polygons.

Senior high and college

For students familiar with vector algebra, the surveyor's method may look analogous to vector cross products. As you may recall, the cross product of two vectors yields a vector perpendicular to the plane of the two vectors and whose magnitude is equal to the area of the parallelogram determined by the two given vectors.

For example,

$$(a\vec{i} + b\vec{j}) \times (c\vec{i} + d\vec{j})$$

$$= \begin{vmatrix} \vec{i} & \vec{j} & \vec{k} \\ a & b & 0 \\ c & d & 0 \end{vmatrix} = (ad - bc)\vec{k}.$$

Consider the special case of a rectangle whose sides are parallel to the edges of the geoboard.

$$\vec{A} \times \vec{B} = \begin{vmatrix} \vec{i} & \vec{j} & \vec{k} \\ c & b & 0 \\ c & d & 0 \end{vmatrix} = (cd - bc)\vec{k}.$$

The magnitude is

$$|\vec{A} \times \vec{B}| = (cd - bc)$$

and thus $\tfrac{1}{2}(cd - bc)$ is $\tfrac{1}{2}$ the area of the parallelogram formed by $\vec{A}$ and $\vec{B}$. This area is shaded in figure 3. Taking the four

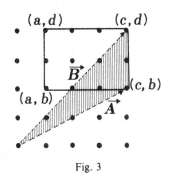

Fig. 3

vertices pairwise and consecutively, we can generate three other vector products, as in figure 4.

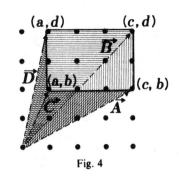

Fig. 4

$$\vec{A} \times \vec{C} = \begin{vmatrix} \vec{i} & \vec{j} & \vec{k} \\ c & b & 0 \\ a & b & 0 \end{vmatrix} = (cb - ab)\vec{k}$$

$$\vec{B} \times \vec{D} = \begin{vmatrix} \vec{i} & \vec{j} & \vec{k} \\ c & d & 0 \\ a & d & 0 \end{vmatrix} = (cd - ad)\vec{k}$$

$$\vec{C} \times \vec{D} = \begin{vmatrix} \vec{i} & \vec{j} & \vec{k} \\ a & b & 0 \\ a & d & 0 \end{vmatrix} = (ad - ab)\vec{k}$$

Note also that the area of the rectangle in terms of the shaded regions is

(▥ + ▤) − (▧ + ▨)

In terms of one-half the magnitude of the vectors we have

$\tfrac{1}{2}(|\vec{A} \times \vec{B}| + |\vec{B} \times \vec{D}|)$
$\qquad\qquad -\tfrac{1}{2}(|\vec{A} \times \vec{C}| + |\vec{C} \times \vec{D}|)$
$= \tfrac{1}{2}[(cd - bc) + (cd - ad)$
$\qquad\qquad - (cb - ab) - (ad - ab)]$

$= \tfrac{1}{2}[c(d - b) + d(c - a)$
$\qquad\qquad - b(c - a) - a(d - b)]$
$= \tfrac{1}{2}[(d - b)(c - a) + (c - a)(d - b)]$
$= \tfrac{1}{2} \cdot 2(d - b)(c - a)$
$= \quad [(d - b)(c - a)].$

Using the surveyor's method with $\begin{smallmatrix} a & c & c & a & a \\ b & b & d & d & b \end{smallmatrix}$ yields precisely the same expressions as the foregoing, as can easily be verified by the reader.

Extensions and Questions

Many questions about the surveyor's method for finding area can be posed and explored.

1. Does it make any difference which vertex is chosen as the starting point?

2. Does it make any difference where the origin is chosen?

3. Is there a three-dimensional extension of the method to determine volumes?

4. Must the fractions be written in consecutive order of the vertices? Can the fractions be written inverted?

5. Do surveyors really use this method? Yes, indeed! In fact, surveying teams have been very busy plotting grid points on the U.S. geoboard (see photograph).

REFERENCE

Hiatt, A. A. "Problem Solving in Geometry." *Mathematics Teacher* 66 (November 1972): 595–600.

Honeycomb Geometry: Applied Mathematics in Nature

By WILLIAM J. ROBERTS, Plymouth State College, Plymouth, NH 03264

"Why do the bees make such funny looking holes?" asked one inquisitive child during a recent visit to our apiary. When I looked at the question seriously, it was clear that the reason for the hexagonal shape could be understood by a high school class in geometry and that exploring its application would be interesting toward the end of the semester. We make use of four ideas from plane geometry:

1. The fact that each angle of a regular polygon of n sides is of measure $(n - 2)180°/n$;

2. The fact that the measure of an exterior angle of a regular polygon is $360°/n$;

3. Relationships involving the $30°$–$60°$ triangle;

4. Formulas for the areas of squares, circles, equilateral triangles, and regular hexagons.

Regular Shapes That Cover the Plane

First, we show that only three polygons tessellate the plane (i.e., cover the plane without leaving any open regions). The sum of the angle measures about any vertex is $360°$. Now, let k be the number of regular polygons of n sides that meet at some vertex. Then, since each interior angle has measure $(n - 2)180°/n$, we conclude that

$$((n - 2)180°/n)k = 360°.$$

A little algebra quickly leads to the relationship that $(n - 2)k = 2n$; hence,

$$nk - 2k - 2n + 4 = 4,$$

or

$$(n - 2)(k - 2) = 4.$$

Since only positive integral solutions are sought, a check shows that the only solutions are $n = 3$ and $k = 6$, $n = 4$ and $k = 4$, $n = 6$ and $k = 3$, corresponding to the equilateral triangle, the square, and the regular hexagon.

Let us consider only these polygons and the circle as possible shapes for cells in the comb. The circle is included as a possible shape since it is the plane figure that encloses maximal area for a fixed perimeter. For given perimeter p, the areas of the figures under consideration are shown in table 1.

TABLE 1

Areas of Figures with Perimeter p

Figure	Area in Square Units
Equilateral triangle	$p^2\sqrt{3}/36 \approx 0.05p^2.$
Square	$p^2/16 \approx 0.06p^2.$
Regular hexagon	$p^2\sqrt{3}/24 \approx 0.07p^2.$
Circle	$p^2/4\pi \approx 0.08p^2.$

The equilateral triangle and the square are less suitable, as table 1 illustrates, since they enclose less area than the regular hexagon or the circle. Furthermore, as shown in figure 1, the formation of cells

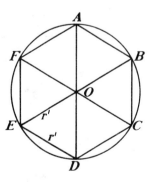

Fig. 1.   Equilateral cells

from equilateral triangles would result in the creation of hexagonal cross sections with radial segments $\overline{OA}, \overline{OB}, \overline{OC}, \overline{OD}, \overline{OE},$ and $\overline{OF}$ included. We should recognize that this choice would necessitate the use of twice the amount of wax for construction when compared to the bounding regular hexagon $ABCDEF$.

The two-cell configurations remaining to be compared are the circle and the hexagon. A circle would appear at first thought to be the more appropriate if the only constraint were to maximize the cross-sectional area. But a question regarding the shaded region illustrated in figure 2(a) arises. Suppose that the bees were to construct a comb using a circular format with spaces between the cells as illustrated. Any configuration for the comb must allow for the passage of the bee within the cell yet not be too large, that is, a circle of fixed diameter can be inscribed in the region created by the bees. Langstroth (1977), the leading pioneer in the design of modern hives, states:

The size of the cells in which workers are reared never varies. The same may substantially be said of the drone (male bee) cells, which are very considerably larger; the cells in which honey is stored often vary exceedingly in depth, while in diameter they are of all sizes from that of the worker-cells to that of the drones.

(*Note:* Langstroth's invention of the movable-frame hive revolutionized beekeeping from a hobby to a lucrative commercial enterprise.)

The restriction of size to usable cells means that we can minimally inscribe a circle of radius b yet not larger than $1.25b$ (where b means a worker can fit and $1.25b$ means a drone will pass). Any cell of a size outside this interval would be unusable by the bees, since it would be either too small or too large. Essentially, if the bees were to use the structure of figure 2(a), then a bee would have to fit into the shaded region to make maximum use of available space. One can see by referring to figure 2(b) that a circle of radius b must then be inscribed in the region. Since $\triangle PQR$ is equilateral,

$$\triangle PRS \cong \triangle PSQ \cong \triangle QSR,$$

therefore $m \angle SQR = 30°$. We find, recalling a few facts from the 30°–60° right triangle, that

$$\frac{r}{(r + b)} = \frac{\sqrt{3}}{2};$$

hence, $r = \sqrt{3}b/(2 - \sqrt{3})$, or approximately $6.46b$. This result greatly exceeds the $1.25b$ radial restriction on the size of a cell. Thus, the bees' constraints would eliminate the pattern illustrated in figure 2(a).

The efficiency of the hexagonal cell over the circular cell is illustrated in figure

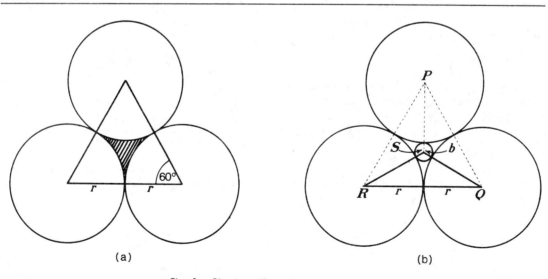

(a)   (b)

Fig. 2.   Circular cells produce wasted space.

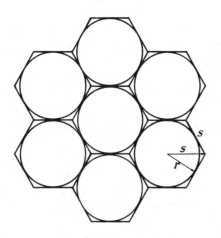

Fig. 3. Hexagonal cells are the most efficient.

3. The hexagonal pattern makes use of the shaded region of figure 2(a). The comparative efficiency of the hexagonal cell versus the circular cell is shown in table 2.

We can demonstrate from figure 3 that the construction of seven circles uses more wax than the construction of seven hexagons. Seven hexagons can be constructed from six outer cells, yielding the central cell without using additional wax—that is, one free hexagon! In addition, the sharing of sides by the six surrounding hexagons yields another free hexagon. So the bees are

TABLE 2

Areas of Figures with Radius r

Figure	Perimeter	Area
Circle	$2\pi r$	πr^2
Hexagon	$4r\sqrt{3}$	$2r^2\sqrt{3}$

using the perimeters of five hexagons to obtain an area equivalent to seven hexagons. Note that the circumference of seven circles is equal to $14\pi r$, which is greater than $20r\sqrt{3}$, the perimeter of five hexagons.

$$\frac{14\pi r - 20r\sqrt{3}}{14\pi r} \approx 0.2136 = 21.4\%.$$

This calculation shows that the seven circles have greater perimeter than the hexagons by 5.5 percent. Furthermore, since $7\pi r^2$ is less than $14r^2\sqrt{3}$, we see that the region enclosed by seven circles will be about 10.3 percent less than that enclosed by seven hexagons.

$$\frac{7\pi r^2 - 14r^2\sqrt{3}}{7\pi r^2} \approx {}^-0.103 = {}^-10.3\%.$$

We have thus shown that the hexagonal pattern of the comb maximizes the enclosed region while minimizing the wax needed for construction; it furthermore satisfies the bees' utilitarian cell-size constraint. Langstroth (1977, pp. 75–76) notes:

The cells of the bees are found perfectly to answer all the most refined conditions of a very intricate mathematical problem. Let it be required to find what shape a given quantity of matter must take in order to have the greatest capacity and the greatest strength, requiring at the same time the least space, and the least labor in its construction. This problem has been solved by the most refined processes of higher mathematics, and the result is the hexagonal or six-sided cell of the honeybee.... At first sight a circle would seem to be the best shape for the development of the larvae; but such a figure would have caused a needless sacrifice of space, materials, and strength; while honey which now adheres so admirably to the many angles or corners of the six-sided cells would have been more liable to run out!

REFERENCE

Langstroth, Lorenzo L. *Langstroth on the Hive and the Honey-Bee.* Greenfield, Mass.: 1853. Reprint. Medina, Ohio: A. I. Root Co.. 1977.

BIBLIOGRAPHY

Page, Warren. "New beesness" (Reader Reflections). *Mathematics Teacher* 72 (October 1979):486–87.

Root, Amos I., et al. *ABC and XYZ of Bee Culture.* Medina, Ohio: A. I. Root Co., 1981.

Siemens, David F., Jr. "The Mathematics of the Honeycomb." *Mathematics Teacher* 58 (April 1965):334–37.

———. "Of Bees and Mathematicians." *Mathematics Teacher* 60 (November 1967):758–60. ◗

Dirichlet Polygons—an Example of Geometry in Geography

By THOMAS O'SHEA, Simon Fraser University, Burnaby, BC V5A 1S6

The teaching of geometry in the elementary school can be an exciting experience; children are receptive to experimentation, and many activities can be devised to facilitate learning. Generally, however, the use of exploration in geometry decreases as students progress through school and as they begin the study of formal axiomatic systems. In the higher grades we need to present interesting uses of geometry that will allow students to develop their powers of exploration and problem solving. The purpose of this article is to outline an example of how geometry serves as a model in the real world and to suggest how it might be used at the high school level.

Let us consider a simple problem in the geography of human settlement (based on Haggett [1972, 366]). Suppose new territory, perhaps the original forested area in North America, is being settled without the benefit of a survey and a number of homesteads occupy positions as shown in figure 1. Assume that the home (the central point) is the focus of each family unit and that the cleared and cultivated area expands about the home in a circular fashion. Furthermore, assume that the cultivated areas around the homes expand at the same rate. What will the final boundaries between farms look like? The reader is invited to explore and make conjectures as to the result before reading on.

One way to attack the problem is to increase the size of each circle until several begin to overlap. The common chord of overlapping circles becomes the natural boundary, assuming reasonable and conciliatory attitudes among neighbors. On this basis, the boundaries begin to unfold, as shown in figure 2.

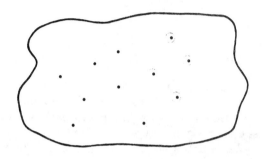

Fig. 1. Farmhouses and surrounding cultivated land in a forested area

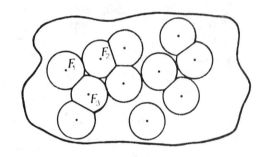

Fig. 2. Homestead boundaries at one time during expansion

If we continue this procedure, we begin to develop the feeling that the boundaries and their relationship to the central farmhouses are special. In particular, by examining farms F_1, F_2, and F_3, one can see that the boundaries formed by the common chords of the three circles are destined to meet at a common point. This point, in fact, is the intersection of the perpendicular bisectors of the segments joining adjacent farmhouses, that is, the circumcenter of the triangle $F_1F_2F_3$. The final boundaries for the entire region are shown in figure 3, and the procedure for constructing them follows.

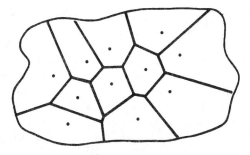

Fig. 3. Final boundaries for the region

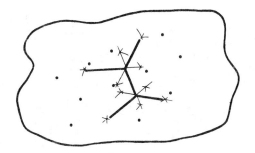

Fig. 5. The compass-and-straightedge construction of the boundaries

To construct the boundaries around any collection of farmhouses, or control points, first join the adjacent control points (see fig. 4). Some doubt may exist about which points should be joined; for example, in the quadrilateral $P_1P_2P_3P_4$ in figure 4, the alternative would be to connect P_1 and P_3 instead of P_2 and P_4. The recommended procedure is to select the shorter diagonal. The result will be a network of triangles, and the circumcenters of the triangles are the vertices of the network.

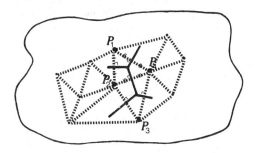

Fig. 4. The boundaries are formed by the perpendicular bisectors of the network's segments.

To determine the location of the circumcenters, the simplest procedure is to use a compass to construct the perpendicular bisectors of the segments of the triangular network. With practice, the segments themselves need not be drawn, thus lessening the confusion in the diagram (see fig. 5). As a general rule, I have found it easiest to begin with the outer points to establish the radiating boundaries and then, after erasing the construction arcs, to work my way into the inner region.

The polygons in figure 3 are called Dirichlet (Deer-ish´-lay) polygons after the German mathematician who first discussed their properties in 1850. One important property of a Dirichlet polygon is that all points within the polygon are closer to its control point than to any other control point. Thus, in the example of the settlement, all portions of the land within a polgon are closer to the enclosed farmhouse than to any other farmhouse. This property has given rise to several interesting applications.

Measuring rainfall using Dirichlet polygons

To determine the mean rainfall over a region containing several rain gauges, the use of the arithmetic average of the gauge readings may not be satisfactory. If the gauges are located fairly uniformly and little variation in rainfall occurs, the mean of the readings will be reasonably accurate. If, however, because of geographic considerations, the gauges are not uniformly distributed, a better approach is to weight each reading by the land area it represents. The use of Dirichlet polygons for this purpose was first suggested by Thiessen (1911).

To illustrate Thiessen's procedure I have chosen the hypothetical problem of determining the mean rainfall for Okanogan County in the state of Washington, as shown in figure 6. Suppose that rain gauges are located at weather stations S_1, S_2, S_3, ..., S_{10}. Suppose the rainfall at each station is R_1, R_2, R_3, ..., R_{10} and the area within Okanogan County dominated by each station is A_1, A_2, A_3, ..., A_{10}. If the area of the county is A, then the weighted

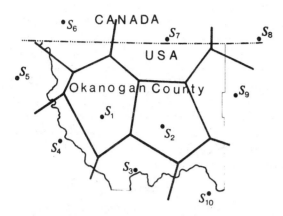

Fig. 6. Dirichlet polygons constructed around a number of weather stations

mean rainfall (R) for the region is given by the following:

$$R = \frac{A_1}{A} R_1 + \frac{A_2}{A} R_2 + \frac{A_3}{A} R_3 + \cdots + \frac{A_{10}}{A} R_{10}$$

$$= \frac{A_1 R_1 + A_2 R_2 + A_3 R_3 + \cdots + A_{10} R_{10}}{A}$$

Another advantage of this method of determining rainfall is that it includes the effect of readings from stations outside the region of interest. In figure 6 these stations are S_4 to S_{10}. Calculations based on readings only from within the region would be less representative of the pattern of rainfall.

The one technical problem in exploring this use of Dirichlet polygons lies in the measurement of irregular areas. A mechanical device admirably suited to this purpose is the polar planimeter, once used extensively in highway design but now largely replaced by the computer. The planimeter is available through drafting equipment suppliers at a cost of approximately $200. Alternatively, schools might contact local engineering offices for used planimeters or donations.

Other uses

Bogue (1948) used Dirichlet polygons to study the economic influence of sixty-seven metropolitan centers across the U. S. By working on the assumption that the economic influence of the centers was equal,

he was able to demarcate each center's region of influence.

In a similar vein, Cole and King (1968) suggested the use of the model to determine how well a system of administrative centers matches the areas for which they are responsible. In essence, they suggested overlaying a system of Dirichlet polygons on a map showing the existing administrative boundaries to see how well the theoretical and actual boundaries coincide.

Apart from the applicability of the model, numerous enrichment activities can be developed (cf. Coxeter [1969]). For example, consider figure 7, in which the control points are located in a grid pattern. Join the adjacent points to produce a network of congruent nonobtuse triangles. Form the Dirichlet region around each control point by joining the circumcenters of the triangles having the control point as a vertex. Continue to construct the Dirichlet region around each control point, and a network of congruent tessellating hexagons is revealed. If the configuration of points is changed so that angle A in figure 7 is increased, two opposite sides of the Dirichlet polygon shrink until, when $m \angle A = 90$, the region becomes rectangular.

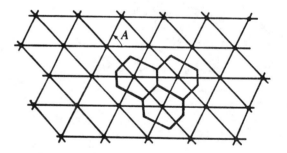

Fig. 7. Dirichlet polygons on a grid yield a tessellating pattern.

The idea can be extended into three-dimensional space. If one visualizes a set of lattice points in space, the Dirichlet polyhedron around a given control point consists of all points in space closer to that point than to any other lattice point. For a basic cubic lattice the Dirichlet polyhedron is a cube. For a face-centered lattice it is a rhombic dodecahedron. For example, if a set of stacked cannonballs were compressed, the result would be a tessellating set of solids, each having twelve rhombic faces. For a body-centered lattice, the Dirichlet polyhedron takes the form of a truncated octahedron, one of the Archimedean solids, which has six square faces and eight hexagonal faces. This form is the one that is produced in the interior of a froth of soap bubbles. A marvelous discussion of these two solids can be found in Thompson (1961, 119–25).

Conclusions

Dirichlet polygons can be introduced at the junior high school level when students first encounter basic geometric constructions. At that level the polygons can provide a rationale for the construction of the perpendicular bisector of a segment. Later on, the property of the perpendicular bisector as the set of points equidistant from two given points can be used to introduce the notion of inequalities in geometry, that is, the perpendicular bisector becomes the boundary separating sets of points that are closer to one given point than to the other.

In the rainfall example, Dirichlet polygons offer a tangible example of weighted averages, a concept that is widely used in practice but not adequately covered in the curriculum.

For those readers intrigued by the use of mathematical models in geography, Haggett's (1972) textbook has a wealth of examples that can be adapted for use at the secondary school level.

REFERENCES

Bogue, Donald J. "The Structure of the Metropolitan Community: A Study of Dominance and Subdominance." Master's thesis, University of Michigan, Ann Arbor, 1948.

Cole, John P., and Cuchlaine A. M. King. *Quantitative Geography: Techniques and Theories in Geography.* New York: John Wiley & Sons, 1968.

Coxeter, H. S. M. *Introduction to Geometry.* 2d ed. New York: John Wiley & Sons, 1969.

Haggett, Peter. *Geography: A Modern Synthesis.* New York: Harper & Row, 1972.

Thiessen, A. H. "Precipitation Averages for Large Areas." *Monthly Weather Review* 39 (November 1911):1082–84.

Thompson, D'Arcy W. *On Growth and Form.* London: Cambridge University Press, 1961.

HOW TO DRAW TESSELLATIONS OF THE ESCHER TYPE

A short, clear discussion showing how you or your students can create tessellation art.

By **JOSEPH L. TEETERS**

University of Wisconsin—Eau Claire
Eau Claire, Wisconsin

THE late Dutch artist M. C. Escher was famous for, among other things, artistic and perplexing tessellations whose nonpolygonal fundamental regions seemed to be beyond the grasp of artists, geometers, and laymen alike. A typical example of Escher's tessellations is the knights on horseback shown on page 57 of Coxeter's *Introduction to Geometry* (1961).

The writer presents here a technique that has proved useful in creating fundamental regions of the Escher type; these in turn yield interesting tessellations. This technique, it is hoped, will enable students and teachers to create fundamental regions for artistically nontrivial tessellations and thereby develop or renew appreciation of art and geometry. At the University of Wisconsin–Eau Claire, for example, a developing interdisciplinary (mathematics and art) course includes a section of Escher art in the syllabus.

Procedure

1. Let A, B, C, D, and N be points such that $\overline{ANB}$ is a straight line. $\angle ANC$ and $\angle NCD$ are right angles. $AN = NB$ and $CD = AB$

2. Let S be a continuous curve connecting A and N as shown in figure 1.

3. Reflect S over in the line $\overleftrightarrow{AN}$ (fig. 2). Let S' represent the reflection of S.

4. Slide S' along $\overleftrightarrow{AN}$ toward B a distance equal to AN (fig. 3). Let S'' represent the curve S' in this position. Let the combined curve of S and S'' be denoted by S_I.

5. Draw the perpendicular bisector $\overleftrightarrow{LM}$ of $\overline{NC}$. Reflect S_I over the line $\overleftrightarrow{LM}$. Let S_I' represent the reflection of S_I (fig. 4).

6. Slide S_I' toward D along the line CD a distance equal to AN. Let the new position of S_I' be called S_II (fig. 5).

7. Let T be a continuous curve connecting A to C as in fig. 6.

8. Slide T down a distance AB so that each point of T moves parallel to $\overleftrightarrow{AB}$ and $\overleftrightarrow{CD}$. Let the final position of T be represented by R as in fig. 6.

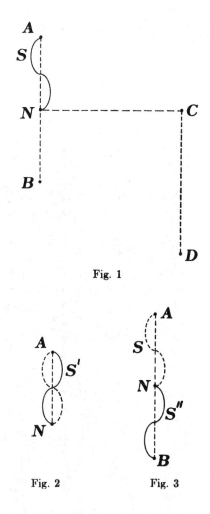

Fig. 1

Fig. 2   Fig. 3

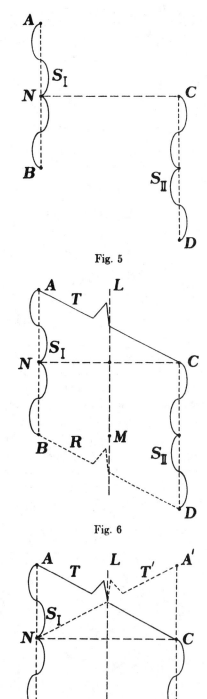

Fig. 5

Fig. 6

9. Next divide the closed region bounded by S_I, S_{II}, T, and R into two congruent parts. This can be done by reflecting T over the line LM, which is the perpendicular bisector of $\overline{NC}$. Let this reflection be represented by T' as shown in fig. 7.

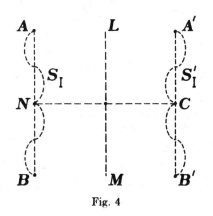

Fig. 4

Fig. 7

10. Slide T' toward B a distance NB so that each point of T' moves parallel to $\overleftrightarrow{AB}$ and $\overleftrightarrow{CD}$. Let this final position of T' be represented by P (fig. 8).

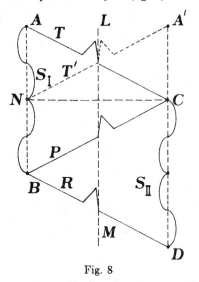

Fig. 8

Why are the closed figures $S_I \cup T \cup P$ and $S_{II} \cup R \cup P$ congruent? How can closed regions such as $S_I \cup T \cup S_{II} \cup R$ be used to form tessellations of the Escher type?

Illustrations

In the same fashion, the curves shown in figure 9 and the completed funda-

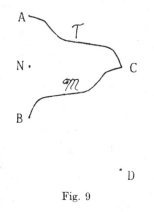

Fig. 9

mental region (fig. 10) yield the tessellation (with appropriate artistic additions) shown in figure 11.

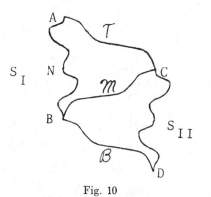

Fig. 10

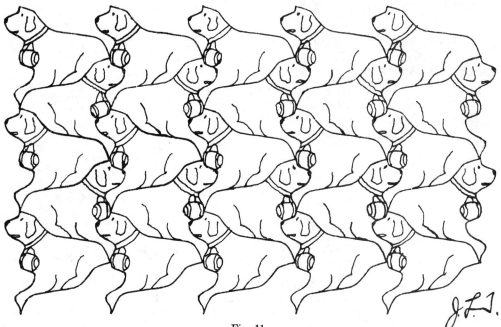

Fig. 11

Additional tessellations, made in the same fashion, are shown in the following figure and the figure on the first page.

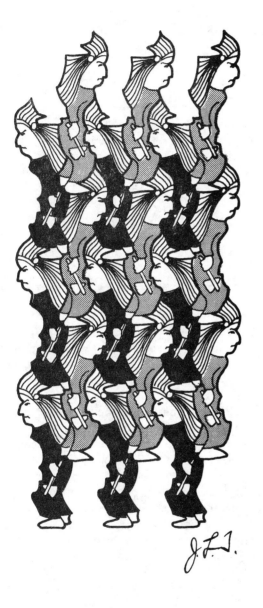

REFERENCES

MacGillavry, C. *Symmetry Aspects of M. C. Escher's Periodic Drawings.* Utrecht: A. Oosthoek, 1965.

Coxeter, H. S. M. *Introduction to Geometry.* New York: John Wiley & Sons, 1961.

DIGRAPHS, MATRICES, AND FOOTBALL-TEAM RATINGS

By ROBERT M. DIEFFENBACH, Miami University—Middletown, Middletown, OH 45042

In Ohio a statewide rating system known as the Harbin Football-Team Rating System determines the high school football teams that are eligible to compete in postseason playoffs. Each team earns points for games it wins and for games that a defeated opponent wins. The teams with the most points "go to state."

The outcome of games played and the procedure for ranking the teams can be illustrated with a directed graph or digraph. Each vertex of the digraph corresponds to one of the teams, and each directed edge corresponds to a win. That is, if team X beats team Y, a directed edge joins vertex X to vertex Y. For example, imagine that teams A through D each played the others with the following results:

Example 1

  Team A beat teams B and D.
  Team B beat teams C and D.
  Team C beat team A.
  Team D beat team C.

The digraph to represent the wins and losses is shown in figure 1. It has one vertex for each team and one directed edge for each win, where, again, an arrow points from a winning team to a losing team.

The rules for ranking Ohio teams award points to each team on two levels. A level-1 point is awarded for each game a team wins; a level-2 point is awarded for each game a defeated opponent wins. Team A in example 1 would receive two points at level 1 for beating teams B and D, two points at level 2 for the two games that B won, and one point at level 2 for the game that D

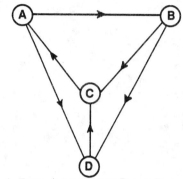

Fig. 1. Team A beat teams B and D; team B beat teams C and D; team C beat team A; and team D beat team C.

won. Altogether, then, team A would receive $2 + 2 + 1 = 5$ points.

Similarly, team B would receive $2 + 1 + 1 = 4$ points; team C would receive $1 + 2 = 3$ points; and team D would receive $1 + 1 = 2$ points. The point totals would determine a ranking of the teams in alphabetical order, even though teams A and B had the same record (2 to 1) as did teams C and D (1 to 2).

Even more remarkably, the rules can result in one team being ranked above another team with a better record. The digraph in figure 2 represents the results of games played by teams A through F.

Winner	Losers
A	D, E, F
B	D, E, F
C	A, B
D	C, F
E	C
F	E

Example 2

The won-lost record for each team is easily compiled by following the arrows:

Winner	Losers		Team	W	L
A	D, E, F		A	3	1
B	D, E, F		B	3	1
C	A, B		C	2	2
D	C, F		D	2	2
E	C		E	1	3
F	E		F	1	3

Fig. 2

$$\mathbf{M} = \begin{array}{c} \\ A \\ B \\ C \\ D \end{array} \begin{array}{cccc} A & B & C & D \\ \left[\begin{array}{cccc} 0 & 1 & 0 & 1 \\ 0 & 0 & 1 & 1 \\ 1 & 0 & 0 & 0 \\ 0 & 0 & 1 & 0 \end{array}\right] \end{array}$$

Not only does a matrix representation of the digraph accommodate any number of teams, but it also allows a team's rating points to be calculated easily.

A team's level-1 points, corresponding to victories, can be found simply by adding the row for that team. More important, the process for calculating a team's level-2 points can also be described in a computational way.

For example, take team A, which receives two level-2 points for beating team B. These two points correspond to the following products:

$$\mathbf{M}[A, B] \cdot \mathbf{M}[B, C]$$
$$= 1 \quad (A \text{ beat } B, \text{ and } B \text{ beat } C)$$

and

$$\mathbf{M}[A, B] \cdot \mathbf{M}[B, D]$$
$$= 1 \quad (A \text{ beat } B, \text{ and } B \text{ beat } D)$$

In the same fashion,

$$\mathbf{M}[A, D] \cdot \mathbf{M}[D, C] = 1,$$

which corresponds to A beating D and D beating C.

However, any other product for team A, like $\mathbf{M}[A, C] \cdot \mathbf{M}[C, D]$, will equal 0 because one or both of the two factors is 0.

The calculations necessary to compute the level-2 points can be organized using matrix multiplication. The product of a single row, say the A row, and a single column, say the D column, is the expression

$$\mathbf{M}[A, A] \cdot \mathbf{M}[A, D] + \mathbf{M}[A, B] \cdot \mathbf{M}[B, D]$$
$$+ \mathbf{M}[A, C] \cdot \mathbf{M}[C, D] + \mathbf{M}[A, D] \cdot \mathbf{M}[D, D]$$
$$= 0 \cdot 1 + 1 \cdot 1 + 0 \cdot 0 + 1 \cdot 0$$
$$= 1,$$

which is the level-2 point that corresponds to A beating B and B beating D.

The matrix product $\mathbf{M}^2$ is obtained by

In this example teams A and B each receive three level-1 points and (2 + 1 + 1 = 4) four level-2 points for beating teams D, E, and F, giving each of them a total of seven points. However, team C receives two level-1 points and (3 + 3 = 6) six level-2 points for beating teams A and B, giving it a total of eight points. A third-place team has the highest ranking! Of course, the ranking system is designed to give a team credit for victories over otherwise successful opponents.

Matrix Representation

In a league (or state) with more teams and more games, drawing a digraph to represent the outcomes of all the games is not practical. However, the results are easily organized in a matrix or array having one row and one column for each team. The entry in the row for team X and the column for team Y will be denoted by $\mathbf{M}[X, Y]$. The value of $\mathbf{M}[X, Y]$ will be "1" if team X beat team Y and "0" otherwise. The matrix is called an adjacency matrix of the digraph.

The games in the first example can be represented with a 4 × 4 matrix.

filling in all sixteen possible row-column products. In particular, the value of the preceding A row–D column product is $1 = \mathbf{M}^2[A, D]$. The entire product matrix is the following:

$$\mathbf{M}^2 = \begin{array}{c} \\ A \\ B \\ C \\ D \end{array} \begin{array}{cccc} A & B & C & D \\ \end{array} \begin{bmatrix} 0 & 0 & 2 & 1 \\ 1 & 0 & 1 & 0 \\ 0 & 1 & 0 & 1 \\ 1 & 0 & 0 & 0 \end{bmatrix} \quad \begin{array}{c} \text{Row Totals} \\ \begin{bmatrix} 3 \\ 2 \\ 2 \\ 1 \end{bmatrix} \end{array}$$

The level-2 points for any team can now be found by adding the row for that team as just illustrated.

Matrix multiplication can also be used to add the rows. For example, the products

$$\mathbf{M} \cdot \begin{bmatrix} 1 \\ 1 \\ 1 \\ 1 \end{bmatrix} = \begin{bmatrix} 2 \\ 2 \\ 1 \\ 1 \end{bmatrix} \text{ and } \mathbf{M}^2 \cdot \begin{bmatrix} 1 \\ 1 \\ 1 \\ 1 \end{bmatrix} = \begin{bmatrix} 3 \\ 2 \\ 2 \\ 1 \end{bmatrix}$$

determine the level-1 and level-2 rating points for each team.

The entire ranking procedure can be described in a single matrix expression using matrix addition. The sum of two matrices is obtained by adding the values in corresponding locations. For example, each value in the matrix $\mathbf{W} = \mathbf{M} + \mathbf{M}^2$ is defined by

$$\mathbf{W}[X, Y] = \mathbf{M}[X, Y] + \mathbf{M}^2[X, Y].$$

In the first example with four teams,

$$\mathbf{W} = \begin{bmatrix} 0 & 1 & 0 & 1 \\ 0 & 0 & 1 & 1 \\ 1 & 0 & 0 & 0 \\ 0 & 0 & 1 & 0 \end{bmatrix} + \begin{bmatrix} 0 & 0 & 2 & 1 \\ 1 & 0 & 1 & 0 \\ 0 & 1 & 0 & 1 \\ 1 & 0 & 0 & 0 \end{bmatrix}$$

$$= \begin{bmatrix} 0 & 1 & 2 & 2 \\ 1 & 0 & 2 & 1 \\ 1 & 1 & 0 & 1 \\ 1 & 0 & 1 & 0 \end{bmatrix},$$

and the points for each team are given by

$$\mathbf{P} = \mathbf{W} \cdot \begin{bmatrix} 1 \\ 1 \\ 1 \\ 1 \end{bmatrix} = \begin{bmatrix} 0 & 1 & 2 & 2 \\ 1 & 0 & 2 & 1 \\ 1 & 1 & 0 & 1 \\ 1 & 0 & 1 & 0 \end{bmatrix}$$

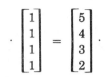

$$\cdot \begin{bmatrix} 1 \\ 1 \\ 1 \\ 1 \end{bmatrix} = \begin{bmatrix} 5 \\ 4 \\ 3 \\ 2 \end{bmatrix}.$$

In other words, the rating points for each team can be obtained from the matrix expression

$$\mathbf{P} = (\mathbf{M} + \mathbf{M}^2) \cdot \begin{bmatrix} 1 \\ 1 \\ 1 \\ 1 \end{bmatrix}.$$

For the second example with six teams,

$$\mathbf{M} = \begin{bmatrix} 0 & 0 & 0 & 1 & 1 & 1 \\ 0 & 0 & 0 & 1 & 1 & 1 \\ 1 & 1 & 0 & 0 & 0 & 0 \\ 0 & 0 & 1 & 0 & 0 & 1 \\ 0 & 0 & 1 & 0 & 0 & 0 \\ 0 & 0 & 0 & 0 & 1 & 0 \end{bmatrix},$$

$$\mathbf{M}^2 = \begin{bmatrix} 0 & 0 & 2 & 0 & 1 & 1 \\ 0 & 0 & 2 & 0 & 1 & 1 \\ 0 & 0 & 0 & 2 & 2 & 2 \\ 1 & 1 & 0 & 0 & 1 & 0 \\ 1 & 1 & 0 & 0 & 0 & 0 \\ 0 & 0 & 1 & 0 & 0 & 0 \end{bmatrix},$$

and

$$\mathbf{P} = \begin{bmatrix} 7 \\ 7 \\ 8 \\ 5 \\ 3 \\ 2 \end{bmatrix}.$$

The Harbin Football-Team Ranking System

The Harbin Football-Team Ranking System also awards fractional points for ties. The same matrix expression will determine the rating points for each team if the value 1/2 is used in both locations $\mathbf{M}[X, Y]$ and $\mathbf{M}[Y, X]$ whenever teams X and Y tie. The effect is to award a team 1/2 point for each game it ties, 1/2 point for each game a defeated opponent ties, 1/2 point for each game a tied opponent wins, and 1/4 point for each game a tied opponent ties.

The rating system also increases the value of points earned for beating teams in a stronger division. The points are multiplied by the factors given in table 1, depending on the division of the team beaten.

TABLE 1

Division	Factor
1	3
2	2.5
3	2
4	1.5
5	1

This modification can also be incorporated into the matrix formula. After the adjacency matrix $\mathbf{M}$ and the product matrix $\mathbf{M}^2$ have been determined, each column is simply multiplied by the factor corresponding to the division for that team.

The rating system illustrates nicely the advantage of using a mathematical model or algorithm to describe a computational process. It also suggests a variety of other ways to rank the teams.

Another Rating Formula

The examples show quite clearly that a team's rating is not affected directly by that team's losses. In particular, if a good team loses to an otherwise miserable team, the rating of the good team is not affected, and the miserable team does not earn enough points to make a difference.

Another point total can be defined for the teams by subtracting points for losses. Just as the values in a team's row of the adjacency matrix $\mathbf{M}$ correspond to victories by that team, so too the values in a team's column represent losses by that team. In other words, a team's losses can be counted by adding the columns of $\mathbf{M}$. Alternatively, we can switch the columns and rows first and then add the rows. The matrix obtained by switching the rows and columns of a matrix $\mathbf{M}$ is called the transpose of $\mathbf{M}$, denoted by $\mathbf{M}^T$, where $\mathbf{M}^T[X, Y] = \mathbf{M}[Y, X]$.

If $\mathbf{W} = \mathbf{M} + \mathbf{M}^2$ were to be called the win matrix, the matrix $\mathbf{L} = (\mathbf{M} + \mathbf{M}^2)^T$ would appropriately be called the loss matrix. An alternate rating that takes wins and losses into account can now be defined by adding the rows of $\mathbf{W} - \mathbf{L}$. A team is awarded points for each win and for each

game that a defeated opponent wins. Likewise, a team loses one point for each loss and for each game that a victorious opponent loses. The effect of this formula on the two examples is easily calculated.

For the teams in example 1,

$$\mathbf{W} = \mathbf{M} + \mathbf{M}^2 = \begin{bmatrix} 0 & 1 & 2 & 2 \\ 1 & 0 & 2 & 1 \\ 1 & 1 & 0 & 1 \\ 1 & 0 & 1 & 2 \end{bmatrix},$$

$$\mathbf{L} = \mathbf{W}^T = \begin{bmatrix} 0 & 1 & 1 & 1 \\ 1 & 0 & 1 & 0 \\ 2 & 2 & 0 & 1 \\ 2 & 1 & 1 & 2 \end{bmatrix},$$

and

$$(\mathbf{W} - \mathbf{L}) \begin{bmatrix} 1 \\ 1 \\ 1 \\ 1 \end{bmatrix} = \begin{bmatrix} 0 & 0 & 1 & 1 \\ 0 & 0 & 1 & 1 \\ -1 & -1 & 0 & 0 \\ -1 & -1 & 0 & 0 \end{bmatrix}$$

$$\cdot \begin{bmatrix} 1 \\ 1 \\ 1 \\ 1 \end{bmatrix} = \begin{bmatrix} 2 \\ 2 \\ -2 \\ -2 \end{bmatrix}.$$

For the teams in example 2,

$$(\mathbf{W} - \mathbf{L}) \cdot \begin{bmatrix} 1 \\ 1 \\ 1 \\ 1 \\ 1 \\ 1 \end{bmatrix}$$

$$= \begin{bmatrix} 0 & 0 & 1 & 0 & 1 & 2 \\ 0 & 0 & 1 & 0 & 1 & 2 \\ -1 & -1 & 0 & 1 & 1 & 1 \\ 0 & 0 & -1 & 0 & 1 & 1 \\ -1 & -1 & -1 & -1 & 0 & -1 \\ -2 & -2 & -1 & -1 & 1 & 0 \end{bmatrix}$$

$$\cdot \begin{bmatrix} 1 \\ 1 \\ 1 \\ 1 \\ 1 \\ 1 \end{bmatrix} = \begin{bmatrix} 4 \\ 4 \\ 1 \\ 1 \\ -5 \\ -5 \end{bmatrix}.$$

In these two examples, the ranking determined by adding the rows of $\mathbf{W} - \mathbf{L}$ agrees exactly with the traditional won-lost standings. This outcome is not unusual

TABLE 2							
		Standings			Rating Scores		
Winner	Losers	Team	W	L	Team	Harbin	Alternate
A	C, E, F	A	3	1	A	8	4
B	D, E, F	B	3	1	B	8	5
C	B, D	C	2	2	C	7	2
D	F, G	D	2	2	D	4	−1
E	C, G	E	2	2	E	5	1
F	G	F	1	3	F	2	−5
G	A	G	1	3	G	4	−6

with this ranking formula. In fact, it is unavoidable when each team plays every other and no game ends in a tie.

More formally, a schedule of games that pairs each team with every other is called a tournament.

THEOREM. *In an N-team tournament if no game ends in a tie, the ranking determined by adding the rows of* **W** − **L** *will agree exactly with the won-lost standings.*

Proof. Let w_X equal the number of games won by team X. Then $N - 1 - w_X$ will equal ℓ_X, the number of games lost by team X, since team X plays exactly $N - 1$ games. The number of games altogether will be the number of pairs that can be chosen from N objects, or $N(N - 1)/2$.

Now, the number of points received by a particular team, let us say team A, is given by the following formula:

$$(w_A - \ell_A) + \left(\sum_{A \text{ beat } X} w_X - \sum_{X \text{ beat } A} \ell_X \right)$$

$$= (w_A - \ell_A) + \left(\sum_{A \text{ beat } X} w_X - \sum_{X \text{ beat } A} (N - 1 - w_X) \right)$$

$$= (w_A - \ell_A)$$
$$+ \left(\sum_{A \text{ beat } X} w_X + \sum_{X \text{ beat } A} w_X - \sum_{X \text{ beat } A} (N - 1) \right)$$

$$= (w_A - \ell_A) + \left(\sum_{A \neq X} w_X - \ell_A \cdot (N - 1) \right)$$

$$= (w_A - \ell_A) + \left(\frac{N(N - 1)}{2} - w_A - \ell_A \cdot N + \ell_A \right)$$

$$= \frac{N(N - 1)}{2} - \ell_A \cdot N$$

$$= w_A \cdot N - \left(\frac{N(N - 1)}{2} \right)$$

This number of points clearly depends only on the number of games that team A wins: the more wins, the higher the number of points. Likewise, in a tournament with no ties, the teams with more wins are higher in the won-lost standings. The rating score ranks the team just as the won-lost standings would. ∎

According to the theorem, then, the ranking determined by adding the rows of the matrix **W** − **L** is "fair" when used to rank teams within a single league, because the ranking will be consistent with the traditional standings whenever each team has played every other and no game ends in a tie.

If each pair of teams does not play or if some games end in ties, the ranking procedure may distinguish between teams with identical records.

Example 3

Suppose seven teams in the same league each play four games with the results in table 2. Teams A and B have equal ratings using the Harbin formula because they have the same number of level-1 and level-2 points. However, team A's only loss was to a weak team (G), whereas team B's only loss was to a strong team (C). The difference is reflected in the alternate rating scores with team B receiving the higher rating.

Other Possibilities

The description of the rating formula as a matrix expression suggests many other formulas. One, proposed by Don Small at Colby College, is obtained by adding the rows of $2\mathbf{M} + \mathbf{M}^2$. With this formula the games a team wins contribute two points to the team's rating score, whereas games a defeated opponent wins contribute only one point.

Another possibility is to add the rows of $\mathbf{M} + \mathbf{M}^2 + \mathbf{M}^3$, although the meaning of $\mathbf{M}^3$ is not entirely clear. A team could receive a point for a game it lost!

No matter how the win matrix, $\mathbf{W}$, is defined, be it $2\mathbf{M} + \mathbf{M}^2$ or whatever, an alternative ranking can be obtained by adding the rows of $\mathbf{W} - \mathbf{W}^\mathsf{T}$. Simple programs for a microcomputer can be written to evaluate and compare the effect of these and other formulas.

REFERENCE

"Ohio Football's 1986 Guide to Football, Why the Computer Reigns Supreme." *Ohio Football* 1 (January 1986): 84–87. ♣

WHAT IS THERE SO MATHEMATICAL ABOUT MUSIC?

Interview with Eli Maor

After twenty years of teaching, Eli Maor still finds exciting the search for new applications of mathematics. His teaching experience reflects a long standing interest in science and in music in particular. In 1968 he gave sixteen lectures on music and science on the Israeli State Radio. The essay contest offered him an excuse to write on one of his favorite topics and he shared top honors. We think you will enjoy reading his reflections on the nature of mathematics and on the trends in mathematics education.

Editorial Panel

MT: *You have published other articles on music. How did your interest begin in this area?*

EM: Well, the subject has fascinated me since high school. I recall my physics teacher talking about the vibrations of a string in connection with simple harmonic motion. At that moment it occurred to me that here was a beautiful relation between science and music—the frequency of the vibrations determining the pitch of the tone. It is an interest that continued through my doctoral work.

MT: *Do some of your feelings about music and other applications affect the sorts of things that you try to accomplish in your teaching?*

EM: Yes, I would say so, in a broad sense. Basically, I think I belong to the old school in thinking that mathematics should be approached from an applied point of view with applications from physics, astronomy, chemistry, and so on. I feel that the new math contained many interesting ideas but that overall it removed students from down-to-earth mathematics. Fortunately I can sense a sort of counterrevolution begin-

ning to take place away from the new math and from the overemphasis on definitions, formalisms, and pure mathematics.

I think the change is a very healthy one. For example, let's take a look at the function concept. Originally, a function was regarded as a way of describing a dependence between two variables, and, in fact, we called them the independent and dependent variable. The function concept is actually based on change and variation. Today, one doesn't hear any of that. One hears about pairs of numbers taken from the domain and from the range; the result is that the student is overwhelmed with definitions.

MT: *Because of your interest in applications, did you ever consider a career as a scientist or engineer? How did you happen to end up teaching mathematics?*

EM: Well, actually I began in physics. My undergraduate degree was in physics with a mathematics minor. I really don't know at what stage I decided to call myself a mathematician. I am inclined to think in terms of these narrow labels. I prefer to see myself as a person working in the broad area of applied mathematics. Wherever there's something interesting in mathematics, that's where I'd like to stick my nose.

MT: *Do you feel that your interest in applications effects the attitudes that your students have toward mathematics?*

EM: Well, that depends on which students and what course you are referring to. In the precalculus course you don't have much choice. You have to cover the syllabus. On the other hand, I am currently teaching a course on the nature and relevance of mathematics. Essentially it is a historical survey where I try to convey something of the flavor of mathematics, especially the difference between the pure and applied approach. I like to impress my students by the vastness and the universality of mathematics in relation to music, art, architecture, and science.

MT: *In light of the large amount of writing you have done, what advice would you offer to teachers who are not accustomed to writing?*

EM: The first thing is to keep an eye open for interesting ideas. My thesis advisor once told me that from the moment he gets up in the morning to the moment he falls asleep, he is on the alert, watching what goes on around him and trying to theorize or ask himself questions. And I think I somehow inherited that attitude. Essentially the key to writing is to find interesting things to write about. I like to share my excitement about things. At the same time, I try to be self-critical; I ask myself if the idea will really be of interest to other people.

The works of the great authors in mathematics are a continuous source of inspiration and ideas—for example, Felix Klein's "Elementary Mathematics from an Advanced Standpoint: Arithmetic, Algebra, Analysis," and David Hilbert's [and Stephen Cohn-Vossen] "Geometry and the Imagination." The power of these works is that with very simple mathematics, a wide variety of beautiful phenomena can be described (even without calculus). It seems to me that one can learn so much more from these sources than from a textbook. I think the current back-to-basics attitude should be complemented by a back-to-the-great-masters approach.

MT: *Are there some other topics that you would like to mention?*

EM: I feel that the calculator is going to have a profound influence on mathematics and mathematics teaching. It works with numbers and not with sets or definitions, unless you want to think of numbers as abstract concepts. With calculator prices getting lower all the time, I think that people who before were never really interested in numbers will become involved. We can really anticipate dramatic changes in the way people view numbers, calculations, and in turn, other aspects of mathematics.

Musical form is close to mathematics—not perhaps to mathematics itself, but certainly to something like mathematical thinking and relationship.
—*Igor Stravinsky (1882-1971)*

Historical Perspectives

Ever since Pythagoras's investigations into the laws of the vibrating string in the sixth century B.C., mathematicians have been fascinated by the subtle relations and analogies that exist between music, the queen of art, and mathematics, the queen of science. From a mystical belief that the laws of musical harmony govern the motion of the heavenly bodies in their orbits, through a mathematical study of the physical laws underlying musical theory, to the deliberate application of mathematical principles to musical composition, the affinity between these two great creations of human thought has continued uninterruptedly throughout the entire history of science and art. The mutual relations in this marriage were not always symmetric; until the Renaissance it was mainly music that had influenced mathematics. One only needs to think of how such musical words as *harmonic* have found their way into the mathematical jargon (harmonic motion, harmonic mean, harmonic functions, and many more) to realize what an enormous influence musical ideas have had on mathematical thought. Then, in the eighteenth and nineteenth centuries, another discipline, physics, became the main arena for musicomathematical relations—a result, no doubt, of the immense success that the newly invented differential and integral calculus has had on this science. But not until our own century have mathematical ideas begun to find their way into musical creation, first in the new serial music, then in a direct application of such tools as information theory, computer programming, and stochastic processes to musical composition. There can be no doubt that the future will see this trend—mathematics exerting an influence on music—bear novel and fruitful results, equally beneficial to both disciplines. (For a more elaborate historical background of the musicomathematical relations, see Helm [1967] and Maor [1976].)

What is it, then, that makes music so akin to mathematics? In trying to answer this question, we must first separate the acoustical-physical aspects of music from those that are purely mathematical. This is not easy to do, for all of music is based on one physical phenomenon, vibrations, the description of which itself requires a substantial amount of mathematics. Still, we can draw a line—arbitrary as it may be—between the two. I shall concentrate in this article on those aspects of music that can be classified as purely mathematical—in other words, aspects that involve musical form. I will restrict myself only to concepts that can be understood with secondary mathematics.

Some Basic Notions

We must first recall some basic concepts. A musical tone, in the traditional sense, is produced by the regular vibrations of some material body, be it a violin string, the air column in a flute's bore, or the stretched membrane of a drum. By regular vibrations we mean vibrations that repeat themselves in an orderly, periodic manner. By contrast, nonmusical sounds or noises involve irregular, random vibrations. I said "in the traditional sense," because with today's music, including such masterpieces as a concerto for vacuum cleaner and orchestra, I am not sure any more as to what should be called musical and what should not. But let us stay in the traditional realm.

Here, then, is our first correlation between music and mathematics: music is the world of *periodic* phenomena. And the simplest periodic phenomenon is none other than the familiar sine curve, called simple harmonic motion by the physicists and pure or simple tone by the musicians. Now when we teach the trigonometric functions in school, we show our students not only the graph of $y = \sin x$ but also of $y = \sin(2x)$, $\sin(x/2)$, and so on. These functions all have the same shape but differ in their period and therefore in their frequency (the reciprocal of the period). In music, these functions all correspond to pure tones of different pitch: the higher the frequency, the higher will the pitch be. The tone A (the standard A played by the oboe as a tuning signal for the orchestra), for example, has the frequency 440 cycles per second or 440 Hertz (fig. 1). Of course, if an

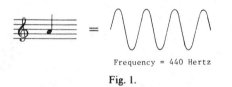

Frequency = 440 Hertz

Fig. 1.

oboe were to sound this note and someone would trace the vibrations on an oscilloscope, we would see a much more complicated shape than a simple sine curve. This is because musical instruments produce not pure tones but compound tones—combinations of many pure tones having different frequencies. The basic shape, however, will still be periodic, with the fundamental frequency always determining the pitch of the entire tone. A pure tone, strictly speaking, is a mathematical abstraction: it can only be produced electronically (i.e., artificially), although the vibrations of a tuning fork are very nearly pure sine vibrations.

Consider now two tones of different pitch, played simultaneously or in succession. The distance between them, as written on the horizontal lines of the staff, constitutes a musical *interval*, just as the distance between two real numbers constitutes an interval on the number line. There is, however, this important difference: although a mathematical interval corresponds to the difference between the two numbers, a musical interval corresponds to the ratio of the frequencies of the two tones. Thus, a fifth (say, from A to D) corresponds to a frequency ratio of $3:2$, a fourth to a ratio of $4:3$, and so on. Most important, the octave, the fundamental unit of musical intervals, corresponds to the ratio $2:1$. That is, tones that are equally separated by octaves (follow an arithmetic progression as written on the staff) really form a geometric progression in their frequencies. By arithmetic progression I mean a collection of notes that are separated by equal intervals in a vertical direction (fig. 2).

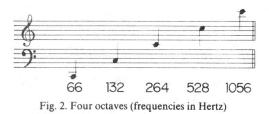

66 132 264 528 1056

Fig. 2. Four octaves (frequencies in Hertz)

Here, then, is a single principle that underlines all musicomathematical relations: *Arithmetic progressions in music correspond to geometric progressions in mathematics;* that is, the relation between the two is logarithmic. This should come as no surprise. In 1860 the German physiologist Theodor Gustav Fechner (1801–1887) formulated a general law that governs the relation between a physical stimulus and the psychological sensation it causes: according to

Fechner, this relation is logarithmic. But although his law is of such a general nature that it applies to most of our senses (the brightness of a source of light, the sensation of pain following a physical pressure, etc.), it is nowhere more pronounced than in music, because here we can measure the physical stimulus (the frequency of vibrations) and the resulting psychological sensation (the sense of pitch) with extreme accuracy and objectivity. It is this fact, above all, that makes it possible to put the sensation of musical tones on a quantitative footing.

Let me now mention a few consequences of this principle. We have seen that a progression of equally spaced musical notes corresponds to a geometric progression in its frequencies. But what if we take a progression of tones whose frequencies are equally spaced? Such is the case with the vibrating string, whose overtones vibrate in frequencies that are 1, 2, 3, 4, ... times that of the fundamental tone (fig. 3). What mu-

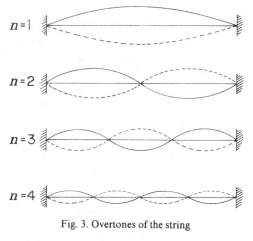

Fig. 3. Overtones of the string

sical intervals correspond to this progression? The answer is shown in figure 4. This progression of tones, shown here for C as the fundamental tone, is called the harmonic series and plays a profound role in musical theory. It is from this series that the basic intervals of Western (and to a certain extent also Oriental) music are derived, such as the octave ($2:1$), the fifth ($3:2$), the fourth ($4:3$), the major third ($5:4$), and so on. But there is more mathematics to this series than just these ratios: if

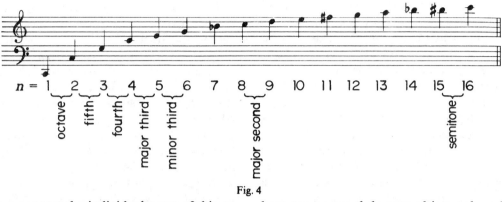

Fig. 4

we connect the individual notes of this series by a smooth curve, we get something that most of us will immediately recognize—the graph of the logarithmic function. This is a direct consequence of Fechner's law. The musical staff, then, actually serves as a logarithmic coordinate system, similar to the familiar logarithmic graph paper.

Of course, the name harmonic series is no stranger to us, but few know that we owe that name to the harmonic series, musical style. In fact, if we consider the reciprocals of the frequencies of this series (i.e., the periods of vibrations) and reduce them so that the first equals one, we get the harmonic sequence, mathematical style:

$$1, 1/2, 1/3, 1/4, 1/5, \ldots$$

Can any other art, or nonscientific discipline for that matter, claim such an intimate relationship to mathematics?

Transformations: Musical versus Mathematical

The notion of transformation is rooted in music as deeply as it is in mathematics. A musical transformation does to a musical figure (e.g., a melody) what a mathematical transformation does to a geometric figure: in both cases a new figure is derived, which nonetheless bears some resemblance to the old.

Consider, for example, melodic inversion. A melody (i.e., a succession of intervals) is inverted with respect to a given note if every interval in the melody reverses its vertical direction: an upward interval

becomes an equal downward interval, and vice versa. An example is shown in figure 5.[1] Now suppose we invert an interval

J. S. Bach's Two-Part Invention No. 1

Fig. 5

whose tones have the frequencies f_1 (the lower tone) and f_2. The inverted interval will have the frequencies f_1 (the upper tone) and f_3 (fig. 6). By definition, the mag-

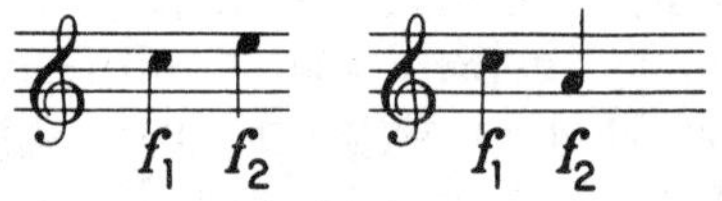

Fig. 6

nitude of the two intervals is the same, only their sense reverses; thus, $f_2{:}f_1 = f_1{:}f_3$ or $f_2 \times f_3 = f_1^2$. This shows that the reference note (the note with respect to which the inversion was done) is the geometric mean between the two other notes—not entirely surprising, considering the logarithmic nature of the pitch-frequency relation. However, let's think for a moment about the term *inversion* as we know it: Inversion in a circle of center O and radius $\overline{OR}$ is a transformation that carries every point $P \neq O$ to an image point Q such that $OP \times OQ = OR^2$. Now put $OP = f_2$, $OQ = f_3$, and $OR = f_1$, and musical inversion becomes mathematical inversion!

---

1. Bach deviated here from strict mathematical inversion in order to keep up with the tones of the scale.

Before we discuss another famous transformation, that of transposition, let me explain briefly the concept of a key in music. (We use here the term *key* as tantamount to tonality; sometimes the term *scale* is also used. See Ammer [1973].) A key is to a musician what a frame of reference or a coordinate system is to a mathematician. It is within the framework of a key that most traditional music had been written, at least until the new notion of atonality came into being in the 1920s (more on this later). Just as a mathematician has the freedom to choose any coordinate system to which to refer a geometric figure, so has a composer the freedom to select the key in which to write a piece. In principle, all keys are equivalent, just as all coordinate systems are. (I shall avoid discussing the emotional connotations that certain keys evoke in some people, this being a purely subjective issue, one that is the source of much controversy.) Now to transpose from one key to another means to carry an entire piece—a melody, for example, together with its harmonic accompaniment—and translate it to another key, in exact analogy to the translation of a figure from one coordinate system to another. When we perform such a translation in geometry, there are certain features that must remain unchanged; these are the invariants of the transformation. Foremost among these, the distance between two points of the original figure must be the same as that between their image points. The very same principle applies also in music: a transposition must leave all intervals invariant, or the transposed piece will not be identical with the original (see fig. 7).

W. A. Mozart's Symphony No. 41
K. 551 ("Jupiter").

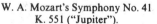
key: C major

key: G major

Fig. 7

Transposition in music is important for precisely the same reasons that translation is important in mathematics: both make the notation simpler. Some instruments—notably the clarinet, the French horn, and the trumpet—play in a written key that differs from what is actually heard. For example, when an A-clarinet plays the written key of C major, the key of A major is actually heard. Since C major has the simplest notation of all keys (no flats or sharps), it is easier for the player to read his piece in this key rather than in A major, the natural key of the instrument. It is, of course, this very same idea that guides us mathematicians when we transform a curve to a new coordinate system where its equation will have a simpler form (e.g., to get rid of the mixed terms in a quadratic expression by shifting to a principal-axes system). In both cases the figure remains the same; only its notation changes (see fig. 8).

Translation, of course, is the simplest of all mathematical transformations; just as transposition is the simplest of all musical transformations. In either case there is no distortion except for a rigid body motion (to use a term from physics) of the entire piece. Inversion is a more drastic transformation: it considerably distorts most figures (e.g., straight lines become circles, major chords become minor chords), yet it leaves invariant the circle of inversion, as well as the tone of inversion. Also, circles concentric to the inversion circle remain concentric to it, just as octaves under inversion remain octaves. There are more drastic transformations yet. Felix Klein (1977), in his famous Erlangen Program of 1872, suggested that geometry be regarded as a hierarchy of transformations—metric, affine, projective, inversive, and topological, in increasing order of their distortive effects—where each transformation is characterized by its invariants. To a large extent, music should be viewed in the same light. Any musical work, from the simplest folk song to Bach's most complex fugues, consists of a basic theme that is then repeated in various forms—different in pitch,

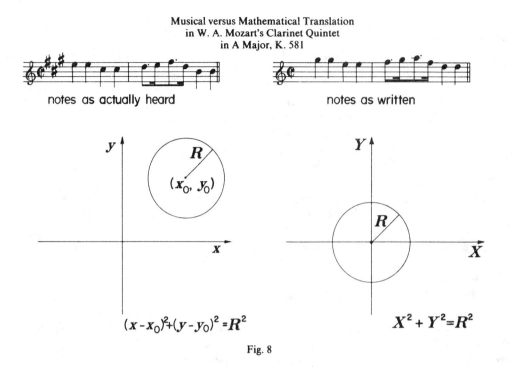

Fig. 8

rhythm, key, or harmony, yet always bearing a distinctive generic relation to the original. It is this feature, more than any other, that is so characteristic of music and distinguishes it from all other forms of art.

The Equal-Tempered Scale

Nowhere, perhaps, do all these ideas combine more coherently into a single musical structure than in the equal-tempered scale. This scale is traditionally attributed to Johann Sebastian Bach, but there are indications that it had already been used before him. In any case, up until Bach's time Western music had used mainly two scales, or variations based on them: the Pythagorean and the just-intonation. Both were based on the natural system of overtones emitted by the vibrating string and were thus correct from the theoretical point of view. But both suffered from a serious disadvantage: not all of their intervals were exactly equal. For example, the two ratios 9:8 and 10:9 were regarded as equal and were both called a major second. True, the difference between these two intervals is very small (although a trained ear can eas-

ily detect it) and not much harm was done by considering them as equal—as long as only simple tunes were sung. But a real difficulty occurred when we wished to transpose a tune from one key to another. Because of the slight difference between the two supposedly equal intervals, the entire system of reference within the key would have been distorted, and a great number of new, intermediate ratios would have become necessary. Bach, in 1722, decided that this slight difference was not worth the trouble, and he sacrificed it in favor of the simplicity of playing. He divided the octave (2:1) into twelve exactly equal intervals, each called a semitone and having the frequency ratio $\sqrt[12]{2}:1$. Now Bach, of course, was not a mathematician; he had no way of calculating the numerical value of this ratio (nor was he ever interested in finding it), but with a pocket calculator we easily find it to be 1.059 . . .—slightly less than the exact semitone 16:15 or 1.066 . . . .

It is, however, not this slight numerical difference that is important but the mathematical principle that stands behind it, the principle of symmetry. All the twelve semi-

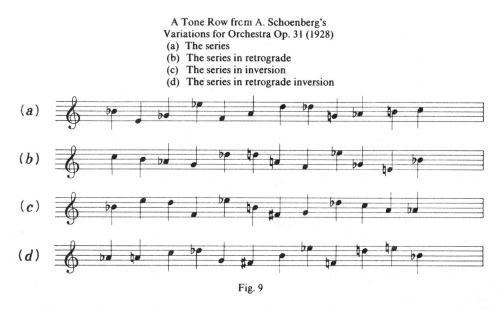

A Tone Row from A. Schoenberg's
Variations for Orchestra Op. 31 (1928)
  (a) The series
  (b) The series in retrograde
  (c) The series in inversion
  (d) The series in retrograde inversion

Fig. 9

tones of the equal-tempered scale are symmetric (equivalent) to each other and therefore play exactly the same role in the scale. This means that we can think of the twelve semitones of the octave as the vertices of a regular twelve-gon inscribed in a circle; transposition from one key to another then simply amounts to a rotation of this circle by the proper amount. (Actually, a logarithmic spiral would be more appropriate than a circle; see Maor [1974].) We really have here a cyclic symmetry group of order 12 that as such becomes subject to the laws of group theory and modular arithmetic (see Metzger-Maor 1967).

But let's not be carried too far into abstract mathematics. The equal-tempered scale had an enormous influence on the development of Western music in the eighteenth and nineteenth centuries. It culminated with the introduction of serial music by Arnold Schoenberg in the 1920s. Essentially, Schoenberg applied the principle of symmetry not only to the technicalities of playing (which was Bach's original intention) but to musical form itself. In his so-called twelve-tone music he abandoned the notions of key and tonality and replaced them with a new structure, the series. Let me quote the excellent description of the series from *Harper's Dictionary of Music*:

In a twelve-tone composition the twelve notes of the chromatic scale appear in a particular order selected by the composer. This order of notes, called the *series* or *tone row*, appears again and again throughout the work, in both melody and chords. No one note can be used again until all eleven of the others have appeared. However, certain modifications of the series are permitted. A tone may appear in any octave; for example, if the original series contains middle C, any other C may be substituted the next time C is to appear. The series may be moved to some other part of the scale, provided all the intervals remain intact. Further, the entire series may be *inverted*. It may appear in *retrograde* (backwards, beginning with the last note of the series and ending with the first), or in *retrograde inversion* (backwards and upside down). These opportunities for change—forty-eight in all—make possible a considerable amount of variety.

Figure 9 is an example of a tone row.

Here, then, the blending of mathematics and music achieves its supreme form; reflections, inversions, invariance, and modulo 12 algebra (invariance under translation by octaves)—indeed much of the vocabulary of the theory of transformations—are all applied here to musical form in its purest sense. There comes to mind Einstein's famous admiration of the fact that mathematics—itself a creation of the mind—so perfectly describes the laws of nature. May not we add to this the laws of music?

REFERENCES

Ammer, Christine. *Harper's Dictionary of Music*. New York: Barnes & Noble, 1973, pp. 172, 309, and 375.

Helm, E. Eugene. "The Vibrating String of the Pythagoreans." *Scientific American* 217 (December 1967):92.

Klein, Felix. "The Erlangen Program." *Mathematical Intelligencer* 0 (August 1977):22.

Maor, Eli. "The Logarithmic Spiral." *Mathematics Teacher* 67 (April 1974):321–27.

———. "Mathematics and the Arts." *Journal of College Science Teaching* 5 (March 1976):223.

Metzger-Maor, Eli. "Musical Scales and Algebraic Groups." *American Journal of Physics* 35 (May 1967):441.

RELATED READINGS
FROM THE *MATHEMATICS TEACHER*

Botts, Truman. "More on the Mathematics of Musical Scales." 67 (January 1974):75–84.

Brown, J. D. "Music and Mathematicians Since the Seventeenth Century." 61 (December 1968):783–87.

Coxeter, H. S. M. "Music and Mathematics." 61 (March 1968):312–20.

Delmar, Morton. "Counterpoint as an Equivalence Relation." 60 (February 1967):137.

Lawlis, Frank. "The Basis of Music—Mathematics." 60 (October 1967):593–96.

Malcolm, Paul S. "Mathematics of Musical Scales." 65 (November 1972):611–15.

O'Keefe, Vincent. "Mathematics—Musical Relationships: A Bibliography." 65 (April 1972):315–24.

BIBLIOGRAPHY

Fritz, Winchel. *Music, Sound and Sensation.* New York: Dover, 1967.

Helmholtz, Hermann. *Sensations of Tone (As a Physiological Basis for the Theory of Music).* New York: Dover, 1954.

Hutchins, Carleen Malery. *The Physics of Music, Readings from Scientific American.* San Francisco: W. H. Freeman & Co., 1978.

Jeans, James. *Science and Music.* New York: Dover, 1968.

Olson, Harry F. *Music, Physics and Engineering.* New York: Dover, 1967.

GEOMETRIC TRANSFORMATIONS AND MUSICAL COMPOSITION

By THOMAS O'SHEA
University of British Columbia
Vancouver, British Columbia V6T 1W5

Music is a hidden exercise in arithmetic, of a mind unconscious of dealing in numbers.

—Leibniz

The purpose of this article is to provide a basis for interdisciplinary activities for students studying transformation geometry. Too often the manipulations of figures that experienced geometry teachers find so attractive do not evoke the same response from their students. I hope that the contents of this article may be used to generate student activities that are both creative and mathematically surprising. These discoveries certainly surprised me when I was investigating the link between mathematics and music.

As you will see, Leibniz' comment on the dependence of music on numbers was conservative; geometry also can play a part. But then Leibniz was unaware of the trends that were to develop in twentieth-century musical composition.

The history of western music is marked

The author is indebted to Lars C. Jansson of the University of Manitoba for initial suggestions that led to the discovery of the relationships described in this article.

by the gradual acceptance of more complex chords and greater harshness or discord. Almost every age had its harmonic pioneers. Monteverdi, just prior to the time of Leibniz, introduced chords that shocked the people of that time. Moussorgsky and Wagner outraged their contemporaries in the same way. Even Beethoven was regarded as a radical in his day.

Nevertheless, all the above composers had the same harmonic theory in common. The reason our own time has been so remarkable is that the traditional theory of harmony was discarded, for a time at least. It became no longer a question of broadening the old harmonic system, but of creating something entirely new. One of the most original of the new composers was Arnold Schoenberg (1874–1951).

In order to make Schoenberg's system accessible to the average high school student, two preliminary problems must be overcome. First, the piano keyboard must be marked in such a way that a piece of music can be played even though the player cannot read music. The following procedure is particularly appropriate for the Schoenberg system; it is mathematically appealing, and it lends itself to other activities related to the number line.

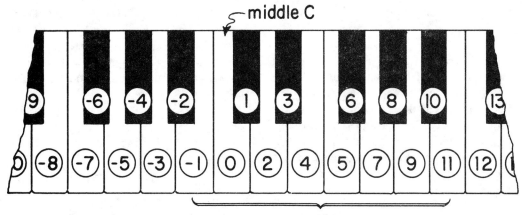

Fig. 1

Using masking tape, label middle C as 0, and then number the keys to the right, including black and white keys, in ascending order: 1, 2, 3,..., 24. Similarly, label the keys to the left of middle C as ⁻1, ⁻2, ⁻3,..., ⁻24. Now if two tones have frequencies p and q in the ratio of 2:1, they are said to be separated by an *octave;* that is, if $p/q = 2$, then p is an octave higher than q. This relationship may be used to partition the notes into *equivalence classes* by the equivalence relation

$$p \sim q \text{ iff } p/q = 2^n, n \in \{\text{integers}\}.$$

Hence two notes belong to the same equivalence class if they are separated by an exact number of octaves (Budden 1967). The numbered keys on the piano thus span four octaves from low C to high C. Notes numbered ⁻24, ⁻12, 0, 12, and 24 all belong to the same equivalence class. This fact is physically reinforced on the piano by the repeated pattern of white and black keys.

Now some means must be found to present the music visually. A convenient representation (Lawlis 1967) is obtained if a graph of time versus note is used as shown in figure 2.

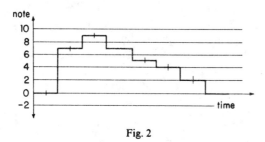

Fig. 2

The graph in figure 2 is that of the first two lines of "Twinkle, Twinkle, Little Star." The unit of the time axis may be taken as the length of a typical note of the melody. Successive notes of the same tone are separated by vertical hash marks. Notice that the seventh and fourteenth notes have been held twice as long as the other notes.

The unit of the vertical axis is the interval from one note to the next in the chromatic scale. Since twelve equal intervals make up an octave and the frequency doubles for each octave, then the frequency of each note must be $\sqrt[12]{2} \doteq 1.0595$ times the frequency of the preceding note lower on the scale (Botts 1974). This means the vertical scale in figure 2 is really a logarithmic scale of frequencies.

Now, having the means both to play a piece and to represent it graphically, Schoenberg's system of *serial composition* can be analyzed. In this system, all twelve notes of the octave are assigned equal importance. No particular note or chord is used as a foundation on which to build, as in traditional composition. There are just five simple rules to follow (Brindle 1966, pp. 18–22).

Rule 1

Set up a row of notes consisting of all twelve notes of the scale, arranged in some specific order. The row must contain all twelve notes, and no note can be repeated. All notes must be used without repetitions, otherwise one might think that the repeated note is more important than the others. Assume that all the notes are held for the same length of time. In actual composition, of course, this would not be done, but it is convenient for graphing purposes.

The row selected might be as follows: 0, 11, 7, 8, 3, 1, 2, 10, 6, 5, 4, 9 (see fig. 3). This row happens to be the one on which Schoenberg's Fourth Quartet is based (Perle 1972, pp. 3–7). Recall that notes an octave apart are elements of the same equivalence class. This implies that the second note could have been ⁻1, or the third ⁻5, without affecting the underlying structure of the composition. Now, with the tone row selected as the basis of the composi-

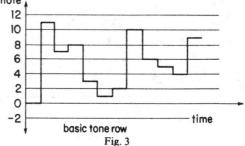

basic tone row
Fig. 3

tion, additional rules are used to produce further notes in the sequence.

Rule 2

The row may be shifted up or down the scale. This operation is called a *transposition* in music. For example, all the notes of the original tone row might be played three steps higher on the scale. Adding 3 to each note in the original sequence results in

original row

0-11-7-8-3-1-2-10-6-5-4-9

transposed row

3-14-10-11-6-4-5-13-9-8-7-12.

Again it must be emphasized that tones 12, 13, and 14 are similar to tones 0, 1, and 2. The latter three could be used if one were actually composing.

The graph of the new sequence following that of the original row appears as shown in figure 4.

It is interesting to note that, if we were dealing with the motion of geometric figures in the plane, the shift of the graph would be a *translation*. All points have

moved an equal distance in the same direction—three units up and twelve units to the right.

A third sequence could be obtained by a second transposition, but a certain musical monotony would surely be the result. Further rules are available to diversify the sound.

Rule 3

The original tone row, or the row obtained from rule 2, may be played backward. This new row is called the *retrograde* of the original row. In the example, the new row based on the original row would result in

original row

0-11-7-8-3-1-2-10-6-5-4-9

retrograde row

9-4-5-6-10-2-1-3-8-7-11-0.

Figure 5 shows the graph of the retrograde row following the original row.

Geometrically, it is evident that the new row is a *reflection* of the original row. The axis of reflection is the vertical line at the end of the last tone of the original row. It

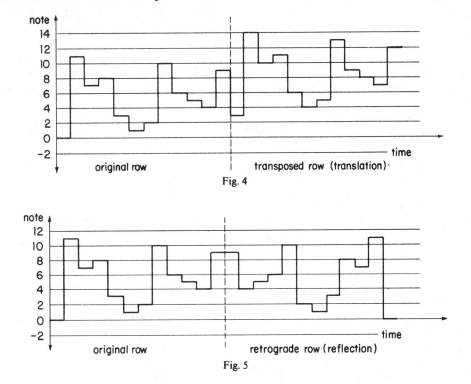

Fig. 4

Fig. 5

may always be considered to be at this location. Consider the case where the axis is a vertical line part of the way along the original row. If the row is reflected about this axis, it must also be translated to the right in order that the notes of the next row follow temporally the notes of the original. There can be no overlapping of the figures.

Rule 4

The original row, or any derived row, may be played upside down. This is a little more complicated. In serial composition it is called an *inversion* of the original row. First, a note must be chosen about which to invert the row. Suppose the selected note is middle C, that is, the zero note of the original row. Then all the new notes following middle C will be the same distance away from middle C going down the keyboard as the notes in the original row were going up the keyboard. Thus, by inverting the original row about middle C, the following rows are produced:

original row

0-11-7-8-3-1-2-10-6-5-4-9

inverted row

0-⁻11-⁻7-⁻8-⁻3-⁻1-⁻2-⁻10-⁻6-⁻5-⁻4-⁻9

The graph of the inverted row following the original row is shown in figure 6.

From a geometrical point of view, the new row is a *glide-reflection* of the original

row. For the particular inversion shown, the original row is reflected about the horizontal axis and then translated parallel to that axis to its new position. In this case, as in the others, it may help to trace the figure on acetate and perform the operations described.

A different note about which to invert the row could have been chosen, for example, note 3. The new notes must be grouped about 3 in the opposite way to the original. In the original, the first note is 0. This is three below the note of inversion 3. Hence, the new first note has to be three above 3, that is, 6. The second note in the original is eight above 3, so the new second note has to be eight below 3, that is, ⁻5. The third is four above 3, so the new third note is four below 3, that is, ⁻1 and so on. Thus the new row following the original row is

original row

0-11-7-8-3-1-2-10-6-5-4-9

inverted row

6-⁻5-⁻1-⁻2-3-5-4-⁻4-0-1-2-⁻3,

and the graph appears as shown in figure 7.

The glide-reflection is not as obvious this time, but consider the original graph attached to the horizontal line through 3 and the whole graph flipped upside down. Then picture this graph shifted to the right to its new position, and it is clear that the combination of reflection and translation results in the glide-reflection.

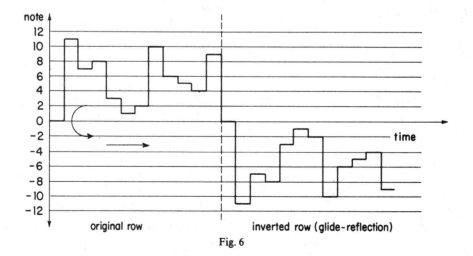

Fig. 6

Rule 5

The original row, or any derived row, may be played upside down and backward. In serial composition the new row is called the *retrograde-inversion* of the original.

The retrograde part presents no problem after a note about which to invert has been selected. Suppose middle C is taken as the note of inversion, as in the first example under rule 4. To get the new row, all that has to be done is to reverse the order of the notes obtained from that inversion. Then the following rows result:

original row

0-11-7-8-3-1-2-10-6-5-4-9

retrograde-inversion row

⁻9-⁻4-⁻5-⁻6-⁻10-⁻2-⁻1-⁻3-⁻8-⁻7-⁻11-0

Figure 8 shows the graph of the original row and the given retrograde-inversion.

It is clear that, geometrically, the result is a *rotation* about the point P, through 180 degrees. The point P will always be located at the intersection of the vertical line at the end of the original tone row and the horizontal line passing through the note of inversion. Hence, if as in the second example under rule 4, note 3 is used as the note of inversion, the point of rotation P′ would be located three units above the point P in figure 8.

Applications

Table 1 summarizes the relationships previously outlined.

There are precisely four permissible operations on a basic tone row in serial composition. There are exactly four types of isometries in transformation geometry. The musical and geometric forms may be placed into a one-to-one correspondence as

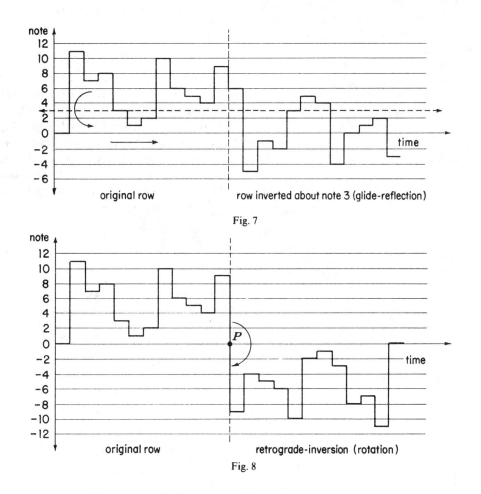

Fig. 7

Fig. 8

TABLE 1

Music	Geometry
basic tone row	basic geometric figure
transposed form	translation
retrograde form	reflection
inverted form	glide-reflection
retrograde-inversion form	rotation

shown in the table. The relationship is remarkable.

Given the clear connection between the musical and the mathematical worlds, the potential for student investigation is considerable. A first step might be to have the students produce a simple serial composition with accompanying graphs based on a shortened tone row of, say, just six notes. A contest to determine whose composition is most attractive musically would ensure that the activity truly combines mathematics and music rather than becoming an academic exercise in numerical and graphical manipulation. More complex compositions using the entire twelve-tone range and variations in the length of time each note is held might be undertaken by students competent in music. Brindle (1966, pp.18–19) provides guidelines for constructing the original tone row.

Reversing the procedure, serial compositions may be analyzed to reveal their underlying geometric form. Variations for Orchestra op. 31 and Canon for String Quartet by Schoenberg and Alban Berg's Lyric Suite for String Quartet are several examples (Brindle 1966, pp. 4–17) that the teacher might prepare for class analysis.

The principles set out by Schoenberg are not new. They have been used to varying extents by other composers. An example of strict inversion is Clementi's canon Gradus ad Parnassum. Bach's Musikalisches Opfer contains a strict retrograde canon. Cherubini's Credo for double choir is written such that the voices of one choir are imitated by the other in reverse order, for example, the treble of the first choir by the bass of the second. Martin Gardner (1978) gives the music for a Mozart composition in which two singers read the same sheet of music from opposite sides, the second melody being the first melody written backward and upside down. Finally the reader may wish to examine Gerald Strang's 1932 composition (Howard and Lyons 1958, p. 68) in which the left and right hands play in strict opposition, and the piece is the same backwards as forwards; it is aptly titled "Mirrorrorrim."

REFERENCES

Botts, Truman. "More on the Mathematics of Musical Scales." *Mathematics Teacher* 67 (January 1974):75–84.

Brindle, Reginald S. *Serial Composition.* London:Oxford University Press, 1966.

Budden, F. J. "Modern Mathematics and Music." *Mathematical Gazette* 51 (October 1967):204–15.

Gardner, Martin. "Mathematical Games." *Scientific American* 238 (April 1978):16–32.

Howard, John T., and James Lyons. *Modern Music: A Popular Guide to Greater Musical Enjoyment.* New York: New American Library, 1958.

Lawlis, Frank. "The Basis of Music—Mathematics." *Mathematics Teacher* 60 (October 1967): 593–96.

Perle, George. *Serial Composition and Atonality.* 3d ed. Los Angeles: University of California Press, 1972.

Editor's Note. Readers interested in music might also wish to explore Eli Maor's "What Is There So Mathematical about Music?" (September 1979).

MEDICAL DIAGNOSIS: A REAL LIFE APPLICATION OF LOGIC

By KENNETH P. GOLDBERG

New York University
New York, NY 10003

Of all the mathematical topics taught at the high school and junior college level, logic must certainly be one of the most frustrating for both students and teachers. On the one hand, the student is told that logic is the necessary basis on which all rational reasoning and decision making rests. On the other hand, since few situations involving human reason are simple enough to permit the application of mathematical logic, it is extremely difficult to discuss and illustrate the use of logic in a believable and interesting manner. In this article we will describe how logic is used as the basis of medical diagnosis and then illustrate this usage with a real example.

Medical Diagnosis

In its most basic form, medical diagnosis consists of the following sequence of steps:

1. A patient has certain symptoms and does not have others.

2. The doctor uses his or her medical knowledge to determine which diseases, if any, correspond to the patient's symptoms and to make a diagnosis.

3. If, given the patient's symptoms, the doctor cannot as yet make a diagnosis, additional tests on the patient may be ordered, or colleagues and medical journals can be consulted in the hope that additional medical knowledge will suggest an accurate diagnosis.

Before describing a mathematical model of this procedure we shall present the system of notation that will be used. We assume a diagnostic situation that concerns m symptoms and n diseases. We make the following definitions.

DEFINITION: *For any integers i, j with $1 \leq i \leq m$ and $1 \leq j \leq n$, let S_i represent the statement,*

Symptom i is present;
and let D_j represent the statement,
Disease j is present.

Now in logic, a statement like "symptom i is present" does not in itself assert that symptom i really *is* present. Rather, it just sits there waiting to be judged true or false. If we really mean that symptom i is present, then we must write that *it is true that* symptom i is present. Such assertions can be neatly abbreviated. Letting "true" and "false" be denoted by 1 and 0 respectively, we will write $S_i = 1$ to indicate that *it is true that* symptom i is present, and similarly $S_i = 0$ to indicate that *it is not true that* symptom i is present (or equivalently that *it is true that* symptom i is not present).

DEFINITION: *By a "symptom complex" we will mean a particular set of assertions about the given set of symptoms. For example,*

$$\{S_1 = 1 \wedge S_2 = 0 \wedge S_3 = 0 \wedge \cdots\}$$

would be a symptom complex, since it tells us whether each symptom in the given set is present or not.

DEFINITION: *By a "disease complex" we will mean a particular set of assertions about the given set of diseases. For example,*

$$\{D_1 = 0 \wedge D_2 = 1 \wedge D_3 = 0 \wedge \cdots\}$$

would be a disease complex, since it tells us whether each disease in the given set is present or not.

DEFINITION: *By a "symptom-disease complex" we will mean a particular set of assertions about the given set of symptoms and diseases. For example,*

$$\{S_1 = 1 \wedge S_2 = 0 \wedge S_3 = 0 \wedge \cdots;$$

$D_1 = 0 \wedge D_2 = 1 \wedge D_3 = 0 \wedge \cdots \}$

would be a symptom-disease complex, since it tells us whether each symptom and each disease in the given set is present or not.

Suppose, for example, that $m = 2$ (two symptoms) and $n = 2$ (two diseases). Then to say that a patient has symptom complex

$$\{S_1 = 0 \wedge S_2 = 1\}$$

is to say that the patient does not have symptom 1 and does have symptom 2. Similarly, to say that the patient has disease complex

$$\{D_1 = 1 \wedge D_2 = 1\}$$

is to say that the patient has disease 1 and also has disease 2. The symptom-disease complex for this patient would then be

$$\{S_1 = 0 \wedge S_2 = 1 \wedge D_1 = 1 \wedge D_2 = 1\}$$

We are now ready to describe the mathematical model of medical diagnosis.

The Medical Diagnosis Model

For simplicity we will assume that we are working in a situation in which there are only two relevant symptoms and two relevant diseases ($m = 2$, $n = 2$). Since each symptom and each disease can either be present or not be present, there is a total of $2^4 = 16$ possible symptom-disease complexes. These sixteen possible symptom-disease complexes are illustrated in figure 1, in which each column represents a different symptom-disease complex. Column 15, for example, represents the particular symptom-disease complex

$$\{S_1 = 0 \wedge S_2 = 1 \wedge D_1 = 1 \wedge D_2 = 1\},$$

mentioned in the previous section. Notice that if we stand the table of figure 1 on end

so that column 1 is at the top and column 16 is at the bottom, then the string of 0's and 1's in any column are just the binary representations for the numbers 0 through 15. Thus, the heading of each column is one more than the number represented by the column itself. This is very handy for purposes of locating the various column arrangements and is made use of in storing tables of symptom-disease complexes like that of figure 1 in computers.

Suppose now that medical knowledge about these two symptoms and two diseases is that anyone who has disease 2 must also have symptoms 1 and 2. In logical notation this medical knowledge would be written

(1) $(D_2 \rightarrow S_1 \wedge S_2)$ is true.

In logic such a statement is false only if $D_2 = 1$ *and* $S_1 \wedge S_2 = 0$. In particular, it is false for the symptom-disease complex

$$\{D_1 = 0 \wedge D_2 = 1 \wedge S_1 = 0 \wedge S_2 = 1\},$$

which is represented by column 1 of the table in figure 1. Thus, our medical knowledge denies the possibility of this symptom-disease complex, and we must consequently delete column 11 from our model. Similarly, we must delete columns 3, 4, 7, 8, and 12 from our model, since each of these symptom-disease complexes is impossible given our medical knowledge. The table of figure 1, with these six "impossible" symptom-disease complexes removed, appears in figure 2 and is called a medical diagnosis model (MDM). The MDM illustrates, for a relevant set of symptoms and diseases and the given medical knowledge relating these symptoms and diseases, which symptom-disease complexes are possible.

	1	2	3	4	5	6	7	8	9	10	11	12	13	14	15	16
D_1	0	1	0	1	0	1	0	1	0	1	0	1	0	1	0	1
D_2	0	0	1	1	0	0	1	1	0	0	1	1	0	0	1	1
S_1	0	0	0	0	1	1	1	1	0	0	0	0	1	1	1	1
S_2	0	0	0	0	0	0	0	0	1	1	1	1	1	1	1	1

Fig. 1. Sixteen possible symptom-disease complexes

Now imagine a patient, Mr. A, who is found to have symptom complex $\{S_1 = 1 \wedge S_2 = 0\}$ (i.e., Mr. A has symptom 1 and does not have symptom 2). From the MDM of figure 2 this symptom complex fits both column 5 (in which case the corresponding disease complex would be $\{D_1 = 0 \wedge D_2 = 0\}$); and column 6 (in which case the corresponding disease complex would be $\{D_1 = 1 \wedge D_2 = 0\}$). In other words, given medical knowledge (1), the best diagnosis we can make for Mr. A is

Symptom Complex
$\{S_1 = 1 \wedge S_2 = 0\}$

Possible Disease   Complexes
$\{D_1 = 0 \wedge D_2 = 0\}$ (column 5)
$\{D_1 = 1 \wedge D_2 = 0\}$ (column 6)

Mr. A definitely does not have disease 2, but he may or may not have disease 1. This is of course an imprecise diagnosis, since there are still two possible disease complexes that Mr. A may have. Suppose, however, that we had the additional medical knowledge

(2) $(D_1 \wedge \sim D_2 \rightarrow \sim S_1 \wedge S_2)$ is true.

(A patient having disease 1 but not disease 2 must not have symptom 1 but have symptom 2.) Then columns 2, 6, and 14 of the MDM of figure 2 are all impossible and must be deleted. A modified MDM corresponding to medical knowledge (1) and (2) is given in figure 3.

	1	2	5	6	9	10	13	14	15	16
D_1	0	1	0	1	0	1	0	1	0	1
D_2	0	0	0	0	0	0	0	0	1	1
S_1	0	0	1	1	0	0	1	1	1	1
S_2	0	0	0	0	1	1	1	1	1	1

Fig. 2. Medical knowledge: The following statement is true (1) $(D_2 \rightarrow S_1 \wedge S_2)$.

With this additional medical knowledge and corresponding MDM we are now able to diagnose Mr. A's disease complex precisely. The only column in the MDM of figure 3 having Mr. A's symptom complex is column 5, and the corresponding disease complex from column 5 is $\{D_1 = 0 \wedge D_2 = 0\}$.

Symptom Complex   Disease Complex
$\{S_1 = 1 \wedge S_2 = 0\}$ $\{D_1 = 0 \wedge D_2 = 0\}$
(Column 5)

In other words, our diagnosis is that Mr. A has neither disease 1 nor disease 2. Notice, however, that although the MDM of figure 3 allows us to diagnose Mr. A's disease complex precisely, there are still symptom complexes for which this would not be true. For example, since the symptom complex $\{S_1 = 0 \wedge S_2 = 1\}$ appears in two different columns in the MDM of figure 3 (columns 9 and 10), there are two different disease complexes that a patient with this symptom complex could have. If, in a given MDM, every symptom complex appears in at most one column of the MDM, then a precise diagnosis is always possible, and the MDM is said to be *complete*. The MDM of figure 3 is not complete, but if we modify it by the additional piece of medical knowledge

(3) $(\sim D_1 \rightarrow \sim S_2)$ is true,

it will become complete, as illustrated in figure 4.

	1	5	9	10	13	15	16
D_1	0	0	0	1	0	0	1
D_2	0	0	0	0	0	1	1
S_1	0	1	0	0	1	1	1
S_2	0	0	1	1	1	1	1

Fig. 3. Medical knowledge: The following statements are true
(1) $(D_2 \rightarrow S_1 \wedge S_2)$
(2) $(D_1 \wedge \sim D_2 \rightarrow \sim S_1 \wedge S_2)$

	1	5	10	16
D_1	0	0	1	1
D_2	0	0	0	1
S_1	0	1	0	1
S_2	0	0	1	1

Fig. 4. Medical knowledge: The following statements are true
(1) $(D_2 \rightarrow S_1 \wedge S_2)$
(2) $(D_1 \wedge \sim D_2 \rightarrow \sim S_1 \wedge S_2)$
(3) $(\sim D_1 \rightarrow \sim S_2)$

Remark: If in an MDM *all* the columns having a particular symptom complex have been eliminated, this simply means that given the available medical knowledge, it is impossible for anyone to have that particular symptom complex.

Medical Diagnosis in Real Life

In the previous section we developed a medical diagnosis model (MDM) for a situation involving two symptoms, two diseases, and a given set of medical knowledge relating these symptoms and diseases. In real-life medical diagnosis, however, the situation is never quite this simple or straightforward. For example, we assumed in developing our MDM that medical knowledge is always of the form, "If a person has such and such diseases then he *must* have such and such symptoms." In reality, medical knowledge is much more likely to be of the form, "If a person has such and such diseases then he will have such and such symptoms *with probability p*," where *p* is some number between 0 and 1 inclusive. Furthermore, since medical knowledge can really be applied with only a limited probability of holding true in a particular case, diagnoses can also be made with only a corresponding probability of being correct. Another implicit assumption that was made in developing the MDM of the previous section was that we could somehow identify exactly those symptoms that were relevant to the given diseases. In reality there are usually many different symptoms that are related to the given diseases to different degrees. These symptoms may include personal and family histories; physical and mental discomforts of the patient; and the results of tests administered to the patient by either the doctor, the hospital, or both. It is up to the person making the diagnosis to decide which symptoms to focus attention on, judging by such considerations as availability of the information (personal histories are usually easy to obtain, whereas hospital tests may take time to arrange for and to evaluate); cost to the patient (some tests are expensive and must be done in a hospital whereas others are relatively inexpensive and may be performed in the patient's home or in a doctor's office); and discomfort to the patient (such as the side effects of a particular drug).

In spite of these real-life difficulties there are situations in which, for a given set of diseases, it is possible to isolate a small number of the most relevant symptoms and for which the medical knowledge relating these symptoms and diseases can be assumed always to hold. One such situation, and the one we will now describe, is that involving back pain. The information used in developing our back pain medical diagnosis model is taken from the two books listed at the end of this article.

The Back Pain Medical Diagnosis Model

Although there are many different types of back pain, we can simplify matters by considering only the three major categories: back strains, disc problems, and arthritic problems. We will therefore concern ourselves exclusively with these three diseases:

D_1: Back strain is present;
D_2: A disc problem is present;
D_3: An arthritic problem is present.

Of the many symptoms that are related to back pains we will consider only the following five:

S_1: Lasegue's Sign is present. (The patient, lying on his back, is asked to stiffen one leg and raise it as high as he can. He then lowers this leg and repeats the procedure with the other leg. If either or both legs cannot be raised to at least 80 degrees without causing pain, we say that Lasegue's Sign is present.)

S_2: The double thigh flexion test causes pain. (In this test the patient bends both knees, presses them together, and draws both thighs simultaneously toward his chest.)

S_3: The patient suffers from a steady, nuisance level of pain that becomes sharply painful when a sudden movement is made.

S_4: The patient has severe pain in the morning and has difficulty bending; the pain decreases as the day wears on but gets worse if the patient remains motionless for an extended period of time.

S_5: The result of a myelogram is positive. (A myelogram is a special procedure, performed in a hospital, for studying the contents of the spinal canal.)

The medical knowledge relating these symptoms and diseases that we will make use of is that the following statements *are all true*.

(1) $\quad (\sim D_1 \wedge \sim D_2 \wedge \sim D_3$
$\rightarrow \sim S_1 \wedge \sim S_2 \wedge \sim S_3 \wedge \sim S_4 \wedge \sim S_5)$

(2) $\quad (D_2 \rightarrow S_1)$

(3) $\quad (\sim D_1 \wedge D_2 \wedge \sim D_3 \rightarrow \sim S_2)$

(4) $\quad (D_1 \rightarrow S_2)$

(5) $\quad ([\sim D_1 \vee D_2] \wedge \sim D_3 \rightarrow \sim S_3)$

(6) $\quad (\sim D_2 \rightarrow \sim S_1)$

(7) $\quad (D_2 \rightarrow S_5)$

(8) $\quad (D_3 \rightarrow S_4)$

For example, medical knowledge (1) tells us that a patient who does not have any of the diseases will not have any of the symptoms; medical knowledge (2) tells us that a patient with a disc problem (D_2) will exhibit Lasegue's Sign (S_1).

If we had no medical knowledge whatsoever relating these symptoms and diseases and since each of the eight symptoms and diseases can either be present or not present in a patient, then there would be a total of $2^8 = 256$ possible symptom-disease complexes. Given our medical knowledge, however, all but thirty-two symptom-disease complexes are eliminated as being impossible and we are left with the thirty-two-column MDM in figure 5.

Notice first that the MDM of figure 5 is not complete. In other words there is at least one symptom complex in the MDM whose corresponding disease complex cannot be precisely diagnosed, given our medical knowledge. For example, consider the symptom complex

$$\{S_1 = 1 \wedge S_2 = 1 \wedge S_3 = 1 \wedge S_4 = 1 \wedge S_5 = 1\}.$$

Since this symptom complex fits both column 255 and column 256, a patient having this symptom complex could have either the disease complex

$$\{D_1 = 0 \wedge D_2 = 1 \wedge D_3 = 1\} \text{ (column 255)}$$

or the disease complex

	1	11	18	50	69	82	85	86	101	114	117	118	139	146	156	178
D_1	0	0	1	1	0	1	0	1	0	1	0	1	0	1	1	1
D_2	0	1	0	0	0	0	0	0	0	0	0	0	1	0	1	0
D_3	0	0	0	0	1	0	1	1	1	0	1	1	0	0	0	0
S_1	0	1	0	0	0	0	0	0	0	0	0	0	1	0	1	0
S_2	0	0	1	1	0	1	1	1	0	1	1	1	0	1	1	1
S_3	0	0	0	1	0	0	0	0	1	1	1	1	0	0	0	1
S_4	0	0	0	0	1	1	1	1	1	1	1	1	0	0	0	0
S_5	0	0	0	0	0	0	0	0	0	0	0	0	1	1	1	1

	197	203	207	210	213	214	220	223	224	229	239	242	245	246	255	256
D_1	0	0	0	1	0	1	1	0	1	0	0	1	0	1	0	1
D_2	0	1	1	0	0	0	1	1	1	0	1	0	0	0	1	1
D_3	1	0	1	0	1	1	0	1	1	1	1	0	1	1	1	1
S_1	0	1	1	0	0	0	1	1	1	0	1	0	0	0	1	1
S_2	0	0	0	1	1	1	1	1	1	0	0	1	1	1	1	1
S_3	0	0	0	0	0	0	0	0	0	1	1	1	1	1	1	1
S_4	1	1	1	1	1	1	1	1	1	1	1	1	1	1	1	1
S_5	1	1	1	1	1	1	1	1	1	1	1	1	1	1	1	1

Fig. 5. Back pain medical diagnosis model

$\{D_1 = 1 \wedge D_2 = 1 \wedge D_3 = 1\}$ (column 256).

That is, such a patient must have disease 2 (a disc problem) and disease 3 (an arthritic problem) but may or may not have disease 1 (a back strain). This is an imprecise diagnosis, and we would need to have additional medical knowledge in order to determine just which of these two is the correct disease complex diagnosis. On the other hand, there are several symptom complexes that appear in exactly one of the columns of the MDM of figure 5, and for any of these symptom complexes a precise diagnosis of the corresponding disease complex is possible. For example, consider the symptom complex $\{S_1 = 1 \wedge S_2 = 0 \wedge S_3 = 1 \wedge S_4 = 1 \wedge S_5 = 1\}$. Since this symptom complex fits only column 239 of our MDM, we can diagnose precisely that anyone having this symptom complex must have the corresponding disease complex of column 239, $\{D_1 = 0 \wedge D_2 = 1 \wedge D_3 = 1\}$. (The patient does not have a back strain but does have both a disc problem and an arthritic problem.) Finally, notice that there are some symptom complexes that do not appear at all in the MDM of figure 5. This indicates that given our medical knowledge, it is impossible for a patient to have these symptom complexes. For example, the symptom complex

$$\{S_1 = 0 \wedge S_2 = 0 \wedge S_3 = 1 \wedge S_4 = 0 \wedge S_5 = 0\}$$

does not appear in our MDM. This should mean that given medical knowledge (1)–(8) inclusive, this particular symptom complex is impossible. Just why this is true is not too difficult to see. From medical knowledge (4) and (8), and the logical equivalence of the general statements $p \rightarrow q$ and $\sim q \rightarrow \sim p$, we see that $\sim S_2$ and $\sim S_4$ imply $\sim D_1$ and $\sim D_3$ respectively. By medical knowledge (5) this would in turn imply $\sim S_3$. Thus, medical knowledge (1)–(8) inclusive implies that $(\sim S_2 \wedge \sim S_4 \rightarrow \sim S_3)$, which shows the impossibility of the symptom complex

$$\{S_1 = 0 \wedge S_2 = 0 \wedge S_3 = 1 \wedge S_4 = 0 \wedge S_5 = 0\}.$$

REFERENCES

Finneson, Bernard E., and Arthur S. Freese. *The New Approach to Low Back Pain*. New York: Berkley Windhover Books, 1975.

Kiernan, Thomas, and Leon Root, *Oh, My Aching Back*. New York: Signet Books, 1973.

4

ALGEBRA

Algebra provides the structure, or rules, for the mathematics we use. From algebra we have numbers (e.g., primes, rational, irrational, complex, and transfinite), equations (e.g., linear, quadratic, and implicit) and their solutions, structures (e.g., groups, rings, and fields), and mathematical extensions of numbers (e.g., matrices).

However, algebra also serves as a language, or notation, for expressing mathematical ideas and relationships. Algebraic notation has become the language of mathematics just as arithmetic notation has become the language of numbers. Today we easily represent variables, expressions, and equations using algebraic notation. Using this notation, we can represent the progression of steps in the solution of many problems.

Algebra is placed after geometry in this text. This is because much of what today is considered algebra was initially considered in, and expressed through, geometry.

An ancient Babylonian clay tablet (fig. 4.1) contains the geometrical representation of the algebraic result $a^2 - b^2 = (a + b)(a - b)$ (Resnikoff and Wells 1984, p. 83).

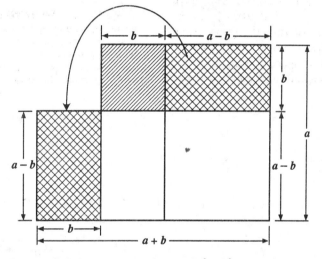

Fig. 4.1. Babylonian representation of $a^2 - b^2 = (a + b)(a - b)$

The Greeks also used such geometric representation. Proposition 4 of Book 2 of Euclid's *Elements* is as follows:

> If a straight line be cut at random, the square on the whole is equal to the squares on the segments and twice the rectangle contained by the segments (Euclid 1956, p. 379).

The diagram in figure 4.2 follows the proposition. The straight line is $\overline{AB}$ with the random cut at point C. *ABDE* and *CBKG* are squares. We introduce the variables a and b to denote the distances AC and CB, respectively. Algebraically, the proposition is expressed

$$(a + b)^2 = a^2 + b^2 + 2ab$$

Using geometry to represent results in algebra continued for over a thousand years. The book *Al-jabr w'al mûqabala* by al-Khwarizmi was published in A.D. 830. The title means the science of reunion and opposition, referring to combining like terms and transposing terms from one side of an equation by using the opposite sign of the term. (See Eves 1983, chap. 15.) The word *algebra* comes from the title of this text. An 1857 Latin translation rendered the author's name as Algorithmi, from which the word *algorithm* evolved. This book still used geometry to represent and solve some algebraic problems. For example, it had the following problem and solution:

Solve (using present-day notation) $x^2 + 10x = 39$.

Solution. Draw a square with sides of length x. Extend two adjacent sides to make rectangles with sides x and 5 as shown in figure 4.3. The total area is $x^2 + 10x$. "Complete the square" by adding a 5 × 5 square as shown. The total area of the figure is 39 + 25, or 64. A square with area 64 has sides of length 8. From the figure,

$$x + 5 = 8,$$

giving

$$x = 3.$$

See Stillwell (1989) for more details of this method.

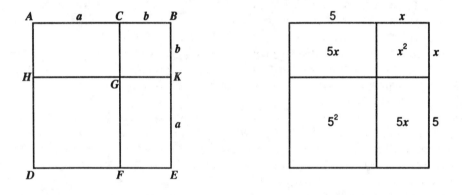

Fig. 4.2. Greek representation of $(a + b)^2 = a^2 + b^2 + 2ab$ Fig. 4.3. Arab solution of $x^2 + 10x = 39$

The algebraic notation we use today, though begun by the Greek Diophantus about A.D. 250 in his book *Arithmetica* and advanced in the book *Al-jabr w'al mûqabala*, was not fully developed until the 1700s.

Babylonian clay tablets give several algebra applications from geometry. Van der Waerden (1963) offers the following Babylonian problem about rectangles:

> Length, width. I have multiplied length and width, thus obtaining the area. Then I added to the area, the excess of length over the width: 3;3. Moreover, I have added length and width: 0;27. Required is the length, width, and area. (Tablet AO 8862)

Here 3;3 represents the Babylonian base-60 notation and indicates 183. For example, 3;5 would equal 3 × 60 + 5 = 185. The problem seems more likely to be a school problem than a real-world application. For example, it adds the measurements of area and the measurements of length. The problem involves two equations with two unknowns. The solution requires the use of the quadratic equation. Try your hand at solving this problem. (Resnikoff and Wells [1984, pp. 80–81] give a solution using modern notation.)

To find numerical solutions using the quadratic equation requires finding square roots. The Babylonians developed a very advanced method for approximating square roots. Using modern notation, let $\sqrt{x}$ denote the square root of a positive number x. Define $a_1 = 1$ and

$$a_{n+1} = \frac{a_n + x/a_n}{2}$$

for $n = 1, 2, \ldots$.

Babylonian clay tablets give multiplication tables, reciprocal tables, and square-root tables. One tablet gives the $\sqrt{2}$ to six places! These tables were useful for arithmetical computations and for solving problems in algebra. One area that required such precision was astronomy, an area in which, as you will see in the section on trigonometry, the Babylonians excelled.

Functions studied in algebra are useful in a wide range of applications. In this section Malone uses applications to introduce quadratic functions. Eisner uses quadratic equations to analyze questions arising in baseball standings. (Martin offers confirming empirical support for Eisner's paper.) Kluepfel gives applications of logarithms in finance, astronomy, physics, and games.

Entire areas of study have opened because of the power that algebra offers to analyze problems. Reagan describes how algebra is used with cryptographs or coded information to both code and decode messages, and Camp uses matrices to code and decode messages. Sloyer uses geometric programming and algebra to study inventory problems.

Algebra has particularly enriched certain fields such as finance. Ruppel uses algebra to analyze equations that arise in consumer financial problems. Soler and Schuster consider compound growth in financial investments. Woodward and Hamel consider the use of calculators in algebra to estimate future prices, populations, and energy reserves. The price estimates are amazingly accurate. Somers considers problems involving yearly and biyearly raises with a surprising algebraic answer. Dunn and Wright use algebra to investigate several models of the U.S. economy.

However, it is the combination of algebraic techniques and equations that are useful in widely diverse modeling and physical applications. Davis and Middlebrooks use algebra to explain a fascinating card trick. Harmeyer uses algebra to answer some questions that arise in flying as a passenger. (McCulloch raises some other questions that arise in flying.) Wagner analyzes fuel consumption for the individual and nation. Sullivan considers the role of mathematics in congressional apportionments. (Shirley provides personal documentation of the effects of mathematical apportionment procedures.) Gonzales and Carr analyze the impact of the Black Death on current and past world population. Haak studies the musical scales produced by a single wire, a monochord. Shoemaker uses algebra to analyze the distance a ball bounces.

REFERENCES

Euclid. *The Elements*. 2d ed. Edited by Thomas L. Heath. New York: Dover Publications, 1956.

Eves, Howard. *Great Moments in Mathematics before 1650*. Washington, D.C.: Mathematical Association of America, 1983.

Resnikoff, H. L., and R. O. Wells, Jr. *Mathematics in Civilization*. New York: Dover Publications, 1984.

Stillwell, John. *Mathematics and Its History*. New York: Springer-Verlag, 1989.

Van der Waerden, B. L. *Science Awakening*. New York: John Wiley & Sons, 1963.

ALGEBRA AND A SUPER CARD TRICK

By EDWARD J. DAVIS
University of Georgia
Athens, GA 30602

and ED MIDDLEBROOKS
First Presbyterian Day School
Macon, GA 31204

Here is a fascinating card trick that can be explained and justified using first-year algebra. We have used this trick with high school classes and mathematics clubs as a motivational device and sometimes as a challenge to students to find or finish the algebraic justification. This procedure makes a good example of the power of mathematics to unmask seemingly complex situations and, therefore, is a good device for teachers to "keep up their sleeves" for some auspicious occasion or a time when interest is lagging. Some related procedures can be found in the bibliography.

Get a standard fifty-two-card deck and work through each step. Later we shall examine the algebra behind the scenes. We assume that jacks, queens, and kings have values of 11, 12, and 13, respectively, whereas aces have a value of 1.

1. Shuffle the deck and begin placing cards faceup all in one stack on a desk top. Claim that you are memorizing the sequence of cards displayed. Challenge the spectators to perform this great mental feat as well!

2. As you are placing cards faceup in step one (say after you have dealt about a dozen cards), secretly pick out and remember one card. Then continue the dealing process so that you place exactly *ten* more cards faceup on top of your secretly selected card (see fig. 1).

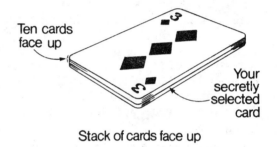

Ten cards face up

Your secretly selected card

Stack of cards face up

Fig. 1

3. Have each of three students select one card at random from the cards in your hand. Have these three cards placed faceup in three separate locations on the desk top. Let's assume the students selected a 4, an 8, and a jack.

4. Turn over the face-up pile of cards containing your secretly selected (and memorized) card and place it under the stack of cards in your hand. You now have three cards, each facing up, and one stack of cards in your hand.

5. Now work with each face-up card separately. Place additional cards facedown on top of each of the three face-up cards. Start with the value of each face-up card and add cards until you reach a count of thirteen. Let the bottom face-up card stick out a little so you can use it in the next step (see fig. 2).

Face-down cards counted as shown

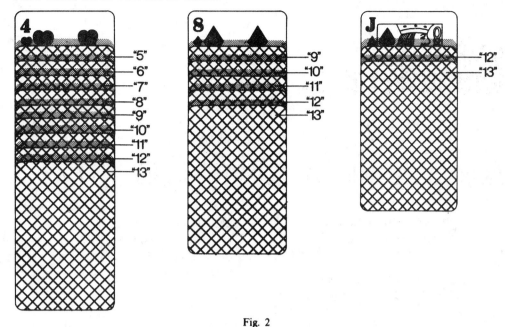

Fig. 2

6. Now, out loud, add the values of the three face-up cards on the bottom of the piles in view. We shall call this sum S. (In our example we have $S = 4 + 8 + 11 = 23$.)

7. Ask if anyone knows the value of the Sth card in your hand. Pretend you are struggling to recall it—remember, you claimed to have memorized a long sequence of cards—and announce it as if you were able to remember it! Count out S cards, and you can't miss!

A Rationale

Let's begin by finding an expression for the total number of cards in each of the three piles of cards left in view. We had piles on top of 8, 4, and a jack.

On the 8 pile, we had $6 = 14 - 8$ cards.

On the 4 pile, we had a total of $10 = 14 - 4$ cards.

On the jack pile, we had a total of $3 = 14 - 11$ cards.

In general, if n is the value of the face-up card on the bottom, there are $14 - n$ cards in the pile. If n_1, n_2, and n_3 are the values of the face-up cards on the bottom, then there are

$$(14 - n_1) + (14 - n_2) + (14 - n_3)$$

cards on the table. In step 7 you counted $S = n_1 + n_2 + n_3$ cards down into the cards in your hand. Adding the number of cards on the table and S gives

$$(14 - n_1) + (14 - n_2) + (14 - n_3) + (n_1 + n_2 + n_3) = 42.$$

You will always reach card number forty-two.

How many cards are beneath your secretly selected card? Ten—you put them there in the second step! (See fig. 3.) That

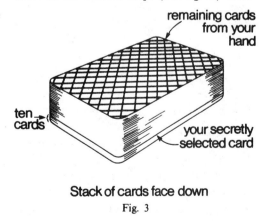

remaining cards from your hand

ten cards

your secretly selected card

Stack of cards face down
Fig. 3

means your secretly selected and memorized card is also card number forty-two.

Teacher's Corner

As with all card tricks, a dash of theatrics can amplify the positive effects. Pretending to struggle to recall the memorized card and claiming to have memorized a long sequence of cards are two such maneuvers. Holding off an explanation or limiting the number of "performances" on a given day are other devices that could spark additional interest. If the class is challenged to find a rationale, they will find it easier if they know all the steps involved. Once students know how to do the trick, they are usually very interested in finding out why it works.

Here are some questions and suggestions we have used to help students find the algebraic explanation.

- Look at the total number of cards in each of the three piles. How can you predict each total if you know the value of the bottom face-up card?

- Think of the cards when they are in the three piles as all being in one stack—this includes the cards in your hand. How far down in the deck is your secret card?

Here are some questions we have posed to get students to look back at their rationales.

- Will the trick always work, or can someone pick three cards at random that will cause it to fail?

- Suppose we count to fourteen instead of thirteen as we place cards on top of the three selected cards. What other change do we have to make?

- Why is the number of cards in each pile $14 - n$? If we count to 13, it seems as if we should have $13 - n$.

- What could happen if four students selected cards in the third step?

- What changes could you make in the trick if you had a double deck (104 cards) to work with?

BIBLIOGRAPHY

Felps, Barry C. "An Old Card Trick Revisited." *Mathematics Teacher* 69 (December 1976):665–66.

Gardner, Martin. *Mathematics: Magic and Mystery.* New York: Dover, 1956. (See chapters 1 and 2.)

Hadar, Nita. "Odd and Even Numbers." *Mathematics Teacher* 75 (May 1982):408–12.

Hays, Katie, and Edward J. Davis. "The 22nd Card Trick." *Illinois Mathematics Teacher* 30 (September 1979):16–17.

Heath, Royal Vale. *Mathemagic: Magic, Puzzles and Games with Numbers.* New York: Dover, 1953.

Stern, Burton L. "Algebra in Card Tricks." *Mathematics Teacher* 66 (October 1973):547.

Trigg, Charles W. "A Card Trick." *Mathematics Teacher* 63 (May 1970):395–96.

Flying in Algebra Class

While flying to Boston aboard a Delta jet, I found a wealth of practical mathematics in the "Delta Air Lines System Route Map." The numbers and formulas were well within the capabilities of second-year algebra students. So I asked to keep the map to use it as the basis for some lessons (table 1).

For our class discussion, the students were given the formula in table 1 and were told to work with the altitude of 10 000 meters. When they saw the chart from the route map, they commented on the unusual choices for altitudes in meters. They decided that the numbers were the result of conversions from altitudes in feet. Since a pilot would not tell passengers they were flying at 9144 meters, we devised table 2. Paying careful attention to significant digits we used hand calculators and generated values to the nearest 100 meters.

"What if you wanted to view a specific span on the surface of the earth? How far up would you need to go?" These questions prompted an introduction to solving equations with radicals. After some discussion, the students understood how to solve an equation like $300 = 3.56 \sqrt{A}$. Our attention turned to more complicated radical equations, which were solved as an assignment.

My favorite exercise using the route map was inspired by a vignette on temperature outside a Delta jet (see table 3). Based on these data, I developed a lesson

on modeling. Students graphed ordered pairs of altitude and temperature (fig. 1). "How," I asked, "could one find the temperature at 2000 meters?" One student said we needed a formula. I told the class a little about mathematical modeling and curve fitting with sets of empirical data. Once they assumed that the curve was linear, we defined the line of best fit and tried to draw the line that seemed closest to the most points on the graph. Then we tried to write an equation for that line.

They knew how to use the intercept and

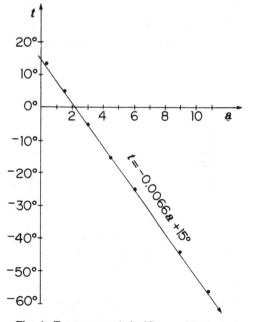

Fig. 1. Temperature (t in °C) vs. altitude (a in thousands of meters)

TABLE 1

It's difficult for most airline passengers, whether they are first fliers or experienced travelers, to cruise above this vast country in clear weather without being impressed by the spectacular panorama below. Few nations in the world have the varied topography of this great land of ours. Anyone who is interested in geography can survey the physical features below . . . forests, grasslands, mountain ranges, deserts, canyons, lakes, rivers, and the cities and farmlands, carved from the earth's surface by the machinery of America. High altitude jet travel affords even the most casual observer, an opportunity to experience America's geographical features from a viewpoint that scholars of yesterday could not imagine.

How far can you see from a Delta jet? VM = √A × 1.22 or VK = √A × 3.56

Cruising in clear weather at 35,000 feet (10,500 meters), it's a long way: a span of 228 miles (368 kilometers) from horizon to horizon.

Your view depends on the curvature of the earth and your height above the earth. The formulas tell you that your view in miles (VM) equals the square

root of your altitude (in feet) multiplied by 1.22 while your view in kilometers (VK) equals the square root of your altitude (in meters) multiplied by 3.56.

But if you've forgotten how to do square roots (and who hasn't?) here's a ready-made table:

Height in Feet	View in Miles*	Height in Meters	View in Kilometers*
1,000	39	305	62
2,000	55	610	88
3,000	67	914	108
5,000	86	1,524	139
10,000	122	3,048	197
15,000	149	4,572	241
20,000	173	6,096	278
25,000	193	7,620	311
30,000	211	9,144	340
35,000	228	10,668	368
40,000	244	12,192	393

* View from either side of plane

slope to write an equation but were concerned about which two points to use for the slope. Not all the data fell on the line of best fit. The class decided to check all pairs of points. Twenty-one values for the slope were computed (seven points, two at a time), and the results were recorded

TABLE 2
$$VK = \sqrt{A} \times 3.56$$

Height in Meters (A)	View in Kilometers (VK)
500	80
1 000	110
2 000	160
3 000	190
4 000	230
5 000	250
7 500	310
9 000	340
10 000	360
11 000	370
12 000	390

TABLE 3

How Cold Is Up?

There you are, bareheaded and with no gloves and in the lightest of summer clothes, eating a cold salad at 69° below (−59° C) zero!

It's routine on Delta jets, summer or any other season, for you to travel in the upper levels of air far from surface heat. It's a case of the higher, the lower. Perhaps you'd like to know exactly how the temperature changes with altitude, how it can be 104° F (40° C) in the sun of the parking lot and well below zero just four miles from the lot, straight up!

The seasons influence lower level temperatures, of course, but on a "standard" day (59° F) (15° C) at sea level) the mercury would drop this way as you went up:

Ft.	Meter	F	C
1,000	300	56°	13°
5,000	1,500	41°	5°
10,000	3,000	23°	− 5°
15,000	4,500	5°	−15°
20,000	6,000	−15°	−26°
30,000	9,000	−47°	−44°
36,087	10,826	−69°	−56°
	(Stratosphere)		

in a table on the chalkboard. The range of the slopes was from −0.0060 to −0.0070 with an average of −0.0066. Curiously, the slope of the line of best fit was −0.0066.

We let t represent the temperature, and a the altitude. Using 15 for the t-intercept and −0.0066, the average slope, the equation became

$$t = -0.0066\,a + 15.$$

We then predicted the temperature at 2000 meters to be

$$t = -0.0066(2000) + 15 \approx 2°.$$

The route map also mentioned that the height of Mt. McKinley was 6194 meters. Replacing a, we found that

$$t = -0.0066(6194) + 15 \approx -26°$$

at the peak.

Students asked what would happen on a nonstandard day, and I sent them off in search of more information. After consulting many books on weather, the students asked a science teacher to explain factors that affect temperature. She explained what clouds, wind velocity, and time of day did to vary the amount of heat in the atmosphere. Then she expanded on modeling in the sciences and told the students that the method we used to find the formula is the same one researchers use to develop empirical formulas.

It is refreshing to note that not all applied mathematics requires facility with differential equations and that algebra need not be advertised as useful only as a preparation for higher mathematics. With simple algebra skills, two practical problems are readily solved. Using applications can make algebra fun again.

Kathleen M. Harmeyer
Maryland State Department
of Education
Baltimore, MD 21201

Tables 1 and 3 appear with permission of Delta Air Lines. A free copy of the route map may be obtained by writing Public Relations, Delta Air Lines, Hartsfield Atlanta International Airport, Atlanta, GA 30320.

High flying

Kathleen M. Harmeyer's article "Flying in Algebra Class" (March 1982) highlighted an exciting and understandable application of mathematical modeling. However, I take issue with the interpretation of the formulas $VM = \sqrt{a} \times 1.22$ and $VK = \sqrt{a} \times 3.56$, stated in the Delta Airlines Chart (table 1) as representing the viewing distance from "horizon to horizon." These formulas represent the sighting distance (v) from the point of observation to the horizon (see figure).

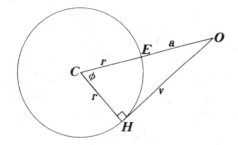

C   represents the center of the earth;
O   represents the point of observation above the surface of the earth;
r   represents the radius of the earth;
v   represents the sighting distance;
a   represents the altitude of the observation;
H   is the point of tangency of the line of sight with the surface of the earth.

Because $\overline{OH}$ is tangent to the earth at point H, the right triangle CHO is formed. Therefore,

$$v = \sqrt{(r + a)^2 - r^2},$$

where r is the radius of the earth (3960 miles) and a is the altitude at which the observation occurs.

$$v = \sqrt{(3960 + a)^2 - 3960^2}$$
$$= \sqrt{(3960^2 + 7920a + a^2) - 3960^2}$$
$$= \sqrt{7920a + a^2}$$

When the altitude is measured in feet, the formula becomes

$$v = \sqrt{7920(a/5280) + (a/5280)^2}$$
$$= \sqrt{1.5a + 3.5 \times 10^{-8}a}.$$

The term $3.5 \times 10^{-8}a$ is insignificant for even the greatest altitudes listed on the chart regarding commercial jet flights—40 000 feet. Therefore, the formula becomes

$$v \approx \sqrt{1.5a} \approx 1.22\sqrt{a}.$$

The length of arc EH may be determined as follows:

$$\tan \phi \approx \frac{1.22\sqrt{a}}{r},$$
$$m \angle \phi \approx \tan^{-1} \frac{1.22\sqrt{a}}{3960},$$
$$m \,\widehat{EH} \approx m \angle \phi.$$

By comparing this arc length with the circumference of the earth.

$$\frac{m \angle \phi}{360} = \frac{m \,\widehat{EH}}{24\ 875},$$

$$m \,\widehat{EH} = \frac{24\ 875 \tan^{-1}\left(\frac{1.22\sqrt{a}}{3960}\right)}{360}$$

$$= 69 \tan^{-1}\left(\frac{1.22\sqrt{a}}{3960}\right) = 69 \tan^{-1}\left(\frac{v}{3960}\right).$$

When a is at its maximum value (40 000 feet), $m\widehat{EH}$ = 243.3 miles compared with v = 244 miles. At lower altitudes the correlation is even greater.

Therefore, for altitudes of commercial jet flights, the length of the line of sight closely approximates the earth arc $\widehat{EH}$. *Twice* this length will represent the view from horizon to horizon.

This development could also be used to verify and illustrate the positioning of communications satellites that are "parked" above the equator at an altitude of 22 300 miles to maintain geosynchronous orbit and overcome the pull of gravity. Three communications satellites are necessary to monitor transmissions around the entire globe as can be easily determined using the previously developed formulas. When the altitude of the satellites is converted to feet, the line of sight varies significantly from the earth arc.

$$v = 1.22\sqrt{1.18 \times 10^8} = 13\ 252 \text{ miles}$$
$$m\widehat{EH} = 5060 \text{ miles}$$
$$2m\widehat{EH} = 10\ 120 \text{ miles}$$

Therefore, each satellite can monitor transmissions across 10 120 miles at the equator, and three will be necessary to monitor the circumference of the earth (24 875 miles).

Diane E. McCulloch
Mount de Chantal Academy
Wheeling, WV 26003

DETERMINING FUEL CONSUMPTION—
AN EXERCISE IN APPLIED MATHEMATICS

*A trillion miles of U.S. driving
consumes gasoline in staggering amounts.*

By CLIFFORD H. WAGNER
The Pennsylvania State University
The Capitol Campus
Middletown, PA 17057

Applied mathematics is more than a convenient pedagogical tool by which we try to motivate our students. It is also a way of cultivating an awareness and understanding of our culture and society. Our students need to understand the *process* of applying mathematics to "real life" problems in order to cope with our technological society and to perform their own personal mathematical applications in everyday life.

Consider the following questions relating to automobile fuel consumption: "Should I buy a Sprint automobile having average gasoline mileage, or should I pay an extra $500 and buy a Spartan automobile having superior gasoline mileage?" "How much gasoline will our country save by improving the fuel efficiency of our cars?"

As we attempt to answer these questions, we will experience the process of applied mathematics.

Fuel Consumption for an Individual Driver

The following series of five questions outlines the process of applied mathematics and should prompt the reader (or, in the context of a classroom discussion, should prompt the student) to make the kinds of decisions and inquiries that are typical of mathematical applications. The answers are not unique; in applied mathematics one must often choose from among several reasonable alternatives. Since we are concerned primarily with the process of applying mathematics, the mathematical level is quite modest.

1. *What specific additional information must we know in order to choose between the Sprint and the Spartan?* Surely we need to know the purchase price and mileage rating of each car. Let's suppose the Sprint costs $3500 and delivers 25 miles per gallon (mpg); the Spartan costs $4000 and delivers 30 mpg.

On further reflection, one realizes that dollars cannot be compared directly with miles per gallon. To determine the cost of consumed gasoline, we must also know the price of gasoline and the number of miles the new car will be driven. The Spartan's lower rate of fuel consumption will offset its extra price only after it has been driven some minimum distance, which we will call the *break-even distance*. Because we cannot be certain of the average price of gasoline during the coming years, let us, at least for the moment, assign a reasonable price such as $1 per gallon and plan to assess the effect of different gas prices before making a final choice between the two cars. Because we are also uncertain of the total distance the car eventually will be driven, let us designate that distance by the variable x.

2. *How can we translate the problem into mathematical terms?* If we designate the costs (in dollars) of driving the Sprint and the Spartan a distance of x miles by $f_1(x)$ and $f_2(x)$ respectively, then it is easy to verify that

$$(1) \quad f_1(x) = 3500 + \left(\frac{1.00}{25}\right) x, \quad \text{and}$$

$$(2) \quad f_2(x) = 4000 + \left(\frac{1.00}{30}\right) x.$$

If $f_1(x) < f_2(x)$, then we would choose to buy the Sprint; if $f_1(x) > f_2(x)$, we would choose the Spartan; and if $f_1(x) = f_2(x)$, then x would be the break-even distance where neither car is preferred.

3. *Before solving the problem, what assumptions have we made so far?* Either explicitly or implicitly, we have assumed that the average price of gasoline will be $1 per gallon, that cost of ownership is to be the basis for choosing between the two cars, and that costs of ownership other than the purchase price and the price of gasoline can be ignored. In effect we are assuming that these other costs, such as depreciation, maintenance, repairs, insurance, and taxes, are comparable for the two cars.

Applied mathematics is not a substitute for human judgment.

We could try to adjust equations (1) and (2) to account for some of these other costs, but we must realize that nearly always there are some uncertainties that can be removed only by making assumptions. Constructing a mathematical model, as in equations (1) and (2), often is like a police artist trying to draw a face without having complete information. For example, the artist who cannot determine the exact shape of a chin must either make assumptions about the chin or abandon the project. Once the assumptions are made and the model has been completed, a rational and informed human judgement must decide if the model is a useful and adequate representation of reality.

That a mathematical model is only an approximation of reality is to be expected. Not only can assumptions and uncertainties lead to approximations, but also the errors inherent in measurement and computer arithmetic often prevent exact representations of reality.

4. *What is the solution? (Which car should I buy?)* By graphing or by solving simultaneously equations (1) and (2), we find the Spartan is preferred to the Sprint if and only if we plan to own the car beyond the break-even distance of 75 000 miles. Notice that if the average price of gasoline were higher than $1 per gallon, the break-

even point would be less than 75 000 miles. The final decision of which car to buy also depends on my degree of confidence in the assumptions made and my degree of certainty in whether or not I will own the car past the break-even distance. Applied mathematics is a resource for human judgement, not a substitute.

5. *Can we generalize these results?* For example, suppose I have chosen the Spartan over the Sprint—should I also be willing to pay another extra $500 for another extra 5 mpg? Perhaps the Spartan has a $4500 diesel model that delivers 35 mpg. One would probably not choose to buy the diesel Spartan, for when comparing the regular Spartan and the diesel Spartan, the break-even point is now 105 000 miles (with gasoline priced at $1 per gallon).

The savings in fuel consumption due to an extra 5 mpg decrease as the fuel economy of a car increases. An intuitive explanation of this relation between fuel consumption and mileage is given in the next section.

Fuel Consumption for a Nation

The same process can be applied to the question, "How much gasoline will our country save by improving the overall fuel efficiency of our cars?" Here we are concerned with cumulative rather than individual fuel consumption.

As before, we must start by obtaining additional information. Congress has mandated in the Motor Vehicle Information and Cost Savings Act that the 1978 model cars of each manufacturer must have an overall average of 18 mpg and that by 1985 this average must be 27.5 mpg. It seems reasonable to expect the average mileage for all cars driven in the United States eventually to reach 27.5 mpg. In the process of improving gas mileage and lowering fuel consumption, how much gasoline will be saved?

If we assume that Americans will continue to drive approximately 10^{12} miles each year (as reported in the *Information Please Almanac, 1977;* p. 85), then the fuel consumption for a given year will be

$$g(m) = \frac{10^{12}}{m} \quad \text{(gallons)},$$

where m is the average mileage of all cars driven that year.

Suppose m is 15 (mpg) this year and that m will be 20 in some future year. How much gasoline will we then be saving? The answer is clearly

$$g(15) - g(20) = 16\ 666\ 666\ 667 \text{ gallons.}$$

As we go from $m = 20$ to $m = 25$, will we save another 16 billion gallons? Unfortunately, we will not, for

$$g(20) - g(25) = 10\ 000\ 000\ 000 \text{ gallons.}$$

This example helps explain why the regular Spartan was preferred over the Sprint but the diesel Spartan was not preferred over the regular Spartan. Fuel consumption is inversely proportional to mileage; therefore as m increases, the slope of $g(m) = 10^{12}/m$ decreases; that is, as m increases, fixed increments in m produce successively smaller decrements in $g(m)$. See figure 1.

Conclusion

The five questions listed above are intended to acquaint the reader with the process of applied mathematics; they are not intended to completely describe every conceivable mathematical application. For example, in many applications, one also performs an experimental analysis to verify

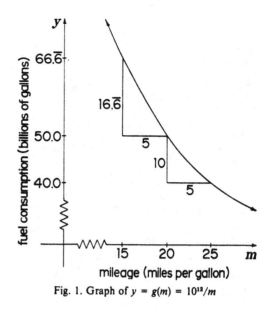

Fig. 1. Graph of $y = g(m) = 10^{12}/m$

the theoretical solution and to justify general conclusions.

Applied mathematics, as well as science in general, depends on the considered assumptions and rational judgements of human beings; it is more important for our students to learn this than to receive the impression that every mathematical problem has an answer in the back of the book.

REFERENCES

Information Please Almanac, 1977. New York: Simon & Schuster, 1977.

United States. *Motor Vehicle Information and Cost Savings Act, U.S. Code,* title 15, section 2002 (1975).

Get the Message?
Cryptographs, Mathematics,
and Computers

By JAMES REAGAN, Stevenson High School, Sterling Heights, MI 48078

Most students realize that functions can be constructed to describe various physical phenomena, but it is not clear when inverses of functions are needed. One appropriate application of functions and their inverses is the coding and decoding of messages and information exchanged among people. Computers can be especially helpful in this process.

Cryptographs

The need for cryptographs, or coded information, is clear. A message intended for selected people should not be meaningful to everyone who intercepts the message. Multinational companies want information about their products and marketing strategies to be internal. Governments want information about policy changes to be private until an appropriate time for their announcement. Even in the private sector, people do not necessarily want their ideas or feelings made public. Letters, telephone conversations, face-to-face meetings, and telecommunications are all susceptible to interception by unintended audiences.

It is not unusual for unauthorized parties to intercept messages; some people make their living doing so. Having computers store, retrieve, and send information does not resolve the problem; some hobbyists pride themselves in being able to invade computer systems and extract information. Many protective schemes are designed at least to discourage these would-be "message pirates" from communicating with a microcomputer. However, it seems to me that it would be more fruitful for young programmers, especially those without sophisticated knowledge of operating systems, to use coded messages rather than to spend time developing elaborate procedures to prevent entry to the system.

Cryptographs and Computers

The computer is an ideal device for coding and decoding messages. It can process data and perform arithmetic very rapidly. A numeric value is assigned to each alphabetic character, numeral, punctuation symbol, special character, and space. Most commonly, these values are those of the American Standard Code for Information Interchange (ASCII); a partial list appears in table 1. Furthermore, most microcomputers have two important built-in functions—one converts characters to ASCII values, and the other converts ASCII values to characters.

Mathematics and Cryptographs

Cryptograms are often found in newspapers and magazines. They are usually puzzles, with clues, in which the letters of a message are replaced by other letters. These letters are to be decoded and the original message deduced. This type of cryptogram does not normally use any of the ten numeric digits, space (a space is a clue to word length), or special characters such as punctuation marks (see fig. 1). As puzzles these cryptograms are entertaining, but if they are to be used to transmit messages, the entire coding table must be sent along with the message. To increase secrecy, we avoid transmitting the coding table by using coding schemes that apply functions. The use of the ASCII values instead of the actual characters permits the use of all characters and requires the passing of the coding function to the receiver.

TABLE 1
Partial List of ASCII Values

Character	Decimal ASCII Value
A	65
B	66
C	67
D	68
E	69
F	70
G	71
H	72
I	73
J	74
K	75
L	76
M	77
N	78
O	79
P	80
Q	81
R	82
S	83
T	84
U	85
V	86
W	87
X	88
Y	89
Z	90
Space	32
0	48
1	49
2	50
3	51
4	52
5	53
6	54
7	55
8	56
9	57

Break the code to give the name of a president and the location of four presidents.

JGPZVT JNZRZP

KGDPL JDQUKGJN

Fig. 1. Sample cryptogram

The following is a discussion of how functions can be applied to the encoding and decoding of messages. I shall progress from some rather simple schemes to one of the most respected and reputedly crack-proof schemes.

For each of the coding schemes, I shall discuss the class of functions and their inverses, encode a message by a function of its ASCII values, and decode it by the inverse function.

An encoding function must have an inverse; the ambiguity associated with not having an inverse would be intolerable. I shall use $E(x)$ to indicate an encoding function and $D(y)$ to indicate the corresponding decoding function. We must choose $y = E(x)$ so that a $D(y)$ exists such that $D(E(x)) = x$. The domain of E is the set of ASCII values of common keyboard symbols (including the space).

Sample Coding Schemes

Linear functions

Linear functions of the form $E(x) = ax + b$ (where $a \neq 0$) can be used to transform the ASCII values of a message into an encoded message. The inverse function is

$$D(y) = \frac{y - b}{a}.$$

To illustrate, the inverse of $E(x) = 4x + 9$ is

$$D(y) = \frac{y - 9}{4},$$

of $E(x) = 2x - 7$ is

$$D(y) = \frac{y + 7}{2},$$

and of $E(x) = 13x - 260$ is

$$D(y) = \frac{y + 260}{13}.$$

This scheme gives beginning algebra students an application of inverse functions and practice in finding them.

Example 1

We begin with the encoding function

$$E(x) = x + 98$$

and this message:

MATH IS FUN

We use the computer's built-in function to produce the ASCII value of each character. Using values for each character as shown in table 1, we obtain the following message:

ASCII: 77 65 84 72 32 73 83 32
        70 85 78

The sender uses the encoding function $E(x)$ on the ASCII values to produce the encoded message (EMessage).

EMessage: 175 163 182 170 130 171
          181 130 168 183 176

These numbers and the encoding function are sent to the receiver.

To decode, the receiver applies the inverse function $D(y)$ on each of the EMessage values to give the values for the decoded message (DMessage):

$$D(y) = y - 98$$

DMessage: 77 65 84 72 32 73 83
          32 70 85 78

Finally, these ASCII values are replaced with corresponding characters from table 1; this procedure returns us to the original message (OMessage):

OMessage: MATH IS FUN

Practice
message 1: 142 132 138 85 118
           135 126 124 125 137

(I used the encoding function $E(x) = x + 53$.)

(Hints and answers are at the end of this article.)

Having to send the encoding function makes it necessary for the scheme to be kept private—the function can be known only to the sender and receiver. The receiver can use the same encoding function to encode return messages to the sender.

Quadratic functions

Finding inverses of quadratic functions illustrates the need for "completing the square." By selecting $a > 0$ and $b > 0$ for our encoding function $E(x) = ax^2 + bx + c$

and by knowing that for the ASCII values $x > 0$, we are assured that our inverse $D(x)$ exists. For example, using $E(x) = x^2 + 4x + 3$, we can obtain the inverse function as follows:

$$y = x^2 + 4x + 4 + 3 - 4$$
$$\text{(completing the square)}$$
$$y = (x + 2)^2 - 1$$

Now, solve for x:

$$(x + 2)^2 = y + 1$$
$$x + 2 = \sqrt{y + 1}$$
$$\text{(since } x > 0 \text{, then } x + 2 > 0)$$
$$x = \sqrt{y + 1} - 2$$

Thus, our decoding function is

$$D(y) = \sqrt{y + 1} - 2.$$

Other pairs of inverses are the following:

$$E(x) = 4x^2 + 8x + 3;$$
$$D(y) = \sqrt{(y + 1)/2} - 1$$
$$E(x) = 3x^2 + 18x - 9;$$
$$D(y) = \sqrt{((y + 36)/3)} - 3$$

Example 2

$E(x) = x^2 + 4x + 3$

Message: WELL DONE

ASCII: 87 69 76 76 32 68 79
        78 69

EMessage: 7920 5040 6083 6083 1155
          4899 6560 6399 5040

DMessage (using $D(y) = \sqrt{(y + 1)} - 2$):
87 69 76 76 32 68 79 78 69

OMessage: WELL DONE

Practice
message 2: 6557 5772 4896 5180
           1221 5925 6720 4757
(I used $E(x) = x^2 + 6x + 5$.)

Notice that in each of the two examples, most of the encoded values are outside the range of ASCII values. Also note that the encoded values remain in the same order as in the original; both the linear and quadratic functions preserve order, that is,

$$a < b \rightarrow E(a) < E(b).$$

For the code breaker, this fact is of substantial benefit; by compressing the encoded values, the characters would divulge themselves rather quickly. We need functions that do not preserve order. Functions in some modulus hold some promise because they do not always preserve order.

Linear Modular Arithmetic Functions

To use modular arithmetic functions, we can find the functional value, then find the remainder when the modulus is used as a divisor. To illustrate, if $f(x) = 3x + 4$ (mod 7), then

$$f(6) \equiv (3)(6) + 4 \quad (\text{mod } 7)$$
$$\equiv 18 + 4 \quad (\text{mod } 7)$$
$$\equiv 22 \quad (\text{mod } 7),$$

or

$$f(6) \equiv 1 \quad (\text{mod } 7);$$
$$f(4) \equiv (3)(4) + 4 \quad (\text{mod } 7)$$
$$\equiv 12 + 4 \quad (\text{mod } 7)$$
$$\equiv 16 \quad (\text{mod } 7),$$

or

$$f(4) \equiv 2 \quad (\text{mod } 7).$$

In general, the outcome of applying functions modulo m is a whole number from 0 to $m - 1$. In addition, the functions are periodic; if K is an integer, then

$$f(x + km) = f(x) \,(\text{mod } m).$$

The function $y \equiv ax + b$ (mod m) has an inverse providing that a and m are relatively prime. For our application the modulus m must be greater than our greatest ASCII value, 90.

Some students may use the addition and multiplication tables to determine the inverse function; others may write computer programs to find the inverse linear modular arithmetic function. To find the inverse function of

$$y \equiv f(x) \equiv 3x + 8 \quad (\text{mod } 115),$$

we need

$$g(y) \equiv ay + b \equiv x$$

or

$$x \equiv a(3x + 8) + b \quad (\text{mod } 115)$$
$$\equiv 3ax + 8a + b \quad (\text{mod } 115).$$

Thus, $3a \equiv 1$ (mod 115) and $8a + b \equiv 0$ (mod 115). A computer program can now be used to help us solve for a and b (see program 1). The solution is $a = 77$ and $b = 74$;

PROGRAM 1

Find the Inverse of a Modular Function

```
100 :    REM COMMODORE PET BASIC
110 :    REM PROGRAM FINDS INVERSES
120 :    REM OF Y=AX + B (MOD M)
121 :
130 :
140 OPEN1,4
200 :
210 :    REM OBTAIN COEFFICIENTS AND
220 :    REM MODULUS; CK FOR FLAG
230 :
240 INPUT"LINEAR COEFFICIENTS
         (A,B)";A,B:IF A=0 AND B=0 THEN 1000
250 INPUT"MODULUS";M
260   PRINT
400 :
410 :REM FIND COEFFICIENT OF Y IN INV
420 :
430 A2=0
440 FOR A1=1 TO M-1
450 A2=A2+A
460 A2=A2-M*INT(A2/M)
470 IF A2=1 THEN 600
480 NEXT A1
490 :
500 :    REM NO INVERSE
510 :
520 PRINT#1,"NO INVERSE"
530 GOTO900
600 :
610 :    REM FIND CONSTANT IN INVERSE
620 :
630 B2=A1*B-1
640 FOR B1=0 TO M-1
650 B2=B2+1
660 B2=B2-M*INT(B2/M)
670 IF B2=0 THEN 800
680 NEXT B1
690 :
700 :    REM NO INVERSE
710 :
720 PRINT#1,"NO INVERSE"
730 GOTO900
800 :
810 :    REM PRINT INVERSE STATEMENT
820 :
830 PRINT#1,"Y="A"X+"B"(MOD"M") HAS
         INVERSE"
840 PRINT#1,"Y="A1"X+";
850 PRINT#1,B1"(MOD"M")"
900 PRINT#1 :PRINT#1 :GOTO240
1000 PRINT#1:CLOSE1:END
```

READY.

our inverse function is $g(y) \equiv 77y + 74$ (mod 115). Some sample combinations of inverses would be these:

$$E(x) \equiv 27x + 19 \quad (\text{mod } 32);$$
$$D(y) \equiv 19y + 23 \quad (\text{mod } 32)$$
$$E(x) \equiv 4x + 5 \quad (\text{mod } 15);$$
$$D(y) \equiv 4y + 10 \quad (\text{mod } 15)$$
$$E(x) \equiv 13x + 28 \quad (\text{mod } 103);$$
$$D(y) \equiv 8y + 85 \quad (\text{mod } 103)$$

Example 3

$E(x) \equiv 3x + 8 \quad (\text{mod } 115)$

Message: THEORY OF NUMBERS

ASCII:
84	72	69	79	82	89
32	79	70	32	78	85
77	66	69	82	83	

EMessage:
30	109	100	15	24	45
104	15	103	104	12	33
9	91	100	24	27	

DMessage (using $D(y) \equiv 77y + 74$ [mod 115]):
84	72	69	79	82	89
32	79	70	32	78	
85	77	66	69	82	83

OMessage: THEORY OF NUMBERS

Practice
message 3:
108	25	71	71	63	88
78	86	88	48	11	10
116	71	48	11	10	131
41	138				

(I used $E(x) \equiv 5x + 37$ [mod 143].)

Exponential Modular Arithmetic Functions

It can be shown that $E(x) \equiv x^3$ (mod p) has the inverse

$$D(y) \equiv y^{(2p-1)/3} \quad (\text{mod } p),$$

where p is prime and $p - 1$ is not divisible by 3. Writing the inverse function itself is quite easy—applying an inverse function with large exponents becomes the challenge. Large exponents can be handled by reducing each intermediate result modulo p (see program 2).

Some sample inverses are these:

$$E(x) \equiv x^3 \ (\text{mod } 41);$$
$$D(y) \equiv y^{27} \ (\text{mod } 41)$$
$$E(x) \equiv x^3 \ (\text{mod } 101);$$
$$D(y) \equiv y^{67} \ (\text{mod } 101)$$
$$E(x) \equiv x^3 \ (\text{mod } 113);$$
$$D(y) \equiv y^{75} \ (\text{mod } 113)$$

Example 4

$E(x) \equiv x^3 \quad (\text{mod } 101)$

Message: MUSIC AND MATHEMATICS

ASCII:
77	85	83	73	67	32	65
78	68	32	77	65	84	72
69	77	65	84	73	67	83

EMessage:
13	45	26	66	86	44	6
54	19	44	13	6	36	53
57	13	6	36	66	86	26

DMessage (using $D(y) \equiv y^{67}$ [mod 101]):
77	85	83	73	67	32	65
78	68	32	77	65	84	72
69	77	65	84	73	67	83

OMessage: MUSIC AND MATHEMATICS

Practice message 4:
72	7	26
31	52	7	19

(I used $E(x) = x^3$ [mod 107].)

Nonprime modulus

If the modulus is the product of two primes p and q, where neither $p - 1$ nor $q - 1$ is divisible by 3, then $E(x) \equiv x^3$ (mod pq) has the inverse

$$D(y) \equiv y^{(2(p-1)(q-1)+1)/3} \quad (\text{mod } pq).$$

The large exponents of the inverse function can be handled as mentioned before, that is, by reducing intermediate results modulo pq.

The great advantage of this scheme is that the large number generated by pq might be extremely difficult to factor into primes. Thus, the number pq can be public; anyone wishing to send messages to me can do so by using the encoding function with my public number pq. Since others will find pq difficult to factor, I have confidence that the message cannot be decoded—only I will have the p and q to use in the decoding function.

To complicate code breaking further, the encoding can be done with larger blocks of digits than the two that represent the ASCII value; for example, by using a nine-digit pq, eight-digit blocks can be encoded, each block representing four

---

PROGRAM 2

Encode and Decode Using
Modular Arithmetic Function

```
10 :      REM COMMODORE PET BASIC        550 V=1
20 :      REM ENCODING AND DECODING      560 :      FOR J=1TO3
             USING                       570 :      V=V*EM(I):V=V−M*(INT(V/M))
30 :      REM E(X)=X^3 MOD M             580 :      NEXTJ
40 :      REM D(X)=X^(2M−1)/3 MOD M      590 EM(I)=V
50 :                                     600 PRINT#1,EM(I);
60 DIM M$(50) ,EM(50) ,DM(50)           610 IF INT(I/10)=I/10 THEN PRINT#1
70 M=149                                620 NEXTI
80 :                                     700 :
100 INPUT"MESSAGE";M$                    710 :      REM DECODE MESSAGE
110 OPEN1,4                              720 :
120 PRINT#1,"MESSAGE:";                  730 PRINT#1:PRINT#1:PRINT#1,"D-
200 :                                           MESSAGE:";
210 :      REM PUT MESSAGE IN ARRAY M$   740 FOR I=1TOL
220 :                                    750 V=1:DM(I)=EM(I)
230 L=LEN(M$)                            760 :      FOR J=1TO(2*M−1)/3
240 FORI=1TOL                            770 :      V=V*DM(I):V=V−M*(INT(V/M))
250 M$(I)=MID$(M$,I,1)                   780 :      NEXTJ
260 PRINT#1,M$(I);                       790 DM(I)=V
270 NEXTI                                800 PRINT#1,DM(I);
300 :                                    810 IF INT(I/10)=I/10 THEN PRINT#1
310 :      REM CONVERT EACH CHARACTER    820 NEXTI
             TO                          900 :
320 :      REM      ASCII VALUES         910 :      REM CONVERT DECODED VALUES
330 :                                    920 :      REM TO OBTAIN ORIGINAL MESSAGE
340 PRINT#1:PRINT#1:PRINT#1,"ASCII:";    930 :
350 FOR I=1TOL                           940 PRINT#1:PRINT#1:PRINT#1,"O-
360 EM(I)=ASC(M$(I))                            MESSAGE:";
370 PRINT#1,EM(I);                       950 FORI=1TOL
380 IF INT(I/10)=I/10 THEN PRINT#1       960 ME$=CHR$(DM(I))
390 NEXT I                               970 PRINT#1,ME$;
500 :                                    980 NEXTI:PRINT#1
510 :      REM ENCODE ASCII VALUES       990 PRINT#1:CLOSE1
520 :                                    1000 END
530 PRINT#1:PRINT#1:PRINT#1,"E-
       MESSAGE:";                        READY.
540 FORI=1TOL
```

---

characters. This method reduces the probability that a statistician will determine the code by analyzing the frequency of the encoded numbers.

Inverses of this type are the following:

$$E(x) \equiv x^3 \pmod{55};$$
$$D(y) \equiv y^{27} \pmod{55}$$
$$E(x) \equiv x^3 \pmod{115};$$
$$D(y) \equiv y^{59} \pmod{115}$$
$$E(x) \equiv x^3 \pmod{187};$$
$$D(y) \equiv y^{107} \pmod{187}$$

Example 5

$$E(x) \equiv x^3 \pmod{187}$$

Message: PROBLEM SOLVING

ASCII: 80   82   79   66   76   69   77   32
         83   79   76   86   73   78   71

EMessage: 181   82   107   77   87
            137   66   43 128 107
             87   69   57 133 180

DMessage   (using $D(y) \equiv y^{107} \pmod{187}$):
            80   82   79   66   76
            69   77   32   83   79
            76   86   73   78   71

Practice
message 5:   363   145   315   84   234   143
             274   274   69 269   146   363
             146   363   269 146
(I used $E(x) \equiv x^3 \pmod{391}$.)

Summary

Sensitive information is often exchanged among people and among computers. To prevent other parties from understanding that information, it can be coded before transmission and decoded upon reception, which entails the use of functions and their inverses. This application of functions is appropriate at several different levels of school mathematics.

Hints for practice messages

1. Use $D(y) = y - 53$.
2. Use $D(y) = \sqrt{y + 4} - 3$.
3. Use $D(y) \equiv 124y + 131 \pmod{143}$.
4. Use $D(y) \equiv y^{71} \pmod{107}$.
5. Use $D(y) \equiv y^{235} \pmod{391}$.

Answers for practice messages

1. YOU ARE RIGHT
2. NICE JOB
3. QUEEN OF MATHEMATICS
4. IN TUNE
5. IS CHALLENGING

BIBLIOGRAPHY

Davenport, H. *The Higher Arithmetic*. New York: Harper & Brothers, 1962.

Smith, John. "Public Key Cryptography." *Byte* 8 (January 1983): 198–218. ◆

Four Labs to Introduce Quadratic Functions

By JIM MALONE

Most high school students get little hands-on experience with mathematics and rarely get an opportunity to see how the techniques they study really work. To remedy this difficulty, I have used four different "labs" in my algebra and precalculus classes.

Students look forward to the labs.

Slowing Down the Acceleration of Gravity

A good way to study an accelerating object in your classroom is to run a taut wire about two inches from one wall, using pipes or nails as points of attachment. One end of the wire should be slightly higher than the other. A pulley placed on the wire at the higher end will accelerate slowly toward the lower end (fig. 1). Students with stopwatches or laboratory timers can record how long it takes for the pulley to reach certain distances along the wire. Have the students graph distance covered as a function of time. With enough data points, the graph will have the familiar appearance of a parabola (fig. 2). The students can use the points to determine the equation of the parabola. This process is simplified because the vertex can be taken as the origin. If you have access to an airtrack (commonly found in physics laboratories), you can use it rather than a wire and a pulley.

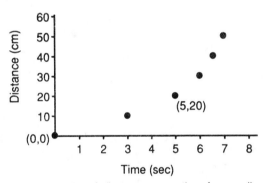

Fig. 2. A plot of distance versus time for a pulley accelerating down a wire. With the vertex at (0, 0), using the point (5, 20) gives the equation $d = 0.8t^2$. Since $d = (1/2)at^2$, the pulley has an acceleration of about 1.6 cm/s/s.

By marking off short intervals at various points along the wire, students can calculate the acceleration of the pulley. I use four intervals, each 10 cm in length, with the midpoint marked. One group of students records how long it takes the pulley to reach the midpoint of each interval from the time it is released. Another group records how long it takes the pulley to pass through each interval. The students can then calculate the average velocity on each interval and make a graph of the velocity of the pulley as a function of time (fig. 3). Discuss with your students the fact that the average velocity on an interval is a very good approximation of

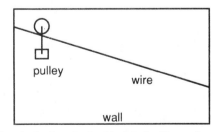

Fig. 1. A wire attached to a wall with a pulley on the wire. When the pulley is released, it will accelerate slowly down the wire.

Jim Malone teaches mathematics and science at the Mercersburg Academy, Mercersburg, PA 17236. He also coaches football and teaches whitewater canoeing and rock-climbing.

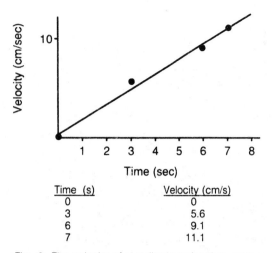

Time (s)	Velocity (cm/s)
0	0
3	5.6
6	9.1
7	11.1

Fig. 3. The velocity of a pulley accelerating down a wire as a function of time. A least-squares line was fit to the points, and its equation was $y = 1.53x + 0.33$. The slope of a velocity-versus-time graph is the acceleration. Therefore, the pulley had an acceleration of about 1.53 cm/s/s.

the instantaneous velocity at the midpoint of the interval. The graph is a straight line,

and its slope is the acceleration of the pulley. This experiment is a beautiful application of the concept of slope. In this example, "change in y divided by change in x" is really "change in velocity divided by change in time," the definition of acceleration.

Calculating the Acceleration of Gravity

An acceleration timer is an inexpensive device that places a mark on a paper tape approximately every sixtieth of a second. By attaching the paper tape to a falling object, such as a metal bar, students can generate a set of points that grow farther apart as the object accelerates. The distance between successive points shows how far the object has fallen in each time interval. Have the students graph the distance the object has fallen as a function of time. A large number of data points result, and the graph is that of a parabola (fig. 4).

By looking at a number of short intervals, students can calculate the acceleration

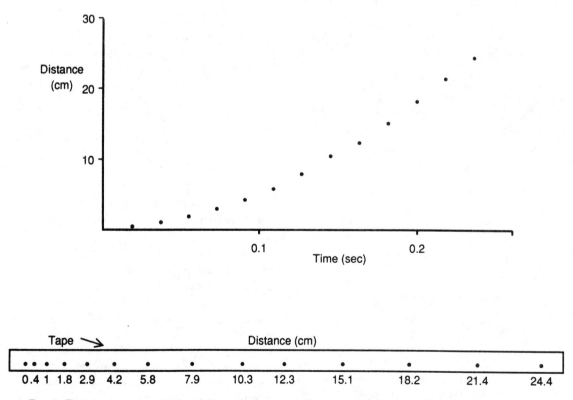

Fig. 4. The tape was generated by a falling object connected to an acceleration timer. The graph shows the distance that the object has fallen as a function of time. The acceleration timer generated fifty-five dots a second.

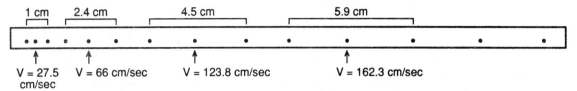

Fig. 5. Use the acceleration timer to determine velocity as a function of time for a falling object. The acceleration timer generates fifty-five dots a second, so it takes the object two-fifty-fifths of a second to pass through each three-dot interval. The average velocity is used as an approximation of the instantaneous velocity at the second point on each of the four intervals.

due to gravity in a manner similar to that mentioned for the pulley. Select three successive points and measure the distance from the first to the third. Since the time interval between points is known, the average velocity on the three-point interval can be calculated. Once again, the average velocity for the whole interval is a good approximation of the instantaneous velocity at the second point on the interval. Have the students calculate the average velocity on several intervals and apply it at the second point of each interval (fig. 5). This procedure allows them to graph velocity as a function of time. The slope of this graph represents the acceleration of the falling object and gives the students an opportunity to compare their calculated values to the known value of the acceleration due to gravity (fig. 6). This comparison, in turn, can lead to a

discussion of possible sources of error in the experiment.

Generating a Parabola

A heavy steel ball rolled across a tilted board follows a parabolic path due to the acceleration of gravity. If graph paper is taped to the board and carbon paper is placed over the graph paper, the path of the ball can easily be recorded (fig. 7). A device called a *Packard apparatus,* usually available in the physics laboratory, is specifically designed for this purpose. Since the path is recorded on graph paper, students can determine the equation of the parabola (fig. 8).

Photographing Projectile Motion

Many high school physics labs have ski-jump-shaped ramps for marbles. I place one of these ramps next to a wall in a darkroom, tape a piece of photographic paper to the

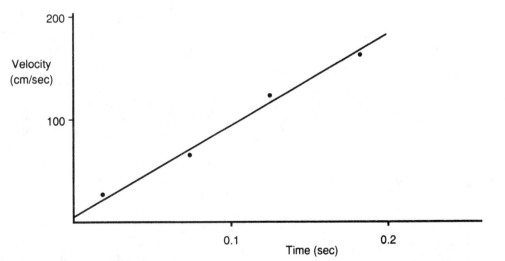

Fig. 6. A graph of velocity versus time for a falling object. The velocities were calculated from the acceleration-timer tape (see fig. 5). The line shown in the graph is a least-squares line that was fit to the points. The slope of a velocity-versus-time graph is the acceleration, and the least-squares line has a slope of 881. This result compares reasonably well (10% error) with the acceleration of gravity, 981 cm/s/s.

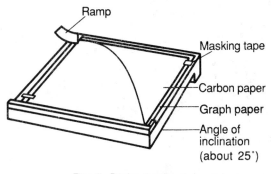

Fig. 7. Packard apparatus

wall, and turn on a strobe light when I release the marble. When the paper is developed photographically, it shows the path that the marble follows. Each time the strobe light flashes, the marble makes a shadow on the photographic paper (fig. 9). I bring my students into the darkroom, four at a time, so that they can observe the process. Each group is in the darkroom for about four minutes. When the pictures are dry the next

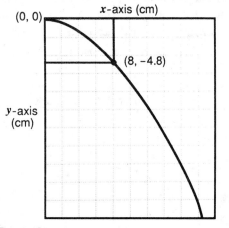

Fig. 8. Choosing an arbitrary point to determine the equation of the parabola generated by the Packard apparatus. In this example, the equation is $y = -0.075x^2$

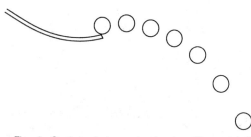

Fig. 9. Strobe photograph showing the parabolic path of a marble coming off a ramp

day, I give the students rulers and ask them to verify that the path of the marble is indeed parabolic. By setting up an appropriate coordinate system and determining the coordinates of the ball at various places, they are able to do this task.

Conclusion

A few practical notes are in order. First of all, it is advisable to try the lab yourself before having students attempt it; otherwise, it is guaranteed to be a flop. With the wire-and-pulley lab it is necessary to adjust the slope so that the rate of acceleration will be appropriate for hand-held timers. If the pulley is moving too fast, it is difficult to time it accurately in a 10-cm interval. It is also worth pointing out to students that Archimedes "diluted" the acceleration of gravity in this manner so that he could measure it with the instruments available to him. Acceleration timers rarely oscillate at exactly one-sixtieth of a second, so they need to be calibrated before the acceleration of gravity can be measured accurately. This calculation can be done by pulling the tape through the timer for a measured amount of time and counting the number of dots produced. Ask a colleague from the science department for help, if necessary. When making strobe pictures, it is necessary to experiment with the exposure setting. I have good success with the strobe light set at 3600 flashes a second. The light should be placed about fifteen feet from the photographic paper and covered with two Kodak #5 Polycontrast filters or their equivalent.

My students often ask when we are going to do more labs. These activities obviously have made an impression on them. It took about a week of class time to do all four of these activities, and the time was well spent. It gave the students an opportunity to generate some real data and then to see if the data were consistent with some mathematical concepts with which they were already familiar. Although I have not done so, these labs can lend a real opportunity for some team teaching with science department faculty, reinforcing the natural association of mathematics and science. ◗

An Application of Quadratic Equations to Baseball

By MILTON P. EISNER, Mount Vernon College, Washington, DC 20007

In baseball, the primary objective of each team is to have the greatest winning percentage in its division at the end of the season. During the season, daily standings list the teams in order of decreasing winning percentages. Beside each team's percentage is the number of games it is behind, a measure of how many games that a team trails the team with the greatest winning percentage. For example, consider the standings of National League teams on the morning of 8 August 1984, as shown in table 1.

The number of games behind (GB) is calculated as follows: Suppose that the leading team has a won-lost record of (A, B) and the trailing team has a won-lost record of (a, b), where

$$\frac{A}{A+B} > \frac{a}{a+b}$$

Then the trailing team is $A - a$ wins behind (or "games behind in the win column") and $b - B$ losses behind (or "games behind in the loss column"). The number of games behind, GB, is calculated as the mean of these two quantities:

$$GB = \frac{(A-a) + (b-B)}{2}$$

Baseball fans and players know that "games behind" is not always a good measure of the deficit between the trailing team and the leading team. A New York Mets fan would look at the standings and think: *We're 3.5 games behind the Cubs but only 2 in the loss column.* That is, if the Cubs lose 2 games, the Mets can catch them by winning as many as the Cubs do over the rest of the season (to use a baseball cliche, the Mets would "control their own destiny"), so the Mets' deficit appears to be *less than* 3.5 games. In contrast, the Atlanta Braves trail the San Diego Padres by 10 in the loss column, although they are only 9.5 games behind. This means that San Diego must lose 10 more games than Atlanta over the rest of the season for the Braves to have a chance, so the Braves' deficit appears to be *greater than* 9.5 games.

Strangely, it is even possible for the leading team to be "behind" the trailing team in games. For example, consider the following standings:

Team	W	L	Pct.	GB
Leaders	18	13	.581	0.5
Trailers	22	16	.579	0.0

Because of the difference in the number of games played, the Leaders are 0.5 games behind the Trailers.

Let's define the deficit D of a trailing

TABLE 1									
Eastern Division					Western Division				
Team	W	L	Pct.	GB	Team	W	L	Pct.	GB
Chicago	67	45	.598	—	San Diego	67	44	.604	—
New York	62	47	.569	3.5	Atlanta	58	54	.518	9.5
Philadelphia	60	51	.541	6.5	Los Angeles	55	58	.487	13
St. Louis	56	56	.500	11	Houston	52	61	.460	16
Montreal	53	58	.477	13.5	Cincinnati	47	65	.420	20.5
Pittsburgh	48	65	.425	19.5	San Francisco	44	65	.404	22

team as the number of times the trailing team would have to beat the leading team for them to be tied in the standings. If the two teams have played the same number of games (i.e., $A + B = a + b$), then GB is equal to D. However, if they haven't played the same number of games, GB and D are not equal. To illustrate, consider the standings of 8 August 1984 given in table 1.

Chicago and St. Louis have both played 112 games. St. Louis is 11 wins behind Chicago and 11 losses behind Chicago. If St. Louis beat Chicago 11 times, both teams would have records of 67–56 and they would be tied. Thus St. Louis has a deficit of 11 games, which is equal to the number of games behind listed in the standings.

In contrast, New York has played 109 games. New York is 5 wins behind Chicago and 2 losses behind Chicago. The mean of these, 3.5, is New York's games behind. But if New York beat Chicago 3.5 times (assuming that such a thing is possible), then New York would have a record of 65.5–47, whereas Chicago would have a record of 67–48.5. New York's winning percentage

---

"Games behind" is not always a good measure.

---

would be .582, whereas Chicago's would be .580, so New York would be ahead of Chicago rather than tied. Thus, the deficit between New York and Chicago is actually *less than* 3.5 games, confirming our intuitive judgment that was based on the loss column.

Now look at the situation in the Western Division between San Diego and Atlanta. Atlanta is 9 wins behind and 10 losses behind, which are averaged to give 9.5 games behind. But if Atlanta beat San Diego 9.5 times (again, assuming it's possible), then Atlanta would have a record of 67.5–54 and San Diego would have a record of 67–53.5. Altanta's winning percentage would be .5556, but San Diego's percentage would be .5560, so Atlanta would still be behind. Thus, Atlanta's deficit is actually *greater than* 9.5 games, again confirming

our intuition that was based on the loss column.

The examples of New York and Atlanta suggest that the relationship between a team's games behind and its deficit is this: *The direction of the inequality between the deficit and the games behind is the same as the direction of the inequality between losses behind and wins behind.* That is, if a team's losses behind are fewer than its wins behind, its deficit is less than its games behind, whereas if its losses behind are greater than its wins behind, its deficit is greater than its games behind.

Having established that games behind does not accurately describe the deficit between teams, we are faced with two mathematical questions: (1) How can we calculate the deficit between teams? (2) Can we use the answer to question (1) to *prove* the relationship between games behind and the deficit just described?

Earlier we said that a team's deficit is the number of times it would have to beat the leading team to become tied in the standings. (The two teams may not actually play that number of games in the remaining schedule.) Returning to the standings, suppose the New York Mets trail the Chicago Cubs by a deficit of D games. Then if the Mets had D more wins (and no more losses) and the Cubs D more losses (and no more wins), they would be tied, that is,

$$\frac{62 + D}{109 + D} = \frac{67}{112 + D}.$$

Solving this proportion, we obtain the following:

$$(62 + D)(112 + D) = 67(109 + D)$$
$$6944 + 174D + D^2 = 7303 + 67D$$
$$D^2 + 107D - 359 = 0$$

Thus, the number of games by which the Mets really trail the Cubs is the solution of a quadratic equation. Solving by the quadratic formula, we have (ignore the negative root)

$$D \approx \frac{-107 + 113.512}{2} \approx 3.26.$$

Thus, the Mets trail the Cubs by 3.26

games. The result confirms that the Mets are actually closer to the Cubs than their 3.5 games behind would indicate.

Similarly, if the Atlanta Braves have a deficit of D games with respect to the San Diego Padres, then

$$\frac{58 + D}{112 + D} = \frac{67}{111 + D},$$

or

$$(58 + D)(111 + D) = 67(112 + D),$$
$$D^2 + 102D - 1066 = 0,$$

and

$$D \approx \frac{-102 + 121.11}{2} \approx 9.56.$$

So the Padres lead the Braves by 9.56 games. The result confirms that the Padres' lead is greater than the Braves' 9.5 games behind would indicate.

These two examples should whet any mathematician's appetite for a proof. Let us restate the relationship in the form of a proposition and try to prove it.

PROPOSITION. *The direction of the inequality between a team's deficit and its games behind is the same as the direction of the inequality between its losses behind and its wins behind.*

Let's define some variables so we can express the proposition with algebraic inequalities. As before, let the leading team have A wins and B losses. Suppose the trailing team is x wins behind and y losses behind. Then its record is $a = A - x$ wins and $b = B + y$ losses. The proposition states that if $x > y$, then the team's deficit D is less than $(x + y)/2$, whereas if $x < y$, D is greater than $(x + y)/2$.

Now by definition, D is the solution to the equation

$$\frac{A - x + D}{A - x + B + y + D} = \frac{A}{A + B + D},$$

which simplifies to

$$D^2 + (A + B - x)D - (Ay + Bx) = 0.$$

Using the quadratic formula and ignoring the negative root, we have

$$D = \frac{\sqrt{(A + B - x)^2 + 4(Ay + Bx)} - (A + B - x)}{2},$$

so

$$D < G = \frac{x + y}{2}$$

if and only if

$$\sqrt{(A + B - x)^2 + 4(Ay + Bx)}$$
$$- (A + B - x) < x + y,$$
$$\sqrt{(A + B - x)^2 + 4(Ay + Bx)} < A + B + y,$$
$$(A + B - x)^2 + 4(Ay + Bx) < (A + B + y)^2,$$

and

$$x^2 - 2(A - B)x < y^2 - 2(A - B)y.$$

Now let $f(t) = t^2 - 2(A - B)t$. The proposition is equivalent to the following statement: If $x > y$, then $f(x) < f(y)$, and if $x < y$, then $f(x) > f(y)$. That is, the proposition is true if x and y belong to an interval on which $f(t)$ is a decreasing function. But $f(t)$ is a quadratic function; it is decreasing on the interval $t \leq A - B$ and increasing everywhere else. Hence, the proposition is true if both x and y are less than or equal to $A - B$, the difference between the leading team's wins and losses. So we can restate the proposition as a theorem:

THEOREM. *Suppose the numbers of games by which a team trails the leading team in the win and in the loss columns are both fewer than or equal to the difference between the leading team's wins and losses. Then the direction of the inequality between the team's deficit and its games behind is the same as the direction of the inequality between its losses behind and its wins behind.*

In most pennant races, this condition will hold. In major league baseball, the leading team usually has a percentage near .600, as both leading teams do in the example. That means that late in the season, the difference between the leading team's wins and losses will be greater than 20. So the relationship will hold for any team that is fewer than 20 games behind in both the win and loss columns. Looking back to the league standings, we see that Chicago's win difference is 22, so that for any team whose wins behind and losses behind are both fewer than or equal to 22, the conclusion of the theorem will apply. For San Diego, the corresponding number is 23.

A final note: If the deficit rather than

the games behind is used as the measure of the distance between teams, the anomaly at the beginning of this article—a team trailing the leader by a negative number of games—cannot occur. The calculation of the deficit between the Trailers and the Leaders requires us to solve the equation

$$\frac{22 + D}{38 + D} = \frac{18}{31 + D},$$

or $D^2 + 35D - 2 = 0$, yielding $D \approx 0.06$, so the Trailers trail by 0.06 games.

In fact, it is easy to prove that D is always positive. Recall that D is the greater of the two solutions (the lesser solution is always negative) of the quadratic equation

$$D^2 + (A + B - x)D - (Ay + Bx) = 0.$$

Replacing x by $A - a$ and y by $b - B$ yields the equivalent equation

$$D^2 + (B + a)D - (Ab - Ba) = 0.$$

This equation has a positive solution if and only if

$$\sqrt{(B + a)^2 + 4(Ab - Ba)} > B + a,$$

that is, $Ab > Ba$. But the relationship of the two teams' winning percentages is

$$\frac{A}{A + B} > \frac{a}{a + b},$$

which is equivalent to $Ab > Ba$. Thus, D is always positive for a team with a lower winning percentage than the leader. We can conclude that a team's deficit D is a better measure of its distance from the leader than its games behind. ♟

Who's in first?

I enjoyed Milton Eisner's creative article (May 1986) on quadratic equations in baseball. I was reminded of a time in 1948 when the Philadelphia A's were in first place in the American League, won a double-header, and wound up in second place!

I do not recall the exact won-lost records, but the following chart will illustrate that it could have happened.

	Before		
	W	L	Pct.
Philadelphia	29	15	.6591
Cleveland	27	14	.6585

	After		
	W	L	Pct.
Cleveland	29	14	.6744
Philadelphia	31	15	.6739

It can be seen that although Philadelphia retained its half-game "edge," the extra two wins and one loss depressed the average once the average exceeded .667. From applying the Eisner deficit formula both before and after, the leader's edge was .02 games, close indeed.

Steven St. Martin
Thomas Jefferson High School
Bloomington, MN 55431

BUSINESS FORMULAS AS CARTESIAN CURVES

By **ELIZABETH RUPPEL**
Madonna High School
Downsview, ON M3K 1V5

In view of recent changes in mathematics curricula emphasizing analytic geometry and applications and the fact that business machine or machine applications courses now teach many of the practical business calculations, it seems inevitable that in a unit on the mathematics of finance, the *main objective ought to be the understanding of mathematical concepts such as the relation of the variables in formulas, the graphical representation, and the power of prediction* associated with these concepts. Morris Kline (1973) has long been urging high school teachers to motivate students by using physical applications when introducing mathematical ideas. This method can also be helpful in teaching business applications. In a unit I have been teaching in a business mathematics course, I found that students gain much greater insight into routine calculations with business formulas when this work is viewed in the light of graphing concepts.

Once the student understands how to compute simple and compound interest, I continue with a unit on graphing having the following specific objectives:

1. Interpret a word problem involving simple business formulas, identify the dependent and independent variables, set up a table of values by using the appropriate formula and function, and then complete a graphical representation of the situation.

2. Find the rise, run, slope, intercepts, maximum or minimum values, range, domain, and intersection and express their meaning in relation to the business application described in the problem.

3. Interpolate and extrapolate values from the graph and check by substituting them into the equation.

Consider the following ten problems that illustrate how these objectives are met.

Problem 1. Brigit Sharp is about to start at a university, and her parents put $4000 into an account paying 5% per annum interest. The $4000 must remain in the account and only the interest can be withdrawn regularly each year to pay for textbooks. How much money will be available for her to spend each year? Show graphically how the money available for books would accumulate over a 4-year period.

Using the formula $I = Prt$, where I is interest, the principal P is 4000, the interest rate r is 5 percent, and the time is t, we have

$$(1) \qquad I = 4000 \times 0.05 \times t = 200t.$$

This equation describes the relation of two variables: time and interest (fig. 1a).

Problem 2. The Ultimate Finance Company offers to lend Brigit $600 for her tuition at 16 ⅔% per annum. Show how the amount A Brigit will owe accumulates each year for her 4 years of undergraduate work.

The appropriate formula is $A = Prt + P$. Substituting values for P, r, and t, we have

$$A = 600 \times \frac{1}{6} \times t + 600$$

or

$$(2) \qquad A = 100t + 600.$$

See figure 1b.

Problem 3. The Tiny Transformer Association found that, for a particular model transformer, when the unit price is $100, the daily supply is 170, but that when the unit price drops to $40, the daily supply is only 90 (Whipkey 1978). Represent this relationship graphically.

Assuming a linear relationship between price P and quantity in supply n, we find that the point-slope method yields the function

(3) $P = 0.75n - 27.5.$

See figure 1c.

Problem 4. When the Tiny Transformer Association sells 90 transformers, the unit price is $10, but when a lot of 20 is sold, the unit price jumps to $80. Represent this price structure graphically assuming a linear relationship between the quantity demanded and unit price.

By the same method used in problem 3, the equation is found to be

(4) $P = {}^{-}n + 100.$

See figure 1d. The graphs in figure 1 do not have restricted domains and ranges.

The independent variables in problems 1–4 are t and n, whereas I, A, and P are the dependent variables. Table 1 shows

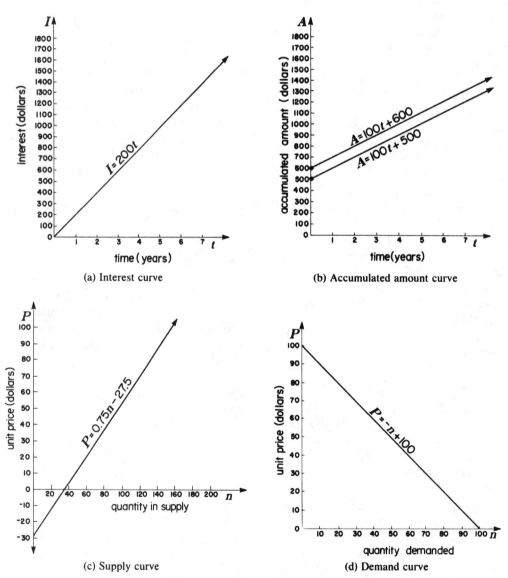

(a) Interest curve

(b) Accumulated amount curve

(c) Supply curve

(d) Demand curve

Fig. 1.

TABLE 1

Function	Domain	Range
$I = 200t$	$0 \leq t \leq 4$	$0 \leq I \leq 800$
$A = 100t + 600$	$0 \leq t \leq 4$	$600 \leq A \leq 1000$
$P = 0.75n - 27.5$	$90 \leq n \leq 170$	$40 \leq P \leq 100$
$P = -n + 100$	$0 \leq n \leq 100$	$0 \leq P \leq 100$

the practical restrictions on the domain and on the range of the variables.

The graph in figure 1a passes through the origin and serves to illustrate direct variation between the variables I and t. This equation is of the form $y = mx$, where m, a constant, is the slope. Problems 2, 3, and 4 yield equations of the form $y = mx + b$ with two constants, the slope m and the y-intercept b. If in problem 2 the interest rate was 20 percent and the amount borrowed was $500, the equation would be $A = 100t + 500$. See figure 1b. Notice that when the t-coefficients (slopes) are the same, the lines are parallel but the y-intercepts are different ($500 \neq 600$).

The graphs in figures 1a, 1b, and 1c have a positive slope (the line is rising toward the right). In figure 1d the slope is negative (the graph is dropping toward the right). In figure 1c the line continues below the x-axis for $0 \leq n \leq 36.7$, but in the practical situation, the domain must be restricted; that is, the unit price must be a positive integer. In figure 1d, the intercepts tell us the maximum unit price (y-intercept) and maximum demand (x-intercept).

Whereas the graphs in figure 1 emphasize the meaning of *slope* and *intercept*, the next two problems and figure 2 concentrate on the *intersection* of lines.

Problem 5. If Brigit borrowed $1000 at 5% per annum for her tuition from a friend of her parents, how long would it take for the interest and principal on this money to accumulate to the same sum as the accumulated amount from the Ultimate Finance Company (problem 2)? What amount would be owed at this time?

This problem is sure to baffle many students. Figure 2a illustrates how graphs help simplify the problem. The information in problem 5 yields the equation

(1) $\qquad A = 50t + 1000.$

The answer to the question is the point of intersection of the two graphs (8, 1400). Algebraically we could solve the problem by setting the two amounts equal.

$$100t + 600 = 50t + 1000$$
$$50t = 400$$
$$t = 8$$

Substituting $t = 8$ in equation (1), we find that after eight years both debts would be $1400.

A comparison of the graphs in figure 2a shows the following:

1. The graph of $A = 100t + 600$ has a greater or steeper slope, and therefore the function increases at a faster rate.

2. The graph of $A = 50t + 1000$ has a greater initial amount of money (or y-intercept) but increases at a slower rate.

Problem 6. Suppose the Tiny Transformer Association wants to know the price at which the quantity demanded is equal to the quantity supplied.

Figure 2b shows the graphs of the equations from problems 3 and 4. The *equilibrium* point is found graphically to be approximately (73, 27). The desirable price for market equilibrium is about twenty-seven dollars per transformer, and the number of transformers sold and produced should be close to seventy-three.

Problem 7. The Thin Soup Company found that at a wholesale price of u cents per can, it can sell $(26 - u)$ million cans of Thin soup each month. What selling price yields the largest revenue for the company (Shockley 1976)?

The total revenue R is

$$R = u(26 - u) = 26u - u^2$$

million cents. The graph of the function ($R = 26u - u^2$) is shown in figure 3a. The revenue drops to zero if the unit price is

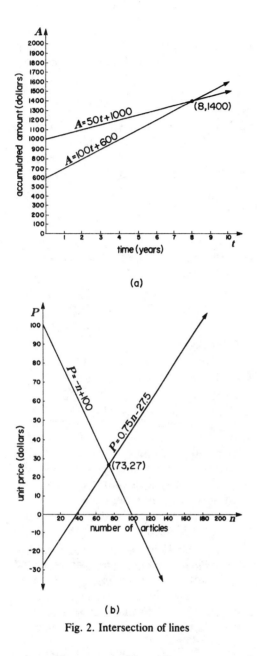

Fig. 2. Intersection of lines

$$A = 60t + 1000,$$

for the case of simple interest. For compound interest, the formula

$$A = P(1 + i)^t$$

applies. Substituting $P = 1000$ and $i = 0.06$ yields

$$A = 1000(1.06)^t.$$

The linear and exponential curves are shown in figure 3b. The difference in the amount after three years is about $5000, a fact that can be determined from the graph.

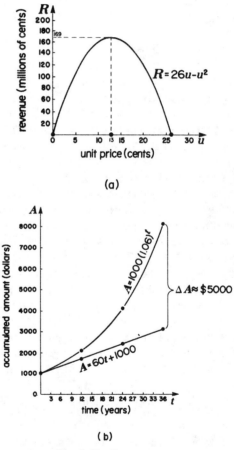

Fig. 3. Nonlinear curves

twenty-six cents, and maximum revenue is attained when the unit price is about thirteen cents, since $u = 13$ is the axis of symmetry of the parabola. The maximum possible revenue is found to be $1 690 000.

Problem 8. If $1000 is invested at 6% per annum for 3 years, what difference does it make if it is calculated as simple interest or if it is compounded annually?

By the method used in problem 2, we obtain the function

The last two problems are intended to emphasize the power of using graphs to make predictions.

Problem 9. A sports shop owner records the amount of sales for 4 years in

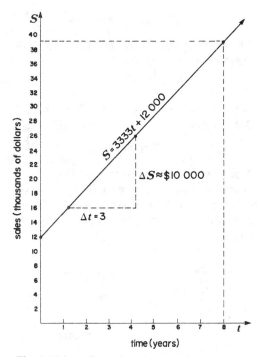

Fig. 4. Using a linear function to make estimates

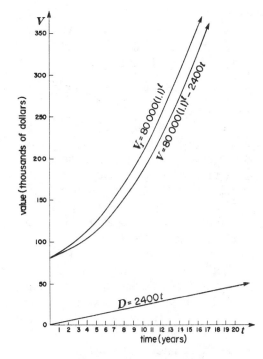

Fig. 5. Appreciation of an $80 000 house

order to discover if there is a pattern for predicting sales. In the first year, sales were $14 900; the second year, $15 000; the third year, $24 000; the fourth year, $25 000. Graph this information (fig. 4).

We can approximate a linear function by plotting the points and drawing a line through two points. Using the first and fourth points, we find the slope is 3333 and the y-intercept is 12 000. We find the equation for sales S is

$$S = 3333t + 12\ 000.$$

Assuming a linear relationship, we find that the sales will reach $40 000 in about 8½ years.

Problem 10. Consider an $80 000 house, an inflation rate of 10%, and a depreciation rate of 3%. What will the value V of this house be in 10 years? in 16 years?

Usually, depreciation D is expressed as a percent of the *original* value, and therefore the formula and calculations are much like the simple interest in problem 1:

$$D = 80\ 000 \times 0.03 \times t = 2400t.$$

See figure 5.

The inflation rate is expressed as a percent of the *present* value, and therefore the formula and calculations are much like the compounded interest in problem 3. The house value V_I, as influenced by inflation, is given by the following function:

$$V_I = 80\ 000(1.1)^t.$$

In table 2 we see $V = V_I - D$; the value V of the house is the difference between the

TABLE 2

t	$V_I = 80\ 000(1.1)^t$	$D = 2400t$	$V = V_I - D$
0	80 000	0	80 000
2	96 800	4 800	92 000
4	117 100	9 600	107 500
6	141 700	14 400	127 300
8	171 500	19 200	152 300
10	207 500	24 000	183 500
12	251 100	28 800	222 300
14	303 800	33 600	207 200
16	367 600	38 400	329 200

inflated value V_I and the amount of depreciation D. This difference can be seen in figure 5.

Assuming constant conditions, we see that a house worth $80 000 now will be worth about \$183 000 in ten years; whereas in sixteen years the same house will be worth about \$329 000. The function that predicts these values is

$$V = 80\ 000(1.1)^t - 2400t.$$

See figure 5.

The power of mathematics to predict and clarify patterns in business problems is accentuated in the mind of the student through solving a collection of related problems. At the same time, computational skills are developed by setting up tables of values. I have included only a few examples here, but temperature scales, arithmetical and geometrical series, commissions, annuities, mortgages (showing how principal paid increases as interest decreases under the equal payment plan), and many other practical problems could also be treated in a very similar fashion. Also, a very important aspect of teaching the applications of mathematics in senior grades is having the student realize that certain qualifications and restrictions are needed in combining the theoretical description with a particular real-life situation. In addition to the restrictions on the domain and the range, which I have discussed in these examples, it is necessary to treat and analyze discrete data as if they were continuous.

The graphs and the related discussions present the student with ideas and insights into practical problems that would otherwise be very difficult for students to comprehend. It is hoped that the student will recognize the significance of the Cartesian coordinate system as a powerful aid for organizing thought as well as a heuristic vehicle for propagating mathematical ideas.

REFERENCES

Kline, Morris. "A Proposal for the High School Mathematics Curriculum." *Mathematics Teacher* 66 (April 1966): 322–30.

Whipkey, Kenneth. *The Power of Mathematics, Applications to Management and the Social Sciences.* New York: John Wiley & Sons, 1978.

Shockley, James. *A Survey of General Mathematics.* New York: Holt, Rinehart & Winston, 1976.

USING THE MONOCHORD: A CLASSROOM DEMONSTRATION ON THE MATHEMATICS OF MUSICAL SCALES

By SHEILA HAAK
1028 S. Washington
Park Ridge, IL 60068

Many students have been told that mathematics and music are strongly related. But have they heard or seen this wonderful relationship? Those who know the musical scale (do-re-mi-fa-sol-la-ti-do) and can handle ratios will be fascinated as they apply mathematics to music. More advanced students will have the opportunity to apply their work with algebra and logarithms to musical scales. A single-stringed instrument, the monochord, demonstrates the mathematics of musical scales.

A monochord is pictured in figure 1.

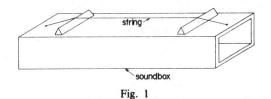

Fig. 1

The monochord in figure 2 is equipped for classroom use. The length of the string between the two bridges vibrates when plucked and produces a tone. Sliding the movable bridge varies the string length and changes the pitch of the tone produced by the vibrations. Directions for making this monochord are given at the end of the article. The cost is minimal and the time required is only a few hours.

The Pythagorean Scale

Pythagoras (sixth century B.C.) was probably the first to apply mathematics to a musical scale. He discovered that two vibrating strings of equal diameter and tension and whose lengths are in the ratio of 1:2 differ in pitch by an octave. The interval of a fifth, do to sol or C to G, results when the string lengths are in the ratio of 2:3. (An *interval of a fifth* is represented by any two notes in which the higher note is seven semitones above the lower note. A *semitone* is the interval between any two adjacent keys on the piano, disregarding the color of tne keys.) The fourth, do to fa or C to F, is sounded by vibrating strings whose lengths are in the ratio of 3:4. (An *interval of a fourth* is an interval of five semitones.) For simplicity, all scales discussed are in the key of C (the white keys of the piano).

Pythagoras was intrigued by the fact that plucked strings whose lengths are in one of these simple ratios (1:2, 2:3, 3:4) produce consonant tones, that is, when two or more of these tones are played at the same time, they sound pleasant. Musicians disagree about whether consonance is determined by the physical properties of the consonant tones or by one's aural perceptions that have been influenced by experience and training.

To demonstrate an octave to your class, slide the loose bridge on the monochord to the 50-centimeter mark and align the edge of the right angle of the movable bridge with the given mark on the tape measure. Pluck the string between the two bridges, the endpoints of the vibrating string. Hence, the relevant string length is 50 centimeters. Slide the bridge to 25 centimeters and pluck the string to discover the octave, low do to high do. Now slide the bridge to the 12.5-centimeter mark. The pitch goes up another octave. Try 6.25 centimeters. You might want to indicate

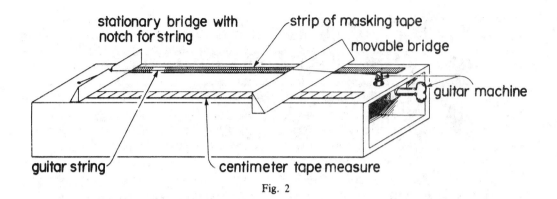

stationary bridge with notch for string

strip of masking tape

movable bridge

guitar machine

guitar string

centimeter tape measure

Fig. 2

on the masking tape lengths of 50 centimeters, 25 centimeters, 12.5 centimeters, and 6.25 centimeters. Label each of these points *do*. Let your students *see* the ratio of 1:2 in these string lengths.

Lengths of 40 centimeters, 20 centimeters, 10 centimeters, and 5 centimeters may also be used. If a piano is available, you might want to pluck strings of varying lengths and compare the pitches to middle C. After middle C is found on the monochord, pluck a string half its length. This pitch should be the first C above middle C on the piano.

To hear the consonance of the octave (low do and high do at the same time), slide the bridge to the 20-centimeter mark. The string length between the two bridges is 20 centimeters; the string length between the movable bridge and the guitar machine is 40 centimeters. At the same time, pluck both the 20-centimeter and 40-centimeter portions of the string. Your students will *hear* the octave and *see* the ratio of 1:2.

In a similar fashion the interval of the fifth can be shown. If do, or C, is produced by a 50-centimeter vibrating string, then sol, or G, is produced by a vibrating string of length (2/3)(50) centimeters, or 33 1/3 centimeters. Have your class do these calculations. Mark sol on the masking tape at 33 1/3 centimeters. Slide the bridge to do at 50 centimeters and pluck the string. Then slide it to sol and pluck the string. The students can hum do-re-mi-fa-sol to verify that the interval is, in fact, do to sol.

Try other string lengths, such as 20 centimeters and 30 centimeters. Have the students try their own measurements.

Try some algebra: If sol is sounded by a 28-centimeter string, how long is the string that produces do? After your students solve the appropriate equation, $2/3\,x = 28$, they can musically check the solution, $x = 42$. Pluck the 42-centimeter string and then the 28-centimeter string. Does it sound like do, then sol? If not, either the solution is incorrect or they have not measured correctly.

Suppose we want to sound do and sol together. We must divide the 60-centimeter string into two portions whose lengths are in the ratio 2:3. Again, algebra helps out. The solution to the equation,

$$2x + 3x = 60,$$

is $x = 12$. So the point at 24 divides the lengths in the ratio 2:3. Test the solution musically. Slide the bridge to 24 centimeters. Pluck the string on both sides of the movable bridge at the same time.

Have the class explain how to use the ratio of 3:4 to produce the pitch interval of a fourth, do to fa or C to F. Where should fa be marked on the masking tape? How do we sound do and fa simultaneously?

The completed Pythagorean scale is shown in table 1. (Note that the frequency of the vibrating string is inversely proportional to its length. To obtain the ratios of the frequencies of various pitches, use the reciprocals of the fractions shown.)

Let L represent 50 centimeters. Have your students calculate the lengths of the strings for all the notes of the scale. In this way, work with fractions, variables, and metric measurements can be reinforced. For your convenience, the string lengths for the Pythagorean scale as well as the other scales discussed in this article are shown in table 5. These string lengths are based on the string lengths given in tables 1–4, using 50 centimeters for the string length of do. Also shown are the decimal equivalents for the ratios of the string lengths. You might prefer to have your students do their calculations with decimals.

For each student, place a clean strip of masking tape on the monochord. Have the student mark the appropriate string lengths for do, re, mi, fa, sol, la, ti, and do according to his or her calculations. As a check, the student should slide the bridge from do to re to mi, and so on, plucking the string each time. It should sound like do-re-mi-fa-sol-la-ti-do. Notes that sound wrong represent an incorrect calculation or measurement.

Other Scales

Although the Pythagorean scale, as played on the monochord, sounds like the scale with which we are familiar, it is not exactly the same as the scale on the piano. One of the drawbacks is that all the whole tone intervals are represented by the same ratio of 8/9, whereas the semitone intervals are not constant. Between E and F (mi and fa) and between B and C (ti and do), each semitone interval is represented

by the ratio of 243/256. Using this ratio, the string length of C# (C sharp), a semitone above C, would be 243/256*L*. D is a semitone above C#, so the ratio of the string lengths of D to C# should also be 243/256. But instead it is 8/9 ÷ 243/256 = 2048/2187 (which is less than 243/256). A tune played in one key would sound different when played in another key.

Singers of the late medieval period found other disadvantages with the Pythagorean scale. They were quite unhappy with its sharp major third, do to mi, and its flat minor third, mi to sol. As the major triad, do-mi-sol, became important in music (it has been the foundation of Western music for several centuries), the *just scale* was developed containing several major triads with string lengths in the ratio 10:12:15. But the scale was never used extensively because some of its fifths (do to sol) were flat and there were two different sizes of whole tone intervals. The just scale appears in table 2.

The *meantone scale* remedied some of the problems of the just scale. It was used for centuries and stood in conflict with the *well-tempered scale* used today. Although most of the fifths were more accepted by musicians, the fifth G#–D# had to be avoided. Known as the *wolf fifth* because it was so unpleasantly out of tune, it was more than a third of a semitone sharp. The meantone scale is shown in table 3.

The class can work with these three scales and, perhaps, draw both musical and mathematical comparisons. The dif-

TABLE 1
Pythagorean Scale

Note	Do	Re	Mi	Fa	Sol	La	Ti	Do
String length	L	$\frac{8}{9}L$	$\frac{64}{81}L$	$\frac{3}{4}L$	$\frac{2}{3}L$	$\frac{16}{27}L$	$\frac{128}{243}L$	$\frac{1}{2}L$

TABLE 2
Just Scale

Note	Do	Re	Mi	Fa	Sol	La	Ti	Do
String length	L	$\frac{8}{9}L$	$\frac{4}{5}L$	$\frac{3}{4}L$	$\frac{2}{3}L$	$\frac{3}{5}L$	$\frac{8}{15}L$	$\frac{1}{2}L$

ferences among these scales, both in terms of mathematical ratios and musical intervals, seem small. The ratios can be easily compared by converting all the ratios to decimals, as done in table 5. The musical intervals can be compared by calculating the string lengths for the monochord and listening to the differences. A perceptive ear will notice that the interval of ti to do, for example, sounds different in each of the three scales.

Students who have not worked with fractional and negative exponents could be given the meantone scale in decimal form.

The Well-tempered Scale

Musicians were troubled by the one major drawback common to all three scales discussed thus far. The mathematical ratio representing a given pitch interval is not everywhere the same. Hence, a given interval in one key will have a different sound when played in another key. This problem is both musical and mathematical. The musicians need any given interval, say the fifth, in which the higher pitch is seven semitones above the lower to sound both *consonant* and *constant* in every key. If the mathematician is to help out with the latter requirement, he must find a sequence of numbers (representing string lengths) in which the ratio of any two numbers, a given number of terms apart, is constant. For the pitch interval of a fifth, the ratio of the eighth and first terms of the sequence must be the same as the ratio of the tenth and third, or sixteenth and ninth. Your advanced algebra classes will recognize that such a sequence must be a geometric sequence. Given that the string lengths of the octave range from L to $(1/2)L$ and that there are twelve semitones in the octave, we can express the first and thirteenth terms of the sequence as $a_1 = 1$ and $a_{13} = 1/2$. If r is the common ratio, then

$$a_1(r^{12}) = a_{13}$$
$$r^{12} = \frac{1}{2}$$
$$r = \sqrt[12]{\frac{1}{2}} = 2^{-1/12}.$$

Hence, every semitone will be represented by the same ratio of $2^{-1/12}:1$. This new scale is called the *well-tempered scale*.

The well-tempered scale, complete with semitones, appears in table 4. Also called the *scale of equal temperament*, it was first proposed by Bartolo Rames, a Spaniard, in 1482 but was not accepted for centuries. In the first half of the eighteenth century, J. S. Bach wrote *The Well-Tempered Clavier*, which includes forty-eight preludes and fugues, to demonstrate the practicality of well-tempered tuning. Preludes and fugues are written in each of the twelve keys—something that could not have been done with the other forms of tuning. Well-tempered tuning was adopted more extensively in the middle of the last century and is the scale that we use to tune our pianos today.

Your advanced algebra classes can go

TABLE 3
Meantone Scale

Note	Do	Re	Mi	Fa	Sol	La	Ti	Do
String length	L	$2(5^{-1/2})L$	$\frac{4}{5}L$	$\frac{5^{1/4}}{2}L$	$5^{-1/4}L$	$2(5^{-3/4})L$	$4(5^{-5/4})L$	$\frac{1}{2}L$

TABLE 4
Well-tempered Scale

Note	Do C	C#	Re D	D#	Mi E	Fa F	F#	Sol G	G#	La A	A#	Ti B	Do C
String length	L	$2^{-1/12}L$	$2^{-2/12}L$	$2^{-3/12}L$	$2^{-4/12}L$	$2^{-5/12}L$	$2^{-6/12}L$	$2^{-7/12}L$	$2^{-8/12}L$	$2^{-9/12}L$	$2^{-10/12}L$	$2^{-11/12}L$	$2^{-1}L$

to work calculating the string lengths of the well-tempered scale. It is hoped that they will see the usefulness of logarithms for this problem if calculators or computers are unavailable. Your students should find the string lengths given in the last column of table 5.

Have the students check their calculations by marking the string lengths of all thirteen notes on the masking tape. To listen for the scale, pluck only the strings for do, re, mi, and so on. Do not pluck C#, D#, and so on. These are the notes played by the black keys on the piano. (In the key of C, only the white notes are played for the scale do-re-mi-fa-sol-la-ti-do. Some students may know that they can play do-re-mi-fa-sol in another key, such as D, by playing the strings for D, E, F#, G, and A.)

Mathematically, and musically, all intervals are constant in every key. Musically, the intervals are very close to perfect, and the problems caused by using the other scales are resolved.

Note the spacing of the thirteen marks on the masking tape. This is logarithmic spacing (or a logarithmic scale, in more than one way!). What might you expect to discover about the spacing of the frets on a guitar or the lengths of organ pipes?

Some students might investigate how the scale is produced by other instruments.

Construction of a Monochord
Materials:

4 27" strips of wood lattice, $\frac{1}{4}'' \times 2\frac{1}{2}''$ (Different widths of lattice may be used.) An extra piece, $\frac{1}{4}'' \times \frac{3}{4}'' \times 3''$, may be needed.

1 6" piece of cant strip, $\frac{3}{4}'' \times \frac{3}{4}''$ (The cross section of cant strip is a right triangle with legs of $\frac{3}{4}''$. Right triangular strips of slightly different dimensions will work.)

1 guitar machine (This string-tightening device is available at musical instrument shops.)

1 steel guitar string, about 0.305 mm (This is also available at musical instrument shops.)

1 centimeter tape measure

1 roll 1" masking tape

nails, screws, wood glue, ruler, hammer, screwdriver, drill, varnish (optional)

Read all the directions before you start.

Approximately $\frac{3}{4}''$ from one end of the piece of lattice that will become the top of the monochord, drill a hole just slightly larger than the rod of the guitar machine.

TABLE 5
Decimal Equivalents of Ratios and String Lengths of Musical Scales

	Pythagorean		Just		Meantone		Well-tempered	
	Length of String	Length of Monochord String in Centimeters	Length of String	Length of Monochord String in Centimeters	Length of String	Length of Monochord String in Centimeters	Length of String	Length of Monochord String in Centimeters
Do C	L	50.00	L	50.00	L	50.00	L	50.00
C#							0.944 L	47.20
Re D	0.889 L	44.45	0.889 L	44.45	0.894 L	44.72	0.891 L	44.55
D#							0.841 L	42.05
Mi E	0.790 L	39.50	0.800 L	40.00	0.800 L	40.00	0.794 L	39.70
Fa F	0.750 L	37.50	0.750 L	37.50	0.748 L	37.40	0.749 L	37.45
F#							0.707 L	35.35
Sol G	0.6667L	33.33	0.6667L	33.33	0.669 L	33.45	0.6674L	33.37
G#							0.630 L	31.50
La A	0.593 L	29.65	0.600 L	30.00	0.598 L	29.90	0.595 L	29.75
A#							0.561 L	28.05
Ti B	0.527 L	26.35	0.533 L	26.65	0.535 L	26.75	0.530 L	26.50
Do C	0.500 L	25.00	0.500 L	25.00	0.500 L	25.00	0.500 L	25.00

Insert the rod of the machine through the hole. Attach the machine to the lattice with screws or nails. See figure 3.

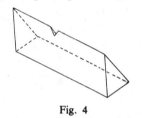

Fig. 3

Cut the cant strip into two pieces: one should be the width of the lattice (approximately $2\frac{1}{2}''$); the other approximately $1''$ longer. These pieces are the bridges. On the shorter bridge, at the midpoint of the edge of an acute angle, tap or cut a slight notch, about $\frac{1}{8}''$ deep. See figure 4. Glue

Fig. 4

and screw the shorter bridge across the top of the monochord, precisely 60 centimeters from the center of the drilled hole. Be sure to position the right angle of the bridge as shown in figure 5.

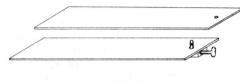

Fig. 5

Nail all four lattice pieces together into an open-ended box, as shown in figure 6. Anchor the looped end of the guitar string to the top of the monochord about $1\frac{1}{2}''$

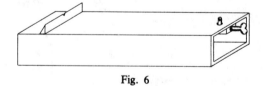

Fig. 6

from the bridge with a screw or nail. It must be anchored very securely. Thread the other end of the string through the small hole of the guitar machine. Guiding the string through the notch of the bridge, tighten slightly by winding the guitar machine. See figure 7.

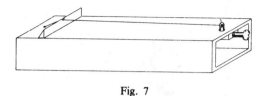

Fig. 7

On the top of the monochord, along one side of the string, glue a 60-centimeter tape measure with the 60 aligned with the center of the drilled hole. On the other side of the string, tape an unmarked strip of masking tape running the length of the tape measure. See figure 8.

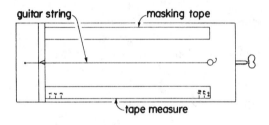

guitar string   masking tope

tape measure

(top view)

Fig. 8

Slip the movable bridge under the string. Be certain that the base of the triangle is one of the legs, as shown in figure 2. Tighten the string. The string must remain very tight or the desired pitch intervals will not be achieved. Depending on the design of the guitar machine, it is possible that the string will not make contact with the movable bridge. If this is the case, remove the bridge and glue a piece of lattice, $\frac{1}{4}'' \times \frac{3}{4}'' \times 3''$, to its underside to increase its altitude. See figure 9.

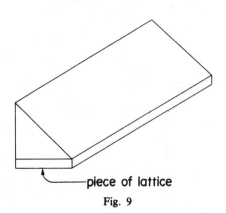

piece of lattice

Fig. 9

Replace the movable bridge on the monochord.

To test your monochord, slide the loose bridge so that the edge of the right angle is at the 50-centimeter mark. Pluck the string between the two bridges. Slide the bridge to 25 centimeters. Pluck the string again. The second pitch should sound an octave above the first (low do, then high do). If it does not, tighten the string and test again.

You may want to varnish your monochord. Remove the string and masking tape when you do so. You may varnish over the tape measure.

Encourage your students to make some monochords. Perhaps you could enlist the help of some shop students. One monochord is sufficient, but several are preferable for classroom use.

BIBLIOGRAPHY

Amir-Moez, Ali R. "Mathematics of Music." *Recreational Mathematics Magazine* 3 (1961):31–36.

———. "Numbers and Music of East and West." *Scripta Mathematica* 22 (1956):268–70.

Backus, John. *The Acoustical Foundations of Music.* New York: W. W. Norton, 1969.

Bell Telephone Laboratories. "The Science of Sound." Folkeways Records and Science Corporation, number FX-6007.

Botts, Truman. "More on the Mathematics of Musical Scales." *Mathematics Teacher* 67 (January 1974):75–84.

Malcom, Paul S. "Mathematics of Musical Scales." *Mathematics Teacher* 65 (November 1972):611–15.

Maor, Eli. "What Is There So Mathematical about Music?" *Mathematics Teacher* 72 (September 1979):414–22.

O'Keeffe, Vincent. "Mathematical-Musical Relationships: A Bibliography." *Mathematics Teacher* 65 (April 1972):315–24.

O'Shea, Thomas. "Geometric Transformations and Musical Composition." *Mathematics Teacher* 72 (October 1979):523–28.

Order from Chaos

As any teacher of geometric progressions would testify, the problem of the bouncing ball and how to handle the troublesome first term is disconcerting to students and requires careful treatment. The different options include working with two infinite series, or summing one doubled series, and then either adding or subtracting the first term. I propose now to suggest another alternative, and by this method, it is hoped, the analysis of the problem will be simplified.

Basically this method involves summing one infinite series, every one of whose terms represents the distance traversed in one fall *and* the subsequent rise of the ball. To be specific, if the ball initially drops *a* units and then rises *ar* units, the distance, *D*, traveled is

$$D = a + 2ar + 2ar^2 + 2ar^3 + \cdots$$
$$= (a + ar) + (ar + ar^2)$$
$$\qquad + (ar^2 + ar^3) + \cdots$$
$$= (a + ar) + (a + ar)r$$
$$\qquad + (a + ar)r^2 + \cdots$$

In this form it is apparent that we have an infinite geometric series with a first term, $a + ar$, and a common ratio, r. The first term is the sum of the distances traveled on the first fall and the first rise of the ball. Each succeeding term also represents the distance from one top position to the next. Aside from recast-ing the nature of each term of the series, we need no new techniques or formulas to solve this problem in a nonmessy fashion.

The person who enjoys formulas (I don't) might continue with the algebra to get

$$D = (a + ar)(1 + r + r^2 + r^3 + \cdots$$

or

$$D = \frac{a(1 + r)}{1 - r}.$$

As an example, consider the golf ball initially falling from a height of 8 feet and rising each time $\frac{3}{4}$ of the distance it just fell. The first term in the geometric progression would be the distance covered in the first drop and rise; that is, $8 + 8 \cdot \frac{3}{4} = 14$ feet: the common ratio is $\frac{3}{4}$. Hence the distance traveled is

$$\frac{14}{1 - \frac{3}{4}} = 56 \text{ feet}.$$

Using the last formula for D, we find that $a = 8$ is the distance of the first fall only, giving

$$D = \frac{8(1 + \frac{3}{4})}{1 - \frac{3}{4}} = 56 \text{ feet}.$$

RICHARD W. SHOEMAKER
University of Toledo
Toledo, OH 43606

Impact of the Black Death (1348-1405) on World Population: Then and Now

By MICHAEL G. GONZALES and WILLIAM J. CARR, Beaver College, Glenside, PA 19038

This article illustrates the use of a simple mathematical model to solve a problem involving the estimation of population. The problem is as follows:

> Estimate the current world population if the Black Death had not occurred in the years A.D. 1348–1405.

We begin by presenting some historical background on the plague and its consequences. Then we describe a model for population growth and give an outline of the method used to predict the current population if the plague had not occurred. Finally we suggest an interpretation of the results: Over the long term, the plague yielded a seemingly overlooked beneficial consequence, namely, it gave us extra time to learn how to cope with the problem of overpopulation.

Historical Background

The bubonic plague, caused by the bacterium *Pasteurella pestis,* is believed to have struck Rome during the second and third centuries (Desmond 1964). But, by far, the greatest of the bubonic plagues occurred in six waves during the fourteenth and fifteenth centuries (1348–1405). Apparently arising in central Asia, it spread throughout India, Asia Minor, northern Africa, Europe, England, Iceland, and perhaps farther west. Historians disagree as to whether it also reached China (Needham 1971; Tuchman 1978). In the regions it is known to have struck, approximately one-third of the population died from the

We wish to express our appreciation to Pamela Chiartas and Susan Roffman for their assistance in the preparation of this manuscript.

disease—20 million in Europe alone (Desmond 1964; Ziegler 1969). As shown in figure 1, the plague actually caused a decrease in the world's population by about 21 percent, from 470 million in 1348 to 370 million by 1400. Indeed, the plague produced the only significant downturn in the otherwise positively accelerated growth curve characterizing the world's human population since A.D. 1000. Tuchman (1978) judged the plague of 1348–1405 to be the greatest natural disaster in recorded history.

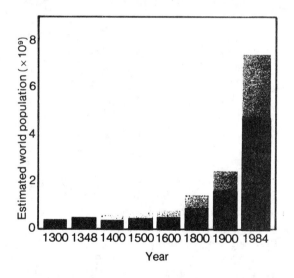

Fig. 1. Estimated world population assuming Black Death did (black bars) or did not (black and colored bars) occur. (No reliable estimate is available for 1700.) The plague struck Europe in 1348. (*Note:* Black-bar data from Desmond [1964] and United Nations Fund for Population Activities [1984]).

In addition to the toll in human lives, the cumulative effects of the six major outbreaks of the plague seriously disrupted the Old World's economy and social structure

(Tuchman 1978; Ziegler 1969). The production of food and other necessities declined, whereas social disorder increased sharply, but these disruptions were relatively short-lived. Even in the regions most seriously affected, population densities recovered to preplague levels within a decade or two, as did the economies (Ziegler 1969).

Some historians have suggested that along with its obviously devastating short-term effects, the plague actually had beneficial long-term effects as well. Ziegler (1969) presented limited evidence for and against the view that the plague's decimation of the population in England strengthened the economic position of the landless laborers, tradespeople, and artisans compared to the landed gentry and the clergy. This benefit, one-sided at best, was

---

The plague yielded a seemingly overlooked beneficial consequence.

---

at least partially offset by legislation aimed at stabilizing wages and prices at preplague levels and at limiting the mobility of laborers. However, some believe that because of the social discontent and "rising expectations" experienced by the landless survivors, the plague ultimately contributed to widespread social and economic changes. Ziegler (1969, 251) concluded that in England the plague "was a catalytic element of the first order, profoundly modifying the economic and social forces on which it operated." Tuchman (1978) makes a similar case for the situation in Europe. But note that these social and economic consequences constitute a mixed blessing, since they merely enhanced the position of some groups at the expense of others.

In the universities of England and Europe, senior faculty members who died during the plague were replaced by younger men who were less steeped in the tradition of using Latin as the major medium of scholarly and legal communication. Therefore, a second consequence attributed by

some to the plague was the increased use of national languages in place of Latin. This, in turn, is said to have fostered an already rising sense of nationalism in England and on the Continent (Tuchman 1978; Ziegler 1969). But given the subsequent violent history of western civilization, one might argue that the emergence of nationalism was, at best, a mixed blessing.

Many would agree with Tuchman's (1978) judgment that the plague of 1348–1405 was the greatest natural disaster in recorded history. Therefore, in the spirit of maximizing the number and radiance of silver linings in the darkest cloud ever to hang over humankind, we propose an additional beneficial consequence that seems to have been overlooked. We suggest that by reducing the world's population (see fig. 1) between 1348 and 1405, the plague has thereby limited the present world population, thus providing us with additional time in which to learn how to deal with what might prove to be the next natural disaster facing humanity—worldwide overpopulation.

The Model and Its Application

To predict current world population if the plague had not occurred, we proceeded as follows. First, as shown in table 1, we collected estimated data on the world's population for the thirteenth through the twentieth centuries.

TABLE 1

Estimated World Population
with Black Death, 1200–1984

Year	Population
1200	0.35×10^9
1300	0.38×10^9
1348 (Black Death begins)	0.47×10^9
1400	0.37×10^9
1500	0.45×10^9
1600	0.49×10^9
1700	No accurate estimate available
1800	0.91×10^9
1900	1.60×10^9
1984	4.80×10^9

Data from Desmond (1946) and United Nations Fund for Population Activities (1984)

Next, the population growth rate was computed for each of the periods in table 2. The model (Boyce and DiPrima 1977) used to compute growth rates was this:

(1) $P_E = P_I\, e^{rt}$

where

   t = duration of period (in years)
   P_I = population at the beginning of the period
   P_E = population at the end of the period
   r = population growth rate

TABLE 2	
Population Growth Rates with Black Death, 1200–1984	
Interval	Growth Rate (r)
1200–1300	0.82×10^{-3}
1300–1348	4.40×10^{-3}
1400–1500	1.96×10^{-3}
1500–1600	0.85×10^{-3}
1600–1800	3.10×10^{-3}
1800–1900	5.64×10^{-3}
1900–1984	13.10×10^{-3}

To get each of the r values in table 2, we used equation (1) and known values for P_I, P_E, and t from table 1. For example, to obtain the growth rate r for the period 1200–1300, we used $P_I = 0.35 \times 10^9$, $P_E = 0.38 \times 10^9$, and $t = 100$. Substitution of these values into equation (1) yields the following:

(2) $0.38 \times 10^9 = (0.35 \times 10^9)e^{(r \times 100)}$

Solving equation (2) for r yields

$$r = 0.82 \times 10^{-3}.$$

Next we use these growth rates and the population figure for 1348 to predict world population if the Black Death had not occurred. To do so, we assumed that all other events between 1348 and 1984 were the same (see question 3 in the suggestions for discussion at the end of the article). The population for 1400 was predicted first by using equation (1) with $P_I = 0.47 \times 10^9$ (population figure for year 1348) and $t = 52$.

In addition we used the r value computed for the interval 1300–1348. We assumed this r value to remain constant throughout the 1300s if the Black Death had not occurred. The predicted population for 1400 is then 0.59×10^9. To predict the population for 1500, we used equation (1) with $P_I = 0.59 \times 10^9$ (the predicted population for 1400 without the plague) and $t = 100$. In addition we used the r value computed for the interval 1400–1500. The predicted population for 1500 is then 0.72×10^9.

We proceeded in a similar manner to predict the populations for 1600, 1800, 1900, and 1984. Table 3 summarizes the results.

TABLE 3	
Predicted World Population without Black Death, 1400–1984	
Year	Predicted Population
1400	0.59×10^9
1500	0.72×10^9
1600	0.78×10^9
1800	1.45×10^9
1900	2.50×10^9
1984	7.50×10^9

The difference between the 1984 estimate with the Black Death and the 1984 estimate without the Black Death is 2.7×10^9. This difference represents $(2.7/4.8) \times 100 = 56$ percent of the current world estimate for 1984.

Suggestions for discussion and further activities

1. Using the method illustrated, provide an estimate of the world's population in 2000 and 2050. Use $r = 13.10 \times 10^{-3}$.

2. Can you think of any other advantages or disadvantages suggested by the results of the modeling?

3. Discuss the importance of the assumptions made in the previous section regarding what would have happened without the plague. How do you think underlying assumptions relate to the applicability or utility of a particular model?

REFERENCES

Boyce, William E., and Richard C. DiPrima. *Elementary Differential Equations and Boundary Value Problems*. New York: John Wiley & Sons, 1977.

Desmond, Annabelle. "How Many People Have Ever Lived on Earth?" In *The Population Crisis and the Use of World Resources*, pp. 27–46, edited by Stuart Mudd. Bloomington, Ind.: Indiana University Press, 1964.

Needham, Joseph. *Science and Civilization in China*. Vol. 4. Part 3. Cambridge: Cambridge University Press, 1971.

Tuchman, Barbara W. *A Distant Mirror: The Calamitous Fourteenth Century*. New York: Alfred A. Knopf, 1978.

United Nations Fund for Population Activities. *State of the World Population: A Report by the Executive Director*. New York: United Nations, 1984.

Ziegler, Philip. *The Black Death*. New York: John Day, 1969. ♥

COMPOUND GROWTH AND RELATED SITUATIONS: A PROBLEM-SOLVING APPROACH

By FRANCISCO deP. SOLER
De Anza College
Cupertino, CA 95014

and **RICHARD E. SCHUSTER**
Space Applications Corporation
Sunnyvale, CA 94086

In the traditional secondary school and junior college curriculum, "practical mathematics" and "college preparatory mathematics" have been treated as non-overlapping courses. Topics that are common mathematical applications have been relegated to courses that are remedial in nature. The outcome is quite predictable: mathematical modeling and the development of algorithms are almost totally ignored and results are presented in cookbook form. As a consequence, two things occur: students in the typical college preparatory curriculum miss being exposed to many practical aspects of mathematics, and students in non–college preparatory courses miss being exposed to the thrill of making mathematics. This latter group frequently believes that mathematics is the use of magic formulas that capriciously appear to work.

Compound growth is one such topic. Compound growth techniques are used to model situations arising in the areas of population studies, radioactive decay, monetary inflation, lending, borrowing, and investing.

The authors are indebted to Zalman Usiskin for the development of similar ideas in *Algebra through Applications* (NCTM 1979) and for his encouragement and inspiration during the time when the authors were exploring the introduction of applications in the high school classroom.

The thrust of this article is to contribute usable examples involving compound growth that emphasize the areas of lending, borrowing, and investing. In the authors' experience, these areas present a wealth of opportunities for mathematical modeling, the development of algorithms, and practical applications.

The examples, exercises, and solutions presented can be fully explored throughout the typical secondary school curriculum. The development and derivation of the mathematics will suggest the appropriate place for their insertion in the syllabus.

Amortized Payments: The Borrower's Approach

The case of someone borrowing money from a bank is an example of compound growth. It illustrates the power of mathematics available to an intermediate algebra student in a real-life situation that has been traditionally introduced as a "magic" formula.

Suppose you borrow $3000 from a bank to be repaid in three years with thirty-six equal monthly payments at a 13 percent annual interest rate. The loan is to be fully amortized; that is, monthly interest is charged on the remaining balance. What is the monthly payment?

Before deriving the solution, we shall use table 1 to illustrate some characteristics of amortized payments. The value of the payment can be computed from the formula to be derived at the end of this section.

Notice that the monthly payment remains constant, the portion of the payment representing interest paid is reduced month to month, and the portion of the payment reducing the remaining balance is increased each month. Observe that, for the third month,

$$101.08 = 31.01 + 70.07;$$
$$2792.03 = 2862.10 - 70.07.$$

In the general case, given an amount borrowed at a certain interest rate and the number of payments to be made, we are looking for the amount of the payment with the properties illustrated in table 1. Let—

known $\begin{cases} r = \text{monthly rate;} \\ P = \text{loan amount;} \end{cases}$

unknown $\begin{cases} M_n = \text{monthly payment for month } n; \ n = 1, 2, 3, \\ \qquad \cdots, 36; \\ P_n = \text{amount of payment against the remaining balance for month } n; \\ \qquad n = 1, 2, 3, \cdots, 36; \\ I_n = \text{amount of interest paid in month } n; \ n = 1, 2, 3, \\ \qquad \cdots, 36. \end{cases}$

In the first month, the interest paid is simply rP since the remaining balance is just the loan amount. Therefore, the first monthly payment may be written as

$$(1) \qquad M_1 = P_1 + I_1 = P_1 + rP.$$

For the second month, the interest paid is calculated on the remaining balance, which is $P - P_1$; therefore

$$M_2 = P_2 + I_2 = P_2 + r(P - P_1).$$

Continuing this way, write

$$M_3 = P_3 + I_3 = P_3 + r(P - P_1 - P_2);$$
$$\cdots$$
$$M_{36} = P_{36} + I_{36}$$
$$= P_{36} + r(P - P_1 - P_2 - \cdots - P_{35}).$$

Using the fact that the monthly payments are equal, we have

$$M_1 = M_2 \rightarrow P_1 + rP = P_2 + r(P - P_1);$$
$$(2) \qquad \therefore P_2 = P_1(1 + r).$$

Likewise,

$$M_2 = M_3 \rightarrow$$
$$P_2 + r(P - P_1) = P_3 + r(P - P_1 - P_2);$$
$$\therefore P_3 = P_2 + r(P - P_1) - r(P - P_1 - P_2)$$
$$= P_2 + rP_2$$
$$= P_2(1 + r),$$

and from (2)

$$P_3 = P_1(1 + r)^2.$$

This pattern generalizes to

$$(3) \qquad P_n = P_{n-1}(1 + r),$$

or

$$P_n = P_1(1 + r)^{n-1}.$$

We know that the sum of the amounts paid against the remaining balance for the thirty-six-month period equal the loan amount. Therefore,

$$(4) \qquad \sum_{n=1}^{36} P_n = P_1 \sum_{n=1}^{36} (1 + r)^{n-1} = P.$$

Notice that once P_1 is found in terms of P in equation (4), we can solve for M_1 in equation (1), and an equation for the monthly payment is found since all monthly payments are the same.

TABLE 1

Month	Payment	Interest Paid	Principal Reduced By	Remaining Loan Balance
1	101.08	32.50	68.58	2931.42
2	101.08	31.76	69.32	2862.10
3	101.08	31.01	70.07	2792.03
...				
36	101.08	1.08	100.00	0.00

From equation (4) and the formula for the sum of a geometric series with a common ratio $(1 + r)$, we have the following:

$$\sum_{n=1}^{36} (1 + r)^{n-1}$$

$$= 1 + (1 + r) + (1 + r)^2 + \cdots + (1 + r)^{35}$$

$$= \frac{(1 + r)^{36} - 1}{r}.$$

Hence,

$$P = P_1 \left[\frac{(1 + r)^{36} - 1}{r} \right],$$

and

$$P_1 = P \left[\frac{(1 + r)^{36} - 1}{r} \right]^{-1}.$$

Since

$$M_1 = P_1 + I_1 = P_1 + rP,$$

it follows that

$$M_1 = P \left[\frac{(1 + r)^{36} - 1}{r} \right]^{-1} + rP,$$

or

$$(5) \quad M_1 = P \left\{ \left[\frac{(1 + r)^{36} - 1}{r} \right]^{-1} + r \right\}.$$

Algebraic manipulation of equation (5) leads to the usual formulation for an amortized thirty-six-month loan,

$$(6) \quad \text{Monthly payment} = \frac{Pr}{1 - (1 + r)^{-36}}.$$

For the example stated at the beginning, $P = 3000$, $r = 0.13/12$, and

Monthly payment

$$= \frac{(3000)(0.13/12)}{1 - (1 + 0.13/12)^{-36}} = 101.08.$$

Amortized Payments: The Lender's Approach

Consider the $3000 of the previous example to be the sum of the amounts the principal was reduced with each monthly payment. From table 1,

$$3000 = 68.58 + 69.32$$
$$+ 70.07 + \cdots + 100,$$

where the nth number in the list represents the amount the principal is reduced in the nth month.

Notice that

$$100 = \frac{101.08}{1 + 0.13/12},$$

$$70.07 = \frac{101.08}{(1 + 0.13/12)^{34}},$$

$$69.32 = \frac{101.08}{(1 + 0.13/12)^{35}},$$

$$68.58 = \frac{101.08}{(1 + 0.13/12)^{36}},$$

and so on.

From the banker's point of view, the $3000.00 is worth $101.08 per month for thirty-six months. The $101.08 the bank will get, say five months from the start of the loan, is not worth $101.08 at the start. It is actually worth only $101.08/(1 + 0.13/12)^5$ at the time the loan is granted.

Generalizing, an investment of D dollars paying interest at a monthly rate r, compounded monthly, will have a dollar value $D(1 + r)$ after one month, $D(1 + r)^2$ after two months, and $D(1 + r)^n$ after n months. Likewise, last month, the value of the investment D was $D(1 + r)^{-1}$, two months ago $D(1 + r)^{-2}$, and n months ago $D(1 + r)^{-n}$.

The total loan value to the banker at the time of the loan is the actual amount of the loan ($3000 in our example). This total may also be written as follows:

$$3000 = \frac{101.08}{(1 + 0.13/12)} + \frac{101.08}{(1 + 0.13/12)^2}$$
$$+ \cdots + \frac{101.08}{(1 + 0.13/12)^{36}},$$

where the first term is the present value of the money to be paid back in the first payment, the second term is the present value of the money to be paid back in the second payment, and so on.

Generalizing and using the same notation as before with the monthly payment for the nth month $M_n = M$ for all n, we have

$$P = \frac{M}{1 + r} + \frac{M}{(1 + r)^2} + \cdots + \frac{M}{(1 + r)^n}$$

$$= M \sum_{k=1}^{n} \frac{1}{(1 + r)^k} = M\left(\frac{1}{1 + r}\right) \sum_{k=0}^{n-1} \frac{1}{(1 + r)^k}$$

$$= M\left[\frac{1}{1 + r}\right]\left[\frac{1/(1 + r)^n - 1}{1/(1 + r) - 1}\right]$$

$$= M\left[\frac{1 - 1/(1 + r)^n}{r}\right],$$

$\rightarrow M = $ Monthly payment

$$= \frac{Pr}{1 - 1/(1 + r)^n}$$

$$= \frac{Pr}{1 - (1 + r)^{-n}},$$

which is identical to equation (6) when $n = 36$.

Some questions to explore, with suggestions of where to introduce them in the curriculum, follow.

1. Find the ending balance after 15 years of saving $100 a month at 8 percent annual interest compounded quarterly. (Algebra II: polynomials, summation of series, exponentiation)

2. A working person is paid every two weeks. She takes advantage of her credit union's automatic deposit plan and has managed to save $25 each pay period for the last six years. If the credit union pays dividends at the rate of 6 percent a year, compounded weekly, what is her present balance? (Algebra II: summation of series, exponentiation)

3. One way to explore noninteger powers would be to consider the following example: A certain bacterium population has a growth rate of 12 percent an hour. Assuming an initial population P_0, what is the population $P_{3.5}$ after 3.5 hours? (Algebra I and II: exponentiation)

4. If the rate of inflation is such that the price of an article doubles in ten years, what happens to the price in five years? What is the annual rate of inflation? (Algebra I and II: square roots and exponentiation)

5. A certain amount of money is deposited in a regular bank account with interest rate r for each compounding period. How long (how many compounding periods) does it take to double the initial investment? (Algebra II: powers and roots)

6. An investor is assured of a 10 percent monthly return on her investment. Given an initial investment of $5000 and assuming she withdraws $100 each month from the account to cover business expenses, how long would it take for her account to reach a balance of approximately $16 190? (Algebra II: polynomials, summation of series, exponentiation, logarithms)

7. Suppose interest is compounded n times a year, at an annual interest rate i, on an initial investment A. Show that the amount in the account at the end of the year is $A(1 + i/n)^n$. What happens when interest is allowed to be compounded continuously? ($n \rightarrow \infty$)? (Calculus: natural logarithm)

8. Suppose John buys a house and the mortgage payment is one-half of his present income. Assume that the dollar amount of the mortgage payment remains constant throughout the life of the loan while John's salary keeps pace with an annual inflation rate of 12 percent. What fraction of his income will John's mortgage payment represent in ten years? (Algebra I and II: exponentiation, ratio)

Answers to Questions

1. 60 quarters, investing $300 a quarter at a rate of interest of 2 percent a quarter:

   Amount = $300[(1.02)^{60} + (1.02)^{59} + \cdots + (1.02) + 1]$

   Amount $= \$300 \left[\dfrac{(1.02)^{61} - 1}{0.02} \right] = \$35\ 199.77.$

2. 1 year = 52 weeks.

   $\dfrac{0.06}{52}$ = weekly interest rate.

   Present balance
   $= 25(1 + 0.06/52)^{312} + 25(1 + 0.06/52)^{310} + \cdots + 25$

   $= 25 \displaystyle\sum_{k=0}^{156} [(1 + 0.06/52)^2]^k$

   $= 25 \left[\dfrac{(1 + 0.06/52)^{2(157)} - 1}{(1 + 0.06/52)^2 - 1} \right] = \$4724.30.$

3. After 1 hour, $P_1 = P_0 + 0.12P_0 = P_0(1 + 0.12)$
   $= 1.12P_0.$

   After 2 hours, $P_2 = P_1 + 0.12P_1 = (1.12)^2 P_0.$

   $\cdots$

   After 3.5 hours, $P_{3.5} = (1.12)^{3.5} P_0.$

4. If P = price of article now,
   $2P$ = price of article in ten years, and
   r = annual rate of inflation,
   then $P(1 + r)^{10} = 2P.$

   We want value of $(1 + r)^5$. So
   $$(1 + r)^5 = \sqrt{(1 + r)^{10}} = \sqrt{2}\,.$$

   In five years prices increase by a factor of $\sqrt{2}$. In one year prices increase by a factor of $2^{1/10}$ (about 7.1 percent a year).

5. If P = present value,
   A = initial investment,
   r = rate of interest for each time period, and
   n = number of time periods A is left in the bank,
   then $P = A(1 + r)^n.$
   We want $P = 2A = A(1 + r)^n$. So
   $$(1 + r)^n = 2 \text{ and } n = \dfrac{\ln 2}{\ln (1 + r)}\,.$$

6. After the 1st month, the amount in the account is
   $$5000(1.1) - 100;$$
   after the 2d month,
   $$[5000(1.1) - 100](1.1) - 100, \text{ or}$$
   $$5000(1.1)^2 - [100(1.1) + 100];$$
   after the 3d month,

   $\{[5000(1.1) - 100](1.1) - 100\}(1.1) - 100, \text{ or}$
   $$5000(1.1)^3 - [100(1.1)^2 + 100(1.1) + 100];$$
   and so on.

   After the nth month, the amount in the account is
   $$5000(1.1)^n - 100 \sum_{k=0}^{n-1} (1.1)^k.$$

   We are looking for the value of n such that
   $$16\ 190 = 5000(1.1)^n - 100 \sum_{k=0}^{n-1} (1.1)^k.$$

   Notice that
   $$\sum_{k=0}^{n-1} (1.1)^k = \dfrac{(1.1)^n - 1}{1.1 - 1}\,.$$

   So $16\ 190 = 5000(1.1)^n - 1000(1.1)^n + 1000$;
   $\quad (1.1)^n = 3.7975$;
   $\quad n = 14.$

7. The interest rate for each compounding period is i/n. The amount P in the account after one compounding period is $P = A (1 + i/n)$. After k compounding periods, $P = A (1 + i/n)^k$, and after n compounding periods (one year), $P = A (1 + i/n)^n$. When the number of compounding periods is allowed to increase without bounds, the amount in the account after one year is
   $$P = \lim_{n \to \infty} \left[A \left(1 + \dfrac{i}{n} \right)^n \right].$$

   Letting $k = n/i$, and using the properties of limits,
   $$P = \left[A \lim_{k \to \infty} \left(1 + \dfrac{1}{k} \right)^k \right]^i.$$

   Since
   $$\lim_{k \to \infty} \left(1 + \dfrac{1}{k} \right)^k = e,$$

   the base of the natural logrithm, it follows that
   $$P = Ae^i.$$

8. I_0 = present income.

   $\dfrac{I_0}{2}$ = amount of mortgage payment (constant).

   $I_{10} = I_0(1 + 0.12)^{10}.$

   Note that this is the future value of a present value I_0.

   The fraction of income represented by the mortgage payment in ten years is
   $$\dfrac{I_0/2}{I_{10}} = \dfrac{I_0/2}{I_0(1 + 0.12)^{10}} \approx 16.1\%.$$

When Less Means More

By KAY B. SOMERS

If you were offered a choice between having your salary raised $200 every six months or $1000 every year, which would you choose? Professor Hiram Bleeker (1983) posed a similar question as reported in the *Chronicle of Higher Education*. He stated that "many people would take the $1000 raise and so deprive themselves of the better deal." In a later issue of the *Chronicle* (1983), several letters to the editor indicated nonbelievers among the readers. We shall see that the answer depends on several factors.

To see how salary raises under each of the described schemes would be computed, we shall look only at the amount of the raise. Since the salary at the beginning of the period when raises begin does not affect the amount of the raise, we can restrict our attention to the amount of additional income resulting from the raise. Assuming salary raises of $200 every six months, we get the results shown in table 1. Notice that the accumulated income column lags by one time period because a raise produces additional income only in the time period after it has been granted. Also note that we are comparing a $1000 raise once a year with a $1000/5 = $200 raise twice a year. Assuming salary raises of $1000 every year, we get the results shown in table 2. After three years, the two schemes yield an equal amount of accumulated income.

The general case can be described as follows. Let $T(n; I, M)$ represent total accumulated income after n years in which a raise of R/I dollars M times a year has been granted, instead of an annual raise of R dollars. We assume that M and n are positive integers and that $I \geq 1$, but I is not necessarily an integer. Then

Kay Somers teaches mathematics at Moravian College, Bethlehem, PA 18018. She is especially interested in applications of mathematics, including operations research and numerical analysis.

$$T(n; I, M) = \sum_{i=1}^{Mn-1} \left(\frac{R}{I}\right)i$$
$$= \left(\frac{R}{I}\right)(1) + \left(\frac{R}{I}\right)(2)$$
$$+ \cdots + \left(\frac{R}{I}\right)(Mn - 1)$$
$$= \left(\frac{R}{I}\right)(1 + 2 + \cdots + Mn - 1);$$

$$(1) \qquad T(n; I, M) = \frac{RMn(Mn - 1)}{2I}.$$

(The index on the summation is $Mn - 1$ because Mn time periods are involved and the total accumulated income lags by one time period.)

We want to compare equation (1) with annual raises of R dollars, in which case $I = 1$ and $M = 1$.

$$T(n; 1, 1) = \sum_{i=1}^{n-1} Ri$$
$$= R(1 + 2 + \cdots + n - 1)$$
$$= \frac{Rn(n - 1)}{2}.$$

To see under what conditions smaller, more frequent raises would be at least as good, we want to determine the relationships among M, I, and n that make the following inequality true:

$$(2) \qquad T(n; I, M) \geq T(n; 1, 1)$$

Equation (2) is true if and only if all the following inequalities are true.

$$\frac{RMn(Mn - 1)}{2I} \geq \frac{Rn(n - 1)}{2}$$
$$M^2n - M \geq nI - I$$
$$M^2n - nI \geq M - I$$
$$(3) \qquad n(M^2 - I) \geq M - I$$

We need consider only the case where $M \leq I$, since if $M > I$, $M^2 > I$ and the inequality is obviously true: frequent raises

	TABLE 1	
y Years	Amount of Raise Granted after y Years	Amount of Accumulated Income after y Years
1/2	$ 200	
1	400	$ 200 = $(1000/5)(1)
3/2	600	600 = (1000/5)(1 + 2)
2	800	1200 = (1000/5)(1 + 2 + 3)
5/2	1000	2000 = (1000/5)(1 + 2 + 3 + 4)
3	1200	3000 = (1000/5)(1 + 2 + 3 + 4 + 5)
7/2	1400	4200 = (1000/5)(1 + 2 + 3 + 4 + 5 + 6)
4	1600	5600 = (1000/5)(1 + 2 + 3 + 4 + 5 + 6 + 7)

sum to more than the annual raise. For example, it is not difficult to decide whether to accept $300 raises four times a year, or $1000 annual raises, since in this case, $M = 4$ and $I = 10/3$ and therefore $M > I$.

Assuming $M \leq I$, we consider three cases.

Case 1. $M^2 - I > 0$. Since $M - I \leq 0$, inequality (3) holds for all n, and frequent raises are better for all n. The question of whether to accept $300 raises two times a year or an annual raise of $1000 should be decided in favor of the smaller, more frequent raises; you will be ahead from the start.

Case 2. $M^2 - I = 0$. For this case, inequality (3) is true:

$$T(n; I, M) > T(n; 1, 1)$$

if $M < I$, and

$$T(n; I, M) = T(n; 1, 1)$$

if $M = I$. Therefore, for $M \leq I$ and $M^2 - I = 0$,

$$T(n; I, M) \geq T(n; 1, 1)$$

for all n, indicating that frequent smaller raises are at least as good as annual raises for any n.

Case 3. $M^2 - I < 0$. Solving inequality (3) for n, we get

$$T(n; I, M) > T(n; 1, 1)$$

if

$$n < \frac{M - I}{M^2 - I}.$$

In this case, frequent raises are better initially. For

$$n > \frac{M - I}{M^2 - I},$$

larger annual raises yield greater total accumulated income. This case is illustrated in tables 1 and 2. In the tables, $I = 5$ and $M = 2$, so $M^2 - I = -1 < 0$. For $n < (M - I)/(M^2 - I) = 3$, the $200 raises twice a year are better, but after three years the larger annual raises will yield greater total accumulated income.

In summary, if $M^2 > I$, smaller, more numerous raises are better every year. If $M^2 < I$, more frequent raises may still be preferred if you plan to collect the raises fewer than $(M - I)/(M^2 - I)$ years.

REFERENCES

Bleeker, Hiram S. "'In' Box." *Chronicle of Higher Education* 26 (27 July 1983):15.

King, Raymond D., and Murray Frost. "Letters to the Editor." *Chronicle of Higher Education* 27 (14 September 1983):34–35. ◗

	TABLE 2	
y Years	Amount of Raise Granted after y Years	Amount of Accumulated Income after y Years
1	$1000	
2	2000	$1000
3	3000	3000
4	4000	6000

A QUALITY INEQUALITY

Good examples of how mathematics can be used in simple real-life situations. Teachers of secondary school mathematics can use the examples found here with their students.

By CLIFFORD W. SLOYER

**University of Delaware
Newark, Delaware**

THE inequality involving the arithmetic and geometric means is a powerful tool in dealing with applications of mathematics. Indeed, it is the cornerstone of a relatively new area of applied mathematics known as *geometric programming*. The purposes of this article are to discuss briefly this inequality and to demonstrate two "real world" applications that secondary teachers in in-service institutes have found interesting and useful. The mathematics used is directly accessible to secondary teachers and students.

We begin with the basic arithmetic mean–geometric mean inequality, which states that

$$(1) \qquad \frac{a + b}{2} \geq \sqrt{ab}$$

where $a, b \geq 0$. Moreover, equality holds in (1) if and only if $a = b$. This result can easily be proved by starting with the known inequality

$$(2) \qquad (a - b)^2 \geq 0.$$

Thus

$$a^2 - 2ab + b^2 \geq 0$$

or (adding $4ab$ to both sides)

$$a^2 + 2ab + b^2 \geq 4ab$$

or

$$\frac{(a + b)^2}{4} \geq ab.$$

Assuming $a, b \geq 0$, we arrive (by taking the square root of each side) at

$$(3) \qquad \frac{a + b}{2} \geq \sqrt{ab}.$$

Moreover, equality holds in (2), and hence in (3), if and only if $a = b$.

The basic arithmetic mean–geometric mean inequality, given by (1), generalizes to

$$(4) \qquad \frac{a_1 + a_2 + \cdots + a_n}{n} \geq \sqrt[n]{a_1 a_2 \cdots a_n}$$

where $a_i \geq 0$ for $i = 1, 2, \ldots, n$. Moreover, equality holds in (4) if and only if $a_i = a_j$ for each i and j. A proof of (4) can be found in Sloyer (1970) or Beckenbach and Bellman (1961), but such proofs are beyond the experience of many secondary students. The student, however, can be made aware that

$$\frac{a_1 + a_2 + a_3}{3} \geq \sqrt[3]{a_1 a_2 a_3}$$

and that equality holds if and only if $a_1 = a_2 = a_3$.

We now consider two applications of the arithmetic mean–geometric mean inequality.

Is Inventory Mandatory?

One frequently hears the expression "low costs through high output." A person who compares the price of a new house in a development to the price of a new custom-built house is aware of this idea. However, there are many business activities in which some costs increase as the manufactured output increases. For example, if large quantities of some product are manufactured and not sold immediately, there may be an inventory cost involving the cost of storage facilities, insurance, and so forth. Consider a steel fabricating company that has to supply 1,600 units of a certain item to a customer during the coming year. This item is unique in the sense that it is purchased only by this customer. Now, there are certain costs involved that do not depend on the number of items to be made: obtaining proper tools from storage, setting up the tools, test production of a few sample items, secretarial time, and so on. Let us suppose that those *setup costs* amount to $100. The cost of producing one unit (labor, material, electricity, repair of machines, etc.) is $3. In addition, there are inventory costs (cost of storage facilities, insurance, etc.) that are determined as follows:

Total inventory costs = $2 × (average
number of units in stock during year)

First, let us suppose that the manager decides to produce all 1,600 units immediately. We assume that these items are sold at a uniform rate during the year. Since the stock will be depleted at the end of the year, the average number of items held in stock during the year is 800. The total cost of this business activity is thus given by

Setup cost	Inventory cost	Production cost
$C = 100\ +$	$2(800)\ +$	$3(1,600)$

or

$$C = \$6,500.$$

Now suppose that the manager decides to produce 800 items immediately and another batch of 800 six months from now. He now has to pay for two *setups*. In addition, there is an average of 400 items in stock during the year. The total cost C of this business activity is now given by

$$C = 2(100) + 2(400) + 3(1,600)$$

or

$$C = \$5,800.$$

Observe that the total cost of the required production has decreased by running two batches rather than one. We might now consider (and possibly compute) what happens to the total cost if four batches of 400 are run, eight batches of 200 are run, five batches of 320 are run, and so on. The diagrams in figure 1 are a conceptual aid in considering the various production schedules that are available.

In particular, we are seeking to discover the process that will minimize the total cost and yet still produce the required number of items. The richness of mathematics, however, enables us to determine an optimal policy without making such numerous considerations. We shall assume that the same number of items is produced at each run. Moreover, we shall assume that the demand for these items remains constant so that the time between production runs is also constant.

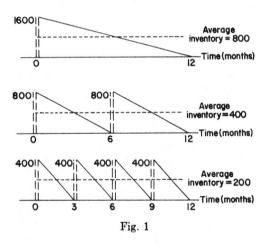

Fig. 1

Let x denote the number of items in the batch produced during each run. If N runs are made, then we want $Nx = 1,600$, and hence the number of runs is given by $1,600/x$. Thus, we have

Number of production runs
in year
$$= \frac{1,600}{x}$$

total setup costs
$$= 100\left(\frac{1,600}{x}\right)$$

average number of items
in stock $= \dfrac{x}{2}$

total inventory costs $= 2\left(\dfrac{x}{2}\right).$

The total cost involved, denoted C, is thus given by

$$C = 100\left(\frac{1{,}600}{x}\right) + 2\left(\frac{x}{2}\right) + 3(1{,}600)$$

or

$$C = \frac{160{,}000}{x} + x + 4{,}800.$$

The \$4,800 is a *fixed cost* over which we have no control. We thus look at

$$\frac{160{,}000}{x} + x.$$

Using the basic arithmetic mean–geometric mean inequality with $a = \dfrac{160{,}000}{x}$ and $b = x$, we have

$$\frac{\frac{160{,}000}{x} + x}{2} \geq \sqrt{160{,}000}$$

or

$$\frac{160{,}000}{x} + x \geq 800.$$

That is, the costs that we can control cannot be less than \$800. Moreover, in order to attain this minimal amount, we must have

$$\frac{160{,}000}{x} = x$$

or

$$160{,}000 = x^2$$

or

$$x = 400.$$

Thus, the *optimal procedure* is to produce 400 items in each run, which means a total of four runs a year, one every three months.

Getting the Most from the Post

The post office limits the size of rectangular boxes sent through the mail by stating that "length plus girth cannot exceed 100 inches." In certain areas this limit is 72 inches. (Recall that *girth* is the perimeter of a cross section.) Our problem is to determine the dimensions of the largest rectangular box (in terms of volume) that can be sent through the U.S. mails, assuming the 100-inch girth limit.

Let l, w, and h denote the length, width, and height, respectively, of a rectangular box (fig. 2).

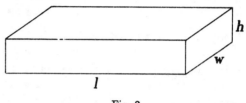

Fig. 2

The girth is $2w + 2h$; so the length plus girth is given by

$$l + 2w + 2h.$$

The volume V is given by

$$V = lwh.$$

Our problem is to find positive numbers l, w, and h, so that

$$l + 2w + 2h \leq 100$$

and $V = lwh$ is as large as possible.

It should be clear that if V is to be as large as possible, then we must have

$$l + 2w + 2h = 100.$$

Suppose $l + 2w + 2h = 90$. Then by increasing l by 10 inches, we have

$$l + 2w + 2h = 100,$$

and we have *increased* the volume.

Thus, we want to find positive numbers l, w, and h, so that

$$(1) \qquad l + 2w + 2h = 100$$

and $V = lwh$ is as large as possible. Using

the arithmetic mean–geometric mean inequality

$$\frac{a_1 + a_2 + a_3}{3} \geq \sqrt[3]{a_1 a_2 a_3} \, ,$$

we have

(2) $$\frac{l + 2w + 2h}{3} \geq \sqrt[3]{4lwh}$$

or

(3) $$\frac{100}{3} \geq \sqrt[3]{4V}$$

or

(4) $$\frac{1}{4}\left(\frac{100}{3}\right)^3 \geq V.$$

Thus it is impossible to construct a rectangular box within the specified limits that has a volume *greater* than $\frac{1}{4}\left(\frac{100}{3}\right)^3$.

Moreover, in order to obtain this *optimal* value, we must have equality in (4) and hence equality in (2), which implies

$$l = 2w = 2h.$$

Substituting into (1), we get

$$3l = 100$$

or

$$l = \frac{100}{3} \, ;$$

so the dimensions of our "largest rectangular box" are given by

length $= \dfrac{100}{3}$ in.

width $= \dfrac{50}{3}$ in.

height $= \dfrac{50}{3}$ in.

REFERENCES

Beckenbach, E., and R. Bellman. *An Introduction to Inequalities*. New York: Random House, 1961.

Sloyer, C. W. *Algebra and Its Applications*. Reading, Mass.: Addison-Wesley Publishing Co., 1970.

CALCULATOR LESSONS INVOLVING POPULATION, INFLATION, AND ENERGY

**By ERNEST WOODWARD
and THOMAS HAMEL**
Austin Peay State University
Clarksville, TN 37040

One of the joys of studying mathematics comes from the surprising results that are often obtained. An example of such a situation is the Rule of 72. This rule states that if money is invested at r percent compounded annually, the amount will double in approximately $72/r$ years. On the other hand, if the interest is compounded semiannually, the doubling time is approximately $70/r$ years; and if the interest is compounded instantaneously, then the doubling time is approximately $69.3/r$ years. In the interesting article "The Rule of 72," which appeared in the November 1966 issue of the *Mathematics Teacher*, Brown argues that these results are appropriate for "small" r. His argument, which makes use of logarithms, is not reproduced here.

The purposes of this article are (1) to show how a hand-held calculator can be used to help students discover the Rule of 72 and (2) to indicate how the Rule of 72 can be used to investigate problems involving population, inflation, and energy reserves. The lessons described in this paper are lessons that each author has used individually with both college and secondary students.

Lesson 1

The first lesson is introduced with the story about the king and the inventor of the chess game. The king wishes to reward the inventor, who is also a mathematician, and asks how he can do this. The mathematician-inventor asks for the wheat obtained by putting one kernel of wheat on the first square of the chessboard, two kernels on the second square, four on the third square, eight on the fourth square, and so on for the entire sixty-four squares of the board.

The observation is made that the total amount of wheat on the chessboard is

$$1 + 2 + 2^2 + 2^3 + \cdots + 2^{63}$$

grains, and

$$1 + 2 = 3 = 2^2 - 1,$$
$$1 + 2 + 2^2 = 7 = 2^3 - 1,$$
$$1 + 2 + 2^2 + 2^3 = 15 = 2^4 - 1,$$
$$1 + 2 + 2^2 + 2^3 + 2^4 = 31 = 2^5 - 1,$$
$$\cdots$$

$$1 + 2 + 2^2 + \cdots + 2^{n-1} = 2^n - 1,$$
$$\cdots$$

and thus,

$$1 + 2 + 2^2 + 2^3 + \cdots + 2^{63} = 2^{64} - 1.$$

The statement is made that 2^{64} kernels of wheat is estimated to be approximately 500 times the total present yearly world wheat production (Bartlett 1976).

The purpose of introducing this story is to emphasize that in the case of a continuous doubling circumstance, the numbers get very large very quickly. Some students are interested in determining how large a number 2^{64} is. For those students having calculators with an x^2 function, the calculation of

$$2^{64} \doteq 1.8447 \times 10^{19}$$

is simple. Students are impressed by the rapid change in the display from 2^{16} to 2^{32} to 2^{64}.

Next, the formula for compound interest with interest compounded yearly is developed. This formula is

$$A_n = p\left(1 + \frac{r}{100}\right)^n,$$

where A_n represents the total amount at the end of n years, p represents the principle, and r percent represents the rate. This result is derived in a typical textbook procedure.

Next, inflation is discussed. The point is made that a constant annual inflation rate is an application of compound interest. Students are asked what they think the cost of a new bicycle would be in the year 2146, assuming it now costs $100 and that there will be a 6 percent annual inflation rate. (Most students predict less than $500, whereas the actual amount is over $1 500 000.)

No attempt is made to find the solution to the problem of the cost of the bicycle in the standard way, that is, an evaluation of $A_{168} = 100(1.06)^{168}$. Such an evaluation would involve the use of logarithms (which some students have not studied) or the use of the exponential function y^x (which some calculators do not have); but these approaches would detract from a strategy that is perhaps more important than the numerical result.

The preferred solution to the bicycle problem, and other similar problems, necessitates introducing the concept of doubling time, that is, the number of years it will take a certain amount of money to double in value when invested at a compound yearly interest rate of r percent. Students are easily convinced that the original amount of money is arbitrary; therefore $1 is used. To find the doubling time, it is necessary to find n such that

$$A_n = 1\left(1 + \frac{r}{100}\right)^n = \left(1 + \frac{r}{100}\right)^n \doteq 2.$$

Students then calculate n's for several given possible r's. For example, if $r = 6$ percent, the following values are obtained with the calculator showing that $n = 12$ when $r = 6$ percent.

$$(1.06)^1 \doteq 1.06$$
$$(1.06)^2 \doteq 1.12$$
$$(1.06)^3 \doteq 1.19$$
$$\cdots$$

$$(1.06)^{11} \doteq 1.90$$
$$(1.06)^{12} \doteq 2.01$$

These data are recorded in table 1. Circled numerals are determined by the use of the calculator and are integral approximations for n. Next, the students are requested to investigate this table. Some students will indicate that in each case the product of the percentage and the doubling time is 72. This conjecture is checked by the class. The question posed is How could we calculate the doubling time, given the rate? Students typically respond that the doubling time is $72/r$.

TABLE 1

r	Doubling Time in Years (Approximately)
3	㉔
4	⑱
6	⑫
8	⑨
9	⑧
12	⑥
18	④
24	③

Returning to the topic of inflation, students are asked to help complete table 2. The entries in the first two columns are given and all others are completed (circled numerals), assuming a 6 percent annual inflation rate. For this example, the doubling period is 12 years (72/6). The entries in the third column are double the corresponding entries in the second column, since one doubling period will have elapsed. The entries in the fourth and fifth columns are derived similarly. The date for the last column, 2146, is 132 years (11 doubling periods) after the date for the previous column. Hence, the entries in the last column are found by multiplying the corresponding entries in the previous column by 2^{11}.

The world population in 1975 was approximately 4 000 000 000, or 4×10^9, and the annual population increase has been fairly constant at about 2 percent (1976 Census, p. 866). Table 3 is then completed, assuming the rate of increase in population will remain at 2 percent. Observe that the

TABLE 2
Costs at a 6 Percent Annual Inflation Rate

Item	1978 Cost	1990 Cost	2002 Cost	2014 Cost	2146 Cost
Soft drink	25¢	50¢	$1	$2	$4096
Movie ticket	$3	$6	$12	$24	$49 152
Bicycle	$100	$200	$400	$800	$1 638 400
Compact automobile	$4000	$8000	$16 000	$32 000	$65 536 000
Modest house	$30 000	$60 000	$120 000	$240 000	$491 520 000

doubling time is 36 years. As before, the circled numerals are calculated by the class. Next, the observation is made that the total land area (including inland lakes and rivers) is approximately 1.36×10^{14} square meters (1976 Census, p. 867). Assuming a constant 2 percent population growth, there would be approximately one person for each square meter in the year 2515. A calculator is not needed to complete this table but it does make the computation easier.

A rather complete class development of this lesson takes approximately one hour. At times, only portions of the previous two tables are completed in class, and the students are asked to complete these tables as an out-of-class assignment. (In one instance this lesson was used alone, without the next lesson, when only one hour of class time was available.)

The first class is ended by presenting the students with the following problem:

Many years ago a fictitious king had 2000 barrels of wine in his cellar. Given that his court consumed 20 barrels of wine last year, and past increases in consumption would indicate a 12% annual increase, how long will the king's wine supply last?

The students are asked to guess at a solution and then challenged to solve the prob-

lem by whatever means they can devise. Most students guess many years more than the actual answer of approximately 22 years. Sometimes students are able to solve the problem correctly prior to the next class

TABLE 3
World Population Assuming 2 Percent Growth Rate

Year	Predicted World Population
1975	4×10^9
2011	8×10^9
2047	1.6×10^{10}
2083	3.2×10^{10}
2119	6.4×10^{10}
2155	1.28×10^{11}
2191	2.56×10^{11}
2515	1.31×10^{14}

meeting but only after considerable effort. The difficulty they have solving the problem generates considerable interest in the methods that are developed in the second lesson.

Lesson 2

The second lesson is involved with the investigation of problems concerning how long energy reserves (coal and petroleum) would last, assuming a constant annual percentage increase in usage. These problems (e.g., the wine problem) are much more complex than the problem of determining how much energy reserves would be used in a given year (e.g., the inflation and population problems). In order to solve these more difficult problems easily, let x be the initial amount of fuel used, x_i the amount of fuel used in the ith year after the initial year, and $r = 6$. Next, the data in table 4 are presented. Of particular interest is the fact that

$$\sum_{i=13}^{24} x_i \doteq 2 \sum_{i=1}^{12} x_i$$

and

$$\sum_{i=25}^{36} x_i \doteq 2 \sum_{i=13}^{24} x_i \doteq 4 \sum_{i=1}^{12} x_i.$$

These data are determined by use of a hand-held calculator. For example, $x_6 = (1.06)^6 x$. Many students recognize that the numbers 1.06, 1.1236, 1.1910, and so on are the same numbers that were obtained in the completion of the doubling-time table of the first lesson, using $r = 6$.

The observation is made that for $1 \le i \le 12$,

$$x_{i+24} \doteq 2x_{i+12} \doteq 4x_i.$$

This result is to be expected since the doubling period is 12 years when $r = 6$. Of particular significance is the fact that $\sum_{i=1}^{12} x_i$ is the amount of fuel used in the first doubling period, that $\sum_{i=13}^{24} x_i$ is the amount of fuel used in the second doubling period, and that $\sum_{i=25}^{36} x_i$ is the amount of fuel used in the third doubling period. Letting $\sum_{i=1}^{12} x_i = y$, the amount of fuel used in the second doubling period is approximately $2y$, the amount of fuel used in the third doubling period is approximately $4y$, the amount of fuel used in the fourth doubling period is approximately $8y$, and the amount of fuel used in the nth doubling period is approximately $2^{n-1}y$. These conclusions suggest that it is important to develop a technique for finding y without using the rather tedious computation presented above.

A point is made that $\sum_{i=1}^{12} x_i$ is the sum of the terms of a geometric progression and that it is easier to approximate this sum by using an appropriate arithmetic series. If $a_1 = x$, $a_{12} = 2x$, and $d = 1/11(x)$, then

TABLE 4

$x_1 \doteq 1.06x$	$x_{13} \doteq 2.1329x \doteq 2x_1$	$x_{25} \doteq 4.2919x \doteq 2x_{13} \doteq 4x_1$
$x_2 \doteq 1.1236x$	$x_{14} \doteq 2.2609x \doteq 2x_2$	$x_{26} \doteq 4.5494x \doteq 2x_{14} \doteq 4x_2$
$x_3 \doteq 1.1910x$	$x_{15} \doteq 2.3966x \doteq 2x_3$	$x_{27} \doteq 4.8223x \doteq 2x_{15} \doteq 4x_3$
$x_4 \doteq 1.2625x$	$x_{16} \doteq 2.5404x \doteq 2x_4$	$x_{28} \doteq 5.1117x \doteq 2x_{16} \doteq 4x_4$
$x_5 \doteq 1.3382x$	$x_{17} \doteq 2.6928x \doteq 2x_5$	$x_{29} \doteq 5.4184x \doteq 2x_{17} \doteq 4x_5$
$x_6 \doteq 1.4185x$	$x_{18} \doteq 2.8543x \doteq 2x_6$	$x_{30} \doteq 5.7435x \doteq 2x_{18} \doteq 4x_6$
$x_7 \doteq 1.5036x$	$x_{19} \doteq 3.0256x \doteq 2x_7$	$x_{31} \doteq 6.0881x \doteq 2x_{19} \doteq 4x_7$
$x_8 \doteq 1.5938x$	$x_{20} \doteq 3.2071x \doteq 2x_8$	$x_{32} \doteq 6.4534x \doteq 2x_{20} \doteq 4x_8$
$x_9 \doteq 1.6895x$	$x_{21} \doteq 3.3996x \doteq 2x_9$	$x_{33} \doteq 6.8406x \doteq 2x_{21} \doteq 4x_9$
$x_{10} \doteq 1.7908x$	$x_{22} \doteq 3.6035x \doteq 2x_{10}$	$x_{34} \doteq 7.2510x \doteq 2x_{22} \doteq 4x_{10}$
$x_{11} \doteq 1.8983x$	$x_{23} \doteq 3.8197x \doteq 2x_{11}$	$x_{35} \doteq 7.6861x \doteq 2x_{23} \doteq 4x_{11}$
$x_{12} \doteq 2.0121x$	$x_{24} \doteq 4.0489x \doteq 2x_{12}$	$x_{36} \doteq 8.1473x \doteq 2x_{24} \doteq 4x_{12}$
$\sum_{i=1}^{12} x_i = 17.8819x$	$\sum_{i=13}^{24} x_i = 35.9832x$	$\sum_{i=25}^{36} x_i = 72.4042x$

$a_1 = 1.00x$

$a_2 = 1.\overline{09}x$

$a_3 = 1.\overline{18}x$

$a_4 = 1.\overline{27}x$

$a_5 = 1.\overline{36}x$

$a_6 = 1.\overline{45}x$

$a_7 = 1.\overline{54}x$

$a_8 = 1.\overline{63}x$

$a_9 = 1.\overline{72}x$

$a_{10} = 1.\overline{81}x$

$a_{11} = 1.\overline{90}x$

$a_{12} = 2.00x$

These values are compared with the corresponding values of x_1 through x_{12}.

$$\sum_{i=1}^{12} a_i = \frac{x + 2x}{2}(12) = \frac{3}{2}x \cdot 12 = 18x.$$

Since $\sum_{i=1}^{12} x_i = 17.8819x$ and $\sum_{i=1}^{12} a_i = 18x$, using $\sum_{i=1}^{12} a_i$ in place of $\sum_{i=1}^{12} x_i$ results in an error of less than 1 percent,

$$\frac{.1181x}{17.8819x}.$$

The important generalization is made that $y \doteq 3/2(xm)$, where m is the length of the doubling period.

Purists are probably shocked that an arithmetic series is used to approximate a geometric series on the basis of a single example, but students are willing and able to accept this obvious impreciseness for the sake of convenience. Also, estimates of available energy reserves are questionable, at best, as a result of ecology constraints, prices of a given resource, and technological advancements. As long as the computed results are accepted for the rough estimates they are, the authors feel justified in using reasonable mathematical approximations.

The lesson is continued by

letting A be the amount of fuel available (estimated reserves) and

letting n be the number of doubling periods the fuel will last.

The contention is that

$$A = y + 2y + 4y + 8y + \cdots + 2^{n-1}y$$
$$= y(1 + 2 + 4 + 8 + \cdots + 2^{n-1})$$
$$= y(2^n - 1).$$

$$\frac{A}{y} = 2^n - 1 \quad \text{and}$$

$$2^n = \frac{A}{y} + 1.$$

In 1977 the world petroleum reserves were estimated at about 6.46×10^{11} barrels, and about 2.17×10^{10} barrels were consumed that year (*Energy Statistics* 1978). Jointly, table 5 is completed (circled numerals) using the information given in the first three columns.

The only column in table 5 that is difficult to complete is the next-to-last column giving values of n for which $2^n = A/y + 1$. Some students have studied logarithms previously and are able to quickly recall that the solution is given by

$$n = \frac{\log\left(\dfrac{A}{y} + 1\right)}{\log 2}.$$

For those students unable or not wanting to use logarithms, the graph of $f(n) = 2^n$ (fig. 1) is used. To make sure that the students recall what the graph of $f(n) = 2^n$ looks like, a few of the points are plotted before placing a transparency of the graph on the overhead projector. From the value of $A/y + 1$ on the $f(n)$ axis, students are directed to go horizontally to the graph of the function, then down vertically to find the value of n such that $f(n) = A/y + 1$. For example, if $A/y + 1 = 1.55$ then $n \doteq 0.63$. The values of n in the table are those found by using logarithms; therefore, use of the graph may result in values of n being slightly different (but still within 0.1) from those listed in the table. Errors caused by the impreciseness of the graph rarely have a significant effect on the value of mn.

The problem of coal resources is studied next. In 1974 it was estimated that the U.S. coal reserves were about 4.34×10^{11} tons (*Coal Resources of the United States* 1974), and approximately 5.58×10^8 tons were consumed in 1975 (*Monthly Energy Review* 1978). Table 6 is completed by the students as a group.

Recent annual increases in usages have usually been under 5 percent; however, it appears this figure may increase to 10 per-

TABLE 5

Estimated Petroleum Reserves	Annual Use Last Year	Rate of Increase	Doubling Time	Amount Used in First Doubling Period		No. of Doubling Periods	No. of Yrs. Fuel Will Last
A	x	r	$m = \dfrac{72}{r}$	$y = \dfrac{3}{2}(x)(m)$	$\dfrac{A}{y} + 1$	n^*	mn
6.46×10^{11}	2.17×10^{10}	0	**	**	**	**	30
6.46×10^{11}	2.17×10^{10}	2	36	1.17×10^{12}	1.55	0.63	23
6.46×10^{11}	2.17×10^{10}	4	18	5.86×10^{11}	2.10	1.07	19
6.46×10^{11}	2.17×10^{10}	6	12	3.91×10^{11}	2.65	1.41	17
6.46×10^{11}	2.17×10^{10}	9	8	2.60×10^{11}	3.48	1.80	14
6.46×10^{11}	2.17×10^{10}	12	6	1.95×10^{11}	4.31	2.11	13

* Where $2^n = \dfrac{A}{y} + 1$

** Does not apply

cent or above because of the shortage of petroleum.

The last few minutes of the second lesson are spent discussing some of the results obtained and the implications of those results. In particular,

1. if inflation increases at the present rate, the money system will probably need to be replaced by another one prior to the year 2100;

2. famine, war, disease, and so on will not allow population to get to the level projected for 2515; and

3. as reserves of fuel become depleted, the fuel becomes harder to get, thus driving up prices and decreasing usage.

(The students were delightfully perceptive, and a couple of their comments stand out. One student who had solved the wine problem, after considerable effort, said of the procedure developed in class for solving such problems, "Boy, it's a lot easier that way." In a discussion about how inaccurate the estimate of reserves might be, the students deduced that even if there is twice as much of a resource available as the amount estimated, the fuel will be depleted after only one more doubling period. After considering this dilemma for a few seconds, another student said, "Changing the percent (rate of increase) is the only solution." That statement sounds a lot like the message energy experts have been giving.)

The second lesson is closed with a hypothetical example Albert Bartlett used in a talk the authors heard him give. In his example, there is bacteria in a bottle and this bacteria doubles in amount each minute and the bottle is large enough to last one hour. If this situation originates at 11:00 o'clock, then at

11:01 lots of room;

11:02 still lots of room;

. . .

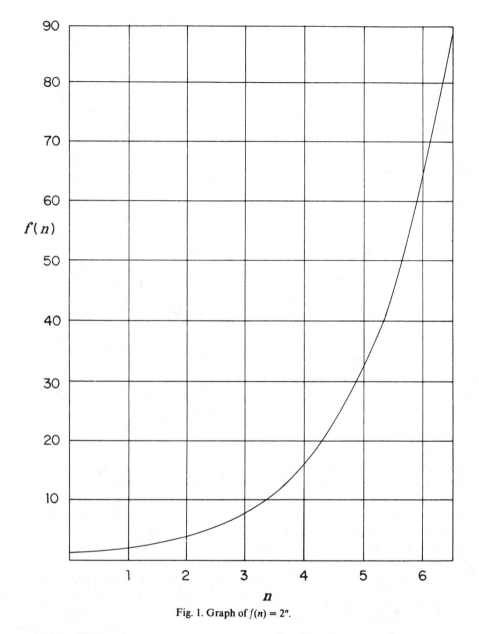

Fig. 1. Graph of $f(n) = 2^n$.

11:59 still lots of room
(only half full);

12:00 full.

Bartlett said that right now in the inflation, population, and fuel situation, it is 11:59.

Evaluations and Conclusions

As indicated earlier, the authors used these lessons with a variety of students (both college students and high school students) and found that the lessons were completed in about two hours. Portions of the tables could be completed in out-of-class assignments, thus cutting down on class time. For the most part, students who were capable of understanding compound interest seemed capable of understanding the lessons. Students did react favorably to the problems studied.

These lessons are recommended in that they

1. concern interesting and vital problems,

TABLE 6

Estimated Coal Reserves A	Annual Use Last Year x	Rate of Increase r	Doubling Time $m = \frac{72}{r}$	Amount Used in First Doubling Period $y = \frac{3}{2}(x)(m)$	$\frac{A}{y} + 1$	No. of Doubling Periods $n*$	No. of Yrs. Fuel Will Last mn
4.34×10^{11}	5.58×10^8	0	**	**	**	**	778
4.34×10^{11}	5.58×10^8	2	36	3.01×10^{10}	15.4	3.94	142
4.34×10^{11}	5.58×10^8	4	18	1.51×10^{10}	29.7	4.89	88
4.34×10^{11}	5.58×10^8	6	12	1.00×10^{10}	44.4	5.47	66
4.34×10^{11}	5.58×10^8	9	8	6.70×10^9	65.8	6.04	48
4.34×10^{11}	5.58×10^8	12	6	5.02×10^9	87.5	6.45	39

* Where $2^n = \frac{A}{y} + 1$

** Does not apply

2. relate mathematics to evaluation of social and scientific problems, and

3. give an example of a situation where use of a hand-held calculator makes the interpretation easier.

The authors suggest the possibility of investigation of similar problems involving the availability and use of other natural resources, such as aluminum and copper. Teachers could give students data on estimated resources and current usage patterns or ask students to find the information in the library.

REFERENCES

Brown, Richard G. "The Rule of 72." *Mathematics Teacher* 60 (November 1966):638–39.

Bartlett, Albert. "The Exponential Function, Part I." *Physics Teacher* 64 (October 1976):393–401.

Department of Energy. *Monthly Energy Review* (November 1978).

Geological Survey Bulletin 1412. *Coal Resources of the United States.* January 1, 1974, p. 33.

Institute of Gas Technology. *Energy Statistics* vol. 1, no. 4. Fourth Quarter 1978, p. 45.

U.S. Bureau of the Census. *Statistical Abstract of the United States: 1976*, 97th ed. (Washington, D.C. 1976): pp. 866–67.

RELATED READINGS

Dunn, Samuel L., and Lawrence W. Wright. "Models of the U.S. Economy." *Mathematics Teacher* 70 (January 1977):102–10.

Dunn, Samuel L., Ruth Chamberlain, Patricia Ashby, and Kenneth Christensen. "People, People, People." *Mathematics Teacher* 71 (April 1978):283–91.

Vest, Floyd. "Secondary School Mathematics from the EPA Gas Mileage Guide." *Mathematics Teacher* 72 (January 1979):10–14.

Wagner, Clifford H. "Determining Fuel Consumption—an Exercise in Applied Mathematics." *Mathematics Teacher* 72 (February 1979):134–36.

Weyland, Jack A., and David W. Ballew. "A Relevant Calculus Problem: Estimation of U.S. Oil Reserves." *Mathematics Teacher* 69 (February 1976):125–28.

The authors are indebted to Mrs. Gene Morgan for her assistance in the preparation of this manuscript.

MODELS OF THE U.S. ECONOMY

By SAMUEL L. DUNN
and LAWRENCE W. WRIGHT

Seattle Pacific College
Seattle, WA 98119

THE field of economics provides many opportunities for applying mathematics. The quantification of economics that has occurred in the last thirty years has made it necessary that economists be trained in the uses of higher mathematics. Algebra, geometry, calculus, probability theory and statistics, higher analysis, linear algebra, and computer science are some of the tools being used in contemporary approaches to economics.

Many of the applications of mathematics and computer science to economics are accessible to secondary school mathematics students. Using examples from economics is one way to convey concepts in mathematics and to make the subject more relevant. The purpose of this article is to suggest some ways that economists and applied mathematicians construct and use models as they study the economy of the United States. Each of the models considered will be described, and the appropriate equations will be developed. A computer program in BASIC designed to test the assumptions is included for each model considered. The testing of assumptions will be done by simulating the appropriate parts of the economy by means of projections into the future. Then the results will be analyzed from the point of view of economics or mathematics. The article concludes with models for further investigation. It is our hope that teachers will become familiar with the language surrounding the concept of a model and will use the language and ideas in the classroom.

The writers are indebted to Professor William Dorn, University of Denver, and his AAAS class in mathematical modeling for stimulating many of the ideas presented in this paper.

One of the major failures of teaching at the secondary and undergraduate college level has been the failure to show students how real-life phenomena are translated into mathematical formulations; much of the teaching effort has been spent in showing them how to proceed once the problem has been set in mathematical terms. Somehow the exercise doesn't come alive because most instruction begins with the mathematics and not the real phenomenon. Fortunately, this situation is gradually changing, partially because of the demand from students for more relevance in their mathematics courses and partially because of the increased attention being given to the modeling process.

It is also our hope that teachers will become more familiar with applications of mathematics outside the physical sciences. It should be pointed out that some people use a great deal of mathematics in the biological, social, and behavioral sciences, whereas others act as if mathematics doesn't exist. Fortunately, some of the applications from these fields are now finding their way into textbooks. We hope that teachers will make a serious attempt to place these applications before their students in order to show the far-ranging usefulness of mathematics in areas other than the "hard" sciences. The reader is referred to the Bibliography for titles of books and articles containing applications of mathematics outside the physical sciences.

Mathematical Models

A general discussion of the concept of *model* is in order. In general, we may define a model of a phenomenon as a *verbal, physical, or mathematical construct that illustrates, embodies, or can be used to analyze one or more aspects of the phenomenon. Mathematical modeling is the process of building a mathematical model from a phenomenon, solving the model, and applying the solution(s) to the phenomenon.* The process is illustrated in figure 1. "Solve" and "apply" must be understood to include the possibility of using the model for simulation of the phenomenon. The modeling process must start with the phenomenon and end with the phenomenon; the cycle must be complete.

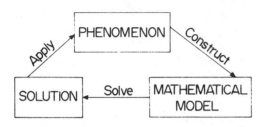

Fig. 1. The mathematical modeling process

One of the first questions to raise about a given model is whether it provides the desired information about the phenomenon under study. In addition, there are at least three tests for goodness of a model, one or more of which may be helpful in determining quality. First, one should test the assumptions that have led to the model. Second, one should determine whether the model has a mathematical solution. Third, one may be able to test the solution(s) against known occurrences of the phenomenon or against experimental evidence to determine whether the solution is describing or predicting those aspects of the phenomenon that are under discussion. If possible, one would want to test a model against all three conditions.

A Brief Economics Lesson

Determining the material well-being of a society—particularly a large one like ours—is a difficult task. Until the late 1920s no measures existed to give us an idea of whether the U.S. economy was expanding, contracting, or remaining relatively constant. An American economist, Simon Kuznets, developed the idea that the best way to determine the economic success or failure of a society was to measure the total amount of *new* goods and services pro-

duced during a given period. The term attached to the amount of new goods and services produced in a given year is *gross national product* (GNP).

Since goods are not normally produced unless buyers are anticipated for them, Kuznets analyzed the economy in terms of who bought (or retained) the new goods. If purchases of any particular product group declined, the sales and income of the sellers (producers) also dropped. (The careful reader will realize that this last statement is a truism; stated in mathematical terms, it would be an identity statement.)

The major buying groups in American society are (1) individual *consumers* (buying food, clothing, movies, cars, housing, etc.); (2) the various units of *government*—local, state, and federal (buying educational services, roads, missiles, etc.); (3) individual *businesses* and corporations (buying new manufacturing equipment, holding—"buying"—some of their own new goods as inventory, etc.); and (4) *foreign purchasers* of American goods. It is important to realize that since Americans buy foreign-made products, we balance the foreign purchase of American goods (exports) against the American purchases of foreign goods (imports) to get what the economists call *net exports.* Purchases of goods and services by business is technically known as *investment.* Note that this use of the word *investment* is not the common meaning of the word.

The sum total of the purchases of these four groups equals exactly the amount of new goods produced each year. How is that always true? Because the new goods that were not purchased by consumers, government, business, and foreign interests were held (or "bought") by the businesses that produced them. Business might not intend those "purchases," but it absorbs the surplus production in the form of inventory buildups.

In summary, then, the major statistics used to analyze the U.S. economy are those involving the gross national product (GNP) and its major components: government spending, domestic consumption, investment, and net exports. The variable names used for them here are as follows:

Y_n GNP of year n
C_n purchases by individual consumers in year n
I_n purchases by businesses in year n, that is, investment in year n
G_n purchases by government in year n
E_n net exports in year n

The U.S. Department of Commerce is the agency of the federal government that is responsible for collecting and analyzing the data that lead to the GNP statistics. The figures are published monthly in the *Survey of Current Business* and other government publications. The figures also appear in almanacs, newspapers, and magazines.

The figures for the GNP and its components for the years 1960–75 are given in table 1. The dollar information in the table and throughout this article will be in terms of *current* dollars rather than *constant value* dollars. Thus, for example, the GNP in 1969 was $935.5 billion as measured in 1969 dollars, and the GNP in 1970 was $982.4 billion as measured in 1970 dollars. On the surface it appears that the GNP of the United States grew by $46.9 billion from 1969 to 1970. However, not all that growth was real growth. Part of the $46.9 billion "increase" is attributable to the inflation that occurred in 1969 and 1970. A dollar in 1970 would purchase less than a dollar in 1969. One must be careful, then, to distinguish the real advance in the economy from the apparent advance as indicated by the figures in the table.

Using current dollars rather than constant value dollars does not seriously hinder applications of the results of the models considered below. It is a straightforward task to convert current dollar information to constant dollar information; all one needs is the actual or predicted inflation rates of the various years in question.

We are now ready to move to a consideration of the models.

Model 1. Exponential projections of the GNP

As we study the data given in table 1, we observe that the GNP went up at a fairly steady rate from year to year during the period 1960–75. For example, the GNP grew $17.3 billion from 1960 to 1961, $40.5 billion from 1961 to 1962, $30.9 billion from 1962 to 1963, and so on. This makes us wonder if there is some average rate of growth that describes the behavior of the GNP. If we could establish such a rate, we might be able to get a fairly accurate projection of what the GNP would be like in 1980. With these observations and questions we come to the assumption of model 1.

TABLE 1
Gross National Product Information*

Year	GNP	C Individual Consumption	I Investment by Business	G Government Spending	E Net Exports
1960	506.0	324.9	76.4	100.3	4.4
1961	523.3	335.0	74.3	108.2	5.8
1962	563.8	355.2	85.2	118.0	5.4
1963	594.7	374.6	90.2	123.7	6.3
1964	635.7	400.4	96.6	129.8	8.9
1965	688.1	430.2	112.0	138.4	7.6
1966	753.0	464.8	124.5	158.7	5.1
1967	796.3	490.4	120.8	180.2	4.9
1968	868.5	535.9	131.5	198.7	2.3
1969	935.5	579.7	146.2	207.9	1.8
1970	982.4	618.8	140.8	218.9	3.9
1971	1063.4	668.2	160.0	233.7	1.6
1972	1171.1	733.0	188.3	253.1	−3.3
1973	1306.3	808.5	220.5	269.9	7.4
1974	1406.9	885.9	212.2	301.1	7.7
1975**	1498.8	963.8	182.6	331.2	21.2

* Dollar information in billions of current dollars. Data taken from (U.S. Department of Labor, 1976, p. 359).
** Preliminary figures.

ASSUMPTION. *The GNP of a given year is a fixed ratio of the previous year's GNP.*

This assumption translates into the equation

$$(1) \qquad Y_n = g \, Y_{n-1},$$

where g is the fixed ratio (called the growth coefficient) mentioned in the assumption. Using the data of table 1, we can determine that the GNP of 1961 was 1.034 times the GNP of 1960. The GNP of 1962 was 1.077 times the GNP of 1961, and so on. For the period 1960–75 it can be shown that the average of the growth coefficient numbers 1.034, 1.077, . . . is 1.075. Using this average, we see that equation (1) becomes, then,

$$(2) \qquad Y_n = 1.075 \, Y_{n-1},$$

and this equation is our first model. It can be shown by induction that the Y values satisfy the relationship

$$(3) \qquad Y_k = 1.075^k Y_0,$$

where Y_0 is the GNP of the initial year considered and Y_k is the projected GNP k years after the initial year.

Equation (3) can be used to provide information about the phenomenon under study, namely, the GNP of the United States. For example, if we start with the initial value of $Y_0 = \$1498.8$ billion for the year 1975, equation (3) gives the GNPs of 1980 and 1985 as $2152 billion and $3089 billion, respectively.

A BASIC program that gives the GNP starting with year N for a period of K years is given in figure 2. Notice that line 100 of the program actually uses the model equation (2) rather than the relationship (3).

Letting $G = 1.075$, $N = 1960$, $K = 20$, and $Y = 506.0$ results in the output in figure 3. (The output has been rearranged for publication purposes.)

Note that the GNP figures provided by the model are fairly close to the actual GNP figures of table 1 at the beginning and end of the period 1960–75 but vary from them considerably during the middle of the period. This is to be expected, since the

```
10   INPUT "GNP GROWTH COEFF.";G
20   INPUT "BEGINNING YEAR";N
30   INPUT "NO. YRS. PROJECTED";K
40   INPUT "GNP OF BEGIN. YR.";Y
50   PRINT
60   PRINT "YEAR","GNP"
70   PRINT
80   PRINT N,Y
90   FOR I = 1 TO K
100  LET Y = G*Y
110  PRINT N + I, Y
120  NEXT I
130  END
```

Fig. 2. Program for computing the GNP from year N for a period of K years (model 1)

```
GROWTH COEFFICIENT FOR GNP?  1.075
BEGINNING YEAR?  1960
NUMBERS OF YEARS TO BE PROJECTED?  20
GNP OF BEGINNING YEAR?  506.0
```

YEAR	GNP	YEAR	GNP
1960	506	1971	1121.1
1961	543.95	1972	1205.18
1962	584.746	1973	1295.57
1963	628.602	1974	1392.74
1964	675.747	1975	1497.19
1965	726.428	1976	1609.48
1966	780.911	1977	1730.19
1967	839.479	1978	1859.96
1968	902.44	1979	1999.45
1969	970.123	1980	2149.41
1970	1042.88		

Fig. 3. Output from the program in figure 2

growth coefficient 1.075 was obtained using figures for the period 1960–75. As a matter of fact, the GNP grew less than 7.5 percent a year during the early part of the period 1960–75 but grew more than 7.5 percent a year during the last part of that period.

When the same N, Y, and K are used in the program, it is interesting to students to see the different GNP numbers that result when the growth coefficient g of equation (1) is varied. As an example, choosing $g = 1.1$, we obtain a 1975 GNP of $2114 billion and a 1980 GNP of $3404 billion. Choosing $g = 1.05$, we obtain a 1975 GNP of $1052 billion and a 1980 GNP of $1343 billion. When we teach this material, it is natural to bring in at this stage the ideas of compounded growth in other areas, such as compound interest, population growth, and so on.

From an economic perspective the chief merit of model 1 is its simplicity. The economist who wishes to project next year's (or the next five or ten years') GNP merely selects the compounded growth rate in the GNP over some past period and applies it to the known base-period value of the GNP. Over long periods of time—for example, decade to decade—this approach makes some sense because the aberrations from a trend tend to offset each other. The figures thus derived might provide order-of-magnitude information on the level of overall economic activity.

For accurate estimates of next year's GNP or for year-by-year projections of economic activity, the model's simplicity creates problems because of the variances in the growth rate of the GNP. For example, during the period of 1960 through 1970 the annual rate of increase in the GNP varied between 3.3 percent and 9.5 percent per annum. Although the compounded rate of increase was 7.5 percent, the standard deviation for the period was nearly two percentage points! This means that if the rates of growth were distributed normally, the ensuing year's growth rate might be expected to fall anywhere between 2 percent above and 2 percent below the projected average of 7.5 percent. Imagine the poor economist who in 1970 projected the 1971 GNP to be $1056 billion on the basis of a 7.5 percent growth rate only to discover that it actually was $1036 billion or $1076 billion (the upper and lower figures of our standard deviation). He would miss by nearly $20 billion in one year alone!

A more basic economic criticism of the model is that it says very little about the underlying behavior of the groups of people who either produce or purchase new goods and services. We know that the compounded rate of increase in the GNP was 7.5 percent during the 1960s. We do not know *why* it was 7.5 percent rather than 5 percent or 9 percent, or, in fact, why the GNP had to grow at all. We do know that there was considerable variation in the annual growth rate during that decade. Perhaps a look at some of the individual spending components of the GNP would help improve the predictive power of the analyst.

Model 2. Exponential projections on components of GNP

This model takes into account variations in the four components of the GNP. Observations similar to those of the previous model lead to the assumption.

ASSUMPTION. *Consumer spending, investment, government spending, and net exports are each a fixed ratio of the previous year's GNP.*

This assumption translates into these equations:

$$(4) \quad \begin{aligned} C_n &= p\,Y_{n-1} \\ I_n &= q\,Y_{n-1} \\ G_n &= r\,Y_{n-1} \\ E_n &= s\,Y_{n-1} \end{aligned}$$

Since the GNP of year n, Y_n, is the sum of the components in year n, that is, $Y_n = C_n + I_n + G_n + E_n$, we get

$$(5) \quad \begin{aligned} Y_n &= pY_{n-1} + qY_{n-1} + rY_{n-1} + sY_{n-1} \\ &= (p + q + r + s)Y_{n-1}. \end{aligned}$$

From table 1 we find that the average values for the constants above during the 1960–75 period were

$$(6) \quad \begin{aligned} p &= 0.6738, \\ q &= 0.1636, \\ r &= 0.2307, \\ \text{and } s &= 0.0072. \end{aligned}$$

Note that the sum of the four constants from (6) is the same as the constant for g in model 1. It can be shown by induction that the Y values for this model satisfy the relationship

$$(7) \quad Y_k = (p + q + r + s)^k Y_0,$$

where Y_0 is the GNP of the starting year.

A program that will allow one to simulate the economy using various values for p, q, r, and s appears in figure 4. The output from this program will be the same as the output given from the program of model 1 if one uses the average values for the constants given in (6). This follows because $p + q + r + s = g = 1.075$ of model 1 (to four significant figures).

```
1Ø  INPUT "CONSUMP. COEFF.";P
2Ø  INPUT "INVEST. COEFF.";Q
3Ø  INPUT "GOV. SPEND. COEFF.";R
4Ø  INPUT "NET EXPORTS COEFF.";S
5Ø  INPUT "BEGINNING YEAR ";N
6Ø  INPUT "NO. YRS. PROJECTED";K
7Ø  INPUT "GNP OF BEGIN. YR.";Y
8Ø  PRINT
9Ø  PRINT
1ØØ PRINT "YEAR","GNP"
11Ø PRINT
12Ø PRINT N,Y
13Ø FOR I = 1 TO K
14Ø LET Y = (P + Q + R + S)*Y
15Ø PRINT N + I, Y
16Ø NEXT I
17Ø END
```

Fig. 4. Program for computing the GNP from year N for a period of K years (model 2)

More interesting results are obtained by holding three of the constants fixed while altering the other constant. For example, suppose government spending is 0.25 of the previous year's GNP rather than 0.2307. Holding the rates of consumer spending, investment, and net exports constant as they are in (6) and starting with a 1960 GNP of $506 billion, we obtain GNP figures from our program of $1963 billion in 1975 and $3085 billion in 1980. On the other hand, decreasing the government spending coefficient to 0.20 while holding the other constants fixed would lead to a 1975 GNP of $973.6 billion and a 1980 GNP of $1211 billion. These results may be compared with the actual 1975 GNP figure of $1498.8 billion and the projections of model 1.

The approach of this model is particularly useful to planners of government programs. Since the amount of government spending can be set within certain limits each year (probably on the order of 0–10 percent increase over the previous year's spending), planners can determine the probable effects of various levels of government spending on GNP. If more produc-

tion and spending is needed to avoid recession and to increase employment, more government spending can be recommended. If overspending and inflation is probable (resulting in too high a GNP), then government spending can be held constant.

Some economic observers believe that the GNP would have been $1036 billion in 1970 if the economy had operated at peak efficiency. You might wish to calculate the r value that would have yielded enough total spending to reach the peak efficiency level. Was this value within the range of political reality (i.e., is the value of r within the historical range for the previous decade)?

Model 3. A Keynesian model

John Maynard Keynes, the British economist, expounded the view that government spending should be used to regulate the economy. He felt that if the economy was not growing fast enough, the government should spend more money in order to induce growth. If the economy was growing too fast, the government should reduce its spending in order to curb unhealthy expansion. All this was to be done relatively independently of the amount of taxes collected. This point of view has been adopted by many governments of the world, including that of the United States. Most U.S. economists and politicians now accept the idea of an economy controlled to a large extent by government fiscal policy.

In this model we shall incorporate the idea that government spending should be used to control the economy. We shall arbitrarily decide that the economy should grow about 5 percent from one year to the next. Our assumptions are these:

ASSUMPTION 1. *Consumer spending, investment, and net exports in a given year are each a fixed ratio of the previous year's GNP.*

ASSUMPTION 2. *If the GNP is not growing fast enough, government spending will be increased. If the GNP is growing too fast, government spending will be decreased.*

Assumption 1 translates into the equations

$$C_n = p\,Y_{n-1},$$
$$I_n = q\,Y_{n-1},$$
$$\text{and } E_n = s\,Y_{n-1},$$

all of which we have seen before. Throughout the discussion of this model we shall use the values

$$(8) \quad \begin{aligned} p &= 0.6738, \\ q &= 0.1636, \\ \text{and } s &= 0.0072. \end{aligned}$$

Assumption 2 is not very specific. We are thus free to consider any reasonable plan for determining the level of government spending. Remember that our goal is to move the GNP ahead at 5 percent a year, and since we do not want erratic behavior in the components, we would hope that the components would move ahead at 5 percent a year as well. Let us consider the following plan:

Since our goal is to increase the GNP at 5 percent a year, let us arbitrarily decide that if the GNP has grown between 3 percent and 7 percent from year $n-2$ to year $n-1$, then the growth rate will be called an acceptable growth, and government spending of year n will be determined by the formula $G_n = 1.05\,G_{n-1}$, which gives us the desired rate of growth in the government spending component of the GNP. On the other hand, if the growth in the GNP from year $n-2$ to year $n-1$ has been less than 3 percent, we shall increase government spending by the formula $G_n = 1.1\,G_{n-1}$. Finally, if the growth in the GNP from year $n-2$ to year $n-1$ has been more than 7 percent, we shall effectively cut government spending by choosing $G_n = G_{n-1}$. In the latter case, government spending just does not go up the normal 5 percent. Thus, government spending in year n is determined by the following formula.

$$(9) \quad G_n = \begin{cases} 1.1\,G_{n-1} & \text{if } Y_{n-1} \le 1.03\,Y_{n-2} \\ 1.05\,G_{n-1} & \text{if } 1.03\,Y_{n-2} \\ & \quad < Y_{n-1} \le 1.07\,Y_{n-2} \\ G_{n-1} & \text{if } 1.07\,Y_{n-2} < Y_{n-1} \end{cases}$$

Our complete model 4 is thus given by the following formula.

$$(10) \quad Y_n = (p + q + s)Y_{n-1} + G_n,$$

where G_n is determined from equation (9).

A program that will allow us to simulate the economy using this model appears in figure 5. Notice that we need information on the GNP for two successive years to get started. This program also prints government spending as a percentage of the GNP and the percentage of increase in the GNP from year to year.

```
1Ø   INPUT "BEGIN. YR. GNP";Y1
2Ø   INPUT "BEGIN. YEAR";N
3Ø   INPUT BEGIN. YR. GOV. SPEND.";G
4Ø   INPUT "NO. YRS. PROJECTED";K
5Ø   INPUT "GNP OF YEAR BEFORE";YØ
6Ø   PRINT
7Ø   PRINT "YEAR","GNP","GOV. SPEND.",
8Ø   PRINT "% GOV.SPEND.","%INC.IN GNP"
9Ø   PRINT
1ØØ  PRINT N-1,YØ
11Ø  PRINT N, Y1, G, G/Y1*1ØØ
12Ø  FOR J=1 TO K
13Ø  IF Y1 > 1.Ø7*YØ GOTO 18Ø
14Ø  IF Y1 <=1.Ø3*YØ GOTO 17Ø
15Ø  LET G=1.Ø5*G
16Ø  GOTO 18Ø
17Ø  LET G=1.1*G
18Ø  LET Y=(.6738+.1636+.ØØ72)*Y1+G
19Ø  LET P = G/Y*1ØØ
2ØØ  LET L = Y/Y1*1ØØ-1ØØ
21Ø  PRINT N+J,Y,G,P,L
22Ø  LET YØ =Y1
23Ø  LET Y1 =Y
24Ø  NEXT J
25Ø  END
```

Fig. 5. Program for computing the GNP from year N for a period of K years (model 3)

Starting with 1961 as the beginning year, we obtain the output in table 2. (The interactive portion of the output has been omitted.)

It should be pointed out that the percentage of increase in the GNP was somewhat over 5 percent throughout the period tested but was approaching 5 percent at the end of the period.

The assumption of this model concerning government spending leads to a well-behaved growth of the GNP. It is interesting

TABLE 2
Keynesian Model Data (Model 3)

YEAR	GNP	GOV. SPEND.	%GOV. SPEND.	%INC. IN GNP
1960	506			
1961	523.3	108.2	20.6765	
1962	555.589	113.61	20.4486	6.1703
1963	588.541	119.29	20.2688	5.93099
1964	622.337	125.255	20.1266	5.74229
1965	657.143	131.518	20.0136	5.59289
1966	693.117	138.094	19.9236	5.47423
1967	730.405	144.998	19.8518	5.37975
1968	769.148	152.248	19.7944	5.30436
1969	809.483	159.861	19.7485	5.24412
1970	851.543	167.854	19.7117	5.19591
1971	895.46	176.246	19.6822	5.15729
1972	941.364	185.059	19.6586	5.12633
1973	989.388	194.312	19.6396	5.1015
1974	1039.66	204.027	19.6243	5.08156
1975	1092.33	214.229	19.6121	5.06556
1976	1147.52	224.94	19.6023	5.0527
1977	1205.38	236.187	19.5943	5.04237
1978	1266.06	247.996	19.588	5.03407
1979	1329.71	260.396	19.5829	5.02739
1980	1396.49	273.416	19.5788	5.02203

to try to vary the inequalities and goals of the assumption to attempt to achieve a 7.5 percent increase in the GNP, thus, on the average, duplicating the actual behavior of the GNP in the period 1960–75.

At this point in using mathematical models to illustrate economic relationships one may wonder whether the models have relevance in policy and decision making. The fact is that whereas much more sophisticated models exist, much of national economic policy is made with no more (and often considerably less) economic sophistication than what we have shown here.

It should be noted that government economic policy is not quite so simple in the real world! Besides economic growth, other goals such as stable prices and high employment levels may also receive priority. Conditions rarely allow simultaneous pursuit of all these goals. Furthermore, economic decisions about government spending are often made in a political context. Congressional representatives running for reelection often find it difficult to support reductions in government spending in their home districts, even if good Keynesian theory suggests that such reductions might be necessary to reduce inflationary pressures.

Models to Be Investigated

We conclude by suggesting further models that bear investigation.

Model 4. An investment model

It seems reasonable to assume that U.S. business leaders will invest more when consumption is increasing and less when consumers are buying less. A simple model to test this assumption can be built by modifying the assumption about investment in model 2, leaving the other assumptions the same. More specifically, the assumption about investment is that *investment is proportional to the rate of change in consumption from the previous year's GNP.* This translates into the equation

$$I_n = w(C_n - C_{n-1}).$$

The equation for the model is

$$Y_n = (p + wp + r + s)Y_{n-1} - wpY_{n-2},$$

where w is the proportionality constant given in the assumption of this model and p, r, and s represent the same constants as in model 2. The average value for w during the period 1960–70 was 3.705. Although the assumption is reasonable, this model is a bad one. The GNP will quickly go negative.

If business leaders really do invest as indicated by the assumption of this model, then there must be some other force in the economy that is keeping it on a more stable path. The reader is referred to Samuelson (1939) for a discussion of this model.

Model 5. A Keynesian investment-predictor model

This model uses the investment assumption of model 4 but uses government spending to correct the erratic behavior caused by the investment assumption. In particular, the effects of a given level of government spending are projected ahead for one year. If the GNP is not behaving correctly (as determined by the goals of the planners), then government spending is changed appropriately. The government spending level that makes the predicted GNP growth acceptable is the level the planners will recommend to the executive and legislative branches of government.

Model 6. A monetarist model

As a complete alternative to the means of determining the GNP in the five models above, students might wish to investigate a monetarist model of the economy. Economists who espouse the monetarist theory of income determination believe that the amount of production is affected directly by the amount of money in circulation. Money in this context is usually thought of as the value of checking accounts plus the amount of currency and coin in circulation. The equation is $Y_n = kM_n$, where M_n is the money supply at the beginning of the year. The values for M_n in Table 3 are for the period 1960–70, given in billions of dollars.

Although this unsophisticated model lacks predictive power as it stands, very complicated variations of it have been used in conjunction with other estimating procedures to project many dimensions of the U.S. economy. Students might be encouraged to play with lags in the GNP's responsiveness to monetary changes as a means of improving the model's conformity to the real world.

TABLE 3
Money Supply (M_n) for Years 1960–70
(Monetarist Model)

Year	M_n
1960	141.9
1961	141.1
1962	145.5
1963	147.6
1964	153.1
1965	159.3
1966	166.8
1967	170.4
1968	183.1
1969	197.4
1970	203.6

Conclusion

Mathematical modeling is very important to the economist. We have presented a few of the more elementary models based on equations that economists have used to study the GNP of the United States. Many more sophisticated and complicated models exist and are used, some of which use concepts and techniques from mathematics other than those used above. We urge the reader to investigate some of the other models and to use the concepts of modeling in the classroom in order that students may see the usefulness of the approach and, most of all, the usefulness of mathematics.

BIBLIOGRAPHY

Anton, Howard, and Bernard Kolman. *Applied Finite Mathematics.* New York: Academic Press, 1974.

Cohen, Jack K., and William S. Dorn. *Mathematical Modeling in Computing.* AAAS Study Guides on Contemporary Problems, no. 8. Washington, D.C.: American Association for the Advancement of Science, 1974.

Dorn, William S., and Daniel D. McCracken. *Introductory Finite Mathematics with Computing.* New York: John Wiley & Sons, 1976.

Malkevitch, Joseph, and Walter Meyer. *Graphs, Models, Finite Mathematics.* Englewood Cliffs, N.J.: Prentice-Hall, 1974.

Mizrahi, Abe, and Michael Sullivan. "Mathematical Models and Applications: Suggestions for the High School Classroom." *Mathematics Teacher* 66 (May 1973): 394–402.

Samuelson, Paul A. "Interactions between the Multiplier Analysis and the Principle of Acceleration." *Review of Economics and Statistics* (May 1939):75–78.

U.S. Department of Labor. *Employment and Training Report of the President.* Washington, D.C.: Government Printing Office, 1976.

APPORTIONMENT—A DECENNIAL PROBLEM

Arithmetic and algebra can help your students understand some of the dilemmas in devising a plan for equitable representation in Washington.

By JOHN J. SULLIVAN
New York State Education Department
Albany, NY 12234

The delegates to the Constitutional Convention in 1787 left us a problem that recurs like a plague every ten years. The Constitution directs that seats in the House of Representatives must be apportioned among the states according to population after each decennial census, but it fails to specify how this is to be done. Consequently throughout most of the life of the Republic, apportionment caused free-swinging legislative battles unrestrained by logic or fair play. Enormous waste resulted. Mathematicians were often recruited to counsel and support various congressional factions and to propose better systems of apportionment. A Harvard mathematician, E. V. Huntington, devised the present method, which has operated smoothly through four apportionments owing, perhaps, more to chance than design. Intensive research in the 1970s demonstrated that Huntington's method has a potentially fatal flaw. Before this faulty method is examined, it will be helpful to review the constitutional mandates on apportionment and some of its history.

What does it mean to apportion representatives according to population? Most objective people would say it means that a state, say Virginia, with 3 percent of the United States population should have 3 percent of the total number of representatives (House size is fixed at 435). Hence Virginia should be assigned 0.03(435), or 13.05, seats in the House. Awarding Virginia 13 seats is done without controversy; few would deny its claim to at least 13

seats. It is the fraction, 0.05, that causes unending difficulty. House seats are integral. Apportionments in the early years of the nation were done using divisors. After protracted logrolling, Congress would agree on a divisor by which the population of each state was divided producing "exact quotas" whose integral parts named the numbers of representatives assigned to the respective states. The fractions were ignored in those days, so congressmen searched for divisors that maximized the integral parts of their exact quotas and minimized the fractional parts. Table 1 shows populations of three states in 1832 and projected apportionments based on several possible divisors.

TABLE 1
Apportionment Computations, 1832
Method of Divisors

State	Population	Exact Quotas Derived from a Divisor of		
		59 000	48 000	47 700
Georgia*	429 811	7.28	8.95	9.01
Kentucky	621 832	10.54	12.95	13.04
New York	1 913 489	32.43	39.86	40.12

* Population data from U.S. Bureau of the Census, Washington, D.C., 1832.

Representative John Quincy Adams described some of the legislative maneuvers of 1832 in his diary. During the debates he "recurred to the constitution, and to a calculation showing that the committee which fixed the ratio [divisor] at forty-eight thousand had taken special care of their own states" (Adams 1876, p. 465). Eventually Congress approved a divisor of 47 700. Adams was distraught. "The effect of this was to give an additional member to each of the states of Georgia, Kentucky, and New York, and it bought the votes . . . to carry the majority. . . . The iniquity of the Apportionment bill and the disreputable means by which so partial and unjust a distribution of the representatives had been effected, agitated me." Adams had cause to mourn. His state, Massachusetts, had an exact quota of 12.80 but received just 12 seats in the House.

Daniel Webster stated the issue clearly.

Daniel Webster also debated on apportionment in 1832. His speech to the Senate, challenging an assignment of seats to New York, contained a crucial point (Webster 1903, pp. 110–11):

If, for example, the House is to contain two hundred and forty members, then the number 240 expresses the representative power of all the States; and a plain calculation readily shows how much of this power belongs to each state . . . . For example, in a House consisting of 240 members, the exact mathematical proportion to which her numbers entitle the State of New York is 38.59; it is certain, therefore, that 39 is the integral or whole number nearest to her exact proportion of the representative power of the Union. Why, then, should she not have thirty-nine? and why should she have forty? She is not quite entitled to thirty-nine; that number is something more than her right. But [by] allowing her thirty-nine, from the necessity of giving her whole numbers, and because that is the nearest whole number, is not the Constitution fully obeyed . . .?

Webster's clear, reasoned argument has lost none of its force. A state should receive at least a number of House seats equal to the integral part of its exact quota, and not more than that number plus one. The present method—Huntington's method of equal proportions—can sometimes fail to do this.

Neither Webster's oratory nor ex-President Adams's influence prevailed in 1832, but their efforts may have helped bring about the adoption of a fairer method of apportionment later. In 1852 a method was adopted that had been proposed by Alexander Hamilton in 1792. As we shall see, it is the best method of apportionment.

Hamilton's Method of Apportionment

Tragically, the turmoil and waste associated with apportionments might have been avoided had President Washington accepted the advice of his Secretary of the Treasury, Alexander Hamilton, when the issue first arose in 1792. A sound method, established after the first census, would have been difficult to refute later. Hamilton certainly knew what the delegates intended. He wrote to Washington (Syrett 1966, p. 228):

II. The number (of representatives) is apportioned among the several states by the following rule— as the *aggregate* numbers of the *United States* are to the *total number* of representatives . . . , so are the *particular numbers of each state* to the number of representatives of such state. But

III. As this second process leaves a residue of eight out of the 120 members unapportioned, these are distributed among the states which upon that second process have the largest fractions or remainders.

Hamilton's method is utterly simple and fair. It uses a proportion,

$$\frac{P}{R} = \frac{p}{r} \quad \text{or} \quad r = \frac{p}{P}\,(R),$$

where p represents a state's population, P, the U.S. population, r, the number of representatives assigned to a state, and R, the total number of representatives. Table 2 shows a hypothetical apportionment by Hamilton's method.

TABLE 2
Hypothetical Apportionment by Hamilton's Method

State	Popul'n	Exact Quota	Lower Quota	Rank	Rep's
Conn.	3 158	8.86	8	3	9
Ga.	685	1.92	1	2	2
Del.	312	0.88	1*	—	1
Md.	5 112	14.34	14	4	14
Mass.	6 085	17.07	17	5	17
N.Y.	20 303	56.94	56	1	57
	35 655		97		100

* Each state must receive at least one seat regardless of its exact quota.

Each state's population is divided by 35 655 and the quotient is multiplied by 100, producing the numbers in the "exact quota" column. To deny a state at least its lower quota of representatives is to deny proportional representation. The sum of the numbers in the "lower quota" column is 97, which leaves just 3 seats to be distributed by some other means. The rank column rates the fractional parts from the largest to the smallest. So New York with the largest, 0.94, is ranked first; Georgia with 0.92 is ranked second, and so on. Those with the highest rank are first entitled to any representatives that have not already been apportioned.

Huntington's method can produce unacceptable apportionments.

It is these extra seats that cause most of the controversy. The critical part of Hamilton's method deals with this residue. He wrote to Washington: "It is of necessity that that residue should be distributed among the several states by some rule and none more equal or defensible can be found than that of giving a preference to the greatest remainders" (Syrett 1966, p. 230).

The fundamental assumptions of Hamilton, and of this article, are these:

1. A state deserves at least the number of representatives equal to the integral part of its exact quota, and not more than this number plus one.

2. The larger the fractional part of a state's exact quota, the stronger is its claim to one of the unassigned seats in the House.

3. No apportionment system is fair, or feasible in the long run, which takes a House seat from one state and gives it to a state with a weaker claim to it.

A minor weakness in Hamilton's method has caused exaggerated concern. In the nineteenth century it sometimes happened that a given state's quota of representatives decreased as the size of the House increased. This wholly normal occurrence was labeled the Alabama paradox by those who felt injured by it (Balinski and Young 1975, p. 704). There is nothing irregular about a state receiving more or fewer House seats depending on changes in its population relative to changes in populations of other states. In fact, proportional representation demands this. Moreover, the issue, today, is a dead one. With a fixed House size, the Alabama paradox is irrelevant.

Hamilton's method was adopted by Congress in 1852. At that time it became known as the Vinton method (Schmeckebier 1941, p. 108). His method served the nation well until it was rashly abandoned in 1911 (ibid., p. 120). Subsequent attempts to apportion representatives in the 1920s were chaotic and threatened the foundations of the government. An entire decade passed with Congress unable to pass an apportionment bill. The unedifying spectacle of Congress deadlocked over apportionment was alarming, considering the dubious constitutionality of leg-

Mathematicians have produced apportionment systems.

islation and the illegality of the presidential electoral vote. The impasse was finally broken in 1929 when a bill was passed providing for automatic apportionment after the 1930 census based on a fixed House size of 435. These provisions were important improvements. In 1941 the present method—equal proportions—was adopted (Ogg and Ray 1948, p. 290).

The Method of Equal Proportions

This method was devised by E. V. Huntington in the 1920s (Huntington 1928). If the populations of two states are A and B and their numbers of representatives are a and b, respectively, then A/a and B/b are the average "sizes" of their congressional districts (the number of people represented by a representative in a district). According to Huntington, in a perfect apportionment the numbers A/a and B/b would be equal; but perfect apportionments are practically impossible. Improvement, though, may be possible. If the amount of inequality between A/a and B/b can be reduced by a transfer of a representative from one state to the other, the transfer should be made. This reasoning lacks any constitutional mandate, but it persuaded Congress to adopt the method of equal proportions. Huntington claimed that if A/a was larger than B/b, then the difference $A/a - B/b$ was less important than the relative difference, which he defined as

$$\frac{\dfrac{A}{a} - \dfrac{B}{b}}{\dfrac{B}{b}}.$$

According to the method of equal proportions, the assignment of an additional representative to state A is correct provided the relative difference in average populations is less than if the additional representative was assigned to state B, or

$$\frac{\dfrac{B}{b} - \dfrac{A}{a+1}}{\dfrac{A}{a+1}} < \frac{\dfrac{A}{a} - \dfrac{B}{b+1}}{\dfrac{B}{b+1}},$$

which can be transformed to an inequality, which is the core of the method:

$$\frac{A}{\sqrt{a(a+1)}} > \frac{B}{\sqrt{b(b+1)}}.$$

The actual working method of equal proportions uses a table of multipliers in which numbers of the form $1/\sqrt{a(a+1)}$ are expressed as decimals (table 3). The multiplier used to assign the second seat, for example, is a decimal approximation of $1/\sqrt{1(2)}$, and the third, $1/\sqrt{2(3)}$. As an illustration of the use of the table, any state A will receive its fourth representative before another state B receives its third provided $A (0.2886751) > B (0.4082483)$. Huntington proved that

when this test is used, it is always possible to arrive at a final apportionment that cannot be improved by any further transfer between any two states (Hungtington 1928, p. 89).

TABLE 3
Equal Proportions Multipliers

Number	Multiplier
2	0.7071068
3	0.4082483
4	0.2886751
.	.
.	.
.	.

Equal proportions (EP) has been used with relatively little controversy, but this peaceful interlude may not last. In 1975 M. L. Balinski and H. P. Young called attention to a major defect in EP. Table 4 illustrates the failing.

The method of equal proportions can produce unacceptable apportionments. State F, with an exact quota of 16.095, receives just 15 seats in the House. State G receives its second representative, making it impossible for State F to receive its sixteenth, because $295(0.7071068) > 3219(0.0645497)$. Balinski and Young have constructed elaborate tables showing apportionments by EP which illustrate its defects clearly. They wrote: "Most seriously, EP does not satisfy quota. . . . While explicitly recognized by the

TABLE 4
Apportionment by Equal Proportions

State	Population	Exact Quota	Number of Representatives
A	325	1.625	2
B	788	3.940	4
C	548	2.740	3
D	562	2.810	3
E	4 263	21.315	21
F	3 219	16.095	15
G	295	1.475	2
	10 000	50	50

many proponents of EP, this flaw was conveniently painted over. It is for them fortunate, indeed, that no census figures since 1930 have provided an example exhibiting the non-quota phenomenon" (Balinski and Young 1975, p. 711).

Conclusions

Can Congress afford to wait until a crisis develops before replacing the method of equal proportions? In the 1920s Congress repeatedly tried and failed to pass an apportionment bill. The waste involved was enormous, and the legal issues endangered the government. Hamilton's method operated successfully during a half century and is, perhaps, the only method that could receive general support. It has irrefutable advantages:

1. It is clearly constitutional; indeed, it is precisely what the delegates to the Constitutional Convention intended.

2. It will assign each state at least its lower quota of House seats and never more than this number plus one.

3. It is a fair method in that the distribution of the extra seats will be "presumably nearly random" (Birkhoff 1976). The process will not favor any states over the long term.

4. It can operate automatically, thereby avoiding controversy, delays, waste, and dangerous governmental crises.

5. It will function perfectly if the House size declines. Many experts believe the House is too large for efficient legislative operations.

6. It can be comprehended easily by most people, which makes for public confidence and popular support.

Alexander Hamilton proposed a fair, constitutional system of apportionment.

Student Investigations

Apportionment has elements that may motivate some students to do individual research. The basic problem is easily grasped and seems to exert fascination. Hundreds of people have tried to invent apportionment systems, including some famous people. The subject will be in the news in 1981–82 and has many interesting historical facets (Meder 1966; Schmeckebier 1941; Sullivan 1972).

The fairest method is to give preference to the larger fractions.

Exercises

1. From information given in the article, determine the population of Massachusetts in 1832. Which of the three divisors in table 1 favored Massachusetts?

2. Use Hamilton's method to complete the following table.

Pop.		House size: 100		House size: 101	
		Quota	Rep.	Quota	Rep.
A	453	45.3	45	45.753	46
B	442				
C	105				
	1000	100	100	101	101

Explain how the table entries demonstrate the Alabama paradox.

3. Two inequalities involving common fractions appear in the section on Huntington's method. Show that they are equivalent.

Answers to Exercises

1. The article states that the population of Massachusetts divided by 47 700 gave a quotient of 12.80. From this we can infer that the population of Massachusetts in 1832 was 610 560. A divisor of 59 000 gives an exact quota of 10.35; a divisor of 48 000 gives an exact quota of 12.72. Either may be defended as "favorable to Massachusetts" depending on your assumptions.

2. The missing entries are

44.2	44	44.642	45
10.5	11	10.605	10

With a House size of 100, state C receives 11 seats. With a House size of 101, state C receives 10 seats, illustrating the Alabama paradox.

3. Separate the fractions in the first inequality:

$$\frac{\dfrac{B}{b}}{\dfrac{A}{a+1}} - \frac{\dfrac{A}{a+1}}{\dfrac{A}{a+1}} < \frac{\dfrac{A}{a}}{\dfrac{B}{b+1}} - \frac{\dfrac{B}{b+1}}{\dfrac{B}{b+1}}$$

Hence

$$\frac{\dfrac{B}{b}}{\dfrac{A}{a+1}} < \frac{\dfrac{A}{a}}{\dfrac{B}{b+1}} \cdot$$

Multiply both members by the denominators:

$$\frac{B^2}{b(b+1)} < \frac{A^2}{a(a+1)}$$

Hence

$$\frac{B}{\sqrt{b(b+1)}} < \frac{A}{\sqrt{a(a+1)}}$$

or

$$\frac{A}{\sqrt{a(a+1)}} > \frac{B}{\sqrt{b(b+1)}} \cdot$$

BIBLIOGRAPHY

Adams, Charles Francis, ed. *Memoirs of John Quincy Adams*. Philadelphia: J. B. Lippincott & Co., 1876.

Balinski, M. L., and H. P. Young. "The Quota Method of Apportionment." *American Mathematical Monthly* 82 (August-September 1975): 701–30.

Birkhoff, Garrett. "House-Monotone Apportionment Schemes." In *Proceedings of the National Academy of Sciences USA*, pp. 684–86. Washington, D.C.: National Academy of Sciences, 1976.

Huntington, E. V. "The Apportionment of Representatives in Congress." In *Transactions of the American Mathematical Society*, pp. 85–110. Providence, R.I.: American Mathematical Society, 1928.

Meder, Albert E., Jr. *Legislative Apportionment*. Boston: Houghton Mifflin Co., 1966.

Ogg, F. A., and O. P. Ray. *Introduction to American Government*. New York: Appleton-Century-Crofts, 1948.

Schmeckebier, Laurence F. *Congressional Apportionment*. Washington, D.C.: The Brookings Institution, 1941.

Sullivan, John J. "The Election of a President." *Mathematics Teacher* 65 (October 1972): 493–501.

Syrett, Harold C., ed. *The Papers of Alexander Hamilton*. New York: Columbia University Press, 1966.

Webster, Daniel. *The Writings and Speeches of Daniel Webster*. Vol. 6. Boston: Little, Brown & Co., 1903.

2/3 of 19

Thanks for the very interesting article on Congressional apportionment (January 1982). I had always assumed that a straightforward method like Hamilton's was used and was surprised to learn that potential complications still exist.

Readers might be interested in the example of Nigeria, where mathematics played a crucial role in politics in 1979. Nigeria was culminating a smooth return to elected, civilian constitutional government after thirteen years of military rule. To encourage national presidential leadership, rather than regional favoritism, the new constitution said that to be elected president, a candidate must (in addition to winning a plurality of votes overall) win at least $\frac{1}{4}$ of the votes in $\frac{2}{3}$ of the states. Since five candidates were seeking election, this was more difficult than it sounds. If no one satisfied the requirements, runoffs were to be held. However, there are 19 states in Nigeria. What does $\frac{2}{3}$ of 19 really mean?

Candidate Shehu Shagari had a clear plurality overall and received $\frac{1}{4}$ of the votes in 12 states. In the 13th state, he had close to $\frac{1}{4}$ of the votes but not quite enough. The electoral commission, and later the courts, ruled that since $\frac{2}{3}$ of 19 is $12\frac{2}{3}$, a candidate could win with $\frac{1}{4}$ of the state totals in 12 states and $\frac{1}{4}$ of $\frac{2}{3}$ (i.e., $\frac{1}{6}$) of the votes in the 13th state. Mr. Shagari satisfied that requirement and was declared the winner.

Both sides had brought forth their university mathematicians to argue this primary mathematics issue. Suddenly the dry arithmetic of multiplying by fractions had become hot politics! Ever since, opening speeches in mathematics meetings regularly refer to "$\frac{2}{3}$ of 19" and the day when mathematics became politics.

As an American application, maybe ERA supporters should have argued that since constitutional amendments need 50 percent support in $\frac{3}{4}$ of the 50 state legislatures, and since $\frac{3}{4}$ of 50 is $37\frac{1}{2}$, the amendment only needed to be approved in 37 states, plus getting 50 percent of $\frac{1}{2}$ (or $\frac{1}{4}$) support in the 38th!

Lawrence Shirley
Ahmadu Bello University
Zaria, Nigeria
West Africa

sharing teaching ideas

SECRET CODES WITH MATRICES

A previous article in the *Mathematics Teacher* by Merrill A. Meneeley (1981) demonstrated how informal modular arithmetic can be applied to coding and decoding messages. The study of cryptography can be further enhanced by the application of matrices. The use of matrix techniques to write secret codes is motivating and can enrich an entire class because the activity does not have to be restricted to the more able students. The sample worksheets included in this article have been used in several algebra and trigonometry classes for college-bound students and can be enjoyed by students who are studying or have studied second-year algebra.

The treatment that follows can be used to introduce the subject of cryptography or, if a student has been exposed to coding and decoding, it can add an exciting new dimension. The method for using matrices is very flexible and can be tailored by the instructor to the class involved. The coding matrices can be changed as long as they are invertible, and the codes themselves can be altered, provided they consist of a prime number of elements.

It is fairly common knowledge that one can crack simple codes by examining the frequencies of encoded characters and comparing them to the frequencies with which we would expect those characters to occur in standard English (or another language). The more coded letters available, the easier it is to establish their frequency. The use of matrices permits the frequencies to be "scrambled" because encoding them in a matrix allows for numerous representations of the same character within a code.

Using the code in table 1, we see that the word *add* is represented as 1, 4, 4. If we put these numbers into a matrix,

$$\begin{bmatrix} 1 \\ 4 \\ 4 \end{bmatrix},$$

and premultiply an invertible matrix,

$$\begin{bmatrix} 0 & 2 & 3 \\ 1 & 4 & 7 \\ 2 & 3 & 6 \end{bmatrix},$$

we no longer have a number occurring twice in the encoded message:

$$\begin{bmatrix} 0 & 2 & 3 \\ 1 & 4 & 7 \\ 2 & 3 & 6 \end{bmatrix} \begin{bmatrix} 1 \\ 4 \\ 4 \end{bmatrix} = \begin{bmatrix} 0 \cdot 1 + 2 \cdot 4 + 3 \cdot 4 \\ 1 \cdot 1 + 4 \cdot 4 + 7 \cdot 4 \\ 2 \cdot 1 + 3 \cdot 4 + 6 \cdot 4 \end{bmatrix}$$

$$= \begin{bmatrix} 20 \\ 45 \\ 38 \end{bmatrix}$$

TABLE 1

A Sample Code

A	B	C	D	E	F	G	H	I	J
1	2	3	4	5	6	7	8	9	10

K	L	M	N	O	P	Q	R	S	T
11	12	13	14	15	16	17	18	19	20

U	V	W	X	Y	Z			.	,
21	22	23	24	25	26	27		28	29

"Sharing Teaching Ideas" offers practical tips on the teaching of topics related to the secondary school curriculum. We hope to include classroom-tested approaches that offer new slants on familiar subjects for the beginning and the experienced teacher.

Notice that the encoded A is 20 and the encoded Ds now take on different values, 45 and 38. The last two numbers can't be converted directly into the code. If, however, they are reduced modulo 29, then we discover that

$$\begin{bmatrix} 20 \\ 45 \\ 38 \end{bmatrix} \equiv \begin{bmatrix} 20 \\ 16 \\ 9 \end{bmatrix} \bmod 29,$$

which would then translate into

$$\begin{bmatrix} T \\ P \\ I \end{bmatrix}.$$

To decode the message we convert the coded message back into numeric form and then premultiply by the inverse of the encoding matrix,

$$\begin{bmatrix} 3 & -3 & 2 \\ 8 & -6 & 3 \\ -5 & 4 & -2 \end{bmatrix}.$$

In so doing, we obtain the following:

$$\begin{bmatrix} 3 & -3 & 2 \\ 8 & -6 & 3 \\ -5 & 4 & -2 \end{bmatrix} \begin{bmatrix} 20 \\ 16 \\ 9 \end{bmatrix}$$

$$= \begin{bmatrix} 3 \cdot 20 + -3 \cdot 16 + 2 \cdot 9 \\ 8 \cdot 20 + -6 \cdot 16 + 3 \cdot 9 \\ -5 \cdot 20 + 4 \cdot 16 + -2 \cdot 9 \end{bmatrix}$$

$$= \begin{bmatrix} 30 \\ 91 \\ -54 \end{bmatrix}$$

$$\equiv \begin{bmatrix} 1 \\ 4 \\ 4 \end{bmatrix} \bmod 29 \rightarrow \begin{bmatrix} A \\ D \\ D \end{bmatrix}$$

Students, if they are provided with the encoding and decoding matrices, can be taught the process with little difficulty, especially if they use a calculator. Using a calculator speeds up the multiplication of the matrix, and the reduction modulo 29 can be accomplished informally by placing 29 in the calculator's memory and adding or subtracting until a number is obtained be-

tween 1 and 29 inclusive (or between 0 and 28 if the code is shifted). Practice in multiplying matrices and reducing modulo 29 can be helpful before students work on the encoding and decoding.

Another example is the following:

S	E	C	R	E	T		M	E	S	S	A	G	E
19	5	3	18	5	20		27	13	5	19	19	1	7	5

If we choose to premultiply by the same three-by-three encoding matrix, the message must be placed in a matrix having three rows. The remaining spaces in any column can be encoded as a blank. Next, the message is translated into a numeric form:

$$\begin{bmatrix} S & R & & S & G \\ E & E & M & S & E \\ C & T & E & & A \end{bmatrix} \rightarrow \begin{bmatrix} 19 & 18 & 27 & 19 & 7 \\ 5 & 5 & 13 & 19 & 5 \\ 3 & 20 & 5 & 1 & 27 \end{bmatrix}$$

The message is then scrambled:

$$\begin{bmatrix} 0 & 2 & 3 \\ 1 & 4 & 7 \\ 2 & 3 & 6 \end{bmatrix} \begin{bmatrix} 19 & 18 & 27 & 19 & 7 \\ 5 & 5 & 13 & 19 & 5 \\ 3 & 20 & 5 & 1 & 27 \end{bmatrix}$$

$$= \begin{bmatrix} 19 & 70 & 41 & 41 & 91 \\ 60 & 178 & 114 & 102 & 216 \\ 71 & 171 & 123 & 101 & 191 \end{bmatrix}$$

$$\equiv \begin{bmatrix} 19 & 12 & 12 & 12 & 4 \\ 2 & 4 & 27 & 15 & 13 \\ 13 & 26 & 7 & 14 & 17 \end{bmatrix} \bmod 29$$

The result, translated from the numeric form, is

$$\begin{bmatrix} S & L & L & L & D \\ B & D & & O & M \\ M & Z & G & N & Q \end{bmatrix},$$

so the coded message is now SBMLDZL GLONDMQ. (Notice now that the R, the space, and the S all are coded as the same letter, L. Also note that the space between words seems to have changed position. Clearly, the use of frequency methods to crack this code has been severely hampered.)

The inverse must be used to decode the message. Students who know, or are taught

NAME _____

Use the following key and decoding matrix and decode the following messages:

A	B	C	D	E	F	G	H	I	J	K	L	M
1	2	3	4	5	6	7	8	9	10	11	12	13

N	O	P	Q	R	S	T	U	V	W	X	Y	Z		.	,
14	15	16	17	18	19	20	21	22	23	24	25	26	27	28	29

Example: Decode LBBFXP using

$$\begin{bmatrix} 11 & -6 & 2 \\ 3 & -2 & 1 \\ 1 & -1 & 1 \end{bmatrix}.$$

$$\begin{bmatrix} L & F \\ B & X \\ B & P \end{bmatrix} \rightarrow \begin{bmatrix} 12 & 6 \\ 2 & 24 \\ 2 & 16 \end{bmatrix}$$

so

$$\begin{bmatrix} 11 & -6 & 2 \\ 3 & -2 & 1 \\ 1 & -1 & 1 \end{bmatrix}\begin{bmatrix} 12 & 6 \\ 2 & 24 \\ 2 & 16 \end{bmatrix} = \begin{bmatrix} 124 & -46 \\ 34 & -14 \\ 12 & -2 \end{bmatrix} \equiv \begin{bmatrix} 8 & 12 \\ 5 & 15 \\ 12 & 27 \end{bmatrix} \rightarrow \begin{bmatrix} H & L \\ E & O \\ L & \end{bmatrix} \rightarrow \text{(HELLO)}.$$

1. Decode A · M_OY using

$$\begin{bmatrix} -7 & 1 & 1 \\ 1 & 0 & 0 \\ 3 & 0 & -1 \end{bmatrix}.$$

(*Hint:* Your first message should be this.)

2. Decode VSNRHWHGYC_R using

$$\begin{bmatrix} 1 & -4 & 2 \\ 2 & -9 & 5 \\ 1 & -5 & 4 \end{bmatrix}.$$

(*Hint:* This is a matrix decoder's best friend.)

3. Decode CKWVGJQFTXJFLVZ using

$$\begin{bmatrix} 0 & 2 & 3 \\ 1 & 4 & 7 \\ 2 & 3 & 6 \end{bmatrix}.$$

(*Hint:* By now you know this.)

Name _____

4. Using the same key as before, *encode* "SECRET_MESSAGE" using

$$\begin{bmatrix} 0 & 2 & 3 \\ 1 & 4 & 7 \\ 2 & 3 & 6 \end{bmatrix}.$$

5. a. Decode SBMLDZL_GLONDMQ using

$$\begin{bmatrix} 3 & -3 & 2 \\ 8 & -6 & 3 \\ -5 & 4 & -2 \end{bmatrix}.$$

   b. What is the relationship between the matrix used to encode problem 4 and that used to decode problem 5?

6. Use

$$\begin{bmatrix} 3 & -3 & 2 \\ 8 & -6 & 3 \\ -5 & 4 & -2 \end{bmatrix}$$

to decode J,I·DJRQ,YOWCIZ.

   a. How is this last message related to the others? b. What conclusions can you draw?

how to find, inverses and when they are possible can generate their own encoding and decoding matrices. Others will have to be supplied with the inverses. Decoding the previous message is accomplished by translating it back into numerical form and pre-multiplying by the inverse of the encoding matrix:

$$\begin{bmatrix} S & L & L & L & D \\ B & D & & O & M \\ M & Z & G & N & Q \end{bmatrix}$$

$$\downarrow$$

$$\begin{bmatrix} 3 & -3 & 2 \\ 8 & -6 & 3 \\ -5 & 4 & -2 \end{bmatrix} \begin{bmatrix} 19 & 12 & 12 & 12 & 4 \\ 2 & 4 & 27 & 15 & 13 \\ 13 & 26 & 7 & 14 & 17 \end{bmatrix}$$

$$= \begin{bmatrix} 77 & 76 & -31 & 19 & 7 \\ 179 & 150 & -45 & 48 & 5 \\ -113 & -96 & 34 & -28 & -2 \end{bmatrix}$$

$$\equiv \begin{bmatrix} 19 & 18 & 27 & 19 & 7 \\ 5 & 5 & 13 & 19 & 5 \\ 3 & 20 & 5 & 1 & 27 \end{bmatrix} \bmod 29$$

This matrix translates to

$$\begin{bmatrix} S & R & & S & G \\ E & E & M & S & E \\ C & T & E & A & \end{bmatrix},$$

or SECRET MESSAGE.

How much time a teacher spends on developing the method depends on the level of the students and how extensively the method will be used. The treatment of encoding and decoding can be a continuing activity, and exercises can be structured for use in those gaps that frequently occur at the end of a class period when something stimulating would be beneficial. If this activity is done over an entire semester, the students can become reasonably proficient. At this point, the journey can end or it can be extended to include changing an en-

coding matrix to a decoding one (by inverting), determining when this step can be done (the determinant is nonzero), and using *n*-by-*n* matrices of different sizes.

Some students may be interested in programming a microcomputer to do the encoding and decoding. If this approach proves worthwhile, they can consider programming a test to see if the encoding matrices are invertible and, if so, investigating a procedure to invert them. Whether or not an extension of the topic is made, the consideration of encoding and decoding with matrices illustrates another fascinating application of mathematics in a practical and recreational activity.

BIBLIOGRAPHY

Mann, Barbara. "Cryptography with Matrices." *Pentagon* 21 (Fall 1961):3–11.

Meneeley, Merrill A. "Decoding Messages." *Mathematics Teacher* 74 (November 1981):629–32.

Peck, Lyman C. *Secret Codes, Remainder Arithmetic, and Matrices.* Washington, D.C.: National Council of Teachers of Mathematics, 1961.

Sinkov, Abraham. *Elementary Cryptanalysis—a Mathematical Approach.* Washington, D.C.: Mathematical Association of America, 1966.

Answers

(1) EASY. (2) CALCULATORS. (3) DECODING IS FUN. (4) SBMLDZL GLONDMQ. (5) (a) SECRET MESSAGE; (b) They are inverses—their product is

$$\begin{bmatrix} 1 & 0 & 0 \\ 0 & 1 & 0 \\ 0 & 0 & 1 \end{bmatrix}.$$

(6) $\begin{bmatrix} S & E & C & R & E \\ T & & M & E & S \\ S & A & G & E & \end{bmatrix}$

(a) They are the same. (b) Messages can be written horizontally. Even if the encoding and decoding matrix pairs are the same, the messages can be scrambled differently.

Dane R. Camp
Downers Grove South
High School
Downers Grove, IL 60516

WHEN ARE LOGARITHMS USED?

By CHARLES KLUEPFEL
New York Telephone Company
Room 9-K6
1166 Avenue of the Americas
New York, NY 10036

With the widespread use of pocket calculators, no one would use a table of logarithms to multiply or raise a number to a power. Of course, the calculator raises numbers to arbitrary powers by using logarithms internally, but why should students learn logarithms if they don't plan to design calculators? Certainly the presence of the log key on many calculators will do away entirely with the need for tables of logarithms. But when is the log key to be used?

I believe that emphasis should be placed on thinking of a logarithm as an inverse operation to raising to a power, just as division is the inverse of multiplication and subtraction is the inverse of addition. Of course, multiplication and addition, being commutative, have only one inverse operation each. Raising to a power has two inverse operations: solving

$$x^y = a$$

for x is taking a root; solving it for y is taking a logarithm (in base x).

Here are some problems whose solutions are logarithms.

Problem 1

Your bank is willing to pay you 5 percent per annum compounded daily, 370 days' worth every year (i.e., about 1.014 days' worth every day), giving an effective annual yield of 5.20 percent per year. You deposit $100 today. How long will it be before this deposit has grown to $200?

Since your amount of money is multiplied by 1.052 every year, you could keep multiplying $1.052 \times 1.052 \times 1.052 \times \cdots$ un-

til the product is over 2, but this is the hard way to find

$$\log_{1.052} 2.$$

The easy way is to derive the formula for converting logarithms from one base to another. Since

$$1.052^x = 2,$$

it follows that

$$x \log 1.052 = \log 2,$$

or

$$x = \frac{\log 2}{\log 1.052},$$

using logarithms to any base so long as we are consistent. If we use base 10 logarithms, we find the logarithm of 2 to base 1.052 by dividing the common logarithm of 2 by the common logarithm of 1.052. We get

$$x = \log_{1.052} 2 = \frac{0.3010299957}{0.0220157398} = 13.673.$$

Your money will double in 13.673 years, or

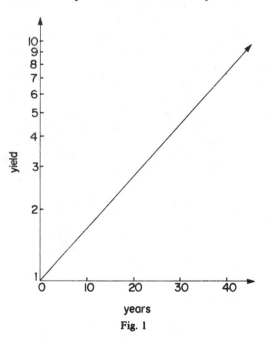

Fig. 1

13 years, 246 days. We see another advantage to this method of finding base 1.052 logarithms—we get the fraction of a year, not just "somewhat more than $13\frac{1}{2}$ years."

Figure 1 has a logarithmic vertical scale, which allows a straight line to represent the exponential function of the 5.20 percent effective annual yield interest rate. The balance rises exponentially, doubling every 13.67 years.

Problem 2

In astronomy, stars are classified for brightness by a system of magnitudes ranging from about 6 for the dimmest stars visible to the unaided eye to 1, 0, or even negative values for the brightest stars. The scheme was designed in such a way that a difference of 5 magnitudes represents a ratio of brightnesses of 100. It is thus a logarithmic scale in which a difference of 1 represents a factor of $\sqrt[5]{100}$, which is therefore a base of logarithms.

If a star of unknown magnitude is measured to be 132 times as bright as one known to be of magnitude 5.37, what is the unknown star's magnitude?

We know that the unknown star is brighter than magnitude 5.37, so its own magnitude is lower numerically than 5.37. The question is, How much lower? The answer is that it is lower by

$$(1) \qquad \log_{\sqrt[5]{100}} 132 = 5.30,$$

and the value of the magnitude is $5.37 - 5.30 = 0.07$.

The value of (1) can be found by dividing the logarithm of 132 by the logarithm of $\sqrt[5]{100}$, the latter being found either by using a power key on the calculator followed by the log key, or by dividing the logarithm of 100 by 5. If common logs are used, the latter method should not require the use of a calculator, as students should know that the common log of 100 is 2 and should be able to do the division by 5 in their heads. The division of the two logs can then be done on the calculator.

The classification of stars into magnitudes 1 through 6 was done originally in the time of Hipparchus and Ptolemy on a subjective basis of what appeared to the eye (and, as we now know, the brain) as somehow equally spaced divisions. It was not until 1850 that the English astronomer Norman Pogson pointed out that each successive magnitude was a constant factor of brightness from the preceding magnitude, thus making the magnitude scale a logarithmic one. He then made the definition to be exactly one magnitude, which represents a brightness ratio of the fifth root of one hundred to one. The fact that this law could be found in the ancient magnitude system attests to the logarithmic nature of the eye's response to light. In fact, other senses respond similarly, and this phenomenon is known variously as Fechner's law or Weber's law. In this way, the eye-brain combination is able to perceive variations in brightness at varied levels of lighting conditions.

Problem 3

The ear's response to sound also follows Fechner's law; thus a logarithmic scale of decibels (dB) is used, one decibel representing a factor of $\sqrt[10]{10}$ in the energy of the sound (this is 1/10 of a bel, which represents a factor of 10). If the lowest sound level audible to a normal ear is given a value of 0 dB at an energy level of 10^{-12} watts per square meter, how many decibels is busy street traffic in which 3×10^{-5} W/m² reach the ear?

The ratio of energies is

$$\frac{3 \times 10^{-5}}{10^{-12}} = 30\,000\,000,$$

and

$$\log_{\sqrt[10]{10}} 30\,000\,000 = 74.8;$$

thus the answer is

$$0 + 74.8 = 74.8 \text{ dB}.$$

Problem 4

On the musical scale, one octave, which represents a factor of 2 in the frequency of sound, is divided into 12 halftones. Since halftones are spaced evenly, each is a factor of $\sqrt[12]{2}$ from the previous one. How many halftones separate a frequency of 440 hertz (a hertz is 1 cycle per second) from one of 329.6 hertz?

$$\log_{\sqrt[12]{2}}\frac{440}{329.6} = 5 \text{ semitones.}$$

Problem 5

In a manually adjusted camera, each step in opening the diaphragm wider allows twice as much light to enter as the preceding opening (called an f-stop), during a given time interval. If the instructions coming with a roll of film give an exposure of 1/50 second at $f/11$ on a sunny day, how many f-stops wider should the camera be set if the light will be only 14 percent as bright as on a normal sunny day (say there is an eclipse in progress)?

Since

$$\log_2 0.14 = -2.8,$$

the camera should be opened up by 2.8 f-stops. Since they are numbered $f/11, f/8, f/5.6, f/4,$ and $f/2.8,$ the correct setting, counting 3 f-stops over, will be about $f/4,$ which is close enough to 2.8 to be handled by the latitude (forgiveness) of the film.

In this instance, direct calculation was also possible, as the numbering of the f-stops is inversely proportional to the square root of the light-gathering power. We seek 1/0.14 times as much power, so we multiply the f-number by $\sqrt{0.14} = 0.374.$

$$11 \times 0.374 = 4.1,$$

so use $f/4.$

Problem 6

Normal atmospheric pressure at sea level is 1013 millibars (mb) and at 11-km altitude is 229 mb, representing a drop in pressure with altitude by a factor of 1.145 each kilometer. If on the ground your barometer reads 1110 mb and a few minutes later in an unpressurized cabin of a small aircraft it reads 1000 mb, how high would you estimate you are above the ground?

$$\log_{1.145}\frac{1110}{1000} = 0.77 \text{ km,}$$

or 770 meters above the ground.

Problem 7

Our last example will involve the game of Master Mind®, and we will use information theory to estimate the relative difficulty levels of three versions: original, Super, and Grand. In original Master Mind®, one person sets up four colored pegs in a row, then the other person tries to find out what the colors were, in the correct order. The way that information is found concerning the colors and positions is by means of guessing a certain combination and being told how many of the four colored pegs in the guess match a peg in the corresponding position in the poser's set, as well as how many are the correct color but are in the wrong position. For example, if the setup is

blue-red-white-black

and the guess is

white-red-red-green,

the poser would tell the guesser he had one correct in the correct position (red) and one correct in the wrong position (white), but would not tell him that the red and white ones were the ones involved. He would convey this information by means of a black peg representing correct color/correct position and a white peg representing correct color/wrong position. The pegs go into an area of four holes available for holding the pegs. Super Master Mind® works similarly except that there are five positions rather than four in the code and guesses, and thus also in the available holes for reply pegs. Grand Master Mind® returns again to four positions, but here each position has both a color and a shape. The details of how the reply is determined need not be given here, but it suffices to say that a completely good correct pair/correct position earns a black peg; half-correct/correct position earns a blue peg; and correct pair/wrong position earns a white peg.

Original Master Mind® uses six colors; Super uses eight; Grand uses five colors and five shapes for twenty-five possible pairs at each position; so the following table shows how many possible codes there are at the outset of the game.

Original: $6^4 = 1296$
Super: $8^5 = 32\,768$ (5 positions)
Grand: $25^4 = 390\,625$

Each trial by the guesser reduces the number of possibilities the setter had originally put into the code. In the example given here, the reply "one black peg, one white peg" would tell the guesser that, for example, "white, green, yellow, yellow" is still a possibility (although we see it is not correct). Something like "white, red, green, blue" is ruled out, as is, for example, "yellow, black, black, yellow." The question is, How much does each answer narrow down the possibilities? We will estimate this as $1/n$, where n is the number of possible replies. In original Master Mind® n is the number of solutions in nonnegative integers of

$$b + w + e = 4,$$

where b represents black pegs, w, white pegs, and e, empty holes. In this case the number n is

$$n = \binom{4 + 3 - 1}{3 - 1} = \frac{6!}{2!\,4!} = 15,$$

where the 4 and the two 3s in the combination symbol are the 4 on the right side of the preceding equation and the number of variables in that equation (b, w, and e) respectively.

So each trial reduces the number of possibilities by a factor of 15. How long does it take to reduce 1296 possibilities to one possibility? The answer:

$$\log_{15}1296 = 2.65 \text{ trials.}$$

To this we must add 1 for actually getting the answer once it is known. Also we must revise the estimate upward, as not all replies are equally likely.

For Super Master Mind® we have:

$$b + w + e = 5$$

$$n = \binom{5 + 3 - 1}{3 - 1} = \frac{7!}{2!\,5!} = 21$$

$$\log_{21}32768 = 3.42 \text{ trials.}$$

For Grand Master Mind® (u is number of blue pegs):

$$b + u + w + e = 4$$

$$n = \binom{4 + 4 - 1}{4 - 1} = \frac{7!}{3!\,4!} = 35$$

$$\log_{35}390625 = 3.62 \text{ trials.}$$

In all three cases we must add 1 and also adjust upward for the uneven distribution of possible replies. So the skill necessary to solve the original Master Mind® in four trials would be about the same as the skill needed to solve the other two versions in five or six trials, with other skill levels requiring proportionately more trials.

The preceding seven problems all have answers that are logarithms. Logarithms can also still be of use for computation, say, of large factorials, and for mental calculations of powers, roots, and products by memorizing two-decimal-place common logarithms of 2, 3, and 7 for purposes of approximation. Thus although you could just say to your students, "If logarithms weren't important, there wouldn't be log keys on calculators," you now have the motivational ammunition of problems that will keep the log keys busy. And you also have a way of giving your students an approximation method for complex problems when a calculator is not at hand.

BIBLIOGRAPHY

Abell, George. *Exploration of the Universe*. 2d ed. New York: Holt, Rinehart & Winston, 1969.

Asimov, Isaac. *Asimov's Biographical Encyclopedia of Science and Technology*. New York: Avon, 1976.

———. *Science, Numbers, and I*. New York: Ace, 1968.

Beck, A. H. W. *Words and Waves*. New York: McGraw-Hill, 1967.

Hodgman, Charles D., editor in chief. *Handbook of Chemistry and Physics*. 39th ed. Cleveland: Chemical Rubber Publishing Co., 1957.

Kastner, Bernice. *Applications of Secondary School Mathematics*. Reston, Va.: National Council of Teachers of Mathematics, 1978.

Purves, Frederick, ed. *The Focal Encyclopedia of Photography*, desk edition. New York: Macmillan, 1960.

5

TRIGONOMETRY AND ELEMENTARY ANALYSIS

Early trigonometry was not used to measure flagpoles or building heights but to measure distances in astronomy. This was useful in navigation and for constructing accurate calendars. Early trigonometry was not plane trigonometry but rather spherical trigonometry.

The oldest surviving trigonometry table is a Babylonian clay tablet now at Columbia University. This tablet has a table of secants of angles between 30° and 45°. It is not clear why or how the table was constructed. But the Babylonians were able to predict eclipses and to construct more accurate calendars than the early Greeks could. Our present-day angle measurement using degrees and minutes originates from the base-60 system developed by the Babylonians. It was also adopted by the Greek astronomers.

The second-oldest surviving trigonometry table is by the Greek Ptolemy (ca. A.D. 85–116). Earlier tables existed but have not survived (see Eves 1983). The table gives chord lengths in a unit circle for angles from 0° to 180° for each ½°. The chord length for an angle θ, written chord (θ), was measured on a unit circle as shown in figure 5.1. The table of chord lengths is equivalent to a table of sine values because

$$\text{chord }(\theta) = 2 \sin \left(\frac{\theta}{2} \right).$$

Kennedy (1989) describes how Ptolemy constructed this table using chord formulas comparable to our trigonometry formulas for the sum and difference of angles and half-angle formulas as well as interpolation. It seems likely that this procedure was used by the Babylonians also, but no surviving record documents their procedure.

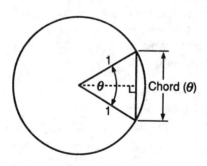

Fig. 5.1. Chord of angle θ

Earlier, the Greek Aristarchus (ca. 310–230 B.C.) made a most impressive application of trigonometry in astronomy. He assumed that the sun, moon, and earth were spherical and that the orbits of the moon around the earth and the sun around the earth were circular. (The fact that the earth moves around the sun does not matter in his computations. However, the fact that the earth's orbit is elliptical lessens the accuracy of his results.) Aristarchus was able to estimate the radius of the moon and the distance of the earth from the moon. This he did by analyzing three astronomy events.

The first situation does not use trigonometry but does introduce the variables. Figure 5.2 shows the arrangement of the sun, the earth, and the moon during a complete lunar eclipse.

The figure is drawn with the centers of the three bodies colinear. There are seven variables. Three of the variables are radii, denoted r_s, r_e, and r_m for the sun, the earth, and the moon, respectively. Three are distances from the centers of the bodies along the line connecting the centers. Observe that the line tangent to the sun and the earth intersects the line through the centers at a point in space denoted O. The distances are as follows: D_{es} between the centers of the earth and the sun, D_{em} between the centers of the earth and the moon, and D between the center of the moon and the point O. The seventh variable is the distance d between the center of the moon and the tangents to the earth and the sun. We treat this distance as the perpendicular distance, though if it were viewed as the point when the moon first became visible again on earth, it would not be the perpendicular distance. Aristarchus analyzed this case also.

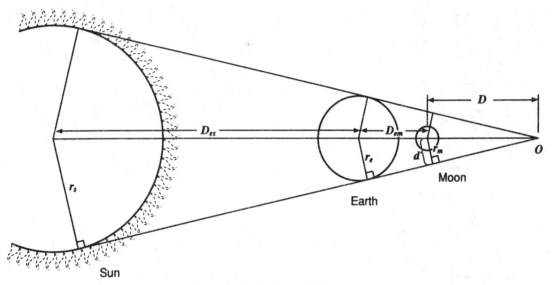

Fig. 5.2. Total eclipse of the moon

To solve for seven variables, seven equations are required. The radius of the earth is known from the method of Eratosthenes and is given as

$$r_e = 25\,000 \text{ miles.}$$

Using similar triangles in figure 5.2 yields two additional equations:

$$\frac{d}{D} = \frac{r_e}{D + D_{em}}$$

$$\frac{d}{D} = \frac{r_s}{D + D_{em} + D_{es}}$$

Aristarchus computed the time between when the moon entered the shadow and when it was completely in the shadow. He also computed the time between when the moon entered the shadow and when it first began to move out of the shadow. Since the ratio of these two measurements was about 2, Aristarchus obtained the following equation:

$$\frac{d}{r_m} = 2$$

The next situation examines the fact that the sun and the full moon appear to be the same size in the sky. This is shown geometrically in figure 5.3.

Aristarchus estimated the angle α between the two tangents drawn between the sun and moon. (Such an arrangement occurs physically during a solar eclipse.) The actual angle is about ½°, although Aristarchus used the inaccurate measure 2°. (Try measuring this angle when the moon is full.) Using the sine of this angle, Aristarchus obtained the following equations:

$$\sin\left(\frac{\alpha}{2}\right) = \frac{r_m}{D_{em}}$$

$$\sin\left(\frac{\alpha}{2}\right) = \frac{r_s}{D_{es}}$$

From his table of sines (or chords), he knew the value of the left-hand side of these equations.

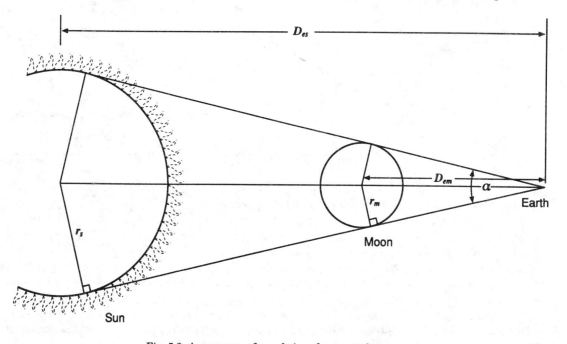

Fig. 5.3. Appearance of equal size of moon and sun

The third event is the rising of the half-moon as shown in figure 5.4. Aristarchus measured the angle β and found the measure of the angle θ using $\theta = 90° - \beta$. He obtained $\theta = 3°$, although the actual value is about $\theta = \frac{1}{6}°$. His seventh equation was

$$\sin(\theta) = \frac{D_{em}}{D_{es}}.$$

Aristarchus then solved these seven equations and obtained $r_m = 1385$ miles. See Resnikoff and Wells (1984, pp. 99–103) for the details. The current values used are $r_m = 1080$ miles and $D_{em} = 238\ 857$ miles. With the correct angle measures, as indicated in the text, Aristarchus' estimate of the radius of the moon would have been accurate to within 10 miles!

Trigonometry was also used to perform arithmetic computations. To illustrate the procedure, consider the following identity:

$$2\cos(A)\cos(B) = \cos(A + B) + \cos(A - B)$$

To find the product of 1732×984, rewrite the problem as $2 \times 0.866 \times 0.984 \times 10^6$. This matches the trigonometric identity and makes the numbers in the product less than 1, which is required for the cosines tables. Using a trigonometry table to find angles with cosines 0.866 and 0.966, we obtain $A = 30°$ and $B = 10°$, respectively. Using these values to find $A + B = 40°$ and $A - B = 20°$ and again using the trigonometry tables, we obtain

$$1732 \times 984 = (0.7631 + 0.9412) \cdot 10^6$$
$$= 1\ 704\ 350.$$

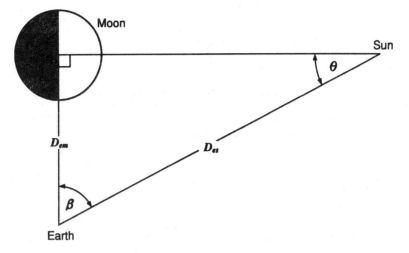

Fig. 5.4. Rise of the half-moon

Use a calculator to verify the accuracy of this computation. Similar computational procedures were known to John Napier (1550–1617) who spent twenty years developing the mathematics of logarithms published in 1614 in his book *Mirifici logarithmorum can· s descriptio*. Logarithms made trigonometric computations obsolete because logarithms could also be used to divide and to raise numbers to powers.

This now-antiquated use of trigonometry illustrates two important points. The first is that many trigonometric identities now taught as algebraic exercises historically had computational applications. The second is that the origin of logarithms lies not so much in an application as in the mathematical structure of another discipline, namely, computational trigonometry. The origins of mathematics are not only from the study of applications but also from the study of the structure of mathematics itself.

The articles in this section sample some of the applications of both trigonometry and elementary analysis. A common application of trigonometry is to estimate distances and angles. Knill shows how to estimate heights of clouds. Jeffrey uses trigonometry to study angles and images formed by lenses.

Trigonometry is a powerful tool when used to analyze angles and distances in geometric figures that arise in applications. Staib studies a medical problem on detecting heartbeat abnormalities. (Robinson's letter to the editor considers an alternative derivation.) Parzynski combines geometry and trigonometry to study the reflective properties of antennas. Lepowsky provides an ingenious application of trigonometry to the study of balances. Palmaccio uses trigonometry to study the problem of estimating winds on a ship in motion.

Trigonometric functions are useful in modeling. Lando and Lando use trigonometric functions to model temperature patterns observed during the year.

Trigonometry, like geometry, does not have to be limited to two-dimensional figures. Jamski uses trigonometry to study the distances on a globe—an introduction to spherical trigonometry. (Sterba gives an alternative solution.)

Like arithmetic computations, trigonometry computations and graphs are often difficult to perform by hand. Demana and Waits use a graphing calculator to analyze questions about parametric trigonometry equations arising in the study of planetary motion. Palmaccio uses parametric trigonometry equations to study weather forecasting.

Elementary analysis studies functions and relations and their properties. Wapner uses difference equations and modeling to study growths of populations that have predators. Sloyer, Crouse, Sacco, and Copes use dynamic programming to study sorting, counting, and coding problems.

REFERENCES

Eves, Howard. *Great Moments in Mathematics before 1650*. Washington, D.C.: Mathematical Association of America, 1983.

Kennedy, Edward S. "The History of Trigonometry." In *Historical Topics for the Mathematics Classroom*. Thirty-first Yearbook of the National Council of Teachers of Mathematics. 2d ed. Reston, Va.: The Council, 1989.

Resnikoff, H. L., and R. O. Wells, Jr. *Mathematics in Civilization*. New York: Dover Publications, 1984.

applications

CLOUD HEIGHT AT NIGHT

Basically, there are two types of pilots' licences—commercial and private. Private pilots whose licences are endorsed for IFR (Instrument Flight Rules) and whose aircraft are suitably equipped with instruments and radios can fly using Instrument Flight Rules in conditions where visibility is restricted.

Some private licences are valid only for flying by VFR (Visual Flight Rules). This permits a pilot to fly an aircraft if the cloud ceiling is 1000 feet or more and the ground visibility is 3 miles or more (fig. 1).

During daylight hours, ground visibility and cloud height can be determined visually by a trained eye. At night ground visibility is determined using the lights from towers and other reference points around the airport. The cloud height at night is determined in the following manner.

An observer is stationed 1000 feet from a light source in a parabolic reflector. This light is directed at the clouds at a constant angle of 70° (fig. 2). The observer measures the angle of elevation θ of the

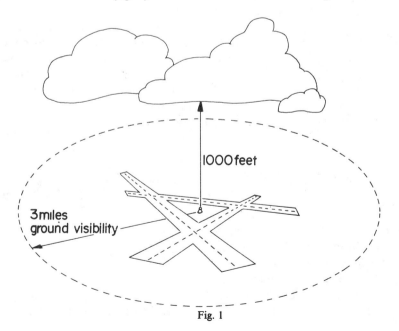

1000 feet

3 miles
ground visibility

Fig. 1

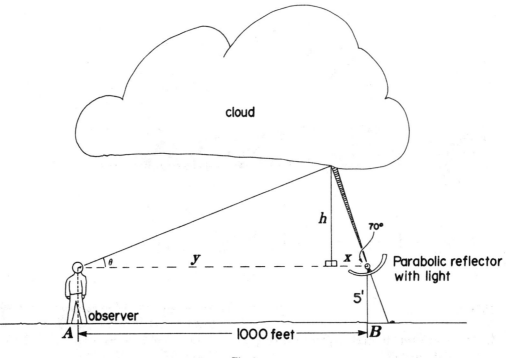

Fig. 2

light reflecting from the clouds. Once $m\angle\theta$ is determined, the height of the clouds may be calculated as follows:

$$\frac{x}{h} = \cot 70$$

(1) $\therefore \quad x = h \cot 70.$

$$\frac{y}{h} = \cot \theta$$

(2) $\therefore \quad y = h \cot \theta.$

Adding (1) and (2) yields

$$x + y = h \cot 70 + h \cot \theta,$$

but

$$x + y = 1000 \text{ ft.},$$

$$\therefore \quad 1000 = h(\cot 70 + \cot \theta),$$

and

$$h = \frac{1000}{\cot 70 + \cot \theta}.$$

Notes: Some airports have an alidade (al'-ah-dād) located at the observer's position. Instead of giving the angle of elevation of the light, the observer reads the altitude of the clouds (to the nearest 100 ft.) directly from the instrument (fig. 3).

If the equation

$$h = \frac{1000}{\cot 70 + \cot \theta}$$

is solved for cot θ, we have

$$\cot \theta = \frac{1000}{h} - \cot 70.$$

By substituting values of the height for h (in multiples of 100 ft.), students can calculate the value of θ that corresponds to these altitudes and then design their own alidade. (For 1000 ft. the angle is approximately 58°, and for 2000 ft. it is approximately 82°.)

Problems

1. Determine the cloud height to the nearest 100 ft. for the following values of θ.

(*a*) 30°
(*b*) 45°
(*c*) 60°
(*d*) 70°

2. Why can the 5-ft. height of the observer's station and light be ignored?

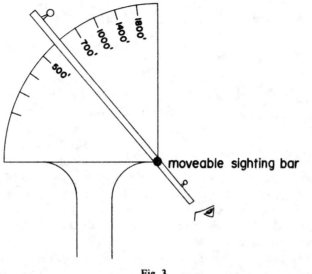

Fig. 3

Answers

1. To the nearest 100 feet: (a) 500, (b) 700, (c) 1100, (d) 1400.

2. Since answers are being rounded to the nearest 100 ft., the 5-ft. height of the observer's stations and light are insignificant.

MATHEMATICS IN PHOTOGRAPHY

By **NEIL J. JEFFREY**
York Mills Collegiate
Don Mills, ON M3B 1W6

One look at the markings on an adjustable camera demonstrates that photography depends heavily on mathematics. On such a camera are marked f-stops, shutter speeds, and distance and ASA scales. In the camera manual are exposure tables and depth-of-field charts. Packed with each roll of film are development times and temperatures. And in the literature are innumerable charts and graphs. In this paper I will attempt to explain some of the mathematics involved in photography.

As a teacher, I have made classroom use of the mathematics in photography to illustrate such conventional topics as geometric sequences and similarity transformations. These ideas have also been the subject of many informal discussions outside of class. Whether a student is an amateur photographer or just curious about the markings on a camera, an understanding of some of the mathematics in photography can be very satisfying. To begin, I will use similar triangles to develop several formulas by a method used in many high school physics courses.

Some standard optics

Consider figure 1, which is a standard ray diagram for a thin converging lens. (Of course, assuming a camera lens to be thin is, at best, questionable; but the formulas developed give surprisingly accurate results.) The physical property of converging lenses involved is that light rays traveling parallel to the axis are refracted through the focus, and vice versa. The focal length of the lens is the distance from its center to the focus. Call this distance f. Let h_o be the height of the object, s_o the distance from the object to the nearer focus, and d_o the distance from the object to the lens. Let h_i, s_i, and d_i be the corresponding quantities for the image.

From a consideration of similar triangles on the image side of the lens, it is clear that

$$(1) \qquad \frac{h_i}{h_o} = \frac{s_i}{f},$$

and on the object side,

$$(2) \qquad \frac{h_i}{h_o} = \frac{f}{s_o}.$$

From (1) and (2) it follows that

$$\frac{s_i}{f} = \frac{f}{s_o},$$

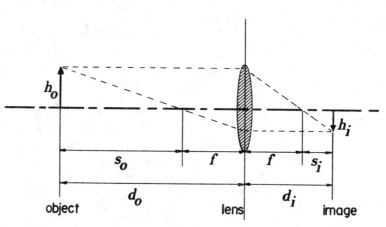

Fig. 1

and

(3) $$s_i \cdot s_o = f^2.$$

Geometry

Photography is essentially a geometric process: it attempts to project a space of three dimensions onto the film plane. In a regular photograph of a person, for example, only the nearest surfaces of the subject are projected onto the film. With an x-ray photograph, the projection is more successful: in addition to surface tissues, organs and bones are projected onto the film.

A frontal photograph of a plane subject produces an image on the film that is similar to the subject. The production of this image is an example of a similarity transformation of the plane. Another similarity transformation is performed when projecting a slide or making an enlargement from a negative. In fact, if this enlargement produces a life-size image of the plane subject, then it is exactly the inverse of the transformation made by the camera.

One problem that can arise when making enlargements is the following one. Common negative sizes are $2\frac{1}{4}'' \times 2\frac{1}{4}''$, 24 mm $\times$ 36 mm, and $4'' \times 5''$. Neither of the first two formats could be mapped onto a sheet of paper $8'' \times 10''$ by a similarity transformation, but the last one can. Either of the first two formats could be mapped onto such a paper by means of different magnifications in the x and y directions, that is, by an affine transformation; but such a distortion is usually not desired. (In practice, the problem is solved by enlarging only a portion of the negative, a portion that is similar to the $8'' \times 10''$ paper.)

Trigonometry

Two important properties of any lens are its focal length and its angle of view. Telephoto, or long focal-length lenses, have a narrow angle of view; short focal-length lenses are commonly referred to as wide-angle lenses. In many lenses the angle of view is the same as the angle subtended by the diagonal of the negative. Figure 2 is a diagram of the simplest situation—a lens of infinitesimal aperture, focused at infinity, where θ represents the angle of view, x is the length of the diagonal of the negative, and f is the focal length of the lens. So we can see that

$$\tan \frac{\theta}{2} = \frac{\frac{x}{2}}{f},$$

$$\frac{\theta}{2} = \tan^{-1} \frac{x}{2f},$$

and

(4) $$\theta = 2\tan^{-1} \frac{x}{2f}.$$

That is, the angle of view of the lens is twice the angle whose tangent equals the length of the negative's diagonal divided by twice the focal length. Table 1 was calculated using (4) and assumes a negative size of 24 mm $\times$ 36 mm for which $x = 12\sqrt{13}$. Focal lengths are in millimeters, angles in degrees. The entries in table 1 may be compared with the focal lengths and angles of view of any 35-mm camera lenses that students and teachers may have.

Ratio and variation

Photography provides several examples of ratios and variations. The f-stop number is simply a ratio:

$$\text{f-stop} = \frac{\text{focal length of lens}}{\text{(effective) diameter of opening}}$$

(Effective diameter is used because the lens is thick and the aperture, inside it, may be equivalent to a slightly different one.) For lenses of fixed focal length, the f-stop number and the effective lens diameter are inversely proportional.

TABLE 1

f	θ
1000	2.48
400	6.19
135	18.21
50	46.79
28	75.38
18	100.48

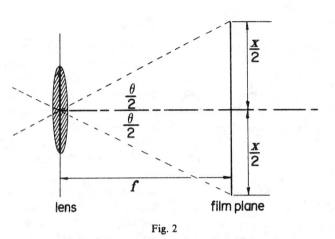

Fig. 2

A moment's consideration should convince most people that the amount of light reaching the film, or the exposure, is proportional to the area of the aperture and to the length of time for which it is open.

$$E \propto At$$

where E is exposure, A is aperture area, and t is the duration of time for which the aperture is open. Furthermore, since the area is proportional to the square of the diameter, d, it follows that

(5) $$E \propto d^2 t.$$

Statement (5) is an example of a joint variation.

Since the diameter is inversely proportional to the f-stop number, one can conclude that

(6) $$E \propto \frac{t}{(\text{f-stop})^2}.$$

Exponential function

Almost as soon as photographic emulsions became standardized, photographers and researchers studied the effect of exposure on film. One of the quantities that they related to exposure was called *density*, which is nearly proportional to the amount of silver deposited on a negative. When they plotted density versus logarithm of exposure, within certain limits, they obtained a reasonably straight line. A rough sketch of such a graph is given in figure 3.

In the straight-line region of the graph,

log exposure = a linear function

of density;

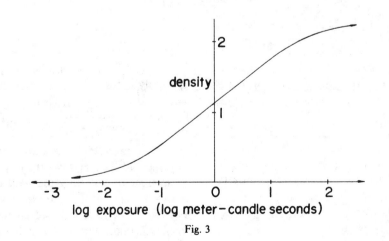

Fig. 3

log exposure = $AD + B$.

For suitable choices of A and B, and where D is density,

$$\text{exposure} = 10^{AD + B}$$
$$\text{exposure} = 10^{AD}(10^{B})$$
$$\text{exposure} = 10^{B}(10^{A})^{D}.$$

Letting 10^{B} be h and 10^{A} be k,

$$\text{exposure} = h \cdot k^{D}.$$

The exposure is, then, an exponential function of density. As a necessary consequence, it follows that equal increments of density will be produced by increasing the exposure by the same factor.

Geometric sequence

It has been observed that equal changes in density are produced by multiplying the exposure by a constant factor. Clearly, then, a succession of equal steps in density can be obtained by a succession of exposures that must form a geometric sequence.

It happens that doubling (or halving) the exposure produces a suitably small change in density. Since the exposure is proportional to the time for which the shutter is open, the sequence of commonly available shutter speeds forms (nearly) a geometric sequence with ratio 2:

$$\frac{1}{500}, \frac{1}{250}, \frac{1}{125}, \frac{1}{60}, \frac{1}{30}, \frac{1}{15}, \frac{1}{8}, \cdots$$

Furthermore, since the exposure is proportional to the square of the diameter, for the exposure to be doubled, the diameter must be multiplied by $\sqrt{2}$. Since the diameter and f-stop number are inversely proportional, it follows that doubling the exposure requires the f-stop number to be divided by $\sqrt{2}$, which creates another geometric sequence:

32, 22, 16, 11, 8, 5.6, 4, 2.8, 2, 1.4, . . .

The use of these two sequences in conjunction is very convenient because shortening the time by one step and opening the aperture by one stop has no net effect on the exposure.

Geometric and arithmetic means

One way often suggested for determining proper exposure is to meter the brightest area and the most deeply shaded area. For example, at 1/8 second, f-stops of $f/90$ and $f/2.8$ might be indicated. Such a scene would have a ten-stop range of brightnesses: 90, 64, 45, 32, 22, 16, 11, 8, 5.6, 4, and 2.8. (Between these eleven f-stops, the exposure is doubled ten times.) In most cases, one would like to use an exposure near the middle, such as $f/16$. Sixteen is, in fact, the geometric mean of 90 and 2.8. Using an exposure too close to either end of the range above would result in either the deepest shades running together or the lightest areas being indistinguishable from one another.

An alternate system of measuring exposures is to use exposure value, or *EV*, numbers. In this system, halving the exposure just increases the *EV* number by one. The range of exposures above corresponds to the following *EV* numbers: 16, 15, 14, 13, 12, 11, 10, 9, 8, 7, and 6, respectively. In this case, the middle exposure is found by taking the arithmetic mean of the two extreme values.

The f-stop ring (or the list of f-stops above) can be used for calculating the geometric mean of the numbers on it: to find the geometric mean of 32 and 8, simply take the number midway between them, 16. Numbers not on the scale can be found roughly by interpolation. The shutter-speed scale can be used in exactly the same way.

A law of exponents

An example of an application of the rule for multiplying powers with the same base arises when using neutral-density filters. (These filters reduce the amount of all colors of light entering the camera.) Each filter has a filter factor associated with it. For example, a factor of 8 indicates that the filter transmits only 1/8 of the light entering it. To maintain the same exposure, the aperture would have to be opened up by three stops. A factor of 4 indicates that the filter transmits only 1/4 of the light entering it. To maintain the same exposure, the aperture would have to be opened up by two stops. If both filters were used at the same time they would transmit only 1/4 × 1/8 or 1/32 of the light; and, in order to maintain the same exposure, a five-stop increase in aperture would be required—that is, the sum of the two individual increases in aperture.

An inverse variation

From (3) it follows that

$$s_i = \frac{f^2}{s_o}.$$

Hence for fixed f,

(7) $$s_i \propto \frac{1}{s_o}.$$

In many lenses, focusing is achieved by moving the entire lens forward or backward as a unit. These lenses are the ones referred to below. (An alternate system of focusing involves moving only part of the lens; this causes its configuration and therefore its focal length to change.) As the focusing ring is rotated, the lens seems to move smoothly in and out; it seems reasonable to suppose that the change in image distance is proportional to the amount of rotation, $\Delta\phi$—

$$\Delta s_i \propto \Delta\phi.$$

Therefore, for a suitable choice of initial angle,

$$s_i \propto \phi.$$

Recall (7),

$$s_i \propto \frac{1}{s_o}.$$

Therefore

(8) $$\phi \propto \frac{1}{s_o}.$$

In fact, the distances marked on the lens barrel are d_o and not s_o, but for most photographic distances, the two are relatively close. Statement (8), therefore, accounts for the location of distance marks on the lens barrel. The amount of rotation needed is inversely proportional to the distance. A particular consequence of (8) is that the amount the lens must be rotated (from the ∞ position) to focus at five feet is twice the amount it must be rotated to focus at ten feet.

Harmonic mean

The location of the image of a point source of light depends on the location of the source. The relationship is given in (3). Points that are not equidistant from the lens produce images that are not equidistant from the lens. Since the film plane can be in only one place, the images of many points must lie either in front of or behind the film plane. At the film plane, the light rays from such points do not quite converge, and they form a small circle on the film. A point is said to be in focus if it is recorded as a suitably small circle, perhaps one whose diameter is less than 0.05 millimeters. Figure 4 shows a pair of rays com-

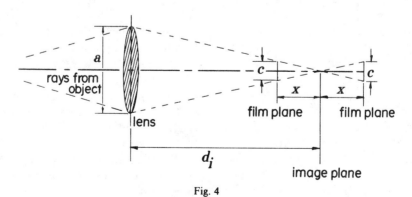

Fig. 4

ing from an arbitrary point whose distance from the lens is d_i, and two possible film plane locations at which the point would be recorded as a circle of diameter c.

Let the effective lens aperture be a, the lens-to-image distance be d_i, the displacement of the film plane from the image be x, and the maximum permissible diameter of the circle of confusion be c. Then in both cases,

$$\frac{a}{d_i} = \frac{c}{x},$$

and hence,

$$\dot{x} = \frac{cd_i}{a}.$$

Notice that x is the same in both directions, Δs_i is the same in both directions, and that $\Delta\phi$ is the same in both directions. That is to say that the lens barrel can be rotated by the same amount from the focused position in either direction before the image goes out of focus. It is for exactly this reason that the depth-of-field scale has pairs of marks that are equidistant from the point of focus, one on either side. Let s_{o-pf} be the object distance on which the lens is focused, and ϕ_{pf} be the corresponding angle of orientation of the lens barrel. Let $s_{o\text{-close}}$ and $s_{o\text{-far}}$ be the distances to the closest and farthest points that remain in focus, and ϕ_{close} and ϕ_{far} be their corresponding lens barrel orientations. Since the point-of-focus mark on the lens barrel is midway between the two depth-of-field marks,

$$(9) \qquad \phi_{pf} = \frac{\phi_{\text{close}} + \phi_{\text{far}}}{2}.$$

So (8) and (9) together imply

$$(10) \qquad \frac{1}{s_{o-pf}} = \frac{\dfrac{1}{s_{o\text{-close}}} + \dfrac{1}{s_{o\text{-far}}}}{2}.$$

That is to say that s_{o-pf} is the harmonic mean of $s_{o\text{-close}}$ and $s_{o\text{-far}}$. Of course, this is a direct consequence of (8).

Evidence that (10) is reasonably accurate, in spite of all the simplifications and assumptions made, can be obtained by referring to a depth-of-field chart. A depth-of-field chart is simply a tabulation of the relationship between the distance focused on and the distances to the closest and farthest things that remain in focus. Some readers might be interested to know that, with the aid of some elementary mathematics and some basic assumptions, it is possible to produce a reasonably accurate depth-of-field chart.

Since in many cases camera lenses are indeed complex, it is surprising that so many of their properties can be understood through mathematics as simple as that presented here. One reason is that, although a lens is complex, it was designed to behave very much in the same way as a thin converging lens, but with several minor improvements. This thin lens, in turn, was intended to act like a pinhole aperture but to allow more light to pass. The result of making some simplifying assumptions about a camera lens is that elementary mathematics can be applied to a very real situation in a way that students can understand.

BIBLIOGRAPHY

Clerc, Louis P. *Photography Theory and Practice.* Edited by D. A. Spencer. London and New York: Focal Press, 1973.

Morgan, Willard D., ed. *The Encyclopedia of Photography.* New York: Greystone Press, 1962.

THE CARDIOLOGIST'S THEOREM

You and your students will enjoy this "Polya" search for an elegant solution to a real problem in diagnosing heart abnormalities.

By JOHN H. STAIB
Drexel University
Philadelphia, PA 19104

A COLLEAGUE from the biomedical engineering department here at Drexel walked into my office recently with a problem in trigonometry. I was surprised, for I knew that his current research interests were in the field of cardiology; in particular, he is working on methods for improving and refining the data that the cardiologist obtains from an electrocardiogram. He explained that the cardiologist does more than just "read" the electrocardiogram: he also measures the heights of, and the distances between, the various peaks that appear. And it was with regard to such measurements that the above-mentioned trigonometry problem had arisen.

The actual problem is as follows: The heights of certain peaks are measured; we shall call these values **a** and **b**. Also, dependent on where the electrodes were attached to the patient (ankle, wrist, and so on), there is a certain angle associated with the given electrocardiogram; we shall call it θ. Then **a**, **b**, and θ, the angle determined by **a** and **b**, are taken as the basis for the vector diagram shown in figure 1. What is then

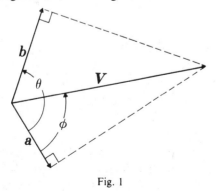

Fig. 1

required is not the usual resultant of the vectors marked **a** and **b** but rather the vector **V** shown in the figure: **V** is the diagonal of the quadrilateral formed by constructing perpendiculars to the given vectors at their tips. A knowledge of **V** and the angle θ that **V** makes with vector **a** gives the cardiologist important information about the path of nerve excitation across the heart that is associated with each heartbeat; the angle is said to determine the "electrical axis" of the heart. Ultimately, this information becomes part of a total diagnostic package that enables the cardiologist to determine specific heart abnormalities.

Currently, cardiologists obtain the length and direction of **V** by graphical means: they simply draw a suitable figure and make the appropriate measurements. My friend had basically come to me with the following:

PROBLEM. *Find an algorithm suitable for minicalculator computation that can compute the length and direction of **V** directly from **a**, **b**, and θ (fig. 1).*

I studied the figure, looking for some elegant solution that would follow from geometry. I noted, for example, that the quadrilateral could be inscribed in a circle. But such investigations led me nowhere. I was thus forced to turn to analytic geometry, where a direct, though tedious, solution was apparent. Introducing a coordinate system (fig. 2), I could determine the coordinates of the tips of the given vectors, then find equations for the perpendiculars, and finally solve those equations to get the coordinates of the tip of **V**. From those coordinates, the length and direction of **V** could easily be found. We shall carry out this solution, leaving some steps for the reader.

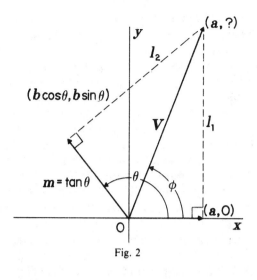

Fig. 2

Equations for the lines l_1 and l_2 are easily obtained. For l_1 we have

$$x = a,$$

and for l_2 we have

$$(y - b \sin \theta) = - \cot \theta \, (x - b \cos \theta).$$

Substituting $x = a$ in this last equation and solving for y gives us the missing y-coordinate of the tip of $\mathbf{V}$. After some simplifying steps, we arrive finally at the following representation for the tip of $\mathbf{V}$:

$$(a, \, -a \cot \theta + b \csc \theta)$$

The length of $\mathbf{V}$ is simply the distance from the point above to the origin; that is,

$$(1) \quad |\mathbf{V}| = \sqrt{a^2 + (-a \cot \theta + b \csc \theta)^2}$$

An ugly expression! But using the "student's trick," replacing "everything" by sines and cosines, formula (1) simplifies to

$$(1') \quad |\mathbf{V}| = \frac{\sqrt{a^2 + b^2 - 2ab \cos \theta}}{\sin \theta}.$$

The solution is completed by calculating ϕ, the direction of $\mathbf{V}$; from figure 2 we see that

$$\phi = \cos^{-1} \frac{a}{|\mathbf{V}|}.$$

Well, not the elegant solution I was first seeking but a good job nevertheless, for the calculations involved are within the range of the typical scientific hand calculator. But

the reader will no doubt have "jumped," as I did, on reading formula (1'). For there in the numerator is the law of cosines. What side of what triangle is the numerator computing? Returning to figure 2, we see that $\sqrt{a^2 + b^2 - 2ab \cos \theta}$ gives the length of the other diagonal of our quadrilateral. Thus, we may conclude that $|\mathbf{V}|$ is obtained by dividing the length of the other diagonal by the sine of θ. But why should that be so?

The analytic solution having thus led me to this curious relationship between the diagonals of a quadrilateral, I was now even more convinced that the problem had an elegant solution. So I returned again to the geometry of the figure.

I decided to first study (that's what Polya does) a special case: $\mathbf{a} = \mathbf{b}$. Also, I included in my considerations the circumscribed circle. Thus we have figure 3. Letting $\theta = 2\alpha$ and exploiting the bilateral symmetry of the figure, we can label it as shown. What we want to show, relative to this figure, is that

$$y + z = \frac{2x}{\sin 2\alpha},$$

or

$$(2) \quad \frac{2x}{y + z} = \sin 2\alpha.$$

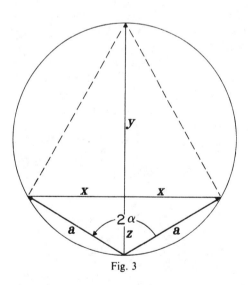

Fig. 3

This turns out to be easy: We note that the four right triangles into which the quadrilateral is divided are all similar. Thus, we

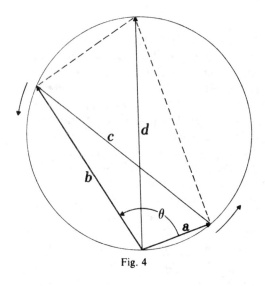

Fig. 4

may use the proportionality of similar triangles to obtain

$$\frac{y}{x} = \frac{x}{z} = \tan \alpha.$$

It follows that $y = x \tan \alpha$ and $z = x \cot \alpha$. Substituting for y and z in equation (2), we obtain

$$\frac{2x}{x \tan \alpha + x \cot \alpha} = \frac{2}{\tan \alpha + \cot \alpha}$$

$$= 2 \sin \alpha \cos \alpha = \sin 2\alpha$$

which is what was to be proved.

Success! But what about the general case where $\mathbf{a} \neq \mathbf{b}$. Well, let us consider figure 4. We wish to prove that $d = c/\sin \theta$. Let us view the figure dynamically: We set it into motion by letting c slide around the circle toward the perpendicular position it had in figure 3. What happens to the quantities that concern us? Well, c/d remains constant because d and c individually remain constant. And θ, hence $\sin \theta$, remains constant because regardless of the position of c, the arc included by θ always has the same measure. Thus, both c/d and $\sin \theta$ remain the same for every position of c. Since in one special position—the perpendicular one—we found that $c/d = \sin \theta$, it follows that for every position of c we shall have $c/d = \sin \theta$. (This proof can easily be cleansed of its motion language.)

Next, recognizing that d is a diameter of the circumscribed circle and that c is a chord, we naturally wish to express our ratio law in a form that relates to the circle rather than to the quadrilateral. To see how this can be done, consider figure 5. Figure 5a is essentially the same as figure 4. To get figure 5b, we delete the dotted lines and slide the triangle in a clockwise direction. We then note that the position of c could be fixed while still permitting the vertex of the angle θ to move. The shape of the triangle would then vary, but the angle θ would

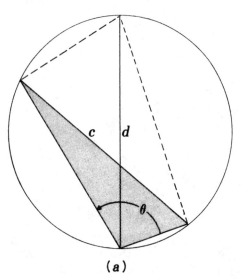

(a)

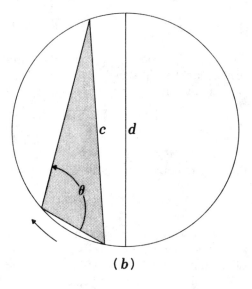

(b)

Fig. 5

remain constant in measure. This is because the arc included by θ remains the same. Thus, we have the following:

THEOREM. *If d and c are a diameter and chord, respectively, of the same circle, then c/d = sin θ, where the measure of θ is 1/2 the measure of either of the arcs determined by c.*

The fact that the corresponding half-arcs are supplementary and that we are dealing with the sine function implies that either arc will satisfy the theorem.

Finally, then, we have arrived at that theorem, which—had I known it at the beginning—would have permitted the elegant solution that I first sought. But I did not know it, nor have I been able to find a source for it. Apparently the reason for its neglect is that it is mathematically uninteresting or without significant application value except, of course, with respect to the cardiologist's problem. To see just how trivial the cardiologist's theorem is, the reader

should prove it again using the diagram of figure 6. The mathematical moral is this: Complicated problems sometimes become

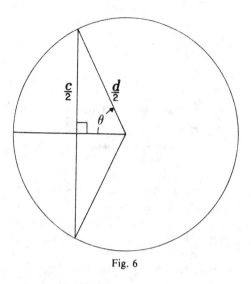

Fig. 6

trivial when looked at in just the right way. And conversely.

Ptolemy prescription

When reading the article "The Cardiologist's Theorem" (January 1977), like all good readers I tried the problem before "reading on" and came up with the following:

The two right angles ensure that the quadrilateral is cyclic, and therefore by Ptolemy's Theorem

(1) $\qquad c \cdot d = a \cdot x + b \cdot y.$

Now
$$a = d \cos \phi$$
$$b = d \cos \psi$$
$$x = d \sin \psi$$
$$y = d \sin \phi$$

giving, on substitution in (1),

$$c \cdot d = d^2 (\cos \phi \cdot \sin \psi + \sin \phi \cdot \cos \psi)$$

$$c = d \sin(\phi + \psi)$$

$$\underline{c = d \sin \theta}$$

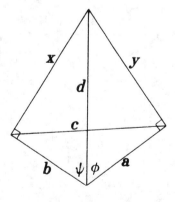

The "Cardiologist's Theorem" is a corollary of Ptolemy's theorem.

Arthur Robinson
International School of Geneva
Geneva
Switzerland

IS THE GRAPH OF TEMPERATURE VARIATION A SINE CURVE? AN APPLICATION FOR TRIGONOMETRY CLASSES

Here's curve-fitting without least-squares techniques. Minicalculators remove the drudgery from the task.

By BARBARA M. LANDO
and CLIFTON A. LANDO

**University of Alaska
Fairbanks, AK 99701**

IN trigonometry courses, students are introduced to the notions of periodic functions and general sine curves. At this point they may be given some examples of trigonometric functions that are used to represent physical phenomena, but they probably do not gain much insight into how these functions are actually developed from the physical data. We found that considerable enthusiasm can be generated at this stage by a project that begins with raw data and ends with a trigonometric function that models the physical situation. There are many familiar phenomena that are periodic, such as sound waves, electrical currents, business cycles, and air pollution levels. For our project we chose the local yearly temperature pattern because the data were readily available and because Alaskans are generally concerned with the weather.

Having introduced a general sine curve to represent

$$f(x) = a \sin [b(x + c)] + d,$$

where a is the amplitude, $2\pi/b$ is the period, c is the horizontal shift, and d is the

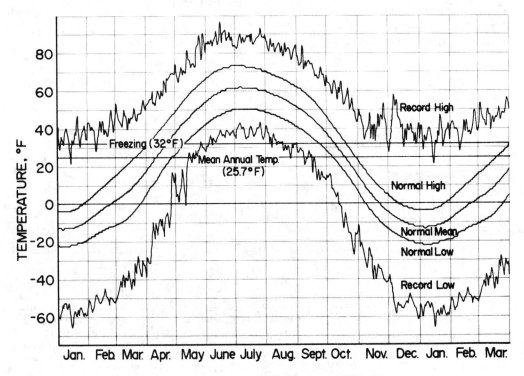

Fig. 1. Air temperature at Fairbanks, Alaska (1941–70)

vertical shift, we presented the students with copies of graphs of Fairbanks air temperature as recorded by the National Weather Service at Fairbanks International Airport (fig. 1). No one hesitated to say that the graphs resembled sine curves. So it was natural to pose these problems:

1. Find a general sine function with the same period, amplitude, and shifts as the normal mean temperature curve.

2. Is the temperature curve really a sine curve; that is, how well does your sine curve approximate the given curve?

3. If the fit is not good, how might it be improved?

4. Could the temperature information in "function form" be more useful in some cases than the same information presented graphically or in tables?

In order to provide some common groundwork, we suggested that the 0° line be taken as the x-axis (other possibilities are the annual mean temperature or 32°), that 1 January be taken as the y-axis, and that units on the x-axis be days and units on the y-axis be degrees. The students were to evaluate their answers by sketching them on their copies of the temperature graph.

To get an accurate sketch, the use of our available calculators or computers was encouraged. When available, a plotter would be highly recommended.

An inspection of the normal mean graph revealed that the temperature varies from about −13° to 61° on this curve, giving an amplitude of $\frac{61 + 13}{2} = 37$. The period is clearly 365, and so the constant b is $2\pi/365$. We estimated that the curve is shifted about 101 days to the right and 25 units upward from the usual positioning of a sine curve. The constants thus obtained yield the function

$$f(x) = 37 \sin \left[\frac{2\pi}{365} (x - 101) \right] + 25.$$

Its graph, with vertical scale increased and the temperature data plotted as points, is shown in figure 2. It appeared that the function $f(x)$ provides an acceptable approximation to the normal mean curve except in September and October.

When the procedure was repeated for the normal low temperature graph, however, we obtained

$$g(x) = 36 \sin \left[\frac{2\pi}{365} (x - 98) \right] + 14,$$

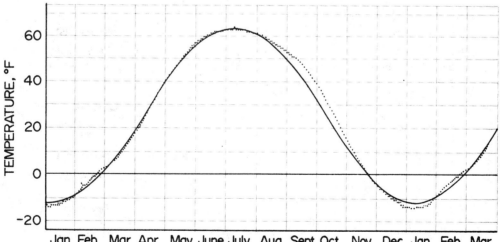

Fig. 2. Normal mean temperatures are plotted as data points; the approximating sine function is

$$f(x) = 37 \sin \left[\frac{2\pi}{365} (x - 101) \right] + 25$$

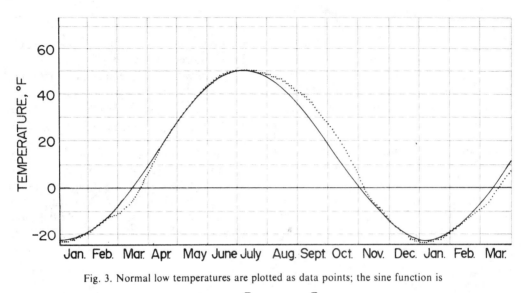

Fig. 3. Normal low temperatures are plotted as data points; the sine function is

$$g(x) = 36 \sin \left[\frac{2\pi}{365} (x - 98) \right] + 14.$$

with poor fit in both spring and fall, presumably due to the lag between ground and air temperatures (fig. 3). We noted that the error was also periodic and so tried to adjust our solution by adding a second sine curve. Since the maximum error appeared to be about 10 degrees, we used 5 for the amplitude and roughly estimated the other constants to arrive at a correction term of

$$5 \sin \left[\frac{2\pi}{365} (x - 182) \right]$$

to be added to $g(x)$ to obtain

$$h(x) = 36 \sin \left[\frac{2\pi}{365} (x - 98) \right] + 14$$

$$+ 5 \sin \left[\frac{2\pi}{365} (x - 182) \right].$$

This result seemed to be a better fit (fig. 4).

It was our intent to use only the tools available to the student, and so we did the curve-fitting by "guessing" a sine curve. It is interesting to note, however, that our guess is quite close to the answer obtained in a least-squares sine approximation. (See Johnson and Hartman [1969].)

In developing this project, we had the advantage of working from an existing temperature graph. In areas where such graph-

ical information is not available, however, it would be a simple project for the class to construct its own graph from readily available weather data. Any weather bureau and most libraries have the references listed in the Bibliography, which are published by the U.S. Weather Bureau and the Environmental Data Service. These publications give the average high, mean, and low for each day of the year. A rough graph can even be constructed using the monthly mean temperatures, which can be obtained by a phone call to the nearest weather station. In this case, you could plot twelve points with the fifteenth day of each month as abscissa and the average mean for that month as ordinate. Using Celsius instead of Fahrenheit presents no problem.

Our students seemed quite impressed with the idea of having developed a mathematical function that represents actual meteorological information. They programmed this sine function into a programmable calculator and were then able to key in the day of the year and immediately obtain the temperature for that day.

We also discussed the usefulness of having temperature information in function form for use in engineering problems. Such functions were used in planning various as-

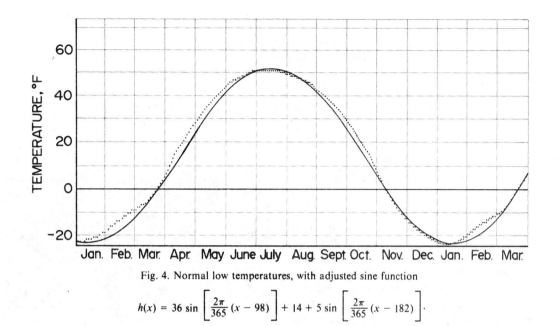

Fig. 4. Normal low temperatures, with adjusted sine function

$$h(x) = 36 \sin\left[\frac{2\pi}{365}(x - 98)\right] + 14 + 5 \sin\left[\frac{2\pi}{365}(x - 182)\right].$$

pects of the Trans-Alaska Pipeline. For example, specifications for the insulating pads, which prevent the hot oil pipeline from melting the permanently frozen tundra (permafrost), were developed by solving a heat equation. A simusoidal representation of annual temperature variation was used as a boundary condition for this partial differential equation.

REFERENCES

Johnson, P., and C. Hartman. *Environmental Atlas of Alaska*. Fairbanks: Institute of Arctic Environmental Engineering, University of Alaska, 1969.

U.S. Department of Commerce, Environmental Data Service. *Climates of the States*. Published annually. Washington, D.C., Government Printing Office.

———. *Climatological Data*. Published monthly with annual summaries. Washington, D.C., Government Printing Office.

U.S. Department of Commerce, U.S. Weath r Bureau. *Local Climatological Data*. Published monthly with annual summaries and comparative data. Washington, D.C., Government Printing Office.

We would like to thank Charles Hartman, Institute of Water Resources, University of Alaska (for Fairbanks temperature data), and John Morack, Physics Department, University of Alaska (for assistance in plotting the graphs).

The Geometry of Microwave Antennas

By WILLIAM R. PARZYNSKI, Montclair State College, Upper Montclair, NJ 07043

Parabolic antennas have become a common sight. Home television antennas can receive more than a hundred channels. Parabolic reflectors are as commonplace as an automobile headlight and as exotic as the solar reflector in the James Bond film *The Man with the Golden Gun.*

Antenna-reflector systems are used extensively in space exploration, communications, and radio astronomy. The antenna shown in figure 1, located in the Mojave desert of California, is sixty-four meters in diameter at its rim. This huge size made possible communication with the Voyager spacecrafts at distances from Earth in excess of 950 million miles, even though Voyager was linked to Earth by a feeble twenty-watt transmitter.

The large reflecting surface (fig. 1) is a paraboloid, and the subreflector at the top is a hyperboloid. Two reflecting surfaces are used so that the incoming microwaves can be focused toward the center of the large reflecting surface, where the electronics are conveniently located to receive the signal. Using only one reflecting surface would put the electronics in an awkward position and would adversely affect the distribution of weight on the large reflecting surface. These surfaces, particularly the larger one, are subject to minor deformations under their own weight as the position of the antenna changes. Since any distortion from the ideal shape impairs performance, the design of a rigid backup structure is an important engineering consideration.

Research on computer-aided structural design of antennas is being conducted at the Jet Propulsion Laboratory in Pasadena, California. This work involves a broad spectrum of undergraduate mathematics,

Fig. 1. An antenna in the Mojave desert

including geometry, algebra, calculus, linear algebra, and numerical methods.

This article describes the geometry of the antenna, particularly the reflective properties of the parabola and hyperbola, which determine the microwave path and concentrate the weak incoming energy.

THEOREM 1. *Let $P(x_0, y_0)$ be a point on the parabola given by $x^2 = 4py$ with $p > 0$, and let α be the acute angle between the tangent line at $P(x_0, y_0)$ and the vertical*

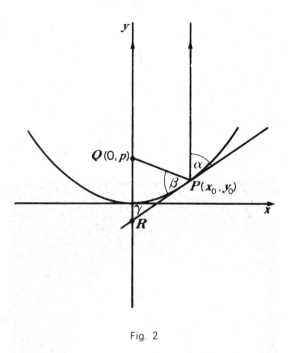

Fig. 2

line through $P(x_0, y_0)$. Let β be the angle between the tangent line and the line connecting the focus $Q(0, p)$ to $P(x_0, y_0)$. Then, $\alpha = \beta$. (See fig. 2.)

Proof. We shall prove that the triangle PQR is isosceles with $QR = PQ$, where R is the intersection of the tangent line and the y-axis. To find the coordinates of R, we find the equation of the tangent line to the parabola at (x_0, y_0). The slope of this line is the derivative of $y = x^2/(4p)$ at x_0; thus, the equation of the tangent line is

$$y - y_0 = (x - x_0)\left(\frac{x_0}{2p}\right).$$

The point R is the y-intercept. With $x = 0$,

$$y = y_0 - \frac{x_0^2}{2p}.$$

Hence, the coordinates of R are

$$\left(0, \frac{y_0 - x_0^2}{2p}\right)$$

The length of $\overline{QR}$ is

$$p - \left(y_0 - \frac{x_0^2}{2p}\right) = p - y_0 + \frac{4py_0}{2p}$$

$$= p + y_0.$$

The length of $\overline{PQ}$ is

$$\sqrt{x_0^2 + (y_0 - p)^2} = \sqrt{x_0^2 + y_0^2 + p^2 - 2py_0}$$

$$= \sqrt{4py_0 + y_0^2 + p^2 - 2py_0}$$

$$= \sqrt{p^2 + 2py_0 + y_0^2}$$

$$= p + y_0.$$

Therefore, $\triangle PQR$ is isosceles with equal base angles β, γ. But by parallelism $\alpha = \gamma$, from which $\alpha = \beta$.

THEOREM 2. *Given the hyperbola $y^2/b^2 - x^2/a^2 = 1$ containing $P(x_0, y_0)$, and with foci $(0, c)$, $(0, -c)$ such that $c^2 = a^2 + b^2$, let L_1 be the line through P and $(0, c)$, and let L_2 be the line containing P and $(0, -c)$. Then, lines L_1 and L_2 intersect the tangent line at P with equal angles α and β. (See fig. 3.)*

Proof. Let m_1 and m_2 be the slopes of L_1 and L_2, respectively. Then,

$$m_1 = \frac{y_0 - c}{x_0}$$

and

$$m_2 = \frac{y_0 + c}{x_0}.$$

Fig. 3

The slope, m_3, of the tangent line $P(x_0, y_0)$ is obtained by implicit differentiation:

$$\frac{y^2}{b^2} - \frac{x^2}{a^2} = 1$$

$$\frac{2yy'}{b^2} - \frac{2x}{a^2} = 0$$

$$y' = \frac{b^2 x}{a^2 y}$$

$$m_3 = \frac{b^2 x_0}{a^2 y_0}$$

Now, from the formula for the angle between two lines,

$$\tan \alpha = \frac{m_3 - m_1}{1 + m_1 m_3}.$$

By substituting for m_1 and m_3 and simplifying using $c^2 = a^2 + b^2$, along with the fact that $y_0^2/b^2 - x_0^2/a^2 = 1$ implies $a^2 y_0^2 - b^2 x_0^2 = a^2 b^2$, we get

$$\tan \alpha = \frac{a^2}{cx_0}, \quad x_0 \neq 0.$$

Next we compute

$$\tan \beta = \frac{m_2 - m_3}{1 + m_2 m_3}$$

in a similar manner to obtain

$$\tan \beta = \frac{a^2}{cx_0}, \quad x_0 \neq 0.$$

Hence, $\alpha = \beta$.

The cross sections of large microwave antenna systems consist of a parabola and a hyperbola, with the focus of the parabola and one focus of the hyperbola coincident (fig. 4). The incoming microwaves that are parallel to the axis of the parabola are reflected from the parabola up toward the hy-

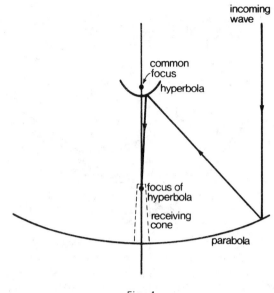

Fig. 4

perbola and back to the other focus of the hyperbola, where the cone of the antenna is located to capture the signal.

BIBLIOGRAPHY

Adler, Jerry. "The Riddles of Saturn." *Newsweek.* 24 November 1982, pp. 60 71.

Larson, Roland E., and Robert P. Hostetler. *Calculus.* 2d ed. Lexington, Mass.: D. C. Heath & Co., 1982, pp. 512 30.

Levy, Roy. "Computer Aided Design of Antenna Structures and Components." *Computers and Structures* 6 (June 1976): 419 28.

Levy, Roy, and Robert Melosh. "Computer Design of Antenna Reflectors." *Journal of the Structural Division, Proceedings of the American Society of Civil Engineers* 99 (November 1973): 2269 85.

Levy, Roy, and William Parzynski. "Optimality Criteria Solution Strategies in Multiple Constraint Design Optimization." *AIAA Journal* 20 (May 1982): 708–15.

Whitt, Lee. "The Standup Conic Presents: The Parabola and Applications." *The UMAP Journal* 3 (1982): 285 313. ◖

THE SUBTLE SCALES OF JUSTICE

A descriptive analysis of a balance scale in use.

By WILLIAM L. LEPOWSKY

**Laney College
Oakland, California**

THE two-pan balance scale is a familiar device. It is commonly used to symbolize the balance of justice, sometimes held by the blindfolded figure of Justice herself. You will find it depicted on every dollar bill in your pocket (on the seal to the right of the portrait). It is, furthermore, a standard device in algebra textbooks in the chapter on the solution of linear equations, and is sometimes found in the mathematics classroom. Yet its simple appearance disguises a surprisingly subtle and intricate structure, and its method of operation is not commonly known. An analysis of the two-pan balance scale provides a fruitful application of high school trigonometry yielding a satisfying result.

Let us first describe how such a scale works. If equal weights are placed in the pans, the scale will balance with the supporting beam horizontal. If the beam is tilted, the scale will oscillate, eventually returning to the horizontal. The horizontal position in this case is termed one of *stable equilibrium*. If unequal weights are used, the scale will come to rest at a tilt, returning to this oblique stable equilibrium position if moved.

It occurs here to ask how we can predict, knowing the two unequal weights, the angle of tilt at which the scale will settle. To answer this question, a detailed analysis of the structure of the scale is necessary.

A principle from physics states that each side contributes a certain *moment of force*, or *torque*, about the point P from which the beam is suspended and that the scale will be in equilibrium when the two moments are equal. The moment of each side is equal to the product of the weight hanging from that side times the horizontal distance from P to the vertical line through the point on the beam from which the weight hangs. (This horizontal distance is termed the *moment arm*.) If the moments are unequal, the side with the larger moment falls.

Figure 1 shows a rigid beam of length $2d$, supported at its midpoint P, with pans of equal weight suspended from its endpoints Q and R. If you think this is how a balance scale is constructed, you are in for a surprise!

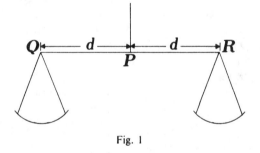

Fig. 1

If equal weights are placed in the pans, the scale will certainly be in equilibrium when the beam is horizontal, since both sides have the same moment $A \cdot d$, where A denotes the total weight of the pan and the object placed in it. However, if the scale is now tilted so that the beam is displaced an arbitrary angle θ from the horizontal (see fig. 2), the two sides still have equal moment arms, $d \cdot \cos \theta$, so both sides still have equal moments, $A \cdot d \cdot \cos \theta$, and the scale is still in equilibrium. Thus, with equal weights in the pans, instead of returning to the horizontal as expected, once tilted, this scale remains tilted! We conclude that figure 1 does not accurately depict a two-pan balance scale, and we must revise our model.

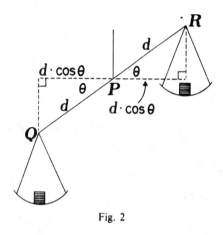

Fig. 2

Before we do, it is striking to note what happens if unequal weights are used. Assuming the weights are *A* and *B*, *A* ≠ *B* (assumed throughout to include the weight of the pans), the moments of the two sides are $A \cdot d \cdot \cos \theta$ and $B \cdot d \cdot \cos \theta$, respectively. These can be equal only if $\cos \theta = 0$, for $\theta = 90°$. We conclude that with unequal weights, in no oblique position will the scale be in equilibrium; it will come to rest only when absolutely vertical, with the lighter weight suspended directly above the heavier one!

A revised structure is shown in figure 3. Now the weights are suspended from the ends of a rigid beam bent so that each arm

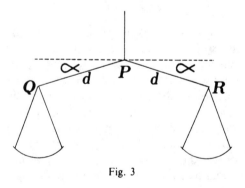

Fig. 3

of length *d* makes an angle α with the horizontal. Observe what a crucial difference this small, subtle change makes!

Figure 4 shows that when this scale is displaced from its rest position, the midpoint *P'* of $\overline{QR}$ is shifted from beneath *P* in the direction of the higher side. Since the distances measured horizontally from *P'* to the verticals through *Q* and *R* are equal, it follows that unlike the scale of figure 1, the moment arms of the two sides, measured horizontally from *P*, are unequal: the higher side has the larger moment arm. Consequently, with unequal weights in the pans, the equilibrium position is one in which the smaller weight is in the higher pan, and the ratio of the moment arms equals the ratio of the weights.

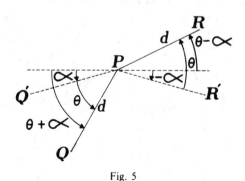

Fig. 4

To determine the angle of tilt θ at this equilibrium position, we must first find expressions for the two moment arms. Figure 5 shows the arms of a scale tilted at angle θ, with *Q'* and *R'* denoting the initial positions of *Q* and *R*. The angles are treated as signed trigonometric angles relative to the horizontal through *P*.

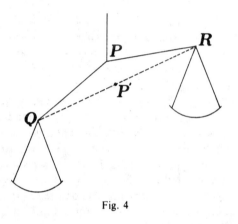

Fig. 5

The angle of rotation from the horizontal to $\overline{PR}$ is $\theta - \alpha$; from the horizontal to $\overline{PQ}$ is $\theta + \alpha$. The moment arms are the magnitudes of the abscissas of R and Q. Since the radius vectors PR and PQ have magnitude d, the moment arms of the higher and lower sides are $d \cdot \cos(\theta - \alpha)$ and $d \cdot \cos(\theta + \alpha)$, respectively.

Assuming the smaller of two weights B on the right and A on the left, the moments of the two sides are $B \cdot d \cdot \cos(\theta - \alpha)$ and $A \cdot d \cdot \cos(\theta + \alpha)$ respectively. Equating the two moments:

$$(1) \quad A \cdot d \cdot \cos(\theta + \alpha) = B \cdot d \cdot \cos(\theta - \alpha)$$

$$A \cdot \cos\theta \cos\alpha - A\sin\theta\sin\alpha$$
$$= B \cdot \cos\theta\cos\alpha + B \cdot \sin\theta\sin\alpha$$

$$(A - B)\cos\theta\cos\alpha = (A + B)\sin\theta\sin\alpha$$

$$\tan\theta = \left(\frac{A - B}{A + B}\right)\cot\alpha$$

The desired result has been obtained: for given weights A and B, the scale will be in equilibrium at the displacement θ given by this formula.

It is a straightforward if somewhat lengthy exercise in trigonometry to show that in any other position, the scale will no longer be in equilibrium and the imbalance of moments will cause it to return to the equilibrium position. The scale now behaves in the expected way. For example, if equal weights are placed in the pans of a tilted scale, the higher side has the greater moment arm, hence the greater moment; so it falls.

The formula obtained above is useful, and just a few points will be noted here:

1. If $A = B$, then $\tan\theta = 0 \cdot \cot\alpha = 0$, and the displacement is 0°.
2. For given A and B, $A \neq B$, the smaller the value of α, the larger the displacement θ.
3. The ratio of A to B (and of course the value of α) suffice to determine θ, since

$$\frac{A - B}{A + B} = \frac{A/B - 1}{A/B + 1}.$$

Table 1 shows the value of θ for various values of A/B and α.

TABLE 1
THE VALUE OF THE DISPLACEMENT θ
IN DEGREES FOR VARIOUS VALUES OF α AND A/B

A/B \ α	5°	10°	15°	20°
2.0	75°	62°	51°	42°
1.8	73°	58°	47°	38°
1.6	69°	53°	41°	32°
1.4	62°	43°	32°	25°
1.2	46°	27°	19°	14°
1.1	29°	15°	10°	7°
1.05	16°	8°	5°	4°
1.0	0°	0°	0°	0°

Now that we have analyzed the proper construction, it is interesting to ask how a scale would work if the points Q and R from which the weights are suspended were *above* P (of course at the same angle and at the same distance from P). You are invited to show that with such a construction—

1. with equal weights in the pans, the scale will be in equilibrium when the pans are at the same height;
2. if unequal weights are used, the equilibrium position is one in which the heavier weight is *higher* than the lighter weight;
3. in either case, the position is one of *unstable equilibrium*; that is, if the scale is displaced from the equilibrium position, it will not return to that position, but will instead move further from it.

You may have noticed an omission in the discussion thus far—we have neglected to consider the weight of the beam and, consequently, its moment. With these factors included, the situation is potentially more complex. A principle from physics states that to compute the moment of the beam about P, multiply its weight W by the horizontal distance from P to its centroid. Now, the beam of figure 1 has its centroid at P; hence, regardless of its orientation, its moment about P is zero, and we are justified in ignoring it.

The centroid C of the beam of figure 3, however, is not at P. It is midway between the midpoints S and T of the two arms, at a distance $c = \frac{a}{2}\sin\alpha$ below P (see fig. 6). When the scale is tilted, the centroid is moved horizontally from beneath P, giving the beam a positive moment about P. To compute the moment of the beam assuming

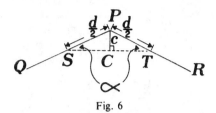

Fig. 6

an angle of tilt θ, note that the horizontal displacement of the centroid is $c \cdot \sin \theta$ (see fig. 7). It follows that a beam of weight W will have a moment $W \cdot c \cdot \sin \theta = W \cdot \frac{d}{2} \cdot \sin \alpha \cdot \sin \theta$ about P. Adding this quantity to the right side of (1) and solving, we find

$$(2) \qquad \tan \theta = \left[\frac{A - B}{A + B + \dfrac{W}{2}} \right] \cot \alpha.$$

This is the desired adjusted result.

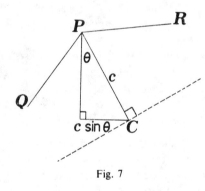

Fig. 7

An actual balance scale is likely to have a beam more irregular than our simplified model, but still symmetric about the vertical through P (see fig. 8). The centroid C of the beam will be at a distance c directly below P, and the moment of the tilted beam will be $W \cdot c \cdot \sin \theta$, just as in figure 7. Adding this to the right side of (1) and solving, we have:

$$(3) \qquad \tan \theta = \frac{(A - B) \, d \cos \alpha}{(A + B) \, d \sin \alpha + cW}.$$

This formula can be rewritten instructively as follows: Let $\overline{PC}$ meet $\overline{QR}$ at M,

and let $PM = h$. Note that $d \cdot \sin \alpha = h$. Dividing both numerator and denominator of the right side of (3) by $d \sin \alpha$ yields

$$\tan \theta = \frac{(A - B) \cot \alpha}{A + B + \dfrac{c}{d \sin \alpha} \cdot W}$$

$$= \left[\frac{A - B}{A + B + \dfrac{c}{h} \cdot W} \right] \cot \alpha.$$

Let $r = \frac{c}{h}$, the ratio that compares the distances from P (the point of support of the scale) to C (the centroid of the beam) and from P to $\overleftrightarrow{QR}$ (the line joining the points of suspension of the pans). We then have the formula:

$$(4) \qquad \tan \theta = \left(\frac{A - B}{A + B + rW} \right) \cot \alpha.$$

This is the general formula that accounts for the weight of the beam. Note that in the scale of figure 3, $r = \frac{1}{2}$; so that in this case, (4) reduces to (2).

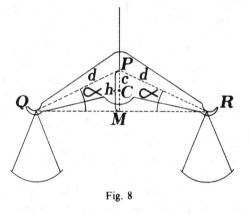

Fig. 8

A balance scale can easily be built using a 12-inch wooden ruler that has 3 holes for looseleaf binders. It can be suspended from its center hole with string or a paper clip, and small pans can be suspended from the holes at the ends, as shown in figure 9. One caution: it will be necessary to cut tiny notches in the wood at all three points of suspension so that the string or hook does not slide along the inner rim of the hole when the scale is tilted.

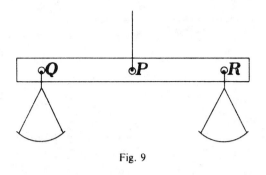

Fig. 9

I built such a scale using a ruler weighing 17 grams, with pans weighing 44 grams each, and $\alpha = 4°$. Since $r = \frac{1}{2}$, when weights

of, let us say, 5 and 10 grams are placed in the pans, the formula yields

$$\tan \theta = \left(\frac{54 - 49}{54 + 49 + \frac{1}{2} \cdot 17} \right) \cot (4°) = 0.64;$$

so the tilt $\theta = 33°$.

REFERENCE

Resnick, Robert, and David Halliday. *Physics, Part I.* New York: John Wiley & Sons, 1966.

SHIPBOARD WEATHER OBSERVATION

By **RICHARD J. PALMACCIO**
Pine Crest School
Fort Lauderdale, FL 33334

On many ships there can be found an anemometer (ăń-ə-mŏḿ-ət-ər) for measuring wind speed, and a wind vane for indicating direction, both mounted together near the bridge area. These two instruments thus indicate the wind velocity, a vector quantity. Even though there are a number of orbiting weather satellites transmitting cloud pictures, meteorologists still depend heavily on surface observations in preparing forecasts. Wind velocity is the most important component of any weather observation, and all ships are strongly urged to radio weather data.

Rotating-cup anemometer and wind vane combine to provide wind velocity readings on meter at the left.

Photograph supplied courtesy of Taylor Instrument Consumer Products Division, Sybron Corp., Arden, NC 28704.

Such reports to the nearest weather service station are pooled internationally and greatly aid the process of forecasting.

How can an observer on a moving ship be expected to furnish an accurate report of wind velocity?

This question will be answered by presenting a method employing vector addition and some simple trigonometry. This procedure uses the ship as a frame of reference for considering three vectors. One of these is the actual wind velocity, which would be measured by a stationary observer. The other two, ship speed and anemometer reading, are easily determined by the shipboard observer. One is the resultant of the other two.

First consider an example that illustrates this vector relationship. Suppose a stationary observer, P, feels a wind blowing, $\vec{a}$, from the north at 10 km/h. A ship at the same location is moving northward, into the wind, at 15 km/h (fig. 1). A

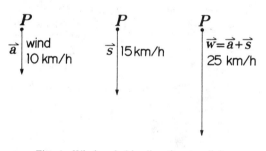

Fig. 1. Wind and ship direction parallel

shipboard observer must experience a wind from the north at 25 km/h. Let $\vec{a}$ be the actual wind velocity reported by the stationary observer at point P. If we let $\vec{s}$ be the *opposite* of the ship's velocity, then the sum of $\vec{a}$ and $\vec{s}$ (which we denote $\vec{w}$) is the wind velocity recorded by the observer aboard the ship. Since the vectors $\vec{a}$ and $\vec{s}$ are parallel and point in the same direction, their magnitudes are related by the equation

(1) $$\|\vec{w}\| = \|\vec{a}\| + \|\vec{s}\|.$$

If we only knew $\|\vec{w}\| = 25$, as recorded by the ship's anemometer, we would obtain $\|\vec{a}\| = 25 - 15 = 10$ km/h as the actual wind speed.

Suppose $\vec{a}$ and $\vec{s}$ are not parallel. Let the actual wind velocity, $\vec{a}$, be directed at a nonzero angle, α, with the ship's axis as shown in figure 2. The arrow on the dotted line indicates the direction of the ship's motion, and P is the ship's position. Next in figure 2b we add to figure 2a the vector $\vec{s}$, indicating the opposite of the ship's velocity vector. Finally, the vector $\vec{w}$, whose magnitude $\|\vec{w}\|$ is the wind speed measured by the ship's anemometer and whose direction angle, θ, is indicated by the wind vane, is shown in figure 2c. This vector is the resultant of vectors $\vec{a}$ and $\vec{s}$.

We now consider the general case of equation (1) in which $\vec{a}$ and $\vec{s}$ are not parallel by rewriting it as equation (2).

(2) $$\vec{w} = \vec{a} + \vec{s}.$$

In order to make the meteorological report, the magnitude and direction of the actual wind vector, $\vec{a}$, must be determined. (In actual shipboard practice, the experienced sailor makes a rather accurate *estimate* of this wind vector from the appearance of the waves. Their amplitude and direction are good indications of the wind's speed and direction, respectively.) Therefore we will develop formulas for $\|\vec{a}\|$ and α in terms of the observable quantities $\|\vec{w}\|$ and θ, which are obtained from the ship's weather instruments, and $\|\vec{s}\|$, the ship's speed. Position an x–y coordinate system with origin at point P as shown in figure 3. Then we can relate the components of $\vec{w}$, $\vec{a}$, and $\vec{s}$ using equation (2).

We have the system

$$\|\vec{w}_x\| = \|\vec{a}_x\| + \|\vec{s}_x\|$$
$$\|\vec{w}_y\| = \|\vec{a}_y\| + \|\vec{s}_y\|,$$

which becomes

$$\|\vec{w}\| \sin \theta = \|\vec{a}\| \sin \alpha$$
$$\|\vec{w}\| \cos \theta = \|\vec{a}\| \cos \alpha + \|\vec{s}\|.$$

Solving for $\sin \alpha$ and $\cos \alpha$ yields

(3) $$\sin \alpha = \frac{\|\vec{w}\| \sin \theta}{\|\vec{a}\|},$$
$$\cos \alpha = \frac{\|\vec{w}\| \cos \theta - \|\vec{s}\|}{\|\vec{a}\|}.$$

Assume for now that θ is measured clockwise from the negative y-axis in figure 3 (this assumption is made only for convenience) and that $0° \leq \theta \leq 180°$. Then it follows that $0° \leq \alpha \leq 180°$. Dividing equations (3), we have

(4) $$\tan \alpha = \frac{\|\vec{w}\| \sin \theta}{\|\vec{w}\| \cos \theta - \|\vec{s}\|},$$

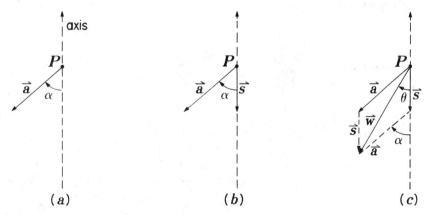

Fig. 2. Wind and ship direction not parallel

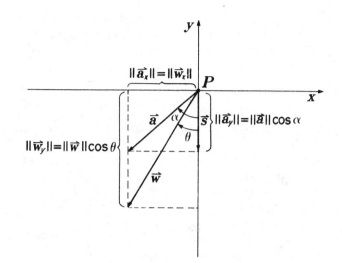

Fig. 3. Horizontal and vertical components of $\vec{a}$ and $\vec{w}$

which we want to solve for α. We must consider carefully how to solve (4) for α. As θ increases, so does α. Since $0° \le \theta \le 180°$, the numerator in (4) is nonnegative. Thus we need only consider the denominator and the three cases in which it is positive, zero, and negative.

An examination of figure 4 shows that when $\cos \theta = \|\vec{s}\|/\|\vec{w}\|$, $\vec{w}$ is the diagonal of the rectangle determined by $\vec{a}$ and $\vec{s}$; so α is clearly 90°. If $\cos \theta > \|\vec{s}\|/\|\vec{w}\|$, θ becomes smaller (since the cosine function is decreasing); so α is acute. When $\cos \theta < \|\vec{s}\|/\|\vec{w}\|$, θ is larger; so α is obtuse. In this latter case we must add the inverse tangent of the right side of (4) to 180° to obtain α. Therefore the solution of (4) for α is

$$(5) \quad \alpha = \begin{cases} \tan^{-1}\left(\dfrac{\|\vec{w}\| \sin \theta}{\|\vec{w}\| \cos \theta - \|\vec{s}\|}\right), \\ \qquad \text{if } \|\vec{w}\| \cos \theta > \|\vec{s}\| \\ 90°, \text{ if } \|\vec{w}\| \cos \theta = \|\vec{s}\|, \\ 180° + \tan^{-1}\left(\dfrac{\|\vec{w}\| \sin \theta}{\|\vec{w}\| \cos \theta - \|\vec{s}\|}\right), \\ \qquad \text{if } \|\vec{w}\| \cos \theta < \|\vec{s}\|. \end{cases}$$

To determine $\|\vec{a}\|$, we can solve system (3) as follows:

$$\left(\frac{\|\vec{w}\| \sin \theta}{\|\vec{a}\|}\right)^2 + \left(\frac{\|\vec{w}\| \cos \theta - \|\vec{s}\|}{\|\vec{a}\|}\right)^2 = 1$$

$$\|\vec{a}\|^2 = \|\vec{w}\|^2 (\sin^2 \theta + \cos^2 \theta) \\ - 2\|\vec{w}\| \cdot \|\vec{s}\| \cos \theta + \|\vec{s}\|^2$$

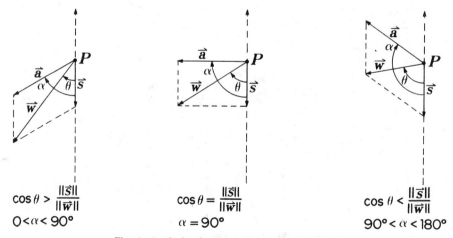

$$\cos \theta > \frac{\|\vec{s}\|}{\|\vec{w}\|} \qquad \cos \theta = \frac{\|\vec{s}\|}{\|\vec{w}\|} \qquad \cos \theta < \frac{\|\vec{s}\|}{\|\vec{w}\|}$$
$$0 < \alpha < 90° \qquad \alpha = 90° \qquad 90° < \alpha < 180°$$

Fig. 4. Analysis of $\cos \theta$ to determine the size of α

(6) $\|\vec{a}\| = \sqrt{\|\vec{w}\|^2 + \|\vec{s}\|^2 - 2\|\vec{w}\| \cdot \|\vec{s}\| \cos \theta}$

Note that (6) can be obtained more directly if students are familiar with the law of cosines.

In the foregoing discussion we assumed $0° \leq \theta \leq 180°$, which meant that the wind observed on the ship was blowing generally from the right of the ship's course line as the observer faces the ship's direction. If the observer finds the wind blowing from the left, then θ can be measured in the counterclockwise direction as indicated in figure 5. Then α is also measured counterclockwise. Once again we can think of θ as $0° \leq \theta \leq 180°$, and equations (5) and (6) still apply.

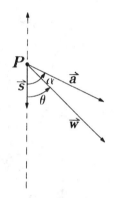

Fig. 5. Wind blowing from the left

These two equations for determining the actual wind vector $\vec{a}$ provide an excellent opportunity for using computers. When teaching programming in BASIC, or any other language, a most important concept for the student to master is that of decision making within a program. The calculation of equation (5) necessitates a certain sequence of IF statements in BASIC that embody typical decision-making logic.

Table 1 includes a BASIC program and table 2 one for the Hewlett-Packard HP-41C programmable calculator. Both programs prompt the user to enter the observed wind (the anemometer reading), the angle of this wind (in degrees) with the ship's path, and the ship's speed. The programs produce the actual wind vector

consisting of the wind speed, $\|\vec{a}\|$, and the actual wind angle, α.

TABLE 1
BASIC Program

```
10 PRINT "WHAT IS THE OBSERVED WIND SPEED";
20 INPUT W
30 PRINT "WHAT IS THE WIND ANGLE";
40 INPUT G
45 LET X = G*3.14159/180
50 PRINT "WHAT IS THE SHIP'S SPEED";
60 INPUT S
65 LPRINT "IF OBSERVED WIND SPEED = ";W;", WIND
       ANGLE = ";G;","
66 LPRINT "AND SHIP'S SPEED = ";S;", THEN"
70 LET A = SQR(W ↑ 2 + S ↑ 2 - 2*W*S*COS(X))
80 LET B = W*COS(X) - S
90 LET C = ATN(W*SIN(X)/B)*180/3.14159
100 IF B > 0 THEN 140
110 IF B = 0 THEN 160
120 LET L = 180 + C
130 GOTO 170
140 LET L = C
150 GOTO 170
160 LET L = 90
170 LPRINT "ACTUAL WIND IS";A;"AT THE
       ANGLE";L;"DEGREES"
175 LPRINT " "
176 GOTO 10
180 END
```

TABLE 2
HP-41C Program

01	LBL "WIND"	36	*
02	LBL 10	37	RCL 02
03	DEG	38	−
04	"WIND OBS?"	39	STO 04
05	PROMPT	40	X=0?
06	STO 00	41	GTO 03
07	"WIND ANGLE?"	42	RCL 01
08	PROMPT	43	SIN
09	STO 01	44	RCL 00
10	"SHIP SPEED?"	45	*
11	PROMPT	46	RCL 04
12	STO 02	47	/
13	RCL 00	48	ATAN
14	X ↑ 2	49	STO 06
15	RCL 02	50	X<0?
16	X ↑ 2	51	GTO 01
17	+	52	RCL 06
18	RCL 01	53	STO 05
19	COS	54	GTO 02
20	RCL 00	55	LBL 01
21	*	56	180
22	RCL 02	57	+
23	*	58	STO 05
24	−2	59	GTO 02
25	*	60	LBL 03
26	+	61	90
27	SQRT	62	STO 05
28	STO 03	63	LBL 02
29	"ACT. WIND="	64	"ACTUAL ∡="
30	ARCL 03	65	ARCL 05
31	AVIEW	66	AVIEW
32	STOP	67	STOP
33	RCL 01	68	GTO 10
34	COS	69	RTN
35	RCL 00	70	END

BIBLIOGRAPHY

Coxford, Arthur. *Trigonometry*, p. 148. New York: Harcourt Brace Jovanovich, 1981.

Crosswhite, Joseph, Lawrence Hawkinson, and Leroy Sachs. *Pre-Calculus Mathematics*, p. 198. Columbus, Ohio: Charles E. Merrill Publishing Co., 1976.

Dolciani, Mary, Edwin Beckenbach, Alfred J. Donnelly, Ray C. Jurgensen, and William Wooten. *Modern Introductory Analysis*, p. 121. Boston: Houghton Mifflin Co., 1964.

Knill, George. "Relative Velocity: Vectors with a Difference." *Mathematics Teacher* 74 (March 1981):209–11.

SPHERICAL GEODESICS

What is the shortest distance between two points on a globe?

By **WILLIAM D. JAMSKI**
Indiana University Southeast
New Albany, IN 47150

Once upon a time the world was flat and the shortest distance between two points was a straight line. Today most people accept a spherical model for the earth, but what is the shortest distance between two points on a sphere? How do you pick an air route between two cities? These are questions for a branch of mathematics known as spherical geodesics.

To begin a study of the problem, we can think of the earth as being intersected by two perpendicular planes each containing the center of the sphere. The intersection of a "horizontal" plane and the earth is the equator. The "vertical" plane and the sphere intersect at the prime meridian (fig. 1). The lines of latitude locate a point in

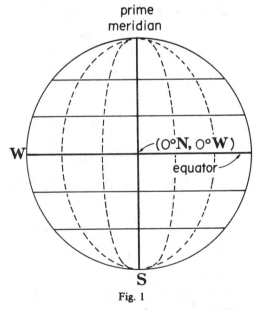

Fig. 1

terms of the number of degrees north or south of the equator. Similarly, lines of longitude are numbered in degrees east or west of the prime meridian. With this system the location of any spot on earth can be designated by giving its latitude and longitude. For example, we locate New Orleans at (30°N, 90°W).

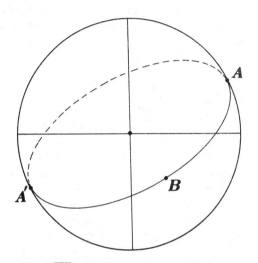

Fig. 2. $\overline{AA'}$ is the diameter of great circle θ containing A and B.

Next we need to know that the intersection of a sphere and a plane containing its center is a great circle. On the earth all lines of longitude and the equator are examples of great circles. They are important to this discussion because these great circles are "straight lines" on a sphere. That is, the shortest distance between any two points on a sphere is the length of the minor arc on the great circle containing them (Moise 1963, pp. 119–20).

How can the coordinate scheme and the great circle-minimum distance relationship be combined? Given a point A at ($x°$N, $y°$E) and a point B, we want to find geodesic AB. We need a great circle θ containing A and B (fig. 2). To obtain θ, antipodal point A' must be found such that $\overline{AA'}$ is a diameter of θ. The question is how to find A'. Imagine a rod from A through the center to A'. Notationally,

$$x°\text{N} \leftrightarrow x°\text{S}, \ 0 \leq x \leq 90;$$

and

$$y°E \leftrightarrow (180 - y)°W, \quad 0 \leq y \leq 180.$$

For example, the point antipodal to New Orleans (30°N, 90°W) is (30°S, 90°E), somewhere in the Indian Ocean. So A' is specified but θ is not. In fact, an infinite number of great circles have diameter $\overline{AA'}$. To find the required one on a globe, $\overline{AA'}$ should be copied with string and rotated until $B \in \overline{AA'}$. If restricted air space, air currents, and fuel allocations are ignored, this would be (and often is) the route an airline would fly from A to B.

Conclusion

The process above illustrates a good application of mathematics and especially solid geometry. Too often the decline of solid geometry has been accompanied by a loss of some imaginative topics that can show both the scope and the power of mathematics. In effect, with this trend we may have thrown out some wheat with the chaff. The following examples are for you and your students to explore. Answers follow the references.

1. Assume the radius of the earth is 3950 miles. What is the maximum spherical distance between a pair of points?

2. Find the air distance between New York and New Orleans.

3. Assuming that great circles on a sphere are equivalent to straight lines on a plane, discuss the following aspects of spherical geometry: determining a sphere, parallel lines, intersecting lines, and degrees in a triangle.

Answers

1. Two antipodal points on a great circle would meet the specified conditions. Therefore the required answer would be one-half of the circumference of a great circle:

$$\tfrac{1}{2}C = \tfrac{1}{2}(2\pi r) = \pi(3950)$$

or approximately 12 400 miles.

2. Using the technique described in the article, a string, and the scale on the globe, you should obtain an answer of approxi-

mately 1170 statute miles. Those interested in spherical trigonometry can consider figure 3 (Palmer et al. 1950, p. 218). From figure 3, we can find

$$a = 49°15' = 49.25°,$$
$$b = 60°3' = 60.05°,$$

and

$$\gamma = 16°4' = 16.066°.$$

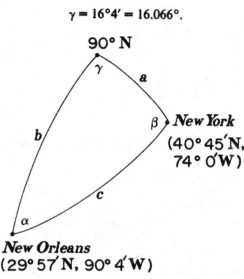

Fig. 3

Using Napier's analogies,

$$\tan \tfrac{1}{2}(\alpha - \beta) = \frac{\cot \tfrac{1}{2}\gamma \sin \tfrac{1}{2}(a - b)}{\sin \tfrac{1}{2}(a + b)}$$

and

$$\tan \tfrac{1}{2}(\alpha + \beta) = \frac{\cot \tfrac{1}{2}\gamma \cos \tfrac{1}{2}(a - b)}{\cos \tfrac{1}{2}(a + b)}$$

We find $\alpha = 46.04°$ and $\beta = 124.58°$. Then from

$$\tan \tfrac{1}{2}c = \frac{\tan \tfrac{1}{2}(a - b) \sin \tfrac{1}{2}(\alpha + \beta)}{\sin \tfrac{1}{2}(\alpha - \beta)},$$

the required length is $c = 16.9270° = 16°56' = 1016'$ or 1016 nautical miles (about 1170 statute miles).

3. In spherical geometry a sphere is a locus of points in space equidistant from a given point; there are no parallel lines; in

fact all lines intersect, and the sum of the measures of the interior angles of a triangle is larger than 180.

REFERENCES

Moise, Edwin E. *Elementary Geometry from an Advanced Standpoint*. Reading: Addison-Wesley Publishing Co., 1963.

Palmer, Claude Irwin, Charles Wilbur Leigh, and Spofford Harris Kimball. *Plane and Spherical Trigonometry*. New York: McGraw-Hill, 1950, pp. 191–222.

Shortest distance

The New York to New Orleans air distance problem in Jamski's article "Spherical Geodesics" (March 1981) can be solved by using a single equation that is the spherical analog of the familiar law of cosines from plane trigonometry. Using the notation and data in the article, we get

$$\cos(c) = \cos(a)\cos(b) + \sin(a)\sin(b)\cos(\gamma),$$

which gives $c = 16.93°$, with a minimum of fuss.

Don Sterba
Villanova Preparatory School
Ojai, CA 93023

Around the Sun in a Graphing Calculator

By FRANKLIN DEMANA and BERT K. WAITS

The topics of polar equations and parametric equations are found in almost all precalculus and calculus textbooks. They furnish important algebraic representations of real-world problems. For example, polar equations are used to describe the elliptical orbit of planets around the sun (Kepler's first law), and parametric equations are frequently used to describe the trajectory of moving objects. These topics are seldom given more than superficial treatment in high school and college precalculus and calculus courses because of the difficulty of obtaining appropriate graphical representations.

Graphs of polar equations and parametric equations are now readily accessible with the aid of hand-held graphing calculators. The speed and power of pocket computer technology turns graphing into a powerful instructional technique and tool for mathematical exploration. NCTM's *Curriculum and Evaluation Standards for School Mathematics* (1989) calls for making mathematical exploration and problem solving a more central focus of instruction in school mathematics. These activities are possible for many more students because of relatively low-cost graphing-calculator technology. Producing polar and parametric graphs by hand takes so long that graphing by hand is rendered useless as a problem-solving or instructional strategy. Graphing calculators can be used to investigate, simulate, and

Franklin Demana and Bert Waits teach mathematics at Ohio State University in Columbus, OH 43210. Demana is especially interested in the use of calculators and computers in mathematics teaching and related curriculum development. Waits's special interests include the design of computer-graphing software, the effective use of technology in the teaching and learning of mathematics, and related curriculum development.

solve important real-world problems. This important shift in instructional emphasis due to technology is illustrated with two examples.

Simple programs can be written for graphing calculators that turn them into powerful, interactive, flexible graphing utilities for polar and parametric equations. An eight-line program for the Casio *fx*-7000G that can be used to graph parametric equations is given in this article. The program requires very little memory and can be stored in one of ten program locations to be quickly recalled as needed. The Casio has a constant-memory feature allowing the program to be retained in memory even when the calculator is turned off. Other graphing calculators (Sharp EL-5200 and HP28C or S) and some computer-graphing software (e.g., Master Grapher [1988]) can be used to obtain similar results.

Parametric Equations

Let C be a curve defined parametrically by $(x(T), y(T))$ for T in the interval $T_{\min} \leq T \leq T_{\max}$. Program 1 draws a graph of C (the line numbers are not part of the program).

Before running the program the user should enter the boundaries for a rectangular portion of the coordinate plane ($X_{\min} \leq$

PROGRAM 1		
The Graph of a Parametric Equation		
		Remark
1.	Cls:Rad	
2.	$0 \to T$	($T_{\min} = 0$)
3.	Lbl 1	
4.	T cos T $\to$ A	($x(T) = T \cos T$)
5.	T sin T $\to$ B	($y(T) = T \sin T$)
6.	T + 0.1 $\to$ T	(increment = 0.1)
7.	Plot A, B	
8.	T $\leq$ 6.28 $\Rightarrow$ Goto 1	($T_{\max} = 6.28$)

$x \leq X_{\max}$ and $Y_{\min} \leq y \leq Y_{\max}$) using the ⃞Range key. This rectangular portion of the coordinate plane is called the viewing rectangle $[X_{\min}, X_{\max}]$ by $[Y_{\min}, Y_{\max}]$. The user edits the program and enters numerical values as desired for $T_{\min}$, increment, and $T_{\max}$ in lines 2, 6, and 8, respectively. The user also enters in the desired $x(T)$ and $y(T)$ in lines 4 and 5. The Casio has natural editing features that make editing easy. When the program is run, the points $(x(T), y(T))$ are plotted for those values of T of the form $T_{\min}$, $T_{\min}$ + increment, $T_{\min}$ + 2(increment), ..., that are less than or equal to $T_{\max}$. This remarkably simple program draws the graph of the curve defined parametrically by

$$x(t) = T \cos T$$

and

$$y(T) = T \sin T$$

in a matter of seconds. This curve is known as the spiral of Archimedes. Figure 1 shows three views of the spiral determined by changing $T_{\min}$ and $T_{\max}$. The values of T that produced the graph are displayed below each figure. The increment is 0.1 unit in each example.

Students can easily and quickly experiment by varying the values of $T_{\min}$, $T_{\max}$, and increment to determine their roles in the program. In this way, students can use graphing calculators as a tool to explore, observe, and make and test conjectures on the basis of their observations. Statements can be added to the program that cause it to pause and request actual inputs, such as $T_{\min}$, $T_{\max}$, or increment, from the user. For example, suppose line 2 of program 1 is changed to

"Tmin="? → T

Then, when the program is executed,

Tmin=?

appears on the screen as a prompt for the user to enter $T_{\min}$. Thus, it is not necessary to edit the program directly to vary the inputs. In addition, the command "Line" can be added between lines 7 and 8 to obtain a connected plot approximating a smooth curve.

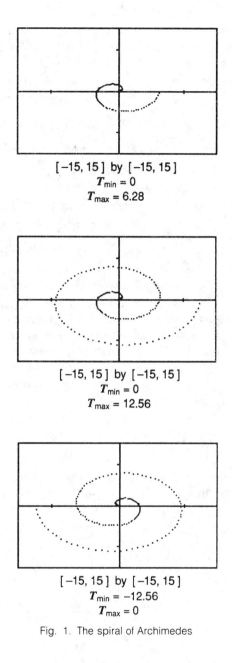

[−15, 15] by [−15, 15]
$T_{\min} = 0$
$T_{\max} = 6.28$

[−15, 15] by [−15, 15]
$T_{\min} = 0$
$T_{\max} = 12.56$

[−15, 15] by [−15, 15]
$T_{\min} = -12.56$
$T_{\max} = 0$

Fig. 1. The spiral of Archimedes

Polar Equations

Suppose we want to draw a graph of the polar equation $r = f(\theta)$. By elementary right-triangle trigonometry, a point with polar coordinates (r, θ) has rectangular coordinates

$$(r \cos \theta, r \sin \theta).$$

The graph of the polar equation $r = f(\theta)$ can be obtained by graphing the parametric equations $x(\theta) = r \cos \theta$ and $y(\theta) = r \sin \theta$.

Thus, the given parametric-graphing program can be used to graph any polar equation $r = f(T)$ by changing lines 4 and 5 to read as follows:

4. f(T) cos T → A

5. f(T) sin T → B

The user must enter $f(T)$. For example, if $f(T) = 10\sin 3T$, lines 4 and 5 would become

4. (10 sin 3T) cos T → A

5. (10 sin 3T) sin T → B,

which produces the graph of the three-leaf rose, $r = 10 \sin 3\theta$. Notice that θ has been replaced by T.

Planetary Motion

Kepler's first law of planetary motion states that all planets move in elliptical orbits about the sun with the sun as one focus of the ellipse. Assume that the major axis of such an ellipse is on the x-axis and the sun is at the origin. Then, the planet's orbit is given by the polar equation

$$r = \frac{b^2}{a + \sqrt{a^2 - b^2} \cos \theta},$$

where a is the semimajor axis length, b is the semiminor axis length, r is the distance from the sun to the planet, and θ is the angle made by the positive x-axis with the line connecting the sun with the planet (fig. 2). Program 2 is an economical way to graph such an ellipse.

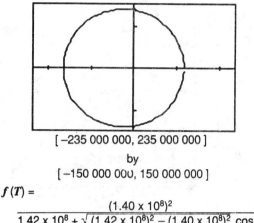

[−235 000 000, 235 000 000]

by

[−150 000 000, 150 000 000]

$f(T) =$

$$\frac{(1.40 \times 10^8)^2}{1.42 \times 10^8 + \sqrt{(1.42 \times 10^8)^2 - (1.40 \times 10^8)^2} \cos T}$$

Fig. 3. A graph of the orbit of Mars about the sun

Now, drawing graphs that represent the orbits of planets around the sun become fascinating problems that are accessible to precalculus students through the use of technology. Mathematics teachers can send their students to the library to search for the values of a and b required to represent the orbit of a given planet around the sun. (This is a delightful opportunity to encourage library use.) Figure 3 is the graph of an orbit with $a = 1.42 \times 10^8$ and $b = 1.40 \times 10^8$, which approximates the orbit of Mars about the sun. Notice that the viewing rectangle is [−235 000 000, 235 000 000] by [−150 000 000, 150 000 000]. The viewing rectangle can be quickly changed on the Casio with the range key. Notice that the elliptical orbit is almost circular, thus offering

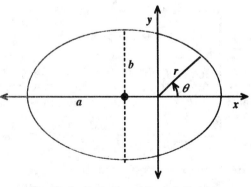

Fig 2. An illustration of Kepler's first law

PROGRAM 2
The Graph of an Ellipse in Polar Form

1.	Cls:Rad
2.	? → A:? → B
3.	0 → T
4.	Lbl 1
5.	$B^2 \div (A + (\sqrt{A^2 - B^2}) \cos T) \to R$
6.	R cos T → M
7.	R sin T → N
8.	T + 0.1 → T
9.	Plot M,N
10.	Line
11.	T ≤ 6.28 ⇒ Goto 1

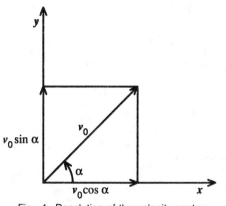

Fig. 4. Resolution of the velocity vector

an opportunity to discuss the concept of eccentricity.

Free-Fall Motion

Suppose that a softball is hit with an initial velocity v_0 ft./sec. at an angle of elevation of α degrees. Neglect air resistance and take the acceleration due to gravity to be 32 ft./sec.^{2}. The initial velocity is a vector with horizontal component $v_0 \cos \alpha$ and vertical component $v_0 \sin \alpha$ (fig. 4). The x-coordinate of the position of the softball at any time T is

$$(v_0 \cos \alpha)T,$$

and the y-coordinate is

$$-16T^2 + (v_0 \sin \alpha)T.$$

Thus, the trajectory of a softball hit with an initial velocity of v_0 ft./sec. at an angle of elevation of α degrees is given by the parametric equations

$$x(T) = v_0 T \cos \alpha$$

and

$$y(T) = v_0 T \sin \alpha - 16T^2,$$

where the point $(x(T), y(T))$ is the position of the ball T seconds after it is hit (fig. 5).

Suppose the ball is hit with an initial velocity of 63 ft./sec. at an angle of elevation of 37 degrees. The parametric equations that describe the path of the ball become

$$x(T) = 63T \cos 37°$$

and

$$y(T) = 63T \sin 37° - 16T^2.$$

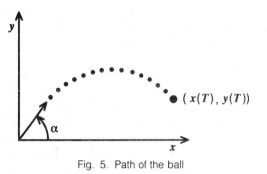

Fig. 5. Path of the ball

Figure 6 is a Casio simulation of the path of the ball for the first two seconds of flight where $T_{\min} = 0$ and $T_{\max} = 2$. Of course, students will need to experiment with several viewing rectangles to come up with figure 6. Be sure to convert 37 degrees to radians if you use program 1.

Graphs generated by graphing calculators can be obtained in seconds, thus allowing students to investigate the problem thoroughly by observing many graphs quickly. Once students have these geometric representations of the problem, they can use the technology to obtain very accurate geometric solutions to the following problems:

1. When will the ball hit the ground?
2. What is the maximum height above ground attained by the ball?
3. When does the ball reach its maximum height?
4. How far does the ball travel in the horizontal direction?

We leave the reader to explore the solution to the foregoing problems by using graph-

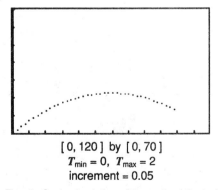

[0, 120] by [0, 70]
$T_{\min} = 0$, $T_{\max} = 2$
increment = 0.05

Fig. 6. Casio simulation of the path of the ball

ing-calculator simulation and zoom-in, a graphing problem-solving procedure (Demana and Waits 1987; Montaner 1987).

Students can use graphing calculators to gain a strong geometric understanding of algebraic ideas and problems. This geometric understanding strengthens the teaching of algebra by serving us a strong base from which algebraic concepts can grow.

Pocket-computer technology has the potential to bring great mathematical power to our students. This article only scratches the surface of important scientific and mathematical situations that are accessible to precalculus students with the aid of technology. Many important topics in science and mathematics can be given more than lip service in a technology-rich curriculum. Problem solving can truly become the focus of a mathematics classroom. Students can explore, conjecture about, and solve nonroutine problems and become active partners in the learning process. Teachers can become facilitators of acquired knowledge rather than purveyors of information.

REFERENCES

Demana, Franklin, and Bert K. Waits. "Solving Problems Graphically Using Microcomputers." *UMAP Journal* 8 (Spring 1987):1–7.

Montaner, F. Rubio. "Use of the Zoom in the Analysis of a Curve." *Mathematics Teacher* 80 (January 1987): 19–28.

National Council of Teachers of Mathematics, Commission on Standards for School Mathematics. *Curriculum and Evaluation Standards for School Mathematics.* Reston, Va.: The Council, 1989.

Waits, Bert K., and Franklin Demana. Master Grapher. Computer software for IBM, Apple II, and Macintosh computers. Reading, Mass.: Addison-Wesley Publishing Co., 1988. ◖

AN APPLICATION OF PARAMETRIC EQUATIONS
TO WEATHER FORECASTING

Forecasting the path of a storm using high school mathematics.

By **RICHARD J. PALMACCIO**

Wellesley Senior High School
Wellesley, Massachusetts

THE purpose of this article is to present a somewhat unusual, but instructive, practical application of mathematics to the field of meteorology. The problem considered will be the prediction of the path of a storm center given certain conditions. Although a little simplified, the problem loses none of its realism and can be easily presented in class at an opportune time. The reader can alter conditions to create new forecasting situations.

Before developing the practical application, a brief meteorological introduction may be helpful. Essentially, the weather observed at ground level is created and governed by two layers of atmospheric circulation. The lower level, below about 18,000 feet, contains the wind patterns associated with the high- and low-pressure areas characterized by clockwise and counterclockwise circulation, respectively, in the Northern Hemisphere. Above 18,000 feet are the so-called steering winds, which direct the motion of the entire lower-level circulatory systems. To illustrate this, suppose, for example, that a spinning top is a low-pressure area or storm. If the top is placed in front of a fan and is blown from point *A* to point *B*, the top represents the low-level circulation and the wind from the fan represents the upper-level steering wind. The locus of points

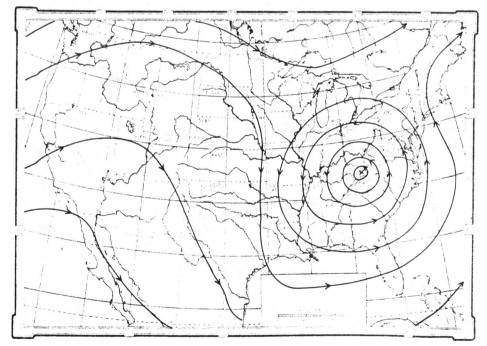

Fig. 1

described by the bottom of the top from *A* to *B* is analogous to the storm path.

Figure 1 indicates a rather typical upper-level wind-flow pattern in winter. It features a high-pressure "ridge" over the western United States and a very intense low-pressure closed circulation centered over Whitesburg, Kentucky. The surface wind pattern induced by the upper-air flow is illustrated in figure 2.

Of great interest in this discussion is the complex low-pressure system of two centers, one over Whitesburg under the upper-air low, the other twenty miles east of Norfolk, Virginia. A major factor in East Coast weather is the development near the coast of secondary storms that often become severe. The primary Whitesburg low forces warm, moist air toward the northeast on its eastern sector. Since this air moves more easily over the ocean, it accelerates with respect to the land air. This creates a circulation in much the same way that an oar paddle makes whirlpools in water.

Prediction of secondary development and movement is often difficult. As a re-

sult, elaborate mathematical models requiring computer-assisted solution have been used increasingly in recent years. In this article a simplified mathematical model for predicting the movement of the Norfolk storm will be exhibited. The primary storm may be neglected because its dissipation follows when the secondary storm cuts off its warm-air supply. In nature, low-level cyclones move only roughly parallel to upper-level patterns. For the purposes of this discussion it will, of course, be assumed that the movement is exactly parallel to the upper-level flow pattern.

To aid in finding the path of the secondary storm, imagine an (x, y) coordinate system placed so that the origin is under the upper-air low at Whitesburg. Since Norfolk is 420 miles due east of Whitesburg, the initial coordinates of the secondary storm are $(420, 0)$. (See fig. 3.) If the upper-air low were stationary, it would steer the storm in a circular path at a linear velocity of, say, 10 mph. Because of ground friction the storm will tend to spiral inward toward the center.

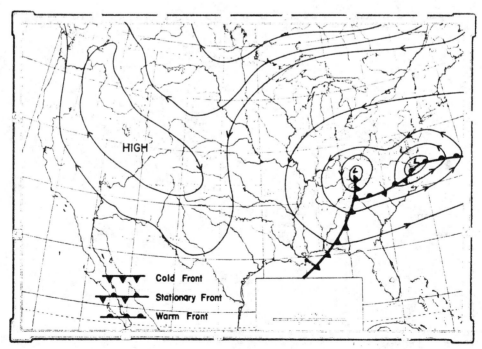

Fig. 2

(This spiraling-inward phenomenon can be dramatically demonstrated by placing grains of sand in a circular bottle half-filled with water. If the water is gently stirred, the sand particles will arrange themselves in a spiral configuration.) Suppose the storm approaches the center at 8 mph. Now assume that the entire upper-air circulation is moving at a velocity of 20 mph on a 60-degree bearing. (The assumed velocity of 060°/20 mph might be based on the extrapolation of past motion of the center or on independent forecasts based on statistical or numerical procedures.) As figure 3 indicates, this may be thought of as a 20-mph translation of co-ordinate axes 30 degrees north of east.

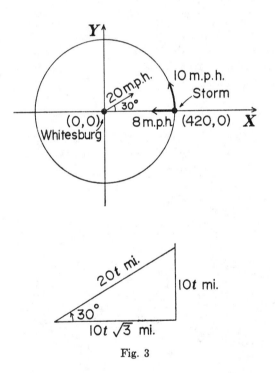

Fig. 3

(The extremely destructive hurricane Agnes of June 1972 offers a superb example of the spiral effect. It moved from Florida into a circulation almost exactly like that of the eastern United States in figure 1 and therefore maintained unusual intensity. Its peculiar looping path over New York and Pennsylvania was the direct result of spiraling toward the vortex

of the almost stationary upper-air circulation.)

In order to construct a system of parametric equations in the Euclidean plane (that is, two equations giving the coordinates x and y as functions of some third variable t), all the conditions assumed above must be accounted for. Let t represent the number of hours after the storm was located at $(420, 0)$. The parametric equations

$$x = r \cdot \cos(\theta)$$

$$y = r \cdot \sin(\theta)$$

describe counterclockwise rotation of the point $P(x, y)$ on a circle of radius r. As θ increases from 0 to 2π radians, P, initially at $(r, 0)$, completes one revolution. For the problem at hand, $r = 420$ miles. Since the circumference of the circle in figure 3 is 840π miles, the time for one complete revolution is $\frac{840\pi}{10} = 84\pi$ hours. In order to replace θ with the correct function of t, compare the domains of θ and t for one revolution.

$$t : 0 \rightarrow 84\pi \text{ hours}$$

$$\theta : 0 \rightarrow 2\pi \text{ radians}$$

Since t and θ are proportional,

$$\frac{\theta}{t} = \frac{2\pi}{84\pi},$$

so that $\theta = \frac{t}{42}$. Now the system

$$x = 420 \cdot \cos(t/42)$$

$$y = 420 \cdot \sin(t/42)$$

describes the rotation of the steering winds. As noted, the storm is drawn toward the center at 8 mph; so the radius of rotation decreases 8 miles each hour. Therefore the equations

(1)
$$x = (420 - 8t)\cos(t/42)$$

$$y = (420 - 8t)\sin(t/42)$$

represent the spiraling motion created by the upper-air circulation. Finally, the movement of the entire circulation must be built into system (1). Examining the triangle in figure 3, one sees the eastward and northward components of the 60-degree bearing. (Any angle could have been chosen, but students prefer working with the popular 30-60-90 triangle.)

In predicting the storm path, the system

(2)
$$x = 10t\sqrt{3} + (420 - 8t)\cos(t/42)$$
$$y = 10t + (420 - 8t)\sin(t/42)$$

accounts for all assumed data affecting the storm movement. For example, if 5 is substituted for t in system (2), the coordinates of the storm 5 hours after its development are obtained.

Note that system (2) is based on the assumption of *constant* forces acting on the storm. The upper-air circulation may intensify or weaken, or it may change shape to become elliptical. If the circulation is elliptical, its major axis could rotate, further complicating the situation. Sometimes closed circulations become open. In this event the air currents become parabolic or hyperbolic and are called low-pressure troughs. If figure 1 is held upside down and the arrows are reversed, the high-pressure ridge becomes a low-pressure trough. One can appreciate how the National Weather Service occasionally errs.

Much information can be extracted from system (2). Consider a forecaster located at the Boston National Weather Service. In addition to being interested in the path, the meteorologist is concerned with the storm's velocity at any point along its track in order to time the arrival of precipitation. In constructing a computer program to calculate values for system (2), let t increase in increments of one hour. Then the distance traveled each hour is also the forward speed. The bearing can be determined as follows. As shown in figure 4, if an object moves from (a, b) to (x, y) along a line L of slope m,

$$m = \frac{y - b}{x - a}, \quad \theta = \arctan(m),$$

and the bearing, β, in degrees, is given by

$$\beta = 90 - \theta.$$

A supplementary aid in timing the approach would be the storm's distance from

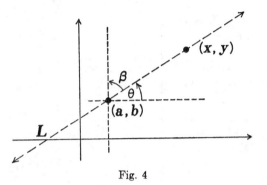

Fig. 4

Boston at the end of each hour. With (0, 0) at Whitesburg, Boston has the coordinates (660, 390). Thus the distance from Boston is given by

$$S = \sqrt{(660 - x)^2 + (390 - y)^2}.$$

The following BASIC computer program was employed in obtaining these statistics and plotting the path:

```
10  LET  A  =  420
13  LET  B  =  0
16  FOR  T  =  1 TO 50
19  LET  X  =  10*SQR(3)*T + (420-8*T)
        *COS(T/42)
22  LET  Y  =  10*T + (420-8*T)*SIN(T/42)
25  LET  V  =  SQR((A-X)↑2 + (B-Y)↑2)
28  LET  S  =  SQR((660-X)↑2 + (390-Y)↑2)
29  LET  M  =  (Y-B)/(X-A)
30  LET  G  =  90-ATN(M)*180/3.14159
31  PRINT "TIME"; T, "X"; X, "Y"; Y,
        "DSTRV"; V, "DSBOS"; S, "BERNG"; G
34  LET  A  =  X
37  LET  B  =  Y
47  NEXT T
50  STOP
55  END
```

Figure 5 shows the path and table 1 contains the computer output by five-hour intervals.

What has been presented here is a greatly simplified picture of the meteorological aspects of the problem discussed. The procedure is not truly a forecasting

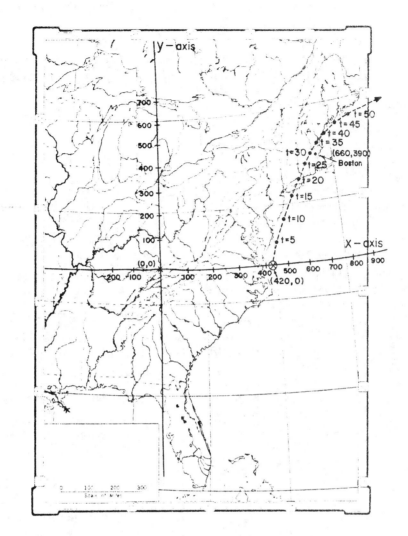

scheme, since it assumes that the cyclone will move with some steering current and that the steering current can be specified, or forecast by some other means. It should also be noted that this article offers a mathematical model of only a comparatively small section of the atmosphere, the eastern half of the United States. Attempts are now under way to construct sophisticated mathematical models of worldwide weather. Such research is leading to longer-range forecasts of improved quality. Computer-drawn prognostic weather maps are issued regularly from Washington, D.C. This is a good example of applied mathematics serving the needs of mankind.

TABLE 1

Hour	X	Y	Speed (mph)	Distance from Boston	Bearing (degrees)
5	464	95	20	354	24.7
10	504	180	18	262	25.4
15	541	255	16	180	28
20	577	319	14	109	31
25	615	373	13	48	38
30	656	418	12	28	46
35	700	453	11	75	55
40	751	481	12	129	68
45	808	503	13	186	73
50	873	519	14	249	78

Modeling with Difference Equations: Two Examples

By LEONARD M. WAPNER, El Camino College, Torrance, CA 90506

Mathematics can stand alone without its applications. The extent to which applications are taught at the secondary level is somewhat arbitrary; nevertheless, I believe that mathematical modeling is both an enjoyable and highly instructive experience for students. Great care should be taken to insure that the models presented are comprehensible and relevant.

Difference equations, as a modeling technique, can be studied at the secondary level. Many differential equation models, normally too advanced for high school algebra students, can be modified using difference equations so that they become accessible to the algebra student.

The two models presented here can be fully understood by students having completed second-year algebra and can also be appreciated, at a somewhat higher level, by calculus students familiar with differential equations.

Modeling

The construction and use of a mathematical model is analogous to physical modeling. As an example, consider the problem of designing, building, and ultimately flying a new type of aircraft. An almost endless list of questions would arise relating to stress and air flow that simply could not be answered directly by building the aircraft and attempting to fly it. Such an approach would be time consuming, costly, and outright dangerous. Instead, a small scale model is built that can be used in wind-tunnel and other tests. One can, of course, question the fact that the model is not an exact replica of the "real thing" and that it differs significantly in overall size, mass,

I wish to thank my wife, Mona, for all her work in preparing the manuscript.

and other features. True! Nevertheless, this price is the one we must pay to obtain quick and easy answers to certain questions regarding the aircraft.

Students will need to be reminded that a model is *only* a model and serves a limited but definite purpose. Consider the following excerpt from *Physics of* the *Atom* (Wehr and Richards 1960, p. 195):

A hollow rubber ball has its center of gravity at its center. Discussion of the motion of the ball can be greatly facilitated by regarding the ball as a point mass with all its mass at the center of gravity. The center of gravity has no objective reality, and if someone cuts the ball open, points to the center and says, "Ha, you see there is no mass there," we calmly reply that the center of gravity makes a poor description of what is at the center of the ball, but that it continues to be useful in describing the motion of the ball. No one description of the ball can ever completely represent what the reality of the ball is....

We do not scoff at maps because they are unreal. We admire them as beautiful descriptions.

So, too, is the case with mathematical models. They describe, in a limited way, a physical reality for purposes of investigation. No one mathematical model will ever be a perfect description for any physical phenomenon. The model will, however, assist us in answering specific questions.

Difference Equations

Difference equations can be thought of as being a finite and discrete approximation to differential equations. Two models that employ these equations follow a brief discussion of difference equations.

Consider, for example, a quantity, y, which increases with time, t, at a rate proportional to its size. If we now consider equally spaced values of t: $t_0, t_1, t_2, \ldots, t_j$, a sequence of y values: $y_0, y_1, y_2, \ldots, y_j$ will correspond such that $y_{n+1} = y_n + ky_n$ for some constant of variation k. This example is one of a first order difference equation and could be equivalently written as

$\Delta y = ky$. The differential equation counterpart would be $dy = \sigma y dt$, or $dy/dt = \sigma y$, the familiar differential equation describing exponential growth. The difference equation and the differential equation say essentially the same thing. Certain advantages derive, however, in using the difference equation approach:

1. A difference equation is easily understood by noncalculus students.

2. The solution of a difference equation, if thought of as a sequence of values y_0, y_1, y_2, ..., can be computed recursively with a minimum of mathematics.

3. Solving a difference equation recursively is easily done by computer. Solving differential equations by computer is more difficult.

Example I: A Predator-Prey Population Model

This example is based on the equivalent differential equation model by Lotka (1956). Imagine a prey population, such as rabbits, interacting with a predator population, such as wolves. We wish to build a mathematical model describing the population of rabbits (r) and the population of wolves (w) that answers the following questions:

1. How will both populations, r and w, behave as functions of time?

2. Specifically, for given initial values of r and w (r_0, w_0), which populations will initially increase and which will decrease?

3. Will the populations r and w change monotonically, or will they have extreme values?

The list could easily be extended.

We construct our model by making the following assumptions:

1. In the absence of wolves, the population of rabbits would grow at a rate proportional to its size.
$$\Delta r = ar \qquad (a > 0)$$

2. In the absence of rabbits, the population of wolves would die at a rate proportional to its size.

$$\Delta w = -dw \qquad (d > 0)$$

3. When the two populations interact, the population of rabbits will be decreased by a term proportional to the number of kills, and the population of wolves will be increased by a term proportional to the number of kills.

Since one can reasonably expect that the number of kills will vary jointly as r and w, we have the following system of difference equations:

$$\left.\begin{array}{ll}\text{rabbits:} & \Delta r = ar - brw \\ \text{wolves} & \Delta w = crw - dw\end{array}\right\} a, b, c, d > 0$$

This system is best written as follows:

(1)
$$\begin{array}{ll}\text{rabbits:} & \Delta r = br\left(\dfrac{a}{b} - w\right) \\[2ex] \text{wolves:} & \Delta w = cw\left(r - \dfrac{d}{c}\right)\end{array}$$

The system in (1) is our model, and we can now begin our investigation. Clearly, if $r_0 = w_0 = 0$, then $\Delta r = \Delta w = 0$ and we would have a stable equilibrium at 0 rabbits and 0 wolves. This information is of no value to us. Note, however, that if $w_0 = a/b$ and $r_0 = d/c$, then once again $\Delta r = \Delta w = 0$. This relationship is of interest and tells us that if the initial populations are as such, then both populations will remain constant through time and we say both populations are at an equilibrium.

So the question now becomes, "What if r_0 and w_0 are such that they are not both equal to their respective equilibrium values?"

From (1) we see that—

if $r > d/c$, then $\Delta w > 0$ (w increases);
if $r < d/c$, then $\Delta w < 0$ (w decreases);
if $w > a/b$, then $\Delta r < 0$ (r decreases); and
if $w < a/b$, then $\Delta r > 0$ (r increases).

So a large population of rabbits gives rise to an increasing population of wolves, and a small population of rabbits causes a decreasing population of wolves. A large population of wolves causes the population of rabbits to decrease, and a small population of wolves will allow the population of rabbits to increase.

It is interesting to note that whether a population increases or decreases is determined *solely by the other population*. Both populations will increase and decrease periodically and behave as illustrated in figure 1. In the figure, $E(d/c, a/b)$ denotes the equilibrium population where $\Delta r = \Delta w = 0$. This result is surprising and not especially intuitive to algebra or beginning calculus students. A proof that these orbits (trajectories) are periodic is given in Goldstein, Lay, and Schneider (1980) along with a proof that the average value of r is d/c and the average value of w is a/b.

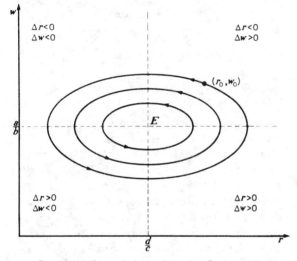

Fig. 1. Wolf population trajectories. Each orbit is determined by an initial value of rabbits (r_0) and an initial value of wolves (w_0).

Students may be intrigued by these unexpected results (periodicity, existence of an equilibrium, etc.), and the instructor will now be faced with the inevitable "what ifs" regarding the model and the physical phenomenon that it describes. Those students having access to a microcomputer should be encouraged to run and modify the program given in table 1 (written in BASIC), which generates, recursively, the solution to our system of difference equations and can assist in answering the "what ifs."

For additional discussion of this model and related models—the differential-

TABLE 1
BASIC Program for Predator-Prey Model

```
10   REM   PREDATOR - PREY MODEL
20   REM   DELTA R = AR-BRW
30   REM   DELTA W = CRW-DW
40   READ A,B,C,D
50   REM   THE VALUES OF A,B,C AND D
60   REM   GIVEN IN THE DATA STATEMENT
70   REM   BELOW WILL GIVE AN EQUILIBRIUM
80   REM   POINT AT 300 RABBITS AND 200 WOLVES.
90   DATA  .04,.0002,.0001,.03
100  PRINT "ENTER INITIAL NO OF RABBITS AND
            INITIAL NO OF WOLVES"
110  INPUT R,W
120  PRINT "RABBITS","WOLVES": PRINT
130  PRINT R,W
140  FOR T = 1 TO 1000
150  R = R + (A * R - B * R * W)
160  W = W + (C * R * W - D * W)
170  PRINT R,W: PRINT
180  NEXT T
999  END
```

equation approach—the instructor is referred to Kemeny and Snell (1962).

Example II: An Arms Race Model

This difference-equation model is based on a differential-equation model of an arms race given in Richardson (1939). As an instructor, I am particularly fond of this model in that it describes a phenomenon in social science that most students would believe could not be described mathematically. Once again, distinct teaching advantages are found in using difference equations as opposed to differential equations, the most significant of which may be that they make the model accessible to algebra students having no calculus background.

Imagine two fictitious countries, Exland and Wyland. Each wants peace with the other but will accumulate armaments to defend themselves against possible attack by the other. We wish to build a model to assist in answering the following:

1. How will Exland's arms expenditures (x) and Wyland's arms expenditures (y) behave as functions of time?

2. Will the expenditures increase without bound, or might they approach some stable equilibrium?

3. Is it conceivable that either country would de-escalate and that perhaps both countries might disarm?

To build the model, we begin by making the following assumptions:

1. Each country is spurred on to increase its expenditures at a rate that is proportional to the other's expenses:

$$\Delta x = ay \qquad (a, d > 0)$$
$$\Delta y = dx$$

2. A country's own expenditures tend to act as a brake and depress its future expenditures. So by modifying the system given in the first assumption, we have

$$\Delta x = ay - bx \qquad (a, b, d, e > 0).$$
$$\Delta y = dx - ey$$

3. Certain underlying (historical) grievances (independent of expenditures) exist that are constant and stimulate expenses.

Now, after one last modification, we have our model:

Exland: $\Delta x = ay \quad - \quad bx \quad + \quad c \, (a, b > 0)$
Wyland: $\Delta y = dx \quad - \quad ey \quad + \quad f \, (d, e > 0)$

$$\underbrace{}_{\substack{\text{spurring}\\\text{term}}} \underbrace{}_{\substack{\text{braking}\\\text{term}}} \underbrace{}_{\substack{\text{grievance}\\\text{term}}}$$

Positive values of c and f would represent a grievance, whereas a negative value of either term could be interpreted as an underlying feeling of goodwill toward the other country.

We can now begin to use the model to answer our questions.

An equilibrium situation will occur if $\Delta x = \Delta y = 0$. Since

$$\Delta x = ay - bx + c$$

and

$$\Delta y = dx - ey + f,$$

we have

$$(2) \qquad \begin{cases} ay - bx + c = 0 \\ dx - ey + f = 0 \end{cases}$$

at equilibrium. We can visualize the solution of (2), if it exists and is unique, as the intersection of two straight lines. For the sake of simplicity, we shall assume the in-

tersection occurs in quadrant I, as illustrated in figure 2. Then if x_0 and y_0, the initial levels of arms expenditures, are such that the point (x_0, y_0) satisfies (2), an equilibrium, E, would exist and neither country would increase or decrease expenditures (see fig. 2). What if x_0 and y_0 are not both at these levels? Two cases result.

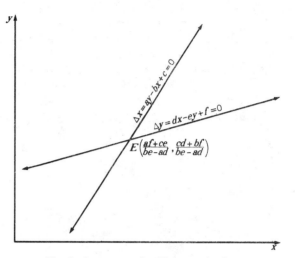

Fig. 2. Arms race—Equilibrium point E

Case 1: Stable equilibrium. By examining figure 3 and noting the signs of Δx and Δy in each of the four regions, one might infer that a stable equilibrium, E, exists at the intersection of the two lines. Such is the case, and several trajectories corresponding to various initial conditions (x_0, y_0) are shown.

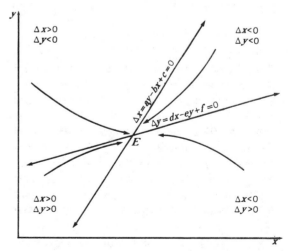

Fig. 3. Arms race—Stable equilibrium

Case 2: Unstable equilibrium. By examining figure 4 and noting the signs of Δx and Δy in each of the four regions, one might conclude that this case represents that of an unstable equilbrium, E, at the intersection of the two straight lines. Various trajectories are shown.

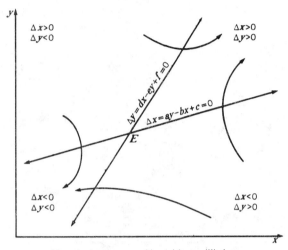

Fig. 4. Arms race—Unstable equilibrium

Summarizing, an equilibrium exists if the two straight lines intersect. If the slope of Exland's line is greater than the slope of Wyland's line,

$$\frac{b}{a} > \frac{d}{e},$$

then a stable equilibrium occurs. If the opposite is true and

$$\frac{b}{a} < \frac{d}{e},$$

then an unstable equilibrium occurs, implying an unlimited escalation or unlimited de-escalation, depending on the initial values x_0 and y_0.

We can extend the preceding discussion to all four quadrants of the plane if we give some meaning to negative values of x and y. We can do so by interpreting a negative value of x or y as an opposite to war preparation, such as units of cooperation, reciprocal assistance, or foreign trade. An indepth discussion of such matters is given in Richardson (1939). The program in table 2

TABLE 2

BASIC Program for Arms Race Model

```
LIST
10   REM   ARMS RACE
20   REM   DELTA X = AY-BX+C
30   REM   DELTA Y = DX-EY+F
40   READ A,B,C,D,E,F
50   REM   THE VALUES OF A,B,C,D,E AND F
60   REM   GIVEN IN THE DATA STATEMENT BELOW
70   REM   WILL RESULT IN A STABLE EQUILIBRIUM
80   REM   AT X = 140, Y = 80.
90   DATA  .01,.02,2,.0125,.1,6.25
100   PRINT "ENTER INITIAL VALUES OF X AND Y"
110   INPUT X,Y
120   PRINT "X","Y": PRINT
130   PRINT X,Y
140   FOR T = 1 TO 1000
150   X = X + (A * Y - B * X + C)
160   Y = Y + (D * X - E * Y + F)
170   PRINT X,Y: PRINT
180   NEXT T
999   END
```

recursively generates a solution for a stable-equilibrium type of arms race.

Conclusion

Mathematical model building is relevant, enjoyable, and instructive. Modeling with difference equations makes innumerable differential-equation models accessible to algebra students. Students learn, often to their surprise, that creativity and mathematical precision go hand in hand when constructing and using models. In addition, difference-equation models can be used to increase a student's computer awareness and sharpen programming skills.

BIBLIOGRAPHY

Goldstein, Larry J., David C. Lay, and David I. Schneider. *Calculus and Its Applications.* Englewood Cliffs: Prentice-Hall, 1980.

Kemeny, John G., and J. Laurie Snell. *Mathematical Models in the Social Sciences.* New York: Blaisdell Publishing Co., 1962.

Lotka, Alfred J. *Elements of Mathematical Biology.* New York: Dover Publications, 1956.

Rapoport, Anatol. *Fights, Games, and Debates.* Ann Arbor: University of Michigan Press, 1960.

Richardson, L. F. "Generalized Foreign Politics." *British Journal of Psychology,* Monograph Supplement XXIII. London: Cambridge University Press, 1939.

Wehr, Mentzer R., and James A. Richards, *Physics of the Atom.* Reading, Mass.: Addison-Wesley Publishing Co., 1960. ✥

Dynamic Programming for Secondary School Students

By CLIFFORD W. SLOYER and RICHARD CROUSE, University of Delaware, Newark, DE 19711
WILLIAM J. SACCO, Tri-Analytics, Inc., Bel Air, MD 21014
WAYNE S. COPES, Tri-Analytics, Inc., Churchville, MD 21028

"It is always fun to learn something entirely new."

"Thank you for making it possible for high school students to do something interesting and challenging for a change."

"Studying this material was a totally new and exciting experience."

"Because the information received was both new and interesting, I felt a sense of accomplishment."

These statements are unedited comments of four of the sixty-four talented secondary students attending a summer institute on applied mathematics at the University of Delaware in June 1982. The comments are *not* isolated but rather are representative of the responses of a majority of the students.

The institute is part of an NSF grant through which we are developing and testing self-teaching enrichment modules for secondary school students (grades 8–12) on several topics in modern applied mathematics, including dynamic programming. The purpose of this paper is to discuss the mathematical content involved, the pedagogy employed, and the results obtained in this introduction of new mathematics into a secondary school program. Our ultimate goal was to develop students' ability in dynamic programming to the point where they could solve an assortment problem at the level of difficulty encountered in the "digitized photograph" problem mentioned later in this article.

This work is supported, in part, by the National Science Foundation under grant no. SED-8025787. Any opinions, findings, conclusions, or recommendations expressed by this publication are those of the authors and do not necessarily reflect the views of the National Science Foundation.

An Introduction

We began with a simple 2 × 2 grid problem as illustrated in figure 1. Students were asked to regard this figure as a diagram of city blocks where the number assigned to a street indicates the time (in minutes) necessary to traverse that block. This time varies for different streets, since the traffic density differs. Consider, for example, a fire engine that wishes to travel from point *A* to point *B* as fast as possible, assuming that at each corner it must go east or north.

The path indicated by the arrows in figure 1 is denoted *ENNE*, where *E* represents a move of one block east and *N* represents a move of one block north. Very quickly students find six paths and list the time required for each, as given in table 1. The shortest time is fourteen minutes, so the optimal path is *NEEN*. This result surprises many students who want to use the "greedy algorithm" and simply move, at each corner, in the direction that requires the least time for the next block. Note that this choice is *not* made at point *A* in the optimal path.

Students are asked to count the number of operations necessary to solve this prob-

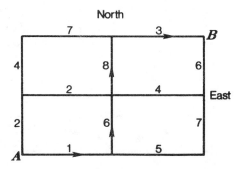

Fig. 1. What is the shortest time from *A* to *B*?

lem. With some instruction in basic combinatorics, students realize that the number of paths, as shown in table 1, can be computed from

$$\binom{4}{2} = \frac{4!}{2!2!} = 6.$$

They are led, if necessary, to the fact that each path has three additions—one less than the number of letters needed to symbolically indicate a path. Hence, a total of $6 \cdot 3 = 18$ additions is necessary. To find the minimum time from the list in table 1, students are asked to "think like a computer." Starting at the top, compare 18 and 19—the smaller is 18; now compare 18 with 17—the smaller is 17; compare 17 with 14—the smaller is 14; compare 14 with 16—the smaller is 14; compare 14 with 15—the smaller is 14. Hence, the minimum time from A to B is fourteen minutes. Note that five comparisons (one fewer than the total number of paths) were required. Thus, one obtains the results that appear in table 2.

TABLE 1	
Paths from A to B in Figure 1	
Path	Time (Min.)
ENNE	1 + 6 + 8 + 3 = 18
EENN	1 + 5 + 7 + 6 = 19
ENEN	1 + 6 + 4 + 6 = 17
NEEN	2 + 2 + 4 + 6 = 14
NNEE	2 + 4 + 7 + 3 = 16
NENE	2 + 2 + 8 + 3 = 15

TABLE 2	
	Number of Operations
Additions	18
Comparisons	5
Total	23

Students are asked to consider a similar grid problem of size 10×10 (fig. 2). When the students are asked how long it would take each of them to solve such a problem, the answer is usually "about four hours."

Let's compute the number of operations necessary to solve such a problem (the stu-

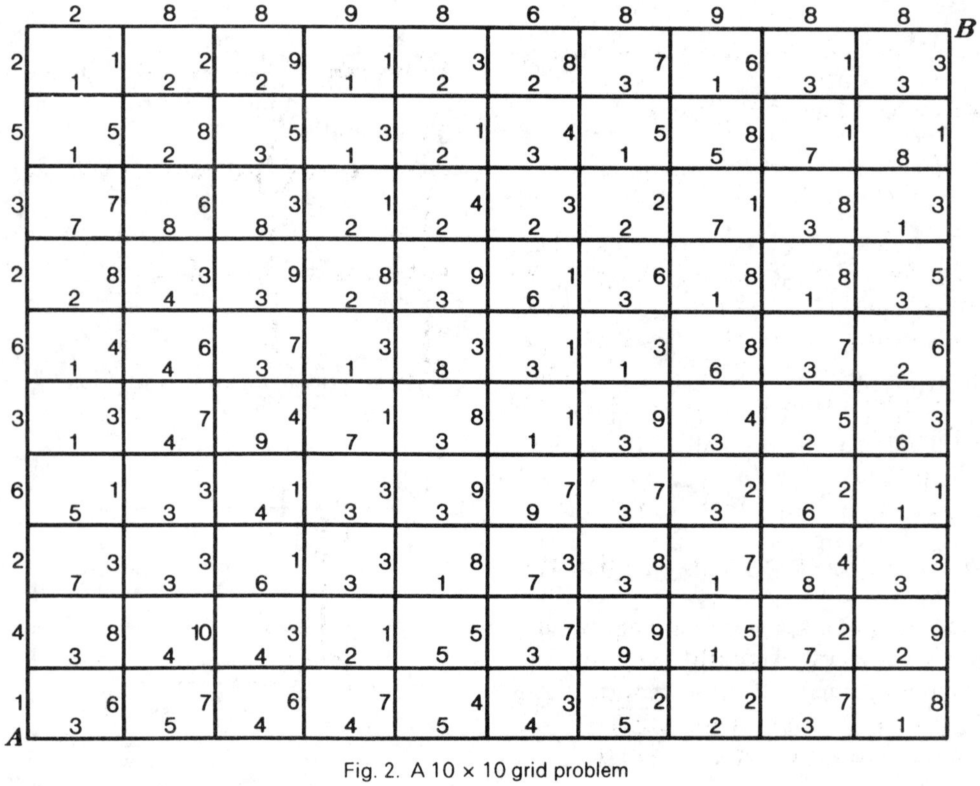

Fig. 2. A 10 × 10 grid problem

dents actually do this calculation). The total number of paths is given by

$$\binom{20}{10} = \frac{20!}{10!10!} = 184\,756.$$

Each path requires nineteen additions. At the end, 184 755 comparisons will be made (see table 3). The solution to this problem requires that an individual work at least forty-five days, provided that time is allowed for eating, sleeping, and so on. A computer operating at 100 000 operations per second would require less than thirty-seven seconds.

TABLE 3

	Number of Operations
Additions	3 510 364
Comparisons	184 755
Total	3 695 119

Limitations of a Computer

Now let us consider a 30 × 30 grid problem. This problem is *not* a large one if, for example, one considers a map of a city such as Phoenix, Arizona, and wants to find an optimal path for a fire engine from one part of the city to another.

The number of paths is given by

$$\binom{60}{30} = \frac{60!}{30!30!} \approx 1.18 \times 10^{17}.$$

Each path has fifty-nine additions; then, comparisons must be made. Clearly, the number of operations exceeds 10^{18}. A computer operating at 100 000 operations per second will perform 3.1536×10^{12} operations a year. Hence, such a computer would require

$$\frac{10^{18}}{3.1536 \times 10^{12}} > \frac{10^{18}}{10^{13}} = 10^5 = 100\,000,$$

or more than 100 000 years to solve this problem.

These numbers are *not* "handed" to students. The students actually carry out all these calculations. At this point, little doubt remains about their anxiety concerning the limitations of a computer.

Dynamic Programming

We introduce students to dynamic programming by considering an example such as that in figure 3. Starting at B and working backward, one asks, at each corner, "If I should arrive here, what direction should I go and how long will it take to reach B?" The results are indicated in figure 4.

Note how a decision is made at vertex $\overline{X}$, which is indicated separately in figure 5. If one goes east from $\overline{X}$, the time required to reach B is $7 + 1 = 8$ minutes; if one goes

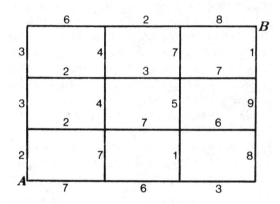

Fig. 3. What is the shortest time from A to B?

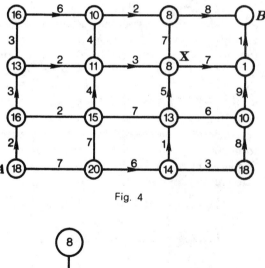

Fig. 4

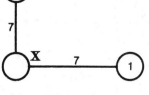

Fig. 5. Decision at $\overline{X}$

north, the time is $7 + 8 = 15$ minutes. The smaller number is 8, which is recorded in the circle, and an arrow indicates that one should go east. A number in a circle indicates the minimum time to go from that vertex to B. Thus, at each corner one performs no more than three operations (fewer at some points on the boundary). From figure 4, we can see that the minimum time from A to B is eighteen minutes, and the optimal path can be found by simply "following the arrows."

With dynamic programming, the size of the grid does not affect the fact that at each corner, no more than three operations are required. A 30×30 grid problem contains $31 \times 31 = 961$ corners; thus, fewer than 3000 operations are required to solve such a problem. A computer working at 100 000 operations a second would require less than 3/100 seconds to accomplish these operations. (Compare this result with the more than 100 000 years required when *all* possible paths had to be considered.) Using Bellman's (1962) principle of optimality, students are led to understand how each decision at a vertex eliminates the need to consider certain paths.

To extend these ideas to the solution of other significant problems, students must be able to write a *functional equation* for the process just described. To achieve this goal, we introduced a coordinate system on the grid so that point A corresponded to $(0, 0)$, and other points were given integral coordinates in a natural way. At vertex (x, y), let $f(x, y)$ denote the minimum time to go from (x, y) to B. At a vertex where a decision must be made, one has the situation shown in figure 6.

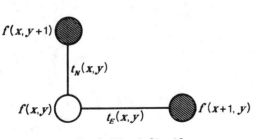

Fig. 6. What is $f(x, y)$?

Here $f(x, y + 1)$ and $f(x + 1, y)$ are known. The symbol $t_N(x, y)$ denotes the time required to move one block north from (x, y), and $t_E(x, y)$ denotes the time to move one block east. Hence,

(1) $f(x, y) = \min \{t_N(x, y) + f(x, y + 1),$
$t_E(x, y) + f(x + 1, y)\}.$

For the students in grades 8–12 with whom we have worked, it was necessary to help them develop this functional equation. It is important for students to understand equation (1), since analogies to it exist in the "assortment problems" that follow.

A Shrub-Covering Assortment Problem

Suppose you are a homeowner anticipating a cold winter and need to protect ten shrubs, each a different size, with individual burlap covers. It seems that the best way to cover them is to buy ten covers, each designed to fit the dimensions of a particular shrub.

Several large department stores are contacted, and none has such covers. However, one store offers to manufacture custom covers for you, but in at most three distinct sizes. Any given cover size will also cover a shrub of a smaller size. For example, a cover with size number 7 will also cover shrubs with size numbers 6, 5, 4, 3, 2, and 1. The store gives you the prices (in dollars) for all ten sizes corresponding to your shrubs, from which you may choose at most three (table 4). Once you have chosen the three sizes to be manufactured, you will be

TABLE 4	
Cover Size	Cost (in Dollars)
i	C_i
1	$C_1 = 1$
2	$C_2 = 4$
3	$C_3 = 5$
4	$C_4 = 7$
5	$C_5 = 8$
6	$C_6 = 12$
7	$C_7 = 13$
8	$C_8 = 18$
9	$C_9 = 19$
10	$C_{10} = 21$

allowed to purchase as many as you like of each size. The objective is to choose the three sizes that will enable you to cover all plants as inexpensively as possible.

A functional equation associated with this problem is also developed with the students' participation. Several additional assortment problems are given, with each one offering students less help in developing the associated functional equation.

Optimal Coding of Digitized Photographs

Photographs obtained from satellites or other space vehicles can be stored or transmitted as numbers. For black-and-white photographs, each number represents one of n gray levels (shades of gray from very white to very black). Each gray level corresponds to the intensity of light reflected from a small region of the original scene.

Such photographs are called digitized photographs. The level of detail that can be observed in the digitized version depends partly on the value of n (the larger the value of n, the better the detail). In many applications, n is either 8, 16, 32, or 64. A typical "photograph" can consist of a million numbers, each number being an integer from the set

$$(0, 1, \ldots, n - 1).$$

These integers are usually represented as binary numbers. For example, if $n = 64$, then the integers 2, 7, and 63 have binary representations:

2	000010
7	000111
63	111111

One photograph can be represented by as many as 6 million bits (0's or 1's) of information. Most applications involve thousands of photographs. This number presents incredible demands on the storage and transmission capabilities of a system. Thus, a design engineer is always interested in techniques that reduce the information required to the least amount necessary.

Imagine the following scenario:

Digitized photographs (of Saturn) with sixty-four gray-level representations (i.e., $n = 64$) begin to arrive at the Jet Propulsion Laboratory. The scientists find these early scenes uninteresting. Until more interesting scenes appear, they will be satisfied with less detail, say, photographs with eight gray levels. Since eight gray levels can be represented by three "bit" binary numbers, we reduce the transmission requirements by one-half. However, on the space vehicle, we have the problem of converting the photographs from sixty-four gray levels to eight gray levels. How would you go about selecting the eight gray levels from among the original sixty-four?

Preliminary Results

Problems having four levels of difficulty are presented to the students:

1. Grid problem
2. Shrub-covering problem
3. Other assortment problems
4. Digitized-photograph problem

We have found the following results:

• Most students in an academic program in grades 8–12, who have completed at least one year of algebra, are capable of handling problems of levels 1 and 2.

• During the summer of 1982, we worked with sixty-four talented students from grades 8–12 who had completed two years of algebra, and we found that 80 percent were able to handle, in a meaningful way, all four levels. It was interesting that achievement did not depend on grade level. Students in grade 8 performed just as well as students in grades 11 and 12.

• Secondary students in general mathematics courses are able to handle problems at level 1, with the exception of the functional equation.

REFERENCE

Bellman, Richard, and Stuart Dreyfus. *Applied Dynamic Programming*. Princeton, N.J.: Princeton University Press, 1962. ◖

6

CALCULUS

Calculus is usually dated from the late 1660s or 1670s when Newton and Leibniz are credited with independently inventing calculus. Such late dating tends to focus on the theoretical formalization of calculus and not on the applied problems that had been considered earlier by many mathematicians. For example, Galileo (1564–1642) had obtained that a projectile thrown (or shot from a cannon) goes a maximum distance when thrown at a 45° angle. Galileo also found that the distance, s, a body falls in time, t, is $s = kt^2$, where k is a constant. Both are now standard applications in most calculus textbooks.

We typically teach calculus in two parts. Differential calculus is taught first and then integral calculus, and the fundamental theorem of calculus gives the surprising link between the two parts: If $f(x)$ is a differentiable function, then

$$\int_a^b \frac{d}{dx} f(x) dx = f(b) - f(a).$$

Historically, integral calculus developed first. The Greeks and Chinese found formulas for the areas of polygons and circles. Euclid derived the formula for the area of a circle in *The Elements*, Proposition 2 of Book 7. These area formulas were obtained by partitioning a figure in clever ways into many small figures and adding the resulting areas—much as we do today in integral calculus. This was called the method of exhaustion, since it exhausted the area of the original figure when the number of small figures increased, that is, went to infinity. Euclid also used the procedure to find the volumes of solids, including pyramids, cones, and spheres. To illustrate the procedure and its difficulty, consider figure 6.1, which is based on the work of Archimedes. Figure 6.1 shows a circle of radius 1 inscribed in a square with another square inscribed in the circle. Compare the perimeters of the three figures. The perimeter of the outer square is $4 \cdot 2$, since each side is of length 2. The circle has perimeter 2π. Using the Pythagorean theorem, we find the inscribed square has sides of length $2 \cdot \sqrt{2}/2$ and thus a perimeter of $4\sqrt{2}$. The lengths of the perimeters increase from the inner figure out, so

$$4\sqrt{2} < 2\pi < 4 \cdot 2,$$

which gives

$$2\sqrt{2} < \pi < 4.$$

By increasing the number of sides of the inscribed and circumscribed regular polygon, the bounds for π come closer and closer together.

By using areas rather than perimeters, the Greeks bounded the area of the circle in their derivation. (The area inside the figure is *exhausted* as more and more sides are added to the polygons.) Archimedes used a ninety-six-sided polygon and obtained the bounds

$$3\frac{10}{71} < \pi < 3\frac{1}{7}.$$

It would be more than 1500 years before better bounds for the value of π were obtained. Boyer (1989, pp. 376–402) shows how Archimedes obtained the volume of a sphere. Hood (1989, pp. 403–5) shows how Archimedes found the area bounded by a chord and a parabola

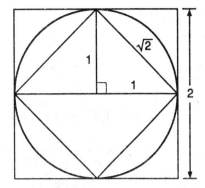

Fig. 6.1. Unit circle with inscribed and circumscribed squares

using triangles and mechanics.

Using the method of exhaustion, the Arab mathematician al-Haytham (ca. 965–1039) found the volume of the figure obtained by rotating a parabola about its base (Stillwell 1989, pp. 102–3).

The development of differential calculus depended on being able to graph functions and relations on a coordinate axis. This became possible when Fermat and René Descartes each developed analytic geometry. Descartes published his development of analytic geometry in 1637 in *Géométrie* (Descartes, 1952). (He also introduced the notation x^n for $n > 2$. The square of x was written as xx.)

In 1679, Fermat published a method for finding the minimum and the maximum of polynomials using

$$\frac{f(x + \Delta x) - f(x)}{\Delta x},$$

the foundation, of course, of the derivative. Using this definition, Fermat solved a number of problems. One problem was the following:

> Given a line of length l, find the point A on the line so that when the two pieces make a rectangle, the area is a maximum.

The resulting figure is, of course, a square. This application, which was worked on by the best mathematicians of the past, is now a standard example in beginning calculus. This occurs because of advances in our understanding of mathematics and the development of teachable mathematical procedures for solving such problems.

Building on previous results but expanding and inventing much, Newton developed calculus in his book *Principia* published in 1687. He found the sums of numerous infinite series including the following,

$$\sin x = x - \frac{x^3}{3!} + \frac{x^5}{5!} - \frac{x^7}{7!} \cdots,$$

for x as an angle measured in radians. An immediate application of this result was that trigonometry tables could now be generated to be accurate to as many figures as desired.

Newton applied calculus to astronomy and mechanics. The *Principia* included Newton's laws of mechanics:

1. Every body persists in its state of rest or of uniform motion in a straight line unless it is compelled to change that state by forces impressed on it.

2. The acceleration caused by one or many forces acting on a body is proportional in magnitude to the resultant force, parallel to it, and inversely proportional to the mass of the body.

3. To every action there is always an opposite and equal reaction.

Another important law was Newton's law of universal gravitation. This states that the force of attraction between two bodies is directly proportional to the product of their masses and inversely proportional to the square of the distance between the [centers of the mass of the] two bodies.

From his four laws, Newton derived Johann Kepler's (1571–1630) laws of planetary motion. Kepler had derived his laws empirically by painstaking computations and observations. Kepler's laws are as follows:

1. Planets move about the sun in elliptical orbits with the sun at one focus.

2. A line joining a planet and the sun sweeps over equal areas in equal intervals of time.

3. The square of the time of one complete revolution of a planet about its orbit is proportional to the cube of the orbit's semimajor axis.

See Eves (1983) for more information on these laws.

Like Euclid in geometry, Newton provided the axioms (or laws) and the mathematics to describe the mechanics of motion. Newton's laws remain the model for mechanics, though Einstein's theory of relativity has necessitated some revisions.

Leibniz independently developed calculus. He too applied it to solve motion problems, though not as extensively as Newton did. Leibniz introduced the words *function, integral,* and *differential* calculus as well as the notation dx.

Calculus is perhaps the most applied mathematics course taught because many of its problems—maximum, minimum, rates of change, and area problems—are applications. The articles in this section sample these applications.

Originally, differential calculus dealt with motion and rates of change. Opp considers projectile motion. Hurley considers the rate of change in the cooling of an object, a problem originally studied by Newton. Ecker looks at rates of change in the optical viewing of pictures on a wall. Austin and Dunning extend the study of optics to show how calculus and physics explain the rainbow. Newton himself first explained the colors in the rainbow.

Applications of integral calculus, as indicated, often involve finding areas. Martin and Ponte find the area of the irregular regions found on golf greens.

Applications of calculus today go beyond the study of motion and problems in science. Brazier considers various models for economics and uses calculus to study minimum and maximum problems. Armstrong and Midgley use calculus and natural logarithms to study medical dosages for radioactive medicines.

REFERENCES

Boyer, Carl B. "The History of the Calculus." In *Historical Topics for the Mathematics Classroom.* Thirty-first Yearbook of the National Council of Teachers of Mathematics. 2d ed. Reston, Va.: The Council, 1989.

Descartes, René. *La Géométrie.* Translated by David Eugene Smith and Marcia L. Lathen. LaSalle, Ill.: Open Court Publishing Co., 1952.

Eves, Howard. *Great Moments in Mathematics before 1650.* Washington, D.C.: Mathematical Association of America, 1983.

Hood, Rodney T. "Archimedes and His Anticipations of Calculus." In *Historical Topics for the Mathematics Classroom.* Thirty-first Yearbook of the National Council of Teachers of Mathematics. 2d ed. Reston, Va.: The Council, 1989.

Stillwell, John. *Mathematics and Its History.* New York: Springer-Verlag, 1989.

GETTING THE BIG PICTURE

By **MICHAEL W. ECKER**
Pennsylvania State University
Dunmore, PA 18512

Problem

A painting on a wall is 5 feet in height, and an observer notes that the bottom of the painting is 2 feet above eye level. How far from the wall should the observer stand to maximize the apparent size of the painting?

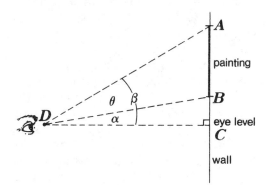

Solution

Consider the side view shown in the diagram. We have $AB = 5$; $BC = 2$; $CD = x$ = distance of observer from the wall; and angles α, β, θ, which are functions of x. We want to maximize $\theta = \theta(x)$. Now $\theta = \beta - \alpha = \cot^{-1} x/7 - \cot^{-1} x/2$. To maximize $\theta(x)$, find $d\theta/dx$, set $d\theta/dx = 0$, and solve for x.

$$\frac{d\theta}{dx} = \frac{^{-}1/7}{1 + (x/7)^2} - \frac{^{-}1/2}{1 + (x/2)^2} = 0.$$

Thus,

$$\frac{1/2}{1 + (x/2)^2} = \frac{1/7}{1 + (x/7)^2}.$$

Cross multiplying and clearing fractions yields

$$98 + 2x^2 = 28 + 7x^2.$$

Hence,

$$5x^2 = 70,$$
$$x^2 = 14,$$

and finally,

$$x = \sqrt{14} \doteq 3.74 \text{ ft.}$$

The reader can check that this critical value does indeed maximize $\theta(x)$.

Problems

1. If the painting were 3 feet above eye level, would you stand closer to or farther from the wall? How far?

2. Generalize: If the painting is height h and is positioned at a level l feet above eye level, determine the distance one should stand from the wall that maximizes the apparent size of the painting as a function of h and l.

3. What if the eye level of the observer falls within the painting?

Solutions

1. Farther; $\sqrt{24} = 2\sqrt{6} \doteq 4.9$ ft.
2. $\sqrt{l(h + l)}$ ft.
3. No maximum; the closer the observer stands, the larger the apparent size.

CALCULUS AND CAPITALISM—
ADAM SMITH REVISITS THE CLASSROOM

A linear and a quadratic equation help determine how a manufacturer can survive in the market place.

By GERALD D. BRAZIER

VPI and State University
Blacksburg, VA 24061

In the March 1975 issue of the *Mathematics Teacher*, Sally Irene Lipsey spoke of applications of mathematics in economics that can enrich the standard curriculum. Such applications are particularly pertinent today, with inflation and business management problems filling the headlines and with news programs discussing economics. Such talk frequently evokes the "gods of the marketplace" that guide the fortunes of a capitalistic, free enterprise system. Many students are unaware of the mathematical basis for the power of these gods and simply treat the laws of capitalism as dogma—to be held to tenaciously or treated with scorn. This article illustrates how elementary differential calculus can "demythologize" some economic situations.

A Mathematical Model

Before an economic situation can be analyzed mathematically, a model must be created. Typically such model building begins with some simplifying assumptions. Our model, based on one of Allen's (1939), assumes the following:

1. The manufacturer is a monopolist, with no competitors.

2. The market demand law relating price P and quantity sold x is a linear equation $P = a - bx$.

3. The manufacturer's cost function relating cost C and quantity sold x is quadratic in form $C = sx^2 + tx + u$.

Let's examine these assumptions to see how closely they reflect the realities of an economic situation.

The first assumption greatly simplifies the analysis by allowing concentration on the basic relationship of the marketplace—the one between manufacturer and consumer. Once the effect of this relationship is understood, then the impact of competition can be more easily analyzed.

> Under one model, the manufacturer should pass on less than half of the tax on his products.

The second assumption, aside from employing a simple function, is a description of a reasonable relationship between quantity and price if a and b are positive. In this case, the graph of this function has negative slope, indicating that a drop in price is accompanied by an increase in quantity sold.

The third assumption is less obvious. It might be helpful to think in terms of the cost per item C/x rather than the total cost C. It is reasonable to expect that the production cost per item would rise sharply as quantity produced becomes small. Conversely, it is expected that cost per item would decrease with increasing production—up to a point. Eventually a point will be reached beyond which it is impossible to increase production without raising the cost per item. Why is that so? Because the manufacturer will eventually put excessive demands on sources of material, labor, and capital—so great that substantially higher prices will have to be paid for the resources needed to increase output. In addition, increased output may measurably increase the rate of depreciation of equipment and so add to production costs. From this point of view, it is understandable that no manufacturing process is suited for unlimited output. Figure 1 is a reasonable graph of a cost-per-item function. The simplest equation for such a graph would be

$$\frac{C}{x} = sx + t + \frac{u}{x}.$$

Multiplying both sides by x gives the quadratic cost function

$$C = sx^2 + tx + u.$$

There are certainly other plausible demand and cost functions (see Allen 1939), but the ones chosen seem to be the simplest that can still reflect some of the complexities.

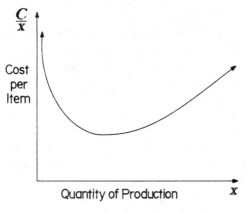

Fig. 1. Graph of the cost-per-item function

$$\frac{C}{x} = sx + t + \frac{u}{x}$$

We will now apply this model to determine how a monopolist manufacturer can maximize profit. In general, profit is simply revenue minus cost. If these two quantities, revenue R and cost C, can be expressed as functions of quantity sold, then the methods of elementary calculus can be employed to investigate the conditions for maximum profit. The function $R - C$ is an expression for profit as a function of quantity. Differentiating this function and setting it equal to zero yields $R' = C'$ as a condition that might provide for maximum profit. In economics, R' is frequently referred to as *marginal revenue* (*MR*) because the derivative

measures the rate of change of revenue for small variations of quantity, that is, marginal changes of quantity or changes "on the margin." Likewise C' is referred to as *marginal cost* (*MC*). Therefore, to find maximum profit it is necessary to find conditions under which marginal revenue equals marginal cost, that is, $MR = MC$.

Revenue is the product of the price per unit and the quantity sold. Under our second assumption it becomes $(a - bx)x$; therefore

$$MR = R' = a - 2bx.$$

Likewise, under the third assumption,

$$MC = C' = 2sx + t.$$

Setting $MR = MC$ and solving for x yields

$$x = \frac{a - t}{2(b + s)}.$$

By standard techniques it is easy to show that this value of x does give an absolute maximum for profit. If $\frac{a - t}{2(b + s)}$ is substituted for x in the demand law $P = a - bx$, the price to set for maximum profit is found to be

(1) $$P = a - \frac{b(a - t)}{2(b + s)}.$$

Taxes

Taxes are one of the most common complicating factors in the economics of manufacturing and sales. Taxes increase the cost of the product to the manufacturer and also, as a consequence, the price to the consumer. The question the manufacturer must answer is how much of the tax should be passed on to the consumer through a price increase. A common notion is that the price to the consumer is simply increased by the amount of the tax. Let's apply our mathematical model to the situation to investigate whether this common notion is correct.

The role of a tax is simplest to see in the case of a unit tax. The federal gasoline tax of 6¢ per gallon and the taxes on liquor are examples of such a tax. In these examples the government imposes a levy of k dollars per unit sold. The effect is to increase the manufacturer's cost by k dollars per unit or by a total of kx dollars. Using the model's assumptions, the relationship $MR = MC$ yields the equation

$$a - 2bx = 2sx + t + k$$

when a unit tax is imposed. Solving for x gives

$$x = \frac{a - t}{2(b + s)} - \frac{k}{2(b + s)}.$$

The price to set for maximum profit is found as before:

$$(2) \qquad P = a - \frac{b(a - t)}{2(b + s)} + k \cdot \frac{b}{2(b + s)}.$$

By comparing equations (1) and (2), the increase in price is seen to be

$$k \cdot \frac{b}{2(b + s)}.$$

Since $b/(b + s)$ is less than one, the increase in price is less than $\frac{1}{2} k$. This means that under this model, the manufacturer should pass on *less than half* of the tax in order to maximize profit. This conclusion runs counter to our intuition and certainly undercuts one myth about the marketplace. Analysis of a percentage tax is more subtle—you are welcome to try that analysis.

The Middleman

The middleman is much maligned as a major culprit in inflation. An idealized situation would be one in which a manufacturer with a cost function of $sx^2 + tx + u$ sells at a price q to a retailer who in turn sells on a market following the demand law, $P = a - bx$. In this situation the retailer is assumed to have *no costs other than purchase from the manufacturer*. The manufacturer's revenue is qx and cost is $sx^2 + tx + u$, so setting marginal revenue equal to marginal cost yields $q = 2sx + t$ for maximum profit. Assuming purchase as the only cost, the retailer then has qx or $(2sx + t)x$

as the cost and $(a - bx)x$ as revenue. Setting $MR = MC$ in this case gives $a - 2bx = 4sx + t$. Solving for x gives

$$x = \frac{a - t}{2(b + 2s)}$$

as the quantity to be sold for maximum profit. Substituting this quantity into the demand law, $P = a - bx$, gives a price

$$(3) \qquad P = a - \frac{b(a - t)}{2(b + 2s)}.$$

The common notion of the middleman's inflationary impact has been upheld . . .

Comparing equations (3) and (1) shows that by merely involving a middleman, the price to the consumer must be larger. Note that the retailer in this situation has no cost other than purchase from the manufacturer. The *presence* of the retailer drives the price up. Such a situation is called a bilateral monopoly and is discussed in detail by Allen (1939). The common notion of the middleman's inflationary impact has been upheld by the mathematical analysis—a myth sustained.

Conclusions

These examples illustrate that elementary differential calculus can be used to analyze relatively complex economic situations. The results of the analyses are in some sense surprising and so help whet the students' interest in mathematics as a valuable tool for them.

REFERENCES

Allen, Roy G. D. *Mathematical Analysis for Economists.* New York: Macmillan, 1939.

Black, J. and J. F. Bradley. *Essential Mathematics for Economists.* London: John Wiley & Sons, 1973.

Daniel, Coldwell, III. *Mathematical Models in Microeconomics.* Boston: Allyn & Bacon, 1970.

Hadar, Josef. *Mathematical Theory of Economic Behavior.* Reading, Mass.: Addison-Wesley Publishing Co., 1971.

Lipsey, Sally Irene. "Adam Smith in the Classroom." *Mathematics Teacher* 68 (March 1975): 189–94.

AN APPLICATION OF NEWTON'S LAW OF COOLING

A fascinating application of Newton's Law of Cooling. The student and the teacher who have some knowledge of logarithms and calculus should find this delightful reading.

By JAMES F. HURLEY

**The University of Connecticut
Storrs, Connecticut**

MANY introductory calculus texts now include a section devoted to applications of the exponential function. The large variety of commonly encountered phenomena whose processes of growth or decay are exponential affords a rich source of interesting and appealing applications. Students who can easily compute the size a century hence of a world population growing continuously at a rate of 2 percent need little further in the way of convincing that calculus can be useful in the real world of today. Problems involving radioactive decay and growth of investments also strike most students as interesting, dealing as they do with questions that, if not familiar, have at least been heard of by most students.

There is often a decline in interest when problems involving Newton's law of cooling are encountered. Some texts omit this topic, but many discuss it and give problems based on it (see, for example, the references cited at the end of this article). Some of these problems involve lifeless situations of the form, "If a body in a room at temperature $n°$ cools from $k°$ to $l°$ in t minutes, how long will it take to cool to $m°$?" Most of the rest involve someone either carrying a thermometer into a deep freeze or plunging it into a pot of hot water. In my experience this sort of problem seems to evoke little interest in the students. The fact that nearly everybody has some experience with, and interest in, mystery stories probably accounts for the interest a class recently showed in the following method for determining the time of death of a murder victim.

If the temperature of a body at time t is given by y and the body is in a room of constant temperature $a < y$, then Newton's law of cooling is usually formulated

$$\frac{dy}{dt} = k(y - a).$$

This yields, on separation of the variables and integration, $ln(y - a) = kt + c$, for some constant c. Given the initial temperature y_0 of the body, c is determined and the formula becomes

$$(1) \qquad ln\frac{y - a}{y_0 - a} = kt.$$

In case the body is that of a murder victim, y_0 can be assumed known ($37°C = 98.6°F$). If the victim is discovered and his body temperature is determined at two different times, then k can be eliminated in (1). The formula for t that results easily yields the time of death, a piece of data every reader (or viewer) of mystery stories recognizes as essential. The following example was successfully given as part of a one-hour examination in a recent calculus course.

The office of the coroner is maintained at $21°C$. While doing an autopsy on a murder victim, the coroner is killed and the victim's body stolen. The coroner's assistant discovers his chief's body and finds its temperature is $31°C$. An hour later, the body temperature is down to $29°C$. Assuming the coroner's body temperature was $37°C$ when he died, find approximately how long after death the body was discovered.

Here (1) gives

$$ln\,\frac{y-21}{16} = kt.$$

The assistant's data give $ln\,\frac{5}{8} = k\bar{t}$ and $ln\,\frac{1}{2} = k(\bar{t}+1)$, where $\bar{t}$ is the desired elapsed time from the coroner's death to discovery of the body. Eliminating k, we obtain

$$-ln\,2 = \frac{ln\,5 - ln\,8}{\bar{t}}\,(\bar{t}+1),$$

$$ln\,8 - ln\,5 - ln\,2 = \frac{ln\,5 - ln\,8}{\bar{t}},$$

$$\bar{t} = \frac{ln\,5 - ln\,8}{ln\,8 - ln\,5 - ln\,2}.$$

A three-place table of natural logarithms gives approximations of -0.470 and -0.223 for the numerator and denominator respectively; so $\bar{t}$ is easily computed to be about 2.11. Thus the coroner was killed about two hours and seven minutes before his body was found.

REFERENCES

Cruise, A., and M. Granberg. *Lectures on Freshman Calculus,* p. 567. Reading, Mass.: Addison-Wesley Publishing Co., 1971.

Flanders, H., R. Korfhage, and J. Price. *Calculus,* p. 438. New York: Academic Press, 1970.

Johnson, R., and F. Kiokemeister. *Calculus with Analytic Geometry,* p. 427. 4th ed. Boston: Allyn & Bacon, 1969.

Leithold, L. *The Calculus with Analytic Geometry,* p. 369. New York: Harper & Row, 1968.

Protter, M., and C. Morrey. *College Calculus with Analytic Geometry,* p. 544. 2d ed. Reading, Mass.: Addison-Wesley, 1970.

Rodin, B. *Calculus with Analytic Geometry,* p. 291. Englewood Cliffs, N. J.: Prentice-Hall, 1970.

A CLASSIFICATION OF PROJECTILE PATHS

Here is an application in analytic geometry.

By **ROGER L. OPP**

**South Dakota School of
Mines and Technology
Rapid City, South Dakota**

WHEN a projectile is fired from $(0, 0)$ (assuming no friction), the equation of its path is given by

$$(1) \qquad \begin{aligned} x &= v_o(\cos \alpha)t, \\ y &= (-g/2)t^2 + v_o(\sin \alpha)t \end{aligned}$$

where v_o is the initial velocity and α is the angle of elevation. The following is a list of questions one might ask:

1. What is the set of all points that can be reached for a given v_o?
2. Which of these points can be found on two different projectile curves?
3. Which points can be reached twice—once by the projectile while still traveling upward, once while it is already traveling downward?
4. What characterization can be given for two curves that contain the same point?

In answer to the preceding questions, the parameter t is eliminated in system (1) to produce

$$(1') \qquad \begin{aligned} gx^2(\tan \alpha)^2 &- 2v_o^2 x(\tan \alpha) \\ &+ 2v_o^2 y + gx^2 = 0. \end{aligned}$$

Next, the foregoing equation is solved for $\tan \alpha$ to obtain

$$(2) \qquad \tan \alpha = \frac{v_o^2 \pm \sqrt{v_o^4 - g(2v_o^2 y + gx^2)}}{gx}.$$

Thus, an angle of inclination exists for every (x, y) such that

$$v_o^4 - g(2v_o^2 y + gx^2) \geq 0.$$

With only $x \geq 0$, $y \geq 0$ considered, this includes all points in the first quadrant on or below the parabola with intercepts $(v_o^2/g, 0)$ and $(0, v_o^2/2g)$. Of course, all these points except the boundary lie on two different projectile curves in that (2) admits to two physically relevant solutions for α.

In answer to question 3, dy/dt is found from equations (1) and equated to zero. This determines that $t = (v_o/g)\sin \alpha$ when the maximum height is attained, and its introduction into equations (1) gives

$$x_m = \frac{v_o^2 \sin \alpha \cos \alpha}{g}, \qquad y_m = \frac{v_o^2 \sin^2 \alpha}{2g}$$

where (x_m, y_m) is the point at which the maximum height is attained.

Next, the parameter α is eliminated by writing

$$x_m^2 = \frac{v_o^4 \sin^2 \alpha (1 - \sin^2 \alpha)}{g^2},$$

which becomes

$$x_m^2 = \frac{2v_o^2}{g} y_m - 4y_m^2$$

when $\sin^2 \alpha$ is replaced by $2gy_m/v_o^2$. This takes the form

$$\frac{x_m^2}{\left(\dfrac{v_o^2}{2g}\right)^2} + \frac{\left(y_m - \dfrac{v_o^2}{4g}\right)^2}{\left(\dfrac{v_o^2}{4g}\right)^2} = 1$$

when the square is completed. Thus, the locus of (x_m, y_m) is an *ellipse*, center at

$(0, v_o^2/4g)$, with one end of its major axis at $(v_o^2/2g, v_o^2/4g)$. Every point inside this ellipse can be reached by the projectile while the projectile rises, yet no point outside the ellipse can be so reached. Since every point below the parabola can be hit exactly twice, the following classification is obvious (see fig. 1):

a. Every point on the parabola can be hit exactly once.

b. Every point inside the ellipse can be hit when the projectile rises and falls.

c. Every point outside the ellipse (and inside the parabola) can be hit twice, downward both times.

d. Every point on the ellipse can be hit once downward and once as an apogee.

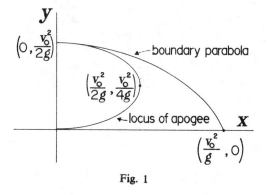

Fig. 1

Finally, consider the locus of all points (targets) struck when $\alpha = 45°$. Every such target can be hit a second time with $\alpha > 45°$. Every point below this locus can be hit with $\alpha < 45°$ and $\alpha > 45°$, respectively, and every point above the 45-degree path can

(must!) be struck by two different α's, each greater than 45°. Intuitively, this doesn't seem possible (consider, for instance, a point directly above the apogee of the 45-degree path; or consider a point far to the right, just beneath the boundary parabola). A further investigation of this situation is now undertaken.

Every projectile path herein under consideration ($\alpha > 45°$) makes tangential contact with the boundary parabola (not including its x-intercept) and conversely. To see this, take any such point on the boundary and note that $x < v_o^2/g$. Now equation (2) becomes $\tan \alpha = v_o^2/gx$ on the boundary so that $\tan \alpha > 1$. Conversely, arbitrary $\tan \alpha > 1$ determines an $x < v_o^2/g$ for which $v_o^4 - g(2v_o^2y + gx^2) = 0$. Let (x_1, y_1) be an arbitrary target point above the projectile path for $\alpha = 45°$ and (x_T, y_T) be the point at which corresponding projectile curves brush the boundary parabola. Since (x_T, y_T) satisfies the equation of the boundary parabola, the radicand of equation (2) becomes zero so that $x_T = (v_o^2/g) \tan \alpha$. When (2) is applied with x and y replaced by x_1 and y_1 respectively, then

$$x_T = x_1 \left[\frac{v_o^2}{v_o^2 \pm \sqrt{v_o^4 - g(2v_o^2 y_1 + g x_1^2)}} \right].$$

Hence, of the two curves passing through (x_1, y_1), one brushes the boundary parabola before passing through (x_1, y_1) and the other brushes the boundary parabola after passing through (x_1, y_1).

THE EXPONENTIAL-DECAY LAW APPLIED TO MEDICAL DOSAGES

By GERALD M. ARMSTRONG, Brigham Young University, Provo, UT 84602
CALVIN P. MIDGLEY, Condell Memorial Hospital, Libertyville, IL 60048

Many drugs are used up by the human body at rates described in terms of exponential decay. Two simple exponential formulas are given in this article. One describes how a therapeutic level of a drug is achieved in terms of its half-life and other parameters. The other describes how this level is maintained.

If the body eliminates a drug so that the rate at which the amount of the drug is changing is proportional to the amount of the drug present, this relationship can be stated in the notation of calculus as

$$f'(t) = kf(t).$$

Students of calculus learn that this equation has a solution of the form

$$f(t) = Ce^{kt}.$$

If H is the half-life of such a drug—the time required for half of it to be used up—and P is the initial dose given, then Pe^{kt}, with

$$k = -\frac{\ln 2}{H},$$

is the amount left in the system after t units of time. (The half-life H is written $t_{1/2}$ and called β *half-life* in medical literature.)

Therapeutic Level and Dosage

Assume now that a drug of half-life H is administered to a patient. If P units of the drug are administered at times $t = 0, \tau, 2\tau, \ldots, (d-1)\tau$, uniform time intervals of length τ, the total amount T of the drug in the body at time $t = d\tau$ is easily found. At time $t = 0$, the first P units are given. Then at time $t = \tau$, the second P units are administered, and the amount left from the first dose is $Pe^{k\tau}$, giving a total of $P + Pe^{k\tau}$ in the

> The administration of drugs is not an exact science, even with representative mathematical models.

system. At time $t = 2\tau$, the total amount in the system is

$$P + Pe^{k\tau} + Pe^{2k\tau},$$

with the terms representing, respectively, the amounts left from the third, second, and first doses. To continue, the amount T of the drug in the system at time $t = d\tau$, one time unit τ after the last dose is given, is

$$T = Pe^{k\tau} + Pe^{2k\tau} + \cdots + Pe^{dk\tau}.$$

Since this expression is the sum of d terms of a geometric sequence with the first term $Pe^{k\tau}$ and constant ratio $e^{k\tau}$,

$$(1) \qquad T = \frac{Pe^{k\tau}(1 - e^{dk\tau})}{1 - e^{k\tau}}.$$

This formula is useful in different ways. As given, T can be obtained in terms of the dose P, the length τ of the time intervals, the total number d of these intervals, and the half-life H, since $k = -(\ln 2)/H$. Among other possibilities, if T, d, and τ are known, P can then be calculated.

The results of continuing the P-unit dose over long periods of time are interesting to consider. We define the steady-state amount of the drug in the system, T_∞, by

$$T_\infty = \lim_{d \to \infty} \frac{Pe^{k\tau}(1 - e^{dk\tau})}{1 - e^{k\tau}}.$$

Since $k < 0$, $e^{dk\tau} \to 0$ as $d \to \infty$, so this limit equals

(2) $$T_\infty = \frac{Pe^{k\tau}}{1 - e^{k\tau}}.$$

Substituting $k = -(\ln 2)/H$ into this equation and simplifying gives us another expression for T_∞:

$$T_\infty = \frac{P}{2^{\tau/H} - 1}.$$

If the half-life H equals the dosage interval τ, then this formula implies that $T_\infty = P$. If H is less than τ, then T_∞ never reaches the value P. But if H is larger than τ, then T_∞ can be considerably larger than P. This idea is illustrated by some values of T_∞ that will be used later; if $H = 2\tau$, then $T_\infty \approx 2.4$ P, and if $H = 9\tau$, then $T_\infty \approx 12.5\ P$.

The steady-state amount T_∞ can also be compared with T. The equation

$$(1 - e^{dk\tau})T_\infty = T,$$

from formulas (1) and (2), shows that the relationship between T_∞ and T depends on the size of $e^{dk\tau}$, which, in turn, depends on the size of $-d\tau(\ln 2)/H$, the exponent. Roughly, the larger $d\tau$ becomes compared with H, the closer T_∞ is to T. And the smaller $d\tau$ is compared with H, the bigger T_∞ is compared with T. More details on such comparisons are found in the examples to follow.

Maintenance Dosage

Now after the therapeutic amount T is obtained by formula (1), this level T of the drug can be maintained in the system. Reduce the size of the dose from P to R, and administer the reduced dose R at the same time intervals as before, at times $t = d\tau$, $(d + 1)\tau$, ... We now determine R. Let R units of the drug be administered at time

$t = d\tau$. Then at time $t = (d + 1)\tau$, but before the next dose of R units is given, require the amount of the drug in the system to again equal T units. This constraint gives

$$T = Re^{k\tau} + \frac{Pe^{2k\tau}(1 - e^{dk\tau})}{1 - e^{k\tau}}.$$

Substitute for T from formula (1) and solve for R. The result is

(3) $$R = P(1 - e^{dk\tau}).$$

Continued administration of R units at time $t = d\tau$, $(d + 1)\tau$, ..., will maintain the amount of the drug in the body at a level that does not fall below T units. The purpose of using the reduced dosage R is to prevent the total amount of the drug in the system from growing too large. This method of treatment, using the dose P for d time units and then reducing it to R according to equation (3), appears to be a new contribution to the theory of drug-dosage regimens.

Some comments are in order before examples of these formulas are presented. The

The half-life of a drug can vary among different patients.

administration of drugs is not an exact science, even with representative mathematical models. The therapeutic amount T must be chosen from a range of empirically determined values. Medical discretion and experience are needed to select proper intervals and durations of time to administer the drug. Even the half-life of a drug can vary somewhat among different patients. Many other factors play a role, such as absorption levels of drugs, their distribution in the system, drug interactions, age of patients, their general health, and the health of such vital organs as the liver and kidneys. So in our model, the variables T, P, d, τ, and even H must be considered at best as approximations to be adjusted to fit individual patients. And we are merely stating the obvious in suggesting that medical practitioners need to account for many variables in administering drugs in general and, particularly, in adapting our formulas. We shall now give two examples of how the formulas can be applied.

Example: Theophylline therapy

The first example concerns the administration of the drug theophylline to a patient with bronchial asthma. Theophylline, a relative of caffeine, is indicated in the treatment of reversible airway obstructions but is a dangerous substance having significant toxic effects. The patient must be monitored carefully, as the minimum toxic level of the drug overlaps the maximum therapeutic level to some extent. (For example, arrhythmias caused by the toxic effects of theophylline can easily be confused with those caused by asthma itself.) Theophylline ther-

---

An alternative to reducing drug dosages is increasing the time between dosages.

---

apy is often continued for two to four weeks after an asthma attack, even if the patient is asymptomatic.

In this example we assume that past experience with the patient dictates that a dose of 100 mg of theophylline every four hours will achieve a desired therapeutic level in twelve hours. But the dose needs to be reduced thereafter to prevent toxicity. We consider the case of a relatively healthy, nonsmoking patient for which the half-life H of the drug is eight hours (H is less than half this value if the patient smokes).

Only the maintenance dose R needs to be calculated here. The units of time are hours, with $\tau = 4$ hours, and $d = 3$. Formula (3) gives

$$R = 100(1 - e^{12k}).$$

With $k = -(\ln 2)/8$, R is close to 65 mg.

It is interesting to compare T and T_∞ in this example. Using formula (1), we find that T is approximately 160 mg. But with either formula (2), or else $T_\infty \approx 2.4P$, T_∞ is about 240 mg. So continuing to give the 100-mg dose instead of reducing it to 65 mg would introduce nearly 50 percent too much theophylline into the system, which could put the patient at a toxic-effects level.

Example: Thyroid therapy

A second example is concerned with thyroid-replacement therapy. Thyroid hormone has two main components, T_4 (thyroxine), the active component, and T_3 (triiodothyronine). This hormone is essential for proper cellular oxygen uptake and proper basal-metabolic rates, for example. Getting too much of this hormone in the system is a real possibility because of its long half-life. Toxic reactions from overdoses include excitability, weak muscles, rapid heartbeat, insomnia, anxiety, psychosis, and even death.

Thyroid deficiency is called hypothyroidism, or myxedema. Now the half-life of T_4 is six to seven days in normal persons and three to four days in hyperthyroid patients. But for persons with myxedema the half-life of T_4 is nine to ten days, the largest value of any drug we have studied.

We assume that tests have indicated that a patient with myxedema must have her or his T_4 blood level increased by 100 μg per liter. If the patient has 5 liters of blood, the therapeutic amount of T_4 to be achieved is 500 μg above the initial level. Take the half-life H of T_4 to be nine days. If we assume that d is 28, formula (1) then gives $P \approx 45$ μg, a dose that by formula (3) also reduces to $R \approx 40$ μg to be given thereafter.

Now for the two solutions given earlier, T_∞ varies considerably. If the 96-μg dose were continued, the level of T_4 would approach $T_\infty \approx 1200$ μg above the initial blood level, which could lead to thyrotoxicosis. If the 45-μg dose were similarly continued, however, the level would approach the more reasonable value of $T_\infty \approx 560$ μg. So an extra margin of safety can be had by building up to the therapeutic level T slowly. (And a slow buildup of thyroid hormone is recommended by the medical profession.)

In conclusion, we should mention some other considerations. Our solution to the problem of overdosing a patient is to reduce the dosage P to R. Another solution is to keep the dose P constant and increase the length of the dosage interval τ. But the mathematics involved is somewhat more difficult, as would be the patient's response—administering T_4 every 1.3 days, for example, is not reasonable! A similar situation is what happens when the dosage regimen requires continuous administration of the drug for a time (e.g., as for an intravenous infusion) and then a periodic dosage afterward. It would be interesting to obtain formulas for dosage schedules in this situation.

BIBLIOGRAPHY

Bochner, Felix, George Carruthers, Jens Kampmann, and Janice Steiner. *Handbook of Clinical Pharmacology*. Boston: Little, Brown & Co., 1978.

Goodman, Louis, and Alfred Gilman. *The Pharmacological Basis of Therapeutics*. 5th ed. New York: Macmillan, 1975. ◗

APPLICATIONS

MATHEMATICS OF THE RAINBOW

By JOE DAN AUSTIN and F. BARRY DUNNING, Rice University, Houston, TX 77251

Figure 1 shows a picture of a rainbow. Have you wondered what causes a rainbow, why it is brighter inside than out, or why more than one rainbow may appear? The answers to these questions involve optics, geometry, trigonometry, and calculus. This article presents some of the optics and mathematics related to these questions.

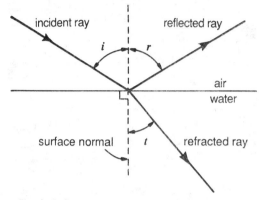

Fig. 2. Reflection and refraction at the boundary between air and water

Fig. 1. The photograph of this rainbow appears through the courtesy of Stanley Jamieson.

Laws of Reflection and Refraction

Rainbows are caused by reflection and refraction of sunlight in raindrops. Figure 2 shows a ray of light incident on a boundary between air and water. Some light is reflected and some transmitted, giving reflected and refracted rays. These rays obey the following basic laws of optics.

i) The incident ray, the reflected or refracted ray, and the normal to the surface lie in the same plane.

ii) The angle of incidence i equals the angle of reflection r (the law of reflection).

iii) The angle of incidence and angle of refraction t are related by

$$(1) \qquad \sin i = n \sin t,$$

where n is the refractive index of water (the law of refraction).

The refractive index of a medium is the ratio of the speed of light in a vacuum to the speed in the medium; the refractive index of air is assumed equal to one. Hecht and Zajac (1974, 72) show that the relative amounts of light reflected and transmitted depend on both i and the polarization of the incident radiation. Indeed, rainbows are polarized. To demonstrate this characteristic, view a rainbow through Polaroid sunglasses and then rotate the lenses. See Nussenzveig (1977).

Reflections in a Raindrop

The mathematical model of reflection by a raindrop assumes the following:

a) Raindrops are spherical.

b) The speed of light is so fast that raindrops can be treated as stationary.

c) Rays of light from the sun are parallel to
one another.

The primary rainbow is formed by a
single reflection in the raindrop (see fig. 3).
Consider a ray of light that strikes the surface of a raindrop at point P with angle of
incidence i. The normal at P, or any other
point on the surface of the raindrop, passes
through the center O. The refracted ray
from P, with angle of refraction t, strikes
the raindrop at Q. The ray reflected from Q
strikes the surface of the raindrop at R, and
a refracted ray emerges from the raindrop.
This ray is weaker than the ray incident at
P because each time light hits a surface,
some is reflected and some is refracted.

The angle between the ray incident at P
and that emerging at R can be derived from
the laws of reflection and refraction and geometry. Using the center O of the raindrop,
construct triangles PQO and RQO (see fig.
3). The triangles are isosceles as $\overline{OP}$, $\overline{OQ}$,
and $\overline{OR}$ are radii of the sphere. By the law
of reflection $m \angle PQO = m \angle RQO$, and the
two triangles are congruent. Thus angles
with vertices on the sphere all have equal
measure t. If the incident and emergent
rays are extended to intersect at point S,
then the angle between them, $\angle PSR$, denoted θ, is given by

(2) $$\theta = 2(2t - i).$$

This result does not depend on the radius of
the raindrop.

Consider now a collection of parallel
rays from the sun incident on a raindrop at
different points on its surface and thus with
different angles of incidence. The paths of
these rays can be traced using the laws of
reflection and refraction and are shown in
figure 4. The ray passing through the
center of the drop is reflected back on itself
and forms a convenient axis. Rays entering
the drop above the axis emerge below the
axis. However, reflected rays do not emerge
at all angles. There is a maximum, θ_{max}, in
the angle θ between the incident and emergent rays. Figure 4 and the Appendix show a
concentration of rays reflected near θ_{max},
resulting in a particularly strong reflection
near this angle. This concentration of reflected light gives rise to the rainbow.

To find θ_{max}, set the derivative of θ with
respect to i from (2) equal to zero. Remem-
ber that t is a function of i. Thus when $\theta =
\theta_{max}$,

$$\frac{d\theta}{di} = 4 \frac{dt}{di} - 2 = 0,$$

or

(3) $$\frac{dt}{di} = \frac{1}{2}.$$

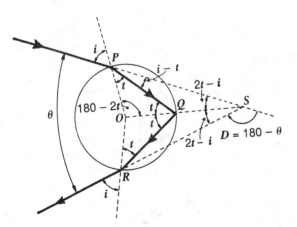

Fig. 3. Single reflection in a raindrop

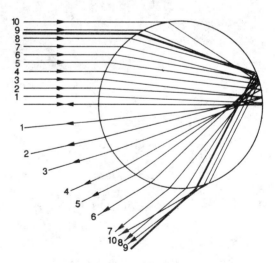

Fig. 4. Reflection of parallel rays by a raindrop. The
heavy line shows the ray for which $\theta = \theta_{max}$.

Differentiating (1) with respect to i gives

$$(4) \qquad \cos i = n \cos t \, \frac{dt}{di}.$$

Substituting (3) into (4) and squaring gives

$$4 \cos^2 i = n^2 \cos^2 t.$$

Using

$$\cos^2 t = 1 - \sin^2 t = 1 - \frac{\sin^2 i}{n^2}$$

(the second equality following from [1]) yields

$$4 \cos^2 i = n^2 - \sin^2 i.$$

Replacing $\sin^2 i$ by $1 - \cos^2 i$ and simplifying gives

$$3 \cos^2 i + 1 = n^2.$$

Solving for $\cos i$ gives that for θ_{max},

$$(5) \qquad \cos i = \sqrt{\frac{n^2 - 1}{3}},$$

from which, given n, θ_{max} can be calculated as shown later.

Reflection in Many Raindrops

In figure 5 an observer at point O is shown viewing raindrops in a rainstorm. To reach O, a ray reflected by raindrop 1 must be deflected through θ_1. This situation is possible if $\theta_1 \leqq \theta_{max}$, which requires that rays from the sun be incident at an angle $\phi < \theta_{max}$. Rainbows are only observed when the sun is behind you and low in the sky; if $\phi > \theta_{max}$, all rays reflected by the raindrops

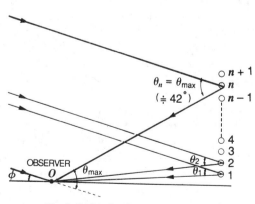

Fig. 5. Reflection by many raindrops

go up and cannot be seen from the surface of the earth. They can be viewed from an airplane! For light from the other raindrops, labeled 2, 3, ..., to reach O it must be reflected through larger angles θ_2, θ_3, ... until, for some raindrop n, $\theta_n = \theta_{max}$. At this point a sharp cutoff occurs because the other raindrops cannot reflect light to O. Rotating the diagram about a line through O parallel to the incident (sun's) rays leaves all angles unchanged. Thus the strong reflection of light occurring near θ_{max} appears as a bright arc (of a circle) in the sky to the observer at O. It has a distinct outer edge (at θ_{max}) and exhibits a gradual fading on the inner side. Figure 5 shows an aligned row of raindrops. A random arrangement of raindrops causes the same bright arc because only the angle, and not the distance, between the observer and the raindrops is important.

Color

The previous discussion describes the formation of a bright arc of reflected sunlight but does not explain why rainbows are colored. Rainbows are colored because sunlight is composed of light of different colors ranging from red through violet, the colors of the rainbow, and because the velocity of light in water, and hence its refractive index, depends on the color of the light—a property termed dispersion. For red light $n \doteq 1.332$ and for violet light $n \doteq 1.344$. From using $n = 1.332$ in (5), the angle of incidence corresponding to θ_{max} requires $\cos i = 0.5080$ and $i = 59°28'$. Then $\sin i = 0.8614$. Using the law of refraction, equation (1), gives $\sin t = 0.8614/1.332 = 0.6467$ and $t = 40°17'$. From (2)

$$\theta_{max} = 2(2t - i) = 42°13'.$$

A similar calculation using $n = 1.344$ yields $\theta_{max} = 40°30'$. Other colors of light have values of θ_{max} between those for red and violet light. The bright arcs produced by reflection of light of different colors are thus displaced relative to each other, giving rise to a series of colored bands—the rainbow! Further, because the value of θ_{max} for red light is greater than that for violet light, the bright arc produced by red light will appear higher in the sky to an observer at O (see fig. 5) and therefore, as evident in figure 1, on the outer edge of the rainbow. The angular width of the rainbow is the difference between the values of $\theta_{\max}$ for red and violet light and is about $1°43'$. Assumption (c) is in effect that the sun is a point source infinitely far away. Newton compensated for the diameter of the sun and computed the width of the rainbow as $2°15'$; see Boyer (1959, 241).

Multiple Rainbows

So far only single reflections of light in a raindrop have been considered. Light can, however, emerge after multiple reflections and produce additional rainbows. Figure 6 shows two and three reflections. For multiple reflections it is convenient to consider the deviation D between the incident and emergent rays (see fig. 6). The angular deviation of a ray introduced by a refraction is $i - t$. Arguments similar to those used with figure 3 show that angles of incidence and

reflection at all points on the inner surface of the raindrop have measure t. Thus each reflection causes a ray to deviate $180° - 2t$. As two refractions necessarily occur, one as the light enters the raindrop and the other as it exits, the total deviation D is

$$(6) \qquad D = 2(i - t) + N(180° - 2t),$$

where N is the number of reflections. One can check this expression for $N = 1$ using (2) and $D = 180° - \theta$. For each N value, light is again only reflected over a limited range of angles. At the extremum

$$\frac{dD}{di} = 2\left(1 - \frac{dt}{di}\right) - 2N\frac{dt}{di} = 0$$

and

$$(7) \qquad \frac{dt}{di} = \frac{1}{1 + N}.$$

Substituting (4) into (7) and squaring gives

$$(1 + N)^2 \cos^2 i = n^2 \cos^2 t.$$

Substituting

$$\cos^2 t = 1 - \sin^2 t = 1 - \frac{\sin^2 i}{n^2}$$

(the second equality from [1]) gives

$$(1 + N)^2 \cos^2 i = n^2 - \sin^2 i.$$

Solving for $\cos i$ (remember $\cos^2 i + \sin^2 i = 1$) at $D = D_{\text{ext}}$ (the extremum value of D) yields

$$(8) \qquad \cos i = \sqrt{\frac{n^2 - 1}{N(N + 2)}}.$$

Let $N = 1$ in (8) and compare to (5). Arguments similar to those given in the Appendix show that for each value of N a concentration of rays is reflected at angles near the extremum D_{ext}. This fact, coupled with the color dependence of n, leads to additional rainbows.

For $N = 2$ reflections, $D_{\text{ext}} \doteq 232°$, which corresponds to an angle θ between the incident and emergent rays of about $52°$. From figure 6, $\theta = D - 180°$. A secondary rainbow appears outside the primary rainbow. It is weaker (fig. 1) because each reflection inside a raindrop causes a loss of light due

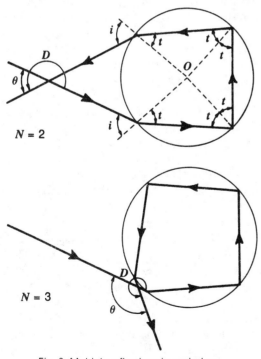

Fig. 6. Multiple reflections in a raindrop

to transmission. The Appendix shows that at D_{ext}, θ is a minimum not a maximum, so the secondary rainbow is sharper on its inner edge. The calculation of D_{ext} for red and violet light shows that the ordering of the colors is reversed in the secondary rainbow. For $N = 3$, the tertiary rainbow, $D_{ext} \doteq 319°$. From figure 6, $\theta = D - 180°$, so $\theta \doteq 139°$. If a tertiary rainbow appears, it appears around the sun! Rainbows from more than three internal reflections are not observed except in laboratory experiments because of loss of light due to the many reflections.

History

The attempt to explain rainbows involved many famous mathematicians. René Descartes, the inventor of analytic geometry, published in 1637 the law of refraction. Snell discovered this law in 1621 but never published his findings; it is often called Snell's law. Descartes drew a figure similar to figure 4 and found the angle between the rainbow and the sun's rays to be between 41° and 42°. He could not explain the colors. Isaac Newton, inventor of the calculus, used a prism to show that white light was made up of different colors. In 1704 he published his results, which had earlier been given in lectures at Cambridge University. He showed that refractive indices depend on color and explained the formation of the rainbow. In 1700 Edmund Halley, of comet fame, became the first person to derive the angle for the third, or tertiary, rainbow, which appears around the sun. People had been looking in the wrong direction for it!

APPENDIX

The concentration of reflected light at angles near θ_{max}, termed the rainbow angle, can be demonstrated by considering how θ depends on the perpendicular distance x between an incident ray and an axis parallel to the ray through the center of the raindrop (see fig. 7). The angle of incidence is

$$\text{(A1)} \qquad i = \sin^{-1} \frac{x}{R},$$

where R is the radius of the drop. From (1)

$$\text{(A2)} \qquad t = \sin^{-1}\left(\frac{\sin i}{n}\right) = \sin^{-1}\frac{x}{nR}.$$

Consider a single reflection in the raindrop. Equation (2) gives

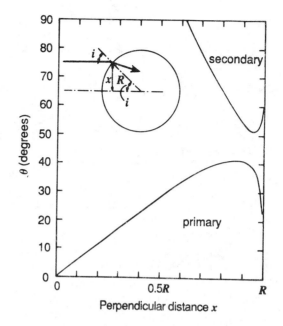

Fig. 7. The dependence of the angle θ on the perpendicular distance x between an incident ray and an axis parallel to the ray through the center of the raindrop. Results for both the primary and secondary rainbows are included.

$$\text{(A3)} \qquad \theta = 2\left(2\sin^{-1}\frac{x}{nR} - \sin^{-1}\frac{x}{R}\right).$$

This angle is plotted for $0 \leq x \leq R$ in figure 7, using a typical refractive index for water $n = 1.336$. A maximum in θ is evident at about 41°. Rays from a sizeable range of x values emerge at angles θ close to the maximum, giving the particularly bright reflections at this angle.

For the secondary rainbow (two reflections),

$$\text{(A4)} \qquad \theta = D - 180° = 180° - 2(3t - i).$$

The verification of (A4) using geometrical arguments similar to those used with figure 3 is an interesting exercise. Using (A1) and (A2) gives

$$\text{(A5)} \qquad \theta = 180° - 2\left(3\sin^{-1}\frac{x}{nR} - \sin^{-1}\frac{x}{R}\right).$$

Plotting this angle (see fig. 7) shows a minimum in the angle θ. Figure 7 also shows that little reflection of light occurs at angles θ between about 41° and 52°. Thus the sky is quite dark in the region between the primary and secondary rainbows. This region is called Alexander's dark band.

REFERENCES

Boyer, Carl B. *The Rainbow*. New York: Sagamore, 1959.

Hecht, E., and A. Zajac. *Optics*. Reading, Mass.: Addison-Wesley Publishing Co., 1974.

Nussenzveig, H. M. "The Theory of the Rainbow." *Scientific American* 236 (April 1977):116–27. (Reprinted in *Light from the Sky*. San Francisco: W. H. Freeman & Co., 1980, 54–65.) ▉

Measuring the Area of Golf Greens and Other Irregular Regions

By W. GARY MARTIN, University of Georgia, Athens, GA 30606
JOAO PONTE, Universidade de Lisboa, Lisboa, Portugal

Much attention is now focused on problem solving as an important activity in the mathematics classroom. Problem solving is a central idea in *An Agenda for Action* (NCTM 1980). One question that may occur to many teachers is, "Where am I supposed to find all these great problems?" In fact, while purely mathematical problems abound, interesting real-life problems are not always so easy to find. Good problems must appear fresh and natural to our students and must tickle their mathematical imaginations. In this article, we examine one such "true life" problem that we have found stimulating.

The Problem

A greenskeeper from a local golf course approached a faculty member in our department with the following problem. Greenskeepers must be very knowledgeable about the kinds and quantities of fertilizers, fungicides, and herbicides to use on various kinds of grass. The quantity to be used is based, of course, on a concentration of the chemical per area unit and on the number of area units. Thus, the greenskeeper has to know, as exactly as possible, the areas of the greens, which are not easy to figure since they are not generally laid out in rectangles, circles, or other familiar geometric regions (see fig. 1).

The greenskeeper who approached us, however, had read an article in a professional journal that outlined two methods developed by Maples (1980). The greenskeeper wanted to know how to tell if the methods worked, short of trying them and seeing if the grass died. To help answer this question, let us turn our attention to the determination of areas of irregular regions.

Some Solutions

A scale-drawing solution

In the mathematics classroom, areas of irregular regions are generally found by considering them on a grid and counting up the number of squares inside the boundary. One of Maples's (1980) ideas may be helpful here. First, he takes measurements from a central point on the green to the boundary in a regular pattern, for example, every ten degrees. Reproducing these radii on a smaller scale on graph paper (fig. 2) serves

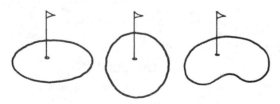

Fig. 1. Typical shapes of golf greens

We thank Edward Davis, University of Georgia, Athens, Georgia, for sharing the original problem and encouraging us to write this article.

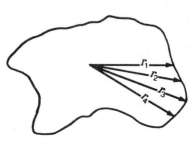

Fig. 2. Constructing a scale model

as a scale model of the green that can be used to approximate the area.

Approximating area by counting squares is often studied in middle school. And, if it is beneficial to learn about area, it is even better actually to compute the areas of real regions as a class project!

Maples's methods

The scale-drawing approach will produce somewhat crude results when used with unusual shapes such as golf greens. Several more exacting, computational methods can be used, including those of Maples. His first method involves averaging the radii, obtained in the manner previously described, and then squaring the answer and multiplying by π. This method is based on the idea that usually greens are nearly circular and that an "average radius" will give a close approximation of the area.

$$(1) \qquad A = \pi((r_1 + r_2 + \cdots + r_{36})/36)^2.$$

Using the values of the radii from table 1 in equation (1), we find that the approximate area is 979.0 m².

Maples's second method calls for squaring the radii before averaging, then multiplying by π, which is a summation of the areas of circular sectors determined by the radii. Recall that the area of a circular sector is given by (measure of central angle/360) $\times \pi r^2$; then the area of the sector

determined by r_i is $(1/36)\pi r_i^2$, since we are using a ten-degree central angle. Summing up the sectors and applying the distributive property yields equation (2).

$$(2) \qquad A = \pi(r_1^2 + r_2^2 + \cdots + r_{36}^2)/36.$$

Again using values of the radii from table 1 in equation (2), we find the approximate area is 1056.1 m².

Using Heron's formula

A similar method, which was not developed by Maples, may also be useful. With this method, the exterior endpoints of consecutive radii are connected to form triangles whose areas can be computed using Heron's formula,

$$A = \mathrm{SQR}(s(s - a)(s - b)(s - c)),$$

where a, b, and c are the lengths of the sides and s is the semiperimeter,

$$s = \tfrac{1}{2}(a + b + c).$$

(See fig. 3a.) Although this approach is more complex computationally, it is manageable using a computer. See program 1 in the Appendix for an example. Using the radii from table 1 in this program produces an approximation of 1040.1 m².

The use of both Maples's methods and Heron's formula can be considered in a geometry course where work is generally limited to regularly shaped figures. Also, many

TABLE 1			
Measures in Meters of Radii of a Golf Green Using Ten Degrees Between Readings			
$r_1 - r_9$	$r_{10} - r_{18}$	$r_{19} - r_{27}$	$r_{28} - r_{36}$
23.2	13.9	22.6	11.6
25.7	13.8	20.4	11.7
28.4	17.1	18.3	14.1
27.4	21.0	15.9	14.8
25.9	23.7	14.4	16.7
18.8	18.7	12.7	17.9
14.0	16.1	11.3	21.4
12.4	16.3	11.2	22.1
11.8	16.7	10.9	22.6

$$\left(\tfrac{1}{36}\sum r_i\right)^2 = 311.6; \quad \tfrac{1}{36}\sum r_i^2 = 336.2.$$

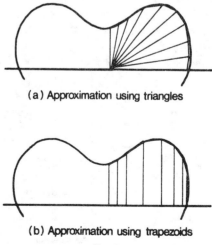

(a) Approximation using triangles

(b) Approximation using trapezoids

Fig. 3.

students will enjoy using Heron's formula to solve a practical problem and may even develop a computer program to obtain the area of irregular polygons. These methods can also be presented in middle school in a simplified manner, relating them to the known formula for the circle.

Checking the Methods Using a Computer

The accuracy of these methods can be tested by using them to find the areas of figures whose areas are known. This approach can be used without computing devices; however, a computer can reduce tedious computation as well as provide a pertinent setting for developing relevant computer algorithms.

All three methods work fairly well with the ten-degree readings recommended by Maples, as long as the figures are not extremely disproportionate, for example, very eccentric ellipses or "narrow" rectangles. Generally, the second method of Maples (hence referred to as method 2) will perform best, followed by the method based on Heron's formula. See programs 2 and 3 in the Appendix for sample programs calculating the areas of rectangles and ellipses.

What is the effect of increasing the number of radii? Although this extra work may not help our greenskeeper, it may suggest whether the methods are mathematically sound. Heron's formula and method 2 become quite accurate, even in extreme cases, if the number of radii is increased sufficiently, say, one per degree, as seen in table 2. At the same time we see that Maples's first method (method 1) is not working well.

Exploring the relative accuracies of the methods with programs 2 and 3 is an interesting task. It is stimulating to explore different mathematical models of a situation, and this problem presents a good forum for comparison. Students will acquire an intuitive notion of limits when they see additional readings produce increasingly accurate answers with method 2 and Heron's formula. Some students may actually enjoy developing the programs underlying these explorations.

Mathematical Discussion

A mathematical analysis of the methods shows that our empirical observations are correct. The radii that we measured can be viewed as a partition of the figure by $360/d$ rays, where d is the number of degrees between radii. Method 2 can be expressed as

$$A = \left(\sum \pi r_i^2 \right)/n,$$

where n is the number of rays. Now $n(dT) = 360$ degrees or 2π radians, where dT is the angle between consecutive radii, since we "went all the way around the circle," and thus $n = 2\pi/dT$. So,

$$(3) \qquad A = \frac{\sum \pi r_i^2}{\dfrac{2\pi}{dT}} = \frac{1}{2} \sum (r_i^2)\, dT.$$

The limit of equation (3) as n approaches infinity is the polar integral

$$\frac{1}{2} \int r^2\, dT,$$

which is the general formula for finding the area of a closed curve in polar coordinates. (See Swokowski 1979, p. 633.) By similar reasoning, the limit of the answers obtained

TABLE 2			
Approximations of the Area of an Ellipse with Semi-major Axis 3 and Semi-minor Axis 1			
Number of Measures	Maples's Method 1	Maples's Method 2	Heron's Formula
36	8.141044	9.424850	9.255012
72	8.141026	9.424778	9.381281
360	8.141026	9.424778	9.423024
$\to \infty$	8.141027	9.424778	9.424778

The exact area is given by $A = \pi ab$, where a and b are the semi-axes. In this case, $A \approx 9.424778$.

using method 1 can be seen as the polar integral

$$\frac{1}{4\pi}\left(\int r\,dT\right)^2,$$

which is not equivalent to the previous expression and does not give the exact area, except in special cases such as the circle.

Indeed, this observation can be verified intuitively. Method 1 presupposes that the area of any region can be computed using its mean radius in the formula for the area of a circle. On the one hand, a circle having the same area as the region does exist, although it does not seem reasonable that the radius of this region should be the mean radius. On the other hand, method 2 is based on an average "slice" of the region. Additional measurements increase the accuracy of this representative slice, thus producing results that approach the correct area.

We also observe that Heron's formula can produce a correct iterative method. Setting up our triangles from the center point actually determines a polygon, as shown in figure 3a. As we use more and more triangles, this polygon becomes closer to the shape of the actual region. If we redraw the figure with vertical lines, as in figure 3b, we see that this process is analogous to two instances of the familiar trapezoidal approximation of the area under a curve, one above and one below the x-axis. Since we know that the trapezoidal method approaches the correct limit (Swokowski 1979, p. 260–61), we are assured that Heron's formula will approach it, too.

As suggested, students of calculus may be able to look at these methods and their mathematical bases. Similarly, preservice teachers can profit greatly from working this problem at several levels, discussing its use in school mathematics as well as in more advanced mathematical analyses.

Conclusion

We have explored a real-world problem involving the determination of the areas of irregular regions. We have discussed the problem on a number of levels, and we invite you to try other approaches. Students will benefit from seeing the real-world uses of mathematics and from having an opportunity to explore mathematical concepts. We hope you and your students will find this a stimulating example.

REFERENCES

Maples, Palmer, Jr. "Maples' Method of Measuring Greens." *Golf Course Management*, June 1980, pp. 41–42.

National Council of Teachers of Mathematics. *An Agenda for Action: Recommendations for School Mathematics of the 1980s*. Reston, Va.: The Council, 1980.

Swokowski, E. W. *Calculus with Analytic Geometry*. 2d ed. Boston: Prindle, Weber & Schmidt, 1979.

APPENDIX

Program 1

```
10  PI = 3.1415926535
20  INPUT "HOW MANY DEGREES BETWEEN
       READINGS?";DB
30  DT = DB / 180 * PI
40  N = 360 / DB
50  FOR T = 0 TO 2 * PI − DT / 2 STEP
       DT
60    INPUT "R = ";R
70    M1 = M1 + R
80    M2 = M2 + R * R
90    IF T <    > 0 THEN 120
100   FR = R
110   GOTO 130
120   GOSUB 200
130   R1 = R
140   NEXT T
150 R = FR:T = DT: GOSUB 200
160 PRINT "HERON: "H
170 PRINT "MAPLE I: "(M1 / N) ^ 2 * PI
180 PRINT "MAPLEII: "M2 / N * PI
190 END
200 REM
210 REM FIGURE AREA OF TRIANGLE
220 X1 = COS (T − DT) * R1
230 Y1 = SIN (T − DT) * R1
240 X2 = COS (T) * R
250 Y2 = SIN (T) * R
260 R2 = SQR ((X1 − X2)  ^ 2 + (Y1 − Y2)  ^ 2)
270 S = (R + R1 + R2) / 2
280 H = H + SQR (S * (S − R) * (S − R1)
       * (S − R2))
290 RETURN
```

Program 2

```
10  PI = 3.1415926535
20  INPUT "ENTER LENGTH AND WIDTH
       .";L,W
30  INPUT "ENTER DEGREES BETWEEN
       RADII.";DB
```

```
40 DT = DB / 180 * PI
50   FOR T = 0 TO PI / 2 STEP DT
60 N = 4
70   IF T = 0 OR T > PI / 2 − DT THEN
       N = 2
80   T1 = T
90 S = L / 2
100  IF T1 < = ATN (W / L) THEN 130
110 T1 = PI / 2 − T1
120 S = W / 2
130 R = S / COS (T1)
140 M1 = M1 + N * R
150 M2 = M2 + N * R ^ 2
160  NEXT T
170  PRINT "I: ";(M1 / (2 * PI) *
       DT) ^ 2 * PI
180  PRINT "II: ";M2 / (2 * PI) *
       DT * PI
190  PRINT "ACTUAL AREA: ";L * W
```

Program 3

```
10 PI = 3.1415926535
20  DIM S(4)
30  PRINT "ENTER SEMI-MAJOR AXIS,
       SEMI-MINOR AXIS:"
40  INPUT A,B
50  INPUT "ENTER DEGREES BETWEEN
       RADII.";DB
60 DT = DB / 180 * PI
70 N = 360 / DB
```

```
80 Q = 2 * PI − DT / 2
90   FOR T = 0 TO Q STEP DT
100 R = A * B / SQR (A ^ 2 + (B ^ 2 − A ^ 2)
       * COS (T) ^ 2)
110 M1 = M1 + R
120 M2 = M2 + R ^ 2
130 R1 = R
140 T1 = T
150  IF FR < > 0 THEN 190
160 FR = R
170 FT = T
180  GOTO 200
190  GOSUB 310
200 R2 = R1
210 T2 = T1
220  NEXT T
230 R1 = FR
240 T1 = FT
250  GOSUB 310
260  PRINT "METHOD I: ";(M1 / N) ^ 2 * PI
270  PRINT "METHOD II: ";M2 / N * PI
280  PRINT "HERON'S FORMULA: ";H
290  PRINT "CORRECT ANSWER: "A *
       B * PI
300  END
310  REM FIND AREA OF TRIANGLE
320 R3 = SQR ((R1 * COS (T1) −
       R2 * COS (T2)) ^ 2 + (R1 *
       SIN (T1) − R2 * SIN (T2)) ^ 2)
330 S = (R1 + R2 + R3) / 2
340 H = H + SQR (S * (S − R1) *
       (S − R2) * (S − R3))
350  RETURN
```

7

PROBABILITY AND STATISTICS

Probability developed initially from the study of games of chance. The earliest book is a posthumous publication *De Ludo Aleae* ("Games of Chance") in 1663 by Girolamo Cardano (1501–1576) (see Ore 1965). Cardano uses the idea of probability as the ratio of the number of favorable outcomes to the total number of outcomes in simple dice problems where the dice have 3, 4, 5, or 6 faces. One problem he considered in his combination mathematics and philosophy meander is the following:

> In *fritillus*, a game like backgammon, two six-sided dice are rolled. You may move a certain number of spaces if the sum of the dice equals the number or at least one die shows that number. Find the probability of being able to move each number of spaces.

We solve the problem for a move of two spaces. Dice rolls allowing a move of two spaces are as follows:

$$(1, 1); (2, 1), (2, 2), \ldots, (2, 6); (1, 2), (3, 2), (4, 2), (5, 2), (6, 2).$$

Since twelve of the thirty-six possible outcomes are favorable, the probability is 12/36. Cardano gives a table with the other possible moves. (Ore [1965] gives the original text and an analysis.)

The mathematical formulation of probability was begun in correspondences between Pascal (1625–1665) and Fermat (1601–1665). The problem that stimulated this interchange is called the problem of points. An example is the following:

> Two players, A and B, are equally skilled in a game. They play until A wins 2 games or B wins 3 games. What are the odds that player A will win the series?

We will follow the type of solution given by Pascal. (For more details, see Eves [1983, chap. 24].) Note that the game will be over in four or fewer plays. Assume that there are four plays and count the outcomes that result in A's winning. A wins if he or she wins two or more of the four plays. Using binomial coefficients from Pascal's triangle, the number of ways player A can win is

$$\binom{4}{2} + \binom{4}{3} + \binom{4}{4}. \tag{1}$$

Here

$$\binom{n}{k} = \frac{n!}{k!(n-k)k!}$$

for n and k nonnegative integers, $n \geq k$, gives the number of combinations of n things taken k at a time (not counting order). The notation $n!$ is n factorial, $n \cdot (n - 1) \ldots 2 \cdot 1$ when $n > 0$ and $0! = 1$. Evaluating (1) shows that player A can win in

$$6 + 4 + 1 = 11$$

ways. The 6 is the number of ways A has exactly two wins in the four plays. Listing these six ways gives

aabb, abab, abba, baab, baba, bbaa,

where *aabb* indicates that player A wins the first two games and B wins the next two. The outcome, of course, is decided when A wins the first two games, so the last two plays do not affect the outcome. A similar analysis for player B gives five ways for B to win. The players are equally skilled, so the outcomes are equally likely. Thus, the odds of A winning are 11 to 5, written 11:5.

A mathematically equivalent variation of the problem is the following:

> Two players, A and B, are equally skilled in a game. They are to play until either wins three games. However, the play is interrupted with A having won one game and B having won none. How should their stakes be divided?

The stakes should be divided with eleven parts to A and five parts to B.

The most important early result in probability was the central limit theorem. This theorem establishes that for repeated independent measurements or outcomes, the normal probability model can be used to approximate probabilities. In 1708, Montmort gave the first empirical demonstration of the result in an analysis of the problem of points. Adams (1974) traced the history of this important result, and most introductory books on probability or statistics discuss it.

An axiomatic foundation of probability, like the one Euclid created in 300 B.C. for geometry, finally occurred in 1933 when Kolmogorov published *Grundbegriffe der Wahrscheinlich-keitrechnung*. An English edition was published in 1950, entitled *Foundations of the Theory of Probability* (Kolmogorov 1950).

The most important early statistical technique was the method of least squares, developed by Legendre (1752–1833) in an 1805 publication on determining the orbits of comets. To illustrate how this method uses calculus to solve estimation problems, consider the following problem:

> The temperature at a certain place is measured for three days at the same time each day giving the following results: 56°, 60°, 59°. Assuming the model
>
> Observed $T = t + E$,
>
> where t is the true temperature and E is the error, how do we estimate t ?

Using the least-square procedure, we find the t-value that minimizes the sum of the errors squared, E^2. This means we minimize the sum S, where

$$S = (56° - t)^2 + (60° - t)^2 + (59° - t)^2.$$

To find the minimum, differentiate S with respect to t and set the resulting derivative equal to 0. Differentiating gives

$$\frac{d}{dt}S = -2(56° - t) - 2(60° - t) - 2(59° - t).$$

Setting the right-hand side equal to 0 and solving for t give

$$t = \frac{56° + 60° + 59°}{3},$$

the average of the three observations, or 58.33°. Legendre gives the general result for any number of observations. The power of the method comes when more than one variable is measured. He used the procedure in this case (with partial derivatives) when the variables were linearly related. (See Stigler [1986] for details on the original paper and applications.)

Much of the mathematical development of statistics was focused on applications. For example, the t test was developed by Gossett in 1908 for detecting variations in small samples at a brewery. (Perhaps the stigma of using mathematics in this application was the reason he wrote under the pseudonym Student, thus giving the statistical procedure its usual name, the Student t test.)

Probability has moved beyond analyzing games of chance to become an important mathematical tool in many areas where chance plays a role. In this section, Knill and Fawcett estimate the size of wildlife populations using probability. Halpern considers how probability has been used to help resolve legal disputes. Austin shows some applications of probability in genetics in "The Mathematics of Genetics." Usiskin uses probability to study voting paradoxes. Austin, in another article, uses probability to study overbooking procedures on airlines. Mathers uses modeling to study time in a queue or waiting line. Rector investigates game theory, a theory widely used in economics or other fields requiring decisions in the presence of uncertainty.

Statistics is a tool for describing and drawing conclusions from data. The computer has stimulated the development of new exploratory statistical procedures appropriate for the classroom and for use outside the classroom. Olson uses stem-and-leaf and box-and-whisker plots to explore patterns in baseball data. Bernklau also considers scores in sporting events and probability models to test hypotheses about these scores. Oakley and Baker use statistical procedures to make predictions about sports records. Barrett, Doyle, and Teague use data-analysis procedures to model cooling rates of warm objects.

REFERENCES

Adams, William J. *The Life and Times of the Central Limit Theorem*. New York: Kaedmon, 1974.

Eves, Howard. *Great Moments in Mathematics after 1650*. Washington, D.C.: Mathematical Association of America, 1983.

Kolmogorov, Andrei Nikolaevich. *Foundations of the Theory of Probability*. Translated by Nathan Morrison. New York: Chelsea Publishing Co., 1950.

Ore, Oystein. *Cardano, the Gambling Scholar*. New York: Dover Publications, 1965.

Stigler, Stephen M. *The History of Statistics*. Cambridge, Mass.: Harvard University Press, 1986.

applications

ESTIMATING THE SIZE OF WILDLIFE POPULATIONS

By GEORGE KNILL
Ministry of Education
Willowdale, ON M2J 1W4

and GEORGE FAWCETT
Board of Education for the
City of Hamilton
Hamilton, ON L8N 3L1

Estimating is a method that can be used where it is impractical to count the actual number. For example, to determine the number of fish in a pond, one could drain the pond and count all the fish; however, the end result—dead fish—would not justify the means. The following is a better alternative.

Catch, tag, and release a number of fish, say x. Thus, there are n fish in the lake, x of which are tagged. Subsequently catch another quantity of fish, say q. If out of this q fish, y of them are tagged, then the assumption is that

$$\frac{y}{q} = \frac{x}{n},$$

enabling us to solve for n.

We can increase the likelihood of our ratios being equivalent if we can make subsequent catches at various locations and use the arithmetic mean of the y's, $\bar{y}$.

So,

$$\frac{\bar{y}}{q} = \frac{x}{n}.$$

This method is called the capture-recapture method.

Example

Give each student or pair of students an envelope containing an unspecified number of plastic chips, $n < 100$. Instruct the students to do the following:

1. Select 10 chips, mark them, and return them to the envelope.

2. Shake the envelope; select a number of chips, say 15; record the number of marked ones; and return all of them to the envelope.

3. Shake the envelope and repeat (a total of 10 times), completing the table.

Number of chips in envelope: n
Number of chips marked: 10

Trial	Number Marked y	Number Selected q
1	4	15
2	1	15
3	7	15
4	3	15
5	5	15
6	4	15
7	4	15
8	6	15
9	2	15
10	3	15
	39	

If $\bar{y} = 39/10 = 3.9$, then

$$\frac{3.9}{15} = \frac{10}{n}$$

and $n = 38.46$. Thus, there were approximately 38 chips in the envelope. The actual number can then be determined by counting.

Teaching Probability— Some Legal Applications

By NOEMI HALPERN, Brooklyn College, Brooklyn, NY 11210

Introducing real-world applications to mathematics classes is one of the best educational ways of motivating students. Probability is an area of mathematics with many interesting applications, and the law is one field to which probability can usefully be applied. In this article some concepts of probability are defined, some categories of legal cases that invite the application of probability are described, and a sample of specific court cases is given.

Many physical phenomena exhibit an element of unpredictability. Even under apparently identical conditions, many observed quantities vary in an uncertain way. For example, the annual amount of snowfall in New Hampshire and the number of heads obtained in three tosses of a single coin vary unpredictably. Probability is the branch of mathematics concerned with making rational statements about phenomena that possess an element of uncertainty.

The term *probability* is used in three ways. *A priori* probability relates to the mathematical calculus of chance, which is exemplified by imaginary games of chance. For example, the probability of obtaining exactly two heads in three tosses of a fair coin is 3/8, since of the eight possible outcomes, precisely three are that of two heads. A priori probability is seldom used in court cases. The second use of the term is statistical and is based on observations of a large sample. Statistical probability is becoming more prevalent in both civil and criminal court cases. This paper will concentrate on this second use of the term *probability*. The third use of the term is simply a statement of credibility, not a precise declaration of frequencies or favorable outcomes. It merely expresses the degree of credence that a rational person will give to something on the basis of available data.

This third kind of probability has hitherto often been used in law. Fact-finding in both civil and criminal cases is for the most part based on reasonable opinions and statements that are nonmathematical and undefinable in scientific terms.

One of the earliest reported instances of the use of mathematical probability in the legal profession is the infamous trial of Alfred Dreyfus in 1899 (Hedrick 1928, 40–41; *Le Petit Temps* 1899). The prosecution attempted to establish that Dreyfus wrote a certain document by citing similarities between the handwriting and the style of the document and those of some letters written by Dreyfus. They claimed that, on the basis of these similarities, the probability was very high that he was the author. Another phase of the prosecution centered on Dreyfus's correspondence. The prosecution maintained that specific correspondence written by him contained coded messages because the letters of the alphabet in it did not occur in the same proportions as in average French prose. The mathematician Henri Poincaré was among the defenders of Dreyfus. He tried, to no avail, to convince the court that it would be highly unlikely for these "average proportions" of letters to occur in any single piece of correspondence or prose. Although most of the people involved in the case did not understand the mathematics presented by the prosecutor, they were swayed by it, and Dreyfus was convicted of treason and deported to Devil's Island.

Many students of elementary probability have difficulty understanding the point that Poincaré was trying to convey. The fact that the most probable event does not necessarily occur very often seems puzzling. If a fair coin is tossed a hundred times, then an even split between heads and tails is the most likely outcome. Yet the probability of this split happening is equal to

$$\binom{100}{50}\left(\frac{1}{2}\right)^{100},$$

which is less than 8 percent. Even a famous mathematician like Poincaré was unable to clarify this point sufficiently and could not convince the court of the fallacies of the prosecutor's "mathematical" arguments.

Probability has been applied to many cases of questionable signatures. One such case concerned the will of W. M. Rice, who left a multimillion-dollar estate (Cullison 1969). An attorney came forward and produced a will bearing Rice's signature on each of its four pages. All four signatures were nearly identical. Rice's relatives questioned the validity of the will on the basis that it was highly improbable for an old man to write his name identically four times in succession. They produced genuine signatures of Rice written at approximately the same time that displayed a great deal of variation. The court ruled that it was improbable that the four signatures were Rice's and that the will must therefore be a forgery. Incidentally, the Rice estate was used to found Rice University.

Students can be helped to understand the court's verdict in the Rice case through the following illustration. Ask them to sign their names on a piece of graph paper ten times in succession. Graph paper with small boxes is preferable. Tell the students that each signature is to be contained in a rectangle of a certain size, say, 5 squares by 25 squares so that a quantitative measure of similarities of two signatures can be established. For example, to compare two signatures, one can count the number of grids in which a marking appears for one signature but not the other. Then the level of similarity of the signatures can be compared in terms of the number of such grids. Two signatures can be considered "identical" if they differ by fewer than some predetermined number of grids. Students can then compute the probability that at least two of the ten consecutive signatures are "identical."

New techniques in spectrography have increased the capability to identify paint pigments and other materials. Probability is often used to help make identifications on the basis of similarities in paint fibers and hairs. For example, in an Australian case, the prosecution advanced evidence that certain paint specks were found on the clothing of both an accused murderer and the victim (Eggleston 1978). The court permitted experts' quantitative statements that the probability of the two specks having a common origin was very high and, on the basis of this evidence, ruled that the two parties must have come into contact.

A small quantity of blood can be used to determine, with high probability, a person's age, sex, and medical history. Blood typing is often used to narrow down possible suspects in murder or assault cases where the assailant's blood has been found on the victim. Blood typing is also employed in paternity cases. When neither paternity nor nonpaternity can be proven, the likelihood of paternity can be determined by probability. Given the probability of the occurrence of the different blood types in the general population and the blood types of the mother and child, the probability of the father having a certain blood type can be established. Students who have learned about blood types in biology classes would find the interrelation of biology, mathematics, and law especially interesting.

Probability theory is widely employed in the evaluation of circumstantial evidence. Generally, when a set of traits is known to be associated with both the perpetrator and the suspect, the probability of an individual possessing the common set of traits is determined. If the probability is one in a million in the general population, then it is concluded that the suspect has but one chance in a million of being innocent. This logic was employed in one of the best-known court cases in which mathematical probability was calculated (*People* v. *Collins; Time* 1968). After a robbery, witnesses testified that the crime was committed by an interracial couple who fled in a yellow car. It was reported that the woman had a

blonde ponytail and that the man was black and had a beard. The Collinses, an interracial couple, were tried for the crime. The prosecutor had a mathematics instructor testify that the probability that the Collinses committed the crime was very high because they fit the description of the perpetrators. The "expert" stated the probability of the occurrence of each of the known characteristics in the general population. He claimed that the probability of a girl having blond hair is 1/3, the probability of a man with a mustache is 1/4, the probability of a black man with a beard is 1/10, the probability of an interracial couple seen together in a car is 1/1000, and so on. He then proceeded to multiply these probabilities to assert that the probability of a couple chosen at random having these characteristics is 1 in 12 million. The prosecutor concluded that there was but 1 chance in 12 million that the defendants were innocent. The Collinses were convicted by the jury, but the decision was reversed on four grounds by the California Supreme Court.

The Collins case is a very good example of the uses and misuses of probability in court cases. It can blend well into a discussion of independent events and Bayes's theorem. First, the California Supreme Court questioned the probabilities of the occurrence of different events, which were stated without any supporting evidence. For example, the claim that the probability of a man having a mustache is 1/4 was not based on concrete evidence. Second, the court pointed out the error made in multiplying the probabilities of each event to compute the probability of the set of events occurring jointly. This procedure is mathematically correct only if the different events are independent. But the events presented to the jury were not independent. Clearly, events such as "a man with a mustache" and "a black man with a beard" are not independent of each other. Therefore, the probability of both events occurring simultaneously is not equal to the product of the probabilities of the two occurring separately. Third, the court claimed that the description of the couple rested merely on the testimony of several witnesses and therefore could not be considered as necessarily correct. Fourth, the court pointed out that if a couple selected at random had only 1 chance in 12 million of bearing the incriminating characteristics, then approximately a 40-percent chance existed that at least one other couple in the Los Angeles area had those traits. The judge indicated a "proof" that was essentially the same as that given for the well-known problem of calculating the probability that in a group of *n* people, at least two will have the same birthday. The court also indicated that because of the jury's lack of mathematical knowledge, they could not be expected to use it correctly.

Although the Collins case points out the

possible problems in invoking mathematical probability in court cases, it also suggests possible correct uses. Naturally, the assumption of independence was wrong, and the probabilities of each of the events should have been supported by empirical evidence. But had the probability been correctly computed (using Bayes's theorem) and its limitations explained to the jury, then it could have been allowed. Even if mathematical evidence is not taken as absolute fact, a quantitative measure can help a jury or a court make a decision.

Mathematical probability is increasingly being introduced in court cases. When used correctly, it is an effective tool in legal decision making. Most students in probability classes will find a discussion of its possible uses and misuses in the legal profession interesting and stimulating. By gaining an idea of the possible applications of probability in nonmathematical contexts, students with little interest in mathematics per se may view the subject with greater interest than they would otherwise. They may also be encouraged to apply mathematics to other nonmathematical situations and disciplines.

BIBLIOGRAPHY

Boyd, W. C. "Tables and Nomogram for Calculating Chances of Excluding Paternity." *American Journal of Human Genetics* 6 (1954):426–33.

Cohen, Laurence Jonathan. *The Probable and the Provable.* Oxford: Clarendon Press, 1977.

Cullison, Alan D. "Identification by Probabilities and Trial by Arithmetic (A Lesson for Beginners in How to Be Wrong with Greater Precision)." *Houston Law Review* 6 (1969):471.

Eggleston, Sir Richard. *Evidence, Proof and Probability.* London: Wiedenfeld and Nicolson, 1978.

Finkelstein, Michael O., and William B. Fairley. "A Bayesian Approach to Identification Evidence." *Harvard Law Review* 83 (January 1971):489–517.

Hedrick, E. R. "The Reality of Mathematics Processes." In *Selected Topics in the Teaching of Mathematics,* Third Yearbook of the National Council of Teachers of Mathematics, pp. 35–41. New York: Bureau of Publications, Teachers College, Columbia University, 1928.

Hooker, S. B., and W. C. Boyd. "Blood-Grouping as a Test of Nonpaternity." *Journal of Criminal Law and Criminology* 25 (1934):187–204.

Jackson, J. D. "Probability and Mathematics in Court Fact-Finding." *Northern Ireland Legal Quarterly* 31 (Autumn 1980):239–54.

Le Petit Temps. Paris: 22 April 1899.

Mode, Elmer B. "Probability and Criminalistics." *American Statistical Association Journal* 58 (September 1963):628–39.

People v. *Collins.* 68 Cal 2d 319, 320, 438. 66 Cal Rptr. 497, (1968).

Shafer, Glenn. *A Mathematical Theory of Evidence.* Princeton, N. J.: Princeton University Press, 1976.

Time, 26 April 1968.

Tribe, Laurence H. "Trial by Mathematics: Precision and Ritual in the Legal Process." *Harvard Law Review* 84 (April 1971):1329–55.

THE MATHEMATICS OF GENETICS

Mendel's classic theory is extended to study "stable" populations and the extinction probabilities of such genetic diseases as cystic fibrosis.

By JOE DAN AUSTIN

Emory University
Atlanta, GA 30322

A PARTICULARLY rich source of applications of high school mathematics is the area of genetics. Many challenging and interesting problems in genetics require only finite probability theory and elementary algebra for their solution. A few such problems are considered in this article.

History of Genetics

The principles of modern genetics were first discovered by the Austrian monk Gregor Mendel. In 1866 Mendel published a paper detailing his nine years of work with the cross-pollination of peas. This paper—the first of his two papers in genetics—remained unnoticed until the year 1900, when Mendel's work was independently reproduced by three biologists, Hugo de Vries in Holland, Carl Correns in Germany, and Erich Tschermak in Austria. The experiment that each of these men completed can be described basically as follows. Initially two types of peas—one with all yellow seeds in the pods and one with all green seeds in the pods—were selected. The seeds from these peas were planted, and the researchers carefully cross-pollinated the resulting plants by hand so that each plant was cross-pollinated with a plant of the opposite-colored seed. The seeds that resulted were *all* yellow in all the pods! Next, these yellow seeds were planted and allowed to cross-pollinate each other in the usual manner. Finally, the second harvest of seeds from these plants was collected and carefully counted according to seed color. Table 1 gives the resulting data obtained by three of the experimenters (Sturtevant 1965, p. 15).

TABLE 1
Cross-Pollination Data for Pea Seeds

Source	Yellow		Green	
	No.	%	No.	%
Mendel, 1866	6022	75.06	2001	24.94
Correns, 1900	1394	75.47	453	24.53
Tschermak, 1900	3580	75.05	1190	24.95
TOTALS	10996	75.11	3644	24.89

Observe that each researcher obtained the same percentages—75 percent yellow seeds and 25 percent green seeds—with such regularity that there must be some way to explain or predict such occurrences; that is, a model must exist! Mendel did propose such a model that does predict these results, and this model is basically mathematical. Subsequent experiments by other geneticists have confirmed the validity of Mendel's model for many other characteristics in both plants and animals.

The author would like to express his appreciation to Professor Charles Ray, Jr., of the biology department of Emory University, for his suggestions and comments in the preparation of this article. The author would also like to express his appreciation to Professor H. Carl Haywood, Professor of Psychology and Special Education, George Peabody College for Teachers, for his very useful comments in his review of an initial version of this article.

Mendel's Model for Genetics

Mendel postulated that the color of the pea seed is determined by something called a *gene*. A gene exists in one or more functional states, and in this case, exactly two states. One state—designated *A*—leads to yellow; the other state—designated *a*—leads to green. In each pea the genes occur in pairs—called genotypes—of which there are four possible types, *AA, aa, aA,* and *Aa.* If the genotype is *AA,* the pea is yellow. If the genotype is *aa,* the pea is green. However, if the genotype is *aA* or *Aa,* the pea is yellow. We therefore call the gene *A* dominant and the gene *a* recessive. We shall not distinguish between *aA* and *Aa*—as we cannot—and shall simply write *Aa* to refer to both these genotypes.

The genotype of each parent is also made up of two genes. In reproduction, each parent contributes one and only one gene to the offspring. Thus the pair of genes of the offspring is made up of one gene from each parent. Mendel assumed that the specific gene a parent contributed was determined by randomly selecting one of the two genes of that parent. Specifically, if a parent had genotype *aa,* then the gene transmitted to the offspring would be *a;* and if the parent genotype was *AA,* then the gene transmitted would be *A.* However, if the parent had genotype *Aa,* the parent would transmit gene *A* with probability 1/2 or gene *a* with probability 1/2.

A second assumption Mendel made was that the selection of the gene transmitted by one parent was independent of which gene was transmitted by the other parent. This permits us to compute the probability of the various genotypes for the offspring if we know the genotypes of the parents. For example, if the two parents' genotypes were *aa* and *Aa,* the probability that the offspring had genotype *aa* would be 1/2, since the first parent contributed type *a* with probability 1 and the second parent contributed type *a* with the probability 1/2; hence 1 × 1/2. Similarly, the offspring would have genotype *Aa* with the probability 1 × 1/2. If both parents had genotype *Aa,* then the probability that the offspring had genotype *AA* would be 1/4, or 1/2 × 1/2. Similarly, the probability the offspring had genotype *aa* would be 1/4. Finally, the probability that the offspring had genotype *Aa* would be 1/2, since the first parent could contribute gene type *a* and the second, type *A* (this has probability 1/2 × 1/2); or the first parent could contribute type *A* and the second, type *a* (this has probability 1/2 × 1/2).

Observe then that in Mendel's experiment we can now predict that exactly 3/4 of the peas in the second generation will be yellow. We do this as follows: The first cross-breeding was between seeds that were all yellow in the pods with seeds that were all green in their pods. The hand cross-pollination assured that one parent was *AA* (pure yellow) and one was *aa* (pure green) genotype. All offspring must be genotype *Aa,* which appears yellow. Thus the first generation is all yellow. For the next generation, both parents are of genotype *Aa,* and the probabilities for the offspring are as previously stated: *aa* with probability 1/4; *Aa* with probability 1/2; and *AA* with probability 1/4. Finally, since *Aa* appears yellow (*A* dominates), the *Aa* and *AA* will appear yellow and only *aa* will appear green. Therefore 3/4, or 1/2 + 1/4, of the offspring appear yellow and 1/4 of the offspring appear green. This is just what Mendel observed in his experiment, as did the other biologists (see table 1) who did the same experiment!

Peas also have the ability to self-pollinate. In this case, the two genes for the offspring are obtained by selecting one of the parent genes at random. Then from another gene pair of the same parent—and thus of the same genotype—a second gene is selected independently and transmitted as the second gene for the offspring. Therefore, if the sole parent has gene type *Aa,* the offspring genotypes occur with the same probabilities as when two parents—each with genotype *Aa*—are involved.

Many human characteristics appear to follow this simple Mendelian model. For example, it is generally true that clear blue eyes are recessive to dark brown eyes, curly hair is dominant to straight hair, red hair is recessive to nonred hair, and blond hair is recessive to dark hair. Recent research has suggested that even eye and hair color may be polygenic and thus not serve as the best example of the Mendelian model for all people.

Certain diseases also follow this model. The "sick" gene is recessive to the "healthy" gene in sickle-cell anemia, Tay-Sachs disease, and cystic fibrosis. However, not every trait is so simple. For example, blood has three possible gene types, A, B, and O, and O being recessive. The possible distinguishable genotypes are then AA, AB, AO, BB, BO, and OO. Since O is recessive, the only possible blood types are usually written A, AB, B, and O. The positive and negative characteristics of blood (Rh factor) are from a different gene. Also, myopia versus normal vision does not follow this simple pattern. However, Mendel's model is a major contribution that explains how many physical characteristics are passed on from parents to offspring.

Population Stability

Using the basic genetic model, we shall consider the question of when the percentages of genotypes in the parent population correspond exactly to the percentages in the offspring population. When this occurs, the population is called *stable*. First we need the concept of *random mating*. This will mean that for the genetic characteristic being considered, the selection of the mating partner (plant or animal) is independent. Assume that for the parent population, p_0 is the fraction of aa genotypes, p_1 the fraction of Aa genotypes, and p_2 the fraction of AA genotypes. Each p_i is nonnegative, and $p_0 + p_1 + p_2 = 1$. We assume that each sex has the same distribution. The probability that we select a male parent of genotype aa is p_0. Under random mating, the probability that both members of the mating pair are aa is $p_0 \cdot p_0$. The probability that the mating pair is aa and Aa is $2(p_0 \cdot p_1)$, since the male could be aa or Aa as long as

the female is the other genotype. Similarly, the probability that the mating pair is aa and AA is $2(p_0 \cdot p_2)$. The probabilities for all possible mating pairs are given in the second column of table 2. Table 2 also gives the probabilities for each of the possible offspring genotypes for the possible mating pairs. In the first row, the mating pair is aa and aa, so that the offspring is also aa. Thus Aa and AA have 0 probability, with both members of the mating pair type aa. Similarly, if the mating pair is aa and Aa, then the offspring are 1/2 aa and 1/2 Aa.

TABLE 2
Mating Pair Probabilities and Offspring Probabilities

Mating Pair	Probability	Offspring Genotype		
		aa	Aa	AA
aa/aa	$p_0 \cdot p_0$	1	0	0
aa/Aa	$2(p_0 \cdot p_1)$	1/2	1/2	0
aa/AA	$2(p_0 \cdot p_2)$	0	1	0
Aa/Aa	$p_1 \cdot p_1$	1/4	1/2	1/4
Aa/AA	$2(p_1 \cdot p_2)$	0	1/2	1/2
AA/AA	$p_2 \cdot p_2$	0	0	1

Hardy-Weinberg Laws

To find the probabilities for the offspring genotypes, we consider all parent pairs in table 2. For the offspring probabilities we obtain the following:

$$(1) \quad P[aa] = p_0^2 \cdot 1 + 2(p_0 p_1)\tfrac{1}{2} + p_1^2 \cdot \tfrac{1}{4}$$
$$= \left(p_0 + \frac{p_1}{2}\right)^2 = \left(\frac{2p_0 + p_1}{2}\right)^2$$

$$(2) \quad P[Aa] = 2(p_0 p_1) \cdot \tfrac{1}{2} + 2(p_0 p_2) \cdot 1$$
$$+ p_1^2 \cdot \tfrac{1}{2} + 2(p_1 p_2) \cdot \tfrac{1}{2}$$

$$(3) \quad P[AA] = p_1^2 \cdot \tfrac{1}{4} + 2(p_1 p_2) \cdot \tfrac{1}{2} + p_2^2 \cdot 1$$
$$= \left(\frac{p_1}{2} + p_2\right)^2 = \left(\frac{p_1 + 2p_2}{2}\right)^2$$

For the population to be stable, the offspring probabilities must be the same as the parent population; that is, $P[aa] = p_0$, $P[Aa] = p_1$, and $P[AA] = p_2$. With this information and $p_0 + p_1 = 1 - p_2$ and $p_1 + p_2 = 1 - p_0$, the first and third equations yield

$$(4) \qquad p_0 = \frac{(p_0 + 1 - p_2)^2}{4}$$

and

$$(5) \qquad p_2 = \frac{(1 - p_0 + p_2)^2}{4}.$$

The expressions inside the parentheses are nonnegative because $p_0 + p_1 + p_2 = 1$. Taking square roots and adding (4) and (5) gives us the final equation:

$$(6) \qquad \sqrt{p_0} + \sqrt{p_2} = 1$$

Equation (6) is necessary for stability. To show it is sufficient as well, assume (6) holds. Then $\sqrt{p_2} = 1 - \sqrt{p_0}$ and $p_2 = 1 + p_0 - 2\sqrt{p_0}$. We show in (1) that $P[aa] = p_0$. From (1) we write

$$P[aa] = \left(\frac{2p_0 + p_1}{2}\right)^2 = \left(\frac{p_0 + 1 - p_2}{2}\right)^2$$
$$= \left(\frac{p_0 + 1 - 1 - p_0 + 2\sqrt{p_0}}{2}\right)^2$$
$$= (\sqrt{p_0})^2 = p_0.$$

A similar derivation gives $P[AA] = p_2$. Then $P[Aa] = p_1$, since $P[Aa] = 1 - P[aa] - P[AA]$. Therefore we have shown that (6) implies stability and proved the following theorem:

THEOREM 1. *Assume that the genotypes aa, Aa, and AA of the parent population have probabilities p_0, p_1, and p_2, respectively, where each p_i is nonnegative and $p_0 + p_1 + p_2 = 1$. Under random mating the population is stable if and only if equation (6) is satisfied.*

The next theorem is quite surprising, since it predicts how long it takes to achieve stability.

THEOREM 2. *Under the assumptions of theorem 1 and random mating, the population is stable after at most one set of offspring.*

Proof: If the parent population satisfies (6), then we have stability after no offspring. Consider the equations (1), (2), and

(3) for the offspring. Taking square roots of equations (1) and (3) and adding gives

$$(7) \qquad \sqrt{P[aa]} + \sqrt{P[AA]} = \frac{2p_0 + p_1}{2}$$
$$+ \frac{p_1 + 2p_2}{2} = \frac{2(p_0 + p_1 + p_2)}{2} = 1.$$

Therefore the offspring probabilities satisfy equation (6), and the population is now stable! (Theorems 1 and 2 are called the Hardy-Weinberg laws.)

Genetic Defects

Next we consider what happens if the genotype *aa* cannot survive. For example, a genetic defect can cause a person to be phenylketonuric. This disease if not detected and treated is characterized by mental retardation (Beadle 1948). The degree of retardation is a function of the quantity of phenylalanine in the system which is related to diet. Individuals with phenylketonuria range in intelligence from being profoundly mentally retarded to being average in intelligence. Even if the disorder is not treated with proper diet, the result is not invariably extreme mental retardation.

Tay-Sachs disease is a nervous degeneration disorder, and *aa* dies in the second or third year of life. Cystic fibrosis, another childhood disorder, is characterized as a lethal or sublethal genetic disease because its victims occasionally survive to adulthood.

If *aa* does not survive, the person with genotype *Aa* is commonly called a carrier (heterozygote), although carriers need not always produce a lethal phenotype. This situation corresponds to a parent population of only *Aa* and *AA* genotypes. Therefore $p_0 = 0$ and $p_1 + p_2 = 1$. With $p_0 = 0$, equations (1), (2), and (3) become

$$(8) \qquad P[aa] = \frac{p_1^2}{4},$$

$$(9) \qquad P[Aa] = \frac{p_1(p_1 + 2p_2)}{2},$$

and

$$(10) \qquad P[AA] = \frac{(p_1 + 2p_2)^2}{4}.$$

Since all aa offspring die, the surviving offspring satisfy

$(11) \quad P[\text{surviving offspring is } aa] = 0,$

$(12) \quad P[\text{surviving offspring is } Aa]$

$$= \frac{P[Aa]}{P[Aa] + P[AA]} = \frac{2p_1}{2 + p_1},$$

and

$(13) \quad P[\text{surviving offspring is } AA]$

$$= \frac{P[AA]}{P[Aa] + P[AA]} = \frac{1 + p_2}{2 + p_1} = \frac{2 - p_1}{2 + p_1}.$$

These last three equations must sum to 1. (For those familiar with conditional probability, these are the conditional probabilities that the offspring is of the genotype, given that it survives.) For stability, the foregoing must be the same as the parent population; so

$$P[\text{surviving offspring is } Aa] = p_1 = \frac{2p_1}{p_1 + 2},$$

or

$$p_1^2 + 2p_1 = 2p_1,$$

or

$$p_1^2 = 0.$$

Thus a necessary condition is $p_1 = 0$. This is sufficient, since it means that $p_2 = 1$ and equation (13) gives

$$P[\text{surviving offspring is } AA] = 1.$$

THEOREM 3. *Under the assumptions of theorem 1, with random mating and the assumption that aa offspring die, then stability occurs if and only if $p_1 = 0$ and $p_2 = 1$.*

Theorem 3 is not a special case of theorem 1 with $p_0 = 0$, since theorem 1 does not assume that aa offspring die. For example, if

$$p_0 = 0 \text{ and } p_1 = p_2 = \frac{1}{2}$$

for the parent population, equations (1), (2), and (3) give

$$P[aa] = \left(\frac{1}{4}\right)^2,$$

$$P[Aa] = \frac{3}{8},$$

and

$$P[AA] = \left(\frac{3}{4}\right)^2$$

for the offspring population. The probabilities for the offspring satisfy equation (6), and the population is now stable.

It is also possible to show that a population will approach the stability conditions given in theorem 3, but the rate is very slow. Table 3 shows the probabilities of the genotypes Aa and AA if the first parent population has $p_1 = 0.10$; that is, if 10 percent of the parent population are carriers of the defective gene. Note how slowly $P[Aa]$ goes to zero!

TABLE 3
Extinction Probabilities for Defective Gene

Generations	$P[Aa] = p_1$	$P[AA] = p_2$
0	.1000	.9000
1st	.0952	.9048
2d	.0909	.9091
5th	.0800	.9200
25th	.0444	.9556
50th	.0286	.9714
100th	.0167	.9833
500th	.0039	.9961

Nonrandom Mating

Finally we consider stability problems when the mating is not random. Suppose that parent genotypes will mate only with their own genotypes. Thus the possible pairs of parents are aa/aa, Aa/Aa, and AA/AA. Table 4 is the same as table 2 but considers only these three parent pairs.

TABLE 4
Nonrandom Mating Pair Offspring
Probabilities

Mating Pair	Probability	Offspring Genotype		
		aa	Aa	AA
aa/aa	p_0	1	0	0
Aa/Aa	p_1	1/4	1/2	1/4
AA/AA	p_2	0	0	1

With table 4, then, the offspring probabilities are simply as follows:

$$(14) \qquad P[aa] = p_0 + p_1 \cdot \frac{1}{4}$$

$$(15) \qquad P[Aa] = p_1 \cdot \frac{1}{2}$$

$$(16) \qquad P[AA] = p_2 \cdot 1 + p_1 \cdot \frac{1}{4}$$

For stability, the offspring probabilities must be the same as the parent population. Looking at equation (15), we find that this requires

$$(17) \qquad p_1 = p_1 \cdot \frac{1}{2} \text{ or that } p_1 = 0.$$

$p_1 = 0$ implies $P[aa] = p_0$ and $p[AA] = p_2$. This is necessary and sufficient for stability under this type of nonrandom mating.

THEOREM 4. *Under the assumptions of theorem 1, but with the assumption that parent genotypes mate only with like genotypes, the population is stable if and only if there are no Aa genotypes, that is $p_1 = 0$.*

It is also possible to prove that the population does approach the stability condition of $p_1 = 0$ in theorem 4.

Summary

In this paper we have considered some very practical problems in genetics. The required mathematics has not been beyond that taught in high school. It is important that students see that there are realistic applications of high school mathematics. The book, *Readings from "Scientific American": Facets of Genetics,* is an excellent source for more detailed information about genetics. For more mathematical models in biology and genetics, the books by Maki and Thompson (1973) and Smith (1968) are recommended.

REFERENCES

Beadle, George W. "The Genes of Men and Molds." *Scientific American,* September 1948. Reprinted in *Readings from "Scientific American": Facets of Genetics,* selected by Adrian M. Srb, Ray D. Owen, and Robert S. Edgar. San Francisco: W. H. Freeman & Co., 1969.

Maki, Daniel P., and Maynard Thompson. *Mathematical Models and Applications.* Englewood Cliffs, N. J.: Prentice-Hall, 1973.

McKusick, Victor A. *Mendelian Inheritance in Man.* Baltimore: Johns Hopkins University Press, 1966.

Readings from "Scientific American": Facets of Genetics. Selected by Adrian M. Srb, Ray D. Owen, and Robert S. Edgar. San Francisco: W. H. Freeman & Co., 1969.

Smith, J. Maynard. *Mathematical Ideas in Biology.* London: Cambridge University Press, 1969.

Sturtevant, A. H. *A History of Genetics.* New York: Harper & Row, 1965.

TWO PREFERENCE PARADOXES

Even under quite reasonable schemes for decision making, some sets of preference choices may not obey transitivity. The specific examples of such sets given here give rise to paradoxes because we so strongly believe transitivity should hold.

By ZALMAN USISKIN

University of Chicago
Chicago, Illinois

GIVEN

and

A is preferred to B

B is preferred to C

under some reasonable scheme for decision making, one normally deduces that, under the same scheme and at the same time,

A is preferred to C.

This note is written to convince the reader that such a deduction is, in general, invalid.

The Voting Paradox

Suppose that three candidates, A, B, and C, run for office. To get the most accurate feeling from each voter, it is decided that each voter should list the three candidates in the order of his own preference. Suppose

30% of the voters list in the order:	A	B	C
5% of the voters list in the order:	A	C	B
5% of the voters list in the order:	B	A	C
25% of the voters list in the order:	B	C	A
30% of the voters list in the order:	C	A	B
5% of the voters list in the order:	C	B	A

Then 65% of the voters have listed A before B, and 60% of the voters have listed B before C. So A is preferred to B and B is preferred to C. One would think

that A is preferred to C. Not so! A full 60% of the voters have listed C before A. Hence we have A preferred to B, B preferred to C, and C preferred to A.

Some Comments on the Voting Paradox

Although one might think that the above paradox does not occur in reality, such a situation happens from time to time. For example, in June 1972, three men—Humphrey, McGovern, and Wallace—were leaders in the race for the Democratic presidential nomination. It was said that those who preferred McGovern seemed to prefer Humphrey next and Wallace least (this order being the public image of how "liberal" each candidate was). Those who preferred Humphrey often preferred Wallace second and McGovern last (perhaps Humphrey represented the established order and McGovern represented the strongest break with the status quo). Yet many who liked Wallace best often wanted McGovern second (dissatisfaction with the status quo meant that any candidate might be better than Humphrey, who signified no change to many). If enough people preferred the candidates in one of these three rankings, it is indeed possible that Humphrey was preferred to Wallace, who was preferred to McGovern, who was preferred to Humphrey. No wonder everyone was so confused then!

This example could be repeated with taste preferences of people, TV watching, public opinion polls, and so on. The

A shorter version of this article appeared in the Illinois Council of Teachers of Mathematics *Newsletter* 22:1 (March 1971).

paradox often occurs in yachting competitions where boats are ranked in order of finish but more than one race is always held. The reader is encouraged to find and study a corresponding situation where four objects are being compared, for it is possible to prefer A to B, B to C, C to D, and D to A.

The paradox also can occur for n objects, $n > 4$. The problem has been studied by a number of people independently, including Black (1958), Trybula (1961), Chien (1962), David (1963), and Usiskin (1964).

How Likely Is the Voting Paradox?

Perhaps the reader feels that the first example was "cooked up," in that the preferences of the voters were arbitrarily ascribed. He should then examine the following situation. Suppose that there were 600 voters and they liked the candidates as evenly as possible. That is, the six possible orders of preference had the numbers of voters shown in table 1. Then, as

TABLE 1

Order	Number of Voters
A–B–C	100
A–C–B	100
B–A–C	100
B–C–A	100
C–A–B	100
C–B–A	100

is backed by intuition, 50% (300) of the voters prefer A to B, 50% prefer B to C, and 50% prefer C to A. But if only *three* voters switch, we can obtain the distribution of preferences in Table 2. Now 301 voters prefer A to B, 301 voters prefer B to C, and 301 voters at the same time

TABLE 2

Order	Number of Voters
A–B–C	101
A–C–B	99
B–A–C	99
B–C–A	101
C–A–B	101
C–B–A	99

prefer C to A. This gives the same paradoxical result as before: A is preferred to B, who is preferred to C, who is preferred to A.

Given n candidates and v voters ranking the candidates randomly, a number of people have studied the probability of obtaining this cyclical type of preference order. For 3 candidates and over 10 voters, the probability is greater than .08, gradually increasing to about .088 as the number of voters increases (see Garman and Kamien [1968] or Sevcik [1969]).

The exact probability for n candidates and v voters seems difficult to compute. In 1970, no simple general formula for the probability was known, though DeMeyer and Plott (1970), Niemi and Weisberg (1968), and Garman and Kamien (1968) give formulas that are complicated and difficult to compute. Pomeranz and Weil (1970) used a computer simulation and obtained estimates for situations with 3 to 40 candidates rated by 3 to 37 voters. (A larger number of voters does not greatly affect the probability.) Some of the estimates may surprise you: Given 5 candidates and 25 voters ranking these, the probability is about .24 that there will be a cyclical preference occurrence. For 11 objects to be rated by 25 people, the probability climbs to over .50.

The reader should keep in mind that these are probabilities based on random rankings. People normally do not rank randomly, and thus such cyclical preference situations will not occur as often in reality. But a second type of cyclical preference seems to occur more frequently, a type called here the "best performer" paradox.

The Best-Performer Paradox

The best-performer paradox is related to, but different from, the voting paradox. Instead of asking individuals to rank objects, let us rate the objects by some performance standard. For instance, suppose three runners, X, Y, and Z, are entered in the 100-yard dash. (I am indebted to Colin Blyth for this example.) Their previous times for this distance give some indication (perhaps the best indication) of how well they will do in the race. Table 3 shows the number of races

TABLE 3

Time	Runner X	Runner Y	Runner Z
9.8			1
9.9	2		
10.0		4	
10.1			2
10.2	1		

in which each runner might have run the distance in a certain time. Who is the best runner? Notice that two-thirds of X's times beat the times of Y (the consistent one). One would expect X to beat Y in a race. X is preferred to Y. Y, in turn, beats Z two-thirds of the time. So Y is preferred to Z.

But Z, when he runs 9.8 (one-third of the time), always beats X. When he runs 10.1 (two-thirds of the time), he has a 1 in 3 chance of beating X. The probability that Z beats X is thus

$$\frac{1}{3} + \frac{2}{3} \cdot \frac{1}{3} = \frac{5}{9}.$$

So Z ought to be preferred to X.

Again we have X preferred to Y, who is preferred to Z, who is preferred to X.

Some Comments on the Best-Performer Paradox

In sports, favorites for a game are often chosen on the basis of past performance against a "common opponent." The above example shows possible pitfalls of such a strategy of choice. It is entirely possible for A to have beaten B over half of the time and for B to have beaten C over half of the time, and yet to have C better than A. What appear to be "upsets" may not be upsets at all.

It should be noted that this example could also be applied to the climates of cities. Given distributions of temperatures and preference for the warmer climate, it

is possible that one might prefer city A to city B, city B to city C, and city C to city A.

This seems to violate common sense. One is forced to ask why this and the other possibilities given above behave so much against our intuition. One reason is that it is more common to compare individual events than distributions of events. We assign *one* number (not a distribution of numbers) as an evaluation of an event (or candidate). Since numbers obey the transitive property, ($a > b$ and $b > c$) implies $a > c$, we expect distributions to do likewise. The above has shown that preferences are not necessarily transitive.

The best-performer paradox also holds for more than three candidates (Usiskin 1964).

Classroom Uses

At some time or another, every high school mathematics student ought to encounter the idea that mathematics is a growing discipline, with some old problems constantly being solved and with new problems constantly being offered for solution.

Every high school student also ought to be given examples of the use of mathematics to shed light on a situation that otherwise seems foggy, if not paradoxical.

These are two types of encounters that most of us would like to do in classrooms; they are also two types of encounters that are very seldom done, because (a) the needed examples require too much mathematics, (b) there is not enough time, or (c) only top students could understand the method of solution. And when we do talk about unsolved problems, often (d) the examples are so old (e.g., Goldbach's conjecture) that we implicitly convince the student that there are no new problems, (e) the problem bears little relationship to any nonmathematical situation, or (f) the solution is trivial or obvious, thus leading students to wonder why anyone would want to spend time on it anyway.

The purpose of this article has been to present a piece of mathematics that does not have weaknesses (*a*) to (*f*). The mathematics needed and the problem itself can be easily explained in a class period even to average students; most of the work is rather recent, having been done in the last ten years; there are immediate yet nontrivial applications; conjectures are easy to test, yet the results are not obvious. One can relate the mathematics to transitivity of relations, to good definitions (e.g., what is meant by "preferring" one candidate over another?), and of course to probability.

REFERENCES

Black, Duncan. *The Theory of Committees and Elections*. New York: Cambridge University Press, 1958.

Chien, C. L. "The Maximum and Minimum Probabilities of Cyclic Stochastic Inequalities." *Chinese Mathematics* 2 (1962): 279–87.

David, H. A. *The Method of Paired Comparisons*. London: Griffin & Co., 1963.

DeMeyer, F., and C. Plott. "The Probability of a Cyclical Majority." *Econometrica* 38 (March 1970): 345–54.

Garman, M. B., and M. I. Kamien. "The Paradox of Voting: Probability Calculations." *Behavioral Science* 13 (July 1968): 306–16.

Niemi, R. G., and H. F. Weisberg. "A Mathematical Solution for the Probability of the Paradox of Voting." *Behavioral Science* 13 (July 1968): 317–23.

Pomeranz, J. E., and R. L. Weil. "The Cyclical Majority Problem." *Communications of the ACM* 13 (April 1970): 251–54.

Sevcik, Kenneth E. "Exact Probabilities of a Voter's Paradox through Seven Issues and Seven Judges." *Institute for Computer Research Quarterly Report* [University of Chicago] 22 (August 1969): section III-B.

Trybula, S. "On the Paradox of Three Random Variables." *Zastosowania Matematyki* 5 (1961): 331–32.

Usiskin, Zalman. "Max-min Probabilities in the Voting Paradox." *Annals of Mathematical Statistics* 35 (June 1964): 857–62.

OVERBOOKING AIRLINE FLIGHTS

By JOE DAN AUSTIN
Rice University
Houston, TX 77001

A practical problem for an airline company is how many reservations should be accepted for a particular flight. If everyone who makes a reservation shows up at the airport to buy a ticket, the solution would be easy. The airline should simply take no more reservations than there are seats on the airplane. However, many people with reservations do not show up at the airport, so there are empty seats on the flight that could be filled if more reservations were accepted.

One solution would seem to be for the airline company to accept as many reservations as possible—that is, not impose a limit on the number of reservations accepted. However, there is a penalty if someone with a reservation shows up at the airport but is unable to purchase a ticket because all seats on the airplane are taken. Specifically, the "denied boarding compensation" is that the airline company must fly the person free on a later flight. For occasions when no one volunteers to fly on a later flight, that is, to be bumped, some airline companies are now offering coupons worth more than the cost of the flight as an incentive for travelers to give up their seats when necessary. (The airline company may also have a public relations problem if too many passengers with reservations cannot fly. However, this will not be considered in the model for this problem.) Thus the problem remains, How many reservations should be accepted for the flight? Assuming that the airline's goal is to maximize its income from the flight, a mathematical model is presented that permits this problem to be solved.

A simplified special case will be considered first. Suppose there are only $k = 3$ seats on the airplane and tickets cost $100

for the flight. Suppose that $n = 4$ reservations are accepted. If three people with reservations show up at the airport to buy a ticket, the airline company collects $300 for the flight. However, if all four people with reservations show up, the airline sells three people tickets but must pay one person $100—that is, give the person a free ticket on a future flight because the airplane is full. The income for the flight is thus $200. The "best" number of reservations for the airline company to accept will be interpreted as the number that maximizes the expected income for the flight.

To find the expected income for a flight for a particular number of reservations, we first make the following assumptions:

1. Only people with a reservation show up at the airport to buy a ticket.

2. The probability that each person with a reservation decides to go to the airport to buy a ticket is p, $0 < p < 1$, and the probability that each person with a reservation decides not to go to the airport is $1 - p$.

3. The people with reservations make their decisions independently of each other.

With these assumptions, the probability that exactly j people go to the airport to buy a ticket, $P[j \text{ show up}]$, for $j = 0, 1, \ldots, n$, is determined by the formula

$$(1) \quad P[j \text{ show up}] = \binom{n}{j} p^j (1 - p)^{n-j},$$

where

$$\binom{n}{j} = \frac{n!}{j!(n - j)!}$$

and

$$n! = n(n - 1) \cdot \cdots \cdot 2 \cdot 1.$$

Formula (1) is the binomial probability distribution. Mosteller, Rourke, and

Thomas (1970, chap. 4) derive this distribution and consider some of its applications.

Using (1), we can find the expected income, E[Income], for the flight in the preceding example if p is known. Suppose that past experience indicates that about 60 percent of the people with reservations for this flight do show up at the airport to buy a ticket, that is, $p = 0.6$. If $n = 4$ reservations are accepted for $k = 3$ seats, the expected income to the airline company is as follows:

$$E[\text{Income}] = 0 \cdot P[0 \text{ show up}]$$
$$+ 100 \cdot P[1 \text{ shows up}]$$
$$+ 200 \cdot P[2 \text{ show up}]$$
$$+ 300 \cdot P[3 \text{ show up}]$$
$$+ 200 \cdot P[4 \text{ show up}].$$

Using the binomial distribution (1), we get

$$(2) \qquad E[\text{Income}] = 0 \cdot 0.026$$
$$+ 100 \cdot 0.154 + 200 \cdot 0.346$$
$$+ 300 \cdot 0.346 + 200 \cdot 0.130 = \$214.40.$$

Table 1 gives the expected income to the airline company for $p = 0.6$ and $k = 3$ seats when $n = 1, 2, \cdots, 7$ reservations are accepted. Observe that the expected income increases until $n = 5$ and then begins to decrease. Thus 5 is the best number of reservations for the airline company to accept; that is, 5 is the number that will maximize the expected income.

It is interesting to note that the best number of reservations does *not* depend on the actual ticket price. For example, if tickets cost $d = \$50$ in the previous example, the expected income if $n = 4$ reservations are accepted is as follows:

$$d/100 \cdot 214.40 = \$107.20,$$

since for any constant d and any random variable X, $E[d \cdot X] = d \cdot E[X]$. The expected income does depend on the ticket price, but the best number of reservations to accept is still $n = 5$.

For a more realistic number of seats on the airplane, the same type of computational procedure as in the previous example can be used. In general, to find the expected income to the airline company, let k be the number of seats on the plane, d the cost of a ticket, p the probability a person with a reservation shows up at the airport to buy a ticket, and n the number of reservations accepted. For $n > k$,

$$(3) \; E[\text{Income}] = d \sum_{j=0}^{k} j \binom{n}{j} p^j (1 - p)^{n-j}$$

$$+ d \sum_{j=k+1}^{n} (2k - j) \binom{n}{j} p^j (1 - p)^{n-j}.$$

If $n \leq k$, the last summation is not included and (3) simplifies to d times the expect-

TABLE 1

Computation of Expected Income for \$100 Ticket Price, $k = 3$ Seats on Airplane, and $p = 0.6$ the Probability a Person with a Reservation Shows Up to Pay for the Reserved Ticket

	Number of People Showing Up to Fly								
	0	1	2	3	4	5	6	7	
				Airline's Income					
	\$0	\$100	\$200	\$300	\$200	\$100	\$0	−\$100	
Number of Reservations									Expected Income
$n = 1$	0.400	0.600							\$ 60.00
$n = 2$	0.160	0.480	0.360						\$120.00
$n = 3$	0.064	0.288	0.432	0.216					\$180.00
$n = 4$	0.026	0.154	0.346	0.346	0.130				\$214.40
$n = 5$	0.010	0.077	0.230	0.346	0.259	0.078			\$217.10
$n = 6$	0.004	0.037	0.138	0.276	0.311	0.187	0.047		\$195.00
$n = 7$	0.002	0.017	0.077	0.194	0.290	0.261	0.131	0.028	\$156.60

ed number of people with a reservation who go to the airport to buy a ticket, that is, $d \cdot n \cdot p$. Unfortunately, the computations in (3) become very tedious when the number of seats k or the number of reservations n is large. If your class has access to a computer, this problem provides a realistic programming exercise. If not, then a calculator would be very useful. When both k and n are small, you can consider using dice or spinners to simulate the problem. Collecting data and then computing average income when various numbers of reservations are accepted can give an approximation to the best number of reservations to accept.

The way to simplify the computation would be to find a simple formula for (3) or for the best number of reservations to accept. Unfortunately, neither seems easy to do. One tempting solution that does not work is the following. If n reservations are accepted, the expected number of people who show up at the airport to buy a ticket is np. Equating np to the number of seats k gives $n = k/p$. For the example given, this gives $n = 3/0.6 = 5$, which is the best number of reservations to accept. However, if the airplane has only $k = 1$ seat and $p = 1/3$, the expected income when $n = 1, 2, 3,$ or 4 reservations are accepted is \$33.33, \$44.44, \$40.74, and \$27.16, respectively. The best number of reservations to accept is $n = 2$ and *not* $n = k/p = 3$. Perhaps you can find a simple formula for the solution.

Observe also that there are several other unanswered mathematical questions even for the numerical solution. In the examples, the expected income increases as n increases to some value and then decreases as n gets larger. A proof that this always occurs would be useful as well as necessary to insure that the solution is indeed best. Also, can some bounds for the best number of reservations be found? These bounds would simplify the computations by limiting the number of reservations that need to be considered. A lower bound is k. Is k/p an upper bound for the best number of reservations?

Final Note

In the model, we implicitly assumed that when a reservation is made, the person buys the ticket at the airport shortly before the airplane departs. However, in reality people often pay for the ticket several days or weeks before the flight. This can be included in the model easily. For example, assume that the plane has $k = 10$ seats and the probability of a person with a reservation showing up at the airport to buy a ticket is $p = 0.6$. Also suppose that seven people pay for their tickets several days or weeks before the flight. Assuming no refunds are given, there are three seats yet to be filled or sold for the flight. To maximize the expected income for the flight, we need only maximize the expected income for these three remaining seats. Hence, we can, in effect, now consider the airplane to have only three seats. If we use the previous example, the airline should accept $n = 5$ reservations for these remaining three seats. Thus if the tickets are paid for enough in advance, the optimal number of reservations to accept can be computed using the number of seats for which tickets have not been paid for in advance in the model for the number of seats in the airplane.

REFERENCE

Mosteller, Frederick, Robert E. K. Rourke, and George B. Thomas, Jr. *Probability with Statistical Applications.* 2d ed. Reading, Mass.: Addison-Wesley, 1970.

EXPLORING BASEBALL DATA

By ALTON T. OLSON, University of Alberta, Edmonton, AB T6G 2G5

I have always been intrigued by the wealth of statistical information that baseball generates. Lately I have found that the techniques of exploratory data analysis (EDA) are quite useful in interpreting such information.

I recently analyzed some of the statistics on the total number of hits of each player on each of the four teams contending for the divisional championships in the American League at the conclusion of the 1985 season. I grouped these individual statistics by team to get a "team hit profile." Since my intent was to find meaning in the data rather than to confirm any predetermined conclusions, I decided that EDA techniques would be most appropriate. The results of my exploration might interest baseball fans of a certain kind, but more important, the techniques may also interest mathematics teachers, particularly those who teach statistics.

It should be noted that the number of data points for each team is not large, which raises questions about the viability of some of the EDA techniques. I make no sweeping claims about these results, only that they are concerned with specific teams at a particular time.

Stem-and-Leaf Plots

Group comparisons can be made by displaying the data in a stem-and-leaf plot. That has been done in figure 1 for the four contending teams—Toronto Blue Jays, New York Yankees, Kansas City Royals, and California Angels.

For small data sets, the stem-and-leaf plot is easy to read, and, fortunately, it is easy to construct. The construction of stem-

	Blue Jays	Yankees	Royals	Angels
21		1		
20				
19				
18			4	
17		2 4		
16	3 7 9		8	
15	1 6			
14			0 6	
13	8	7		7
12		0		4 5
11		0	5	4 4 6 6
10	1 8	5		4
9	0 6	1	0	0 6
8			0 3 5	
7		9		
6		9	4	
5				
4	7 9	0 1	7	1
3		1	0 2 4	
2	3	5	5 6 9	4 7 8 9
1	6 7	7	6	1 8
0	1 3 4 4 7 8	0 2 4 8 8	0 3	1 1 2 5

Stem = Tens   Leaf = Units

Fig. 1. Stems and leaves for hits in 1985

and-leaf plots is best explained by a comparison with simple tallies. As an example, three Blue Jays had between 160 and 170 hits during 1985. In a tally this number could be indicated with a range of 160–170 in the margin to the left of the vertical bar with three tally marks to the right of the bar. Suppose, instead of the range 160–170 written to the left of the bar, we inserted the leading digits 16 and to the right of the bar we inserted the units digits instead of the tally marks. This display retains the visual impact of the tally and, in addition, we have retained the original data. A stem-and-leaf plot is constructed by this procedure. In figure 1 we can see that the three Blue Jays with hit totals between 160 and 170 actually had 169, 167, and 163 hits.

For the data in figure 1, the high was 211 and the low was 0. Thus, stems were written in order from 0 to 21 with the leaves added to the right to complete the numbers.

The stem-and-leaf plot permits easy group comparisons in much the same way as histograms. However, unlike histograms, no data are lost. In short, this display can also be used for archival purposes. With this plot it is possible to make a number of informal comparisons among the groups. We note the following:

1. The spread of the data points for each of the teams

2. How some of the data points are clumped (The California Angels have two distinct clumps.)

3. That the shapes of the data distributions can be noted (The Royals had the most symmetric distribution.)

4. That unusual data points can be highlighted (Don Mattingly of the Yankees had an *unusual* season.)

Box-and-Whisker Plots

Box-and-whisker plots are given for the four teams in figure 2. In these plots the middle half of the distribution is defined by the box. The length of the box is called the *midspread*. The median is noted within the box, and the whiskers extend to the endpoints of the distribution. The box-and-whisker plots are used to highlight the middle parts of distributions because that is generally where the most stable and important data can be found. Likewise it seems plausible that the most important part of a *team* would be in the middle. (Teams don't win with one superstar.)

Deciding how far to count in to determine the middle half, the median, and so on, is easy if we use Tukey's (1977) *grows-to* device. Basically, if a quotient is not an integer, then it should "grow to" the next higher integer, and if a quotient is an integer, then it should "grow to" the integer plus a half. For example, with twenty-one data points in a set, we find the median by dividing by 2 and getting 10.5, which then grows to 11, and so obtain the median by "counting in" eleven data points from the top or the bottom. If a data set contains twenty data points then we divide by 2 and get 10, which then grows to 10.5, and find

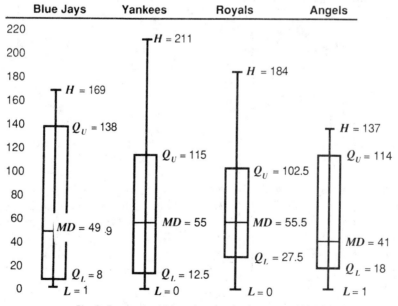

Fig. 2. Box-and-whisker plots for the four teams' hits

the median by computing the average of the tenth and eleventh data points.

We find the middle part of the distribution by "trimming off" the highest quarter and the lowest quarter. Doing so requires that we find the upper quartile (Q_U) and lower quartile (Q_L) values. If n is the number of data points in a set, then these quartile values are determined by finding what $n/4$ grows to; counting down that amount from the top gives the upper quartile, and counting up that amount from the bottom gives the lower quartile.

We can read a number of immediate conclusions from the plots. Initially, we can compare the medians. For example, half of the Angels team had fewer than 41 hits, whereas half of the Yankees had more than 55 hits. To compare the lower echelons of the teams, note that one-quarter of the Jays had fewer than 8 hits, whereas the similar statistic for the Royals is 27.5. By the same token, one-quarter of the Jays had more than 138 hits, whereas the same statistic for the Royals is 102.5. These plots highlight other features of the distributions, such as spread, particularly the spread of the middle parts, and the various asymmetries of the distributions. The use of box-and-whisker plots allows us to be more precise

about some of the characteristics of data sets that can only be hinted at with the stem-and-leaf plots.

A distribution has three distinguishing characteristics—levels, spread, and shape. With the box-and-whisker plot we have been able to make various levels comparisons. Once these comparisons are made, then levels information can be set aside so that other features can be highlighted. The levels feature is set aside by subtracting the group median from each data point in that group.

Box-and-Whisker Plots with Level Removed

Removing the levels allows us to concentrate on the spread features of the teams without being distracted by levels comparisons. Box-and-whisker plots, with each team's median subtracted, are given for the four teams in figure 3. For example, the Blue Jays' median, 49, is subtracted from each Blue Jay's hit total, and then a box-and-whisker plot is constructed. Actually, if we are only interested in the box-and-whisker plot, we can subtract 49 from each of the five summary values in figure 2 and create the plot from those results.

In figure 2 the plots all have about the same lowest value. In figure 3 the plots all

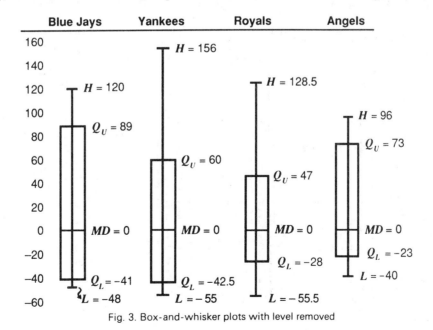

Fig. 3. Box-and-whisker plots with level removed

have the same median. It is then easier to compare the rest of the plots to their respective medians. For instance, the relationships between extreme values and medians are easier to read. In the same way, the positions of the upper quartiles are easily compared with respect to their medians. Note the Angels' and the Blue Jays' upper-quartile positions as compared to the Yankees' and the Royals'. In general it should be better to have the upper-quartile mark high with respect to the median because that would mean that the hit totals are not bunched around the median.

After the levels feature is removed, it is easier to make comparisons based on the spreads. After those comparisons are made, we can set aside the spread features so that we can get a better look at the shape features. We set aside the spreads by dividing each data set by the midspread of that data set. This process results in data sets that have midspreads of one.

Standardized Box-and-Whisker Plots

In practice the data sets are "standardized" by subtracting the median to remove the

levels and then dividing by the midspread to remove the midspread differences. In figure 4 the levels and the midspread have been removed. This is the best view of the shapes of the distributions that we have had. No other features can distract us from the shape features.

The placement of the median within a distribution is an important shape feature. With the standardized plot, we can see more clearly what position the median takes within the midspread for each data set. As an example, the Yankees had the highest placement for the median within the midspread. That feature would have been difficult to see in the previous plots.

The placement of the median within a distribution relative to the extreme values is another important shape feature. Dividing by the midspread of a data set spreads out the distribution if that midspread is relatively small, but doing so makes the distribution more compact if that midspread is large. For example, relative to his team's midspread, George Brett is a bigger standout for the Royals than Don Mattingly is for the Yankees. In a similar vein, the Blue

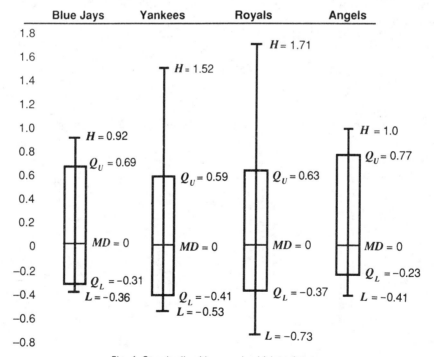

Fig. 4. Standardized box-and-whisker plots

Jays don't have an exceptional standout relative to their midspread.

In essence, we can see the shapes of these four distributions using the same metric for all.

Each of the distributions is asymmetric. They are each skewed toward the lower end of their respective distributions. That much can readily be observed. However, it is not easy to compare degrees of asymmetry only by observing the plots. For that, we will need to compare the transformations that are needed to bring each of the distributions back to near symmetry.

Transforming Plots

When distributions are skewed in a uniform way, it is frequently possible to return them to a symmetric form by the application of a transformation to each of the data points. As an example, the data set {1, 4, 4, 9, 9, 16, 16, 16, 25, 25, 36, 36, 49} is skewed toward the lower numbers; however, it can be made symmetric by using the square root of each of the data points. The resulting data set would be {1, 2, 2, 3, 3, 4, 4, 4, 5, 5, 6, 6, 7}. It is plainly symmetric. The square-root transformation is only one of a number of transformations that can be used in modifying data sets. Of most importance, the shapes of data sets can indirectly be compared by comparing the transformations that are needed to make them symmetric.

As an example of a data-set transformation, the Blue Jays' distribution is brought into near symmetry by using the power transformation with an exponent of 0.44. This transformation is applied to the original data to avoid the problems inherent in transforming negative and zero data points. Summarizing information of the transformed data is given in figure 5. After the transformation, the median is 5.54. To get a sense of symmetry, the median favorably compares to the midpoint of the box, which is 5.61, and to 5.57, which is the midpoint of the interval that is determined by counting 3.5 places in from each end. (Counting in 3.5 places roughly determines one-eighth of the distribution.)

In a similar way the exponents needed

Depth	Low	High	Mid
Blue Jays (0.44)			
11	5.54		5.54
6	2.49	8.74	5.61
3.5	1.84	9.31	5.57
2	1.62	9.50	5.56
1	1.00	9.55	5.27
Yankees (0.48)			
10.5	6.79		6.79
5.5	3.30	9.75	6.53
3	1.95	11.83	6.89
2	1.39	11.89	6.65
1	0.00	13.05	6.53
Royals (0.49)			
10.5	7.14		7.14
5.5	5.07	9.65	7.36
3	3.89	11.49	7.69
2	1.71	12.31	7.01
1	0.00	12.87	6.44
Angels (0.4)			
11	4.41		4.41
6	3.17	6.64	4.91
3.50	1.61	6.78	4.19
2	1.00	6.89	3.94
1	1.00	7.15	4.07

Fig. 5. Summarizing information after data transformations

for the power transformations for the other teams are Yankees (0.48), Royals (0.49), and Angels (0.4). (These transformations were found by trial and error.) For all teams, the midscores were kept as close together as possible. In summary, the Royals needed the weakest transformation, whereas the Angels needed the strongest. It would seem that the distributions did not differ greatly in their shapes, but it should be remembered that these numbers are exponents and cannot be interpreted in a linear way. Also, cross-team comparisons of the results cannot be made because the transformations are different for each of the teams.

With appropriate caution, speculative interpretations can be made about the shape of the Angels' distribution. In a word, the Angels' distribution is most heavily skewed away from symmetry. This feature could have been important when individual Angels judged their own performance levels in comparison to those of the rest of the team. After all, such judgments would likely be in relative terms, not in terms of some absolute standards. In such comparisons the shape of a distribution would be quite important.

Concluding Remarks

A number of beginning techniques of exploratory data analysis have been presented here. The techniques are powerful yet easy to apply. They seem quite appropriate as an introduction to statistical reasoning because of their intuitive plausibility.

In essence, these techniques keep the user close to the data. Can statistics be introduced in a better way?

BIBLIOGRAPHY

Erickson, Bonnie H., and Terry A. Nosanchuk. *Understanding Data.* Toronto: McGraw-Hill Ryerson, 1977.

Landwehr, James M., and Ann E. Watkins. "Stem-and-Leaf Plots." *Mathematics Teacher* 78 (October 1985): 528–31.

Tukey, John W. *Exploratory Data Analysis.* Reading, Mass.: Addison-Wesley Publishing Co., 1977.

Velleman, Paul F., and David C. Hoaglin. *Applications, Basics, and Computing of Exploratory Data Analysis.* Boston: Duxbury Press, 1981. ▪

A Look at Frequency Distributions for Sports Scores

By DAVID BERNKLAU, Long Island University, Brooklyn, NY 11201

Frequency distributions are familiar to almost all sports fans. Most common are one-way distributions in which the frequency of occurrence for each of the related categories is given. Table 1 gives an example of such a distribution. Several basic concepts in statistics and probability can be illustrated here. For example, the mean, median, mode, range, standard deviation, and other sample statistics can be calculated, as well as the a posteriori probability that a certain score occurs (table 2).

> One clear advantage of a two-way table is that it concisely summarizes the scores.

The purpose of this article is to look at various concepts arising from a two-way frequency distribution of game scores. Since such examples appear infrequently in

TABLE 1

Distribution of Scores in Last Round
of 1985 Masters Tournament

Score	Frequency	Cumulative Frequency
65	1	1
66	0	1
67	1	2
68	2	4
69	2	6
70	9	15
71	6	21
72	10	31
73	8	39
74	5	44
75	3	47
76	4	51
77	4	55
78	2	57
79	3	60

TABLE 2

Location and Dispersion
Statistics and Probability
Distribution for Golf Data

Location Statistics	Dispersion Statistics
Mean ($\bar{x}$): 72.7$\bar{6}$	Range: 14
Median: 72	Standard Deviation (s): 3.10
Mode: 72	

Probability Distribution

Score	Probability	Cumulative Probability
65	$\frac{1}{60}$	$\frac{1}{60}$
66	$\frac{0}{60}$	$\frac{1}{60}$
67	$\frac{1}{60}$	$\frac{2}{60}$
68	$\frac{2}{60}$	$\frac{4}{60}$
69	$\frac{2}{60}$	$\frac{6}{60}$
70	$\frac{9}{60}$	$\frac{15}{60}$
71	$\frac{6}{60}$	$\frac{21}{60}$
72	$\frac{10}{60}$	$\frac{31}{60}$
73	$\frac{8}{60}$	$\frac{39}{60}$
74	$\frac{5}{60}$	$\frac{44}{60}$
75	$\frac{3}{60}$	$\frac{47}{60}$
76	$\frac{4}{60}$	$\frac{51}{60}$
77	$\frac{4}{60}$	$\frac{55}{60}$
78	$\frac{2}{60}$	$\frac{57}{60}$
79	$\frac{3}{60}$	$\frac{60}{60}$

newspapers and periodicals, most sports fans probably are not familiar with them, just as many people are confounded when faced with a standard joint-distribution, or contingency, table.

An Example

Table 3 gives the distribution of the scores of the 840 National Hockey League games played in the 1984–85 season. To find the number of games that ended in a particular score, locate the number at the intersection of the appropriate row and column. For example, 35 out of the 840 games ended in a score of 6–4, as that is the intersection of the four-goal row and the six-goal column.

One clear advantage of a two-way table is that it more concisely summarizes the scores. Since 61 different scores are here, a one-way frequency table would be a list of the 61 scores with their corresponding frequencies.

Are ties half as frequent as scores differing by one goal?

Another advantage of having the scores tabulated in this format is the marginal totals, which give the number of times that a particular "winning" or "losing" score occurred. For example, the "winner" had scored two goals in 38 of the games, whereas the "loser" had scored two goals in 217 of the games. However, since 21 of

these games ended 2–2, "winning" and "losing" are not mutually exclusive in a table like this one, and so it would be incorrect to say that in $38 + 117 = 255$ games the winning or losing team scored two goals. We can drop the quotation marks provided we subtract the number of ties, giving $38 - 21 = 17$ games won with two goals and $217 - 21 = 196$ times that a losing team lost with two goals. Therefore, in a total of $17 + 196 + 21 = 234$ games did *either or both* teams score exactly two goals. The reader should recognize this as the addition rule for two events that are not mutually exclusive: $38 + 217 - 21 = 234$.

Conditional Probability

The non–mutually-exclusive row-and-column totals for a particular number of goals scored can be used to form a table giving the frequencies of winning, tying, and losing for the particular number of goals scored. Table 4 is the table formed from these totals.

The table is useful to illustrate the concept of conditional probability. For example, the a posteriori probability that a team won a game given that it scored only two goals is simply $17/255 \doteq 0.067$. The probability of winning rises to over two-thirds given that the team scored exactly five goals ($171/249 \doteq 0.687$) and is certain given that the team scored at least eight goals.

Using the standard notation, we have

$$P(W \mid G) = \frac{P(W \text{ and } G)}{P(G)},$$

	TABLE 3

Distribution of National Hockey League Scores for the 1984–85 Season															

Loser	Winner														
	0	1	2	3	4	5	6	7	8	9	10	11	12	13	Totals
0	0	3	2	5	12	7	5	5	1	0	0	0	0	0	40
1		5	15	27	27	19	13	9	3	2	0	0	1	0	121
2			21	62	48	39	23	14	4	3	1	1	0	1	217
3				29	64	60	36	18	9	5	1	0	1	0	223
4					33	46	35	18	10	2	2	1	0	0	147
5						11	26	19	4	2	2	2	1	0	67
6							3	10	3	3	0	0	0	0	19
7								1	3	2	0	0	0	0	6
Totals	0	8	38	123	184	182	141	94	37	19	6	4	3	1	840

TABLE 4				
Frequencies of Winning, Tying, and Losing for a Particular Number of Goals Scored				
Goals Scored	Winning	Tying	Losing	Total
0	0	0	40	40
1	3	10	116	129
2	17	42	196	255
3	94	58	194	346
4	151	66	114	331
5	171	22	56	249
6	138	6	16	160
7	93	2	5	100
8	37	0	0	37
9	19	0	0	19
10	6	0	0	6
11	4	0	0	4
12	3	0	0	3
13	1	0	0	1
Totals	737	206	737	1680

where W is the event that the game is won and G indicates the number of goals in the win. For the example in the preceding paragraph, we have

$$P(W \mid 2) = \frac{P(W \text{ and } 2)}{P(2)} = \frac{\frac{17}{1680}}{\frac{255}{1680}} = \frac{17}{255}.$$

Table 5 gives the complete listing of such conditional probabilities; similar tables can be formed for tying and losing.

One related idea concerns a law of "partial total probability." The law of total probability, which is used in conjunction with Bayes's theorem, is unnecessary here, since the probability that a team wins (or loses) is simply $737/1680 \doteq 0.439$, with the

numerator and denominator of the fraction obtained directly from the column totals of table 4.

The law of total probability gives the same result as

$$\frac{40}{1680} \cdot \frac{0}{40} + \frac{129}{1680} \cdot \frac{3}{129} + \frac{255}{1680} \cdot \frac{17}{255}$$

$$+ \frac{346}{1680} \cdot \frac{94}{346} + \cdots + \frac{1}{1680} \cdot \frac{1}{1}$$

$$= \frac{0 + 3 + 17 + 94 + \cdots + 1}{1680}$$

$$= \frac{737}{1680}.$$

Using the standard notation, we have

$$P(W) = P(G = 0) \cdot P(W \mid G = 0)$$

$$+ P(G = 1) \cdot P\left(\frac{W}{G} = 1\right)$$

$$+ P(G = 2) \cdot P\left(\frac{W}{G} = 2\right) + \cdots$$

$$+ P(G = 13) \cdot P\left(\frac{W}{G} = 13\right).$$

Now consider a question such as, "What is the probability of winning given that the team scored no more than four goals?" Using the idea of "partial total probability," we have, noting that the sample space has been reduced to $40 + 129 + 255 + 346 + 331 = 1101$,

TABLE 5	
Probability of Winning for a Given Number of Goals Scored	
Goals Scored	Probability of Winning
0	0
1	0.023
2	0.067
3	0.272
4	0.456
5	0.687
6	0.863
7	0.930
≥ 8	1

$$P(W \mid G \leq 4) = P(G = 0) \cdot P\left(\frac{W}{G} = 0\right)$$

$$+ P(G = 1) \cdot P\left(\frac{W}{G} = 1\right)$$

$$+ P(G = 2) \cdot P\left(\frac{W}{G} = 2\right)$$

$$+ P(G = 3) \cdot P\left(\frac{W}{G} = 3\right)$$

$$+ P(G = 4) \cdot P\left(\frac{W}{G} = 4\right)$$

$$= \frac{40}{1101} \cdot \frac{0}{40} + \frac{129}{1101} \cdot \frac{3}{129} + \frac{255}{1101}$$

$$\cdot \frac{17}{255} + \frac{346}{1101} \cdot \frac{94}{346} + \frac{331}{1101} \cdot \frac{151}{331}$$

$$= \frac{0 + 3 + 17 + 94 + 151}{1101}$$

$$= \frac{265}{1101}$$

$$\doteq 0.241.$$

Just as with the law of total probability, this approach is unnecessary, since the result is simply the ratio of the partial column sums:

$$\frac{0 + 3 + 17 + 94 + 151}{40 + 129 + 255 + 346 + 331} = \frac{265}{1101}$$

Nevertheless, these approaches can help the student make the connection between a statistical principle and numerical operations so that an apparently difficult concept in probability is shown to be equivalent to the simple ratio of one sum to another, a common calculation.

Measures of Central Tendency

Now let us consider the mean, median, and mode. The mean, or average, score can be defined as the average winning score (AWS) to the average losing score (ALS). Table 4 gives

AWS

$$= \frac{0 \times 0 + 3 \times 1 + 17 \times 2 + 94 \times 3 + \cdots + 1 \times 13}{737}$$

$$= \frac{3877}{737} \doteq 5.26$$

and
ALS

$$= \frac{40 \times 0 + 116 \times 1 + 196 \times 2 + 194 \times 3 + \cdots + 5 \times 7}{737}$$

$$= \frac{1957}{737} \doteq 2.66,$$

and so the "average score" can be said to be 5.26 to 2.66, or 5–3. However, this result does not take into account the 103 games that ended in ties. Nevertheless, if these games are counted as wins and losses, we have

$$\text{AWS} = \frac{3877 + 346}{737 + 103} = \frac{4223}{840} \doteq 5.03$$

and

$$\text{ALS} = \frac{1957 + 346}{737 + 103} = \frac{2303}{840} \doteq 2.74,$$

and so the average score again rounds to 5–3. (Notice that the revised AWS decreased while the revised ALS increased. The reason is that the average tying score is $346/103 \doteq 3.36$, and ALS $< 3.36 <$ AWS.)

Returning to the concept of conditioning, we see that the average, or expected (E), winning score for a losing score of three goals is

$$E(WS \mid 3)$$

$$= \frac{29 \times 3 + 64 \times 4 + 60 \times 5 + \cdots + 1 \times 12}{223}$$

$$= \frac{1124}{223} \doteq 5.04,$$

which is just about equal to the AWS.

Table 6 gives the complete listing of average winning scores for given losing scores. Notice the higher AWS in the instance of a shutout than in the situation of the loser scoring one or two goals.

How does the average score of 5–3 compare with the median and modal scores? If we define the median score in a similar manner, namely median winning score to median losing score, then it turns out that the median score is also 5–3, since $840/2 = 420$, and, as seen from the marginal totals in table 3, five goals is the average of the 420th and 421st scores for the winner

TABLE 6

Average Winning Score
for Each Losing Score

Losing Score	Number of Games	AWS
0	40	4.45
1	121	4.25
2	217	4.35
3	223	5.04
4	147	5.63
5	67	6.69
6	19	7.32
7	6	8.17

and three goals is the average of the 420th and 421st scores for the loser. (Table 4, which separates the tying scores, gives the same results for the strict median winning and losing scores, but these, of course, are not always the same.)

Regarding the model score, we are again faced with a concept not well defined. Do we define it as usual, namely as the game score that occurs most frequently, or as the modal winning score to the modal losing score? Either way, as table 3 shows, it is 4-3, and so the two are coincidental here. (Nevertheless, the usual definition should be preferred; see Mosteller [1973a] for an example where the two are not the same.)

The sum of diagonal elements in table 3 gives the frequencies of the differences of scores, which are enumerated in table 7. From this table we see that the mean and

TABLE 7

Frequencies of Differences
of Scores

Difference	Frequency	Cumulative Frequency
0	103	103
1	229	332
2	196	528
3	132	660
4	84	744
5	47	791
6	27	818
7	14	832
8	4	836
9	2	838
10	0	838
11	2	840

median scores of 5–3 (difference = 2) correspond to the mean and median differences (the mean difference, computed from the table, is 2.29), as does the modal score of 4–3 (difference = 1) to the modal difference.

Hypothesis Testing

A question that Mosteller (1973b) proposed pertaining to college football scores was whether ties are half as frequent as differences of one point. His argument was that for a given tie score, a–a, are two corresponding scores, $(a + 1)$–a and a–$(a + 1)$, and so for two teams nearly evenly matched we have three nearly equally likely game scores.

(Although a one-point difference in the score of a football game is not per se comparable to a one-goal difference in the score of a hockey game, they each, of course, represent the closest nontying score, and so the argument is appropriate in hockey, too.)

The question here, "Are ties half as frequent as scores differing by one goal?" can be investigated first by considering the ratio of the number of ties to the number of scores differing by one goal and comparing this ratio to one-half. Table 7 gives this ratio as $103/229 \doteq 0.45$, or about 10 percent under one-half.

Testing the hypothesis that the ratio is equal to one-half against the alternative that it is not is equivalent to testing the hypothesis that the ratio of the number of ties to the number of scores differing by zero or one goal is equal to one-third against the alternative it is not. The statistic $\hat{p}$ is equal to $103/332 \doteq 0.31$ here, which results in a z-score of about -0.89, which is clearly not significant. Thus, the hypothesis that ties are half as frequent as scores differing by one goal is a good one.

As an interesting follow-up consider the fact that of the 229 one-goal differences, 48 of them occurred in overtime; that is, without the overtime period (instituted at the start of the 1983–84 season was a five-minute sudden-death overtime period to be played in regular-season games in the event a game is tied at the end of regulation time) 48 more ties and 48 fewer one-goal differences would have occurred a priori. Thus, the data would now give $\hat{p} = 151/332 \doteq 0.45$ with a corresponding z-score of 4.70, which is highly significant. (It looks as if the institution of the overtime period in hockey not only cut down on the number of ties but also made the close scores conform more to what should be expected based on Mosteller's argument.)

The Chi-Square Goodness-of-Fit Test

Looking back at table 3, we can ask, "How well does the table conform to what is expected for its given marginal totals?" For example, did the modal score of 4–3, which occurred 64 times, occur much too frequently? To help answer this question, we can find the expected frequency for the score of 4–3 and compare it to the observed frequency of 64.

One way to look at this question is to consider the winner's column of four goals as the distribution of losing scores for a winning score of 4. If we do so, then as a winning score of 4 occurred 184 times while the corresponding nonwinning scores of 0, 1, 2, 3, and 4 occurred a total of $40 + 121 + 217 + 223 + 147 = 748$ times, a weight of 184/748 can be applied to this distribution. Therefore, the expected frequency for the score 4–3 is

$$\frac{184}{748} \times 223 \doteq 54.8.$$

Table 8 gives the observed and expected frequencies for the distribution of losing scores for a winning score of 4. Applying

TABLE 8

Observed and Expected Frequencies of Losing Scores for a Winning Score of 4

Losing Score	Observed Frequency	Expected Frequency
0	12	9.8
1	27	29.8
2	48	53.4
3	64	54.8
4	33	36.2

the chi-square test for goodness of fit, we have

$$\chi^2 \doteq \frac{(12 - 9.8)^2}{9.8} + \frac{(27 - 29.8)^2}{29.8} + \frac{(48 - 53.4)^2}{53.4}$$
$$+ \frac{(64 - 54.8)^2}{54.8} + \frac{(33 - 36.2)^2}{36.2}$$
$$\doteq 3.13.$$

Since

$$P(\chi_4^2 < 3.36) \doteq \frac{1}{2},$$

the fit for this particular distribution is good.

Table 9 gives the expected frequencies for losing scores in each of the thirteen winning-score distributions. In general, each jth-column entry, E_{ij}, was obtained from table 3 by

$$E_{ij} = \frac{\sum_{i=0}^{j} a_{ij}}{\sum_{i=0}^{13} \sum_{j=i}^{} a_{ij}} \times \sum_{j=i}^{13} a_{ij}$$

TABLE 9

Expected Frequencies

	0	1	2	3	4	5	6	7	8	9	10	11	12	13
0	0.0	2.0	4.0	8.2	9.8	8.9	6.8	4.5	1.8	0.9	0.3	0.2	0.2	0.0
1		4.0	12.2	24.8	29.8	27.0	20.5	13.5	5.3	2.8	0.9	0.6	0.4	0.1
2			21.8	44.4	53.4	48.5	36.7	24.3	9.6	4.9	1.5	1.0	0.8	0.3
3				45.6	54.8	49.8	37.7	25.0	9.8	5.0	1.6	1.1	0.8	0.3
4					36.2	32.8	24.8	16.4	6.5	3.3	1.0	0.7	0.5	0.2
5						15.0	11.3	7.5	2.9	1.5	0.5	0.3	0.2	0.1
6							3.2	2.1	0.8	0.4	0.2	0.1	0.1	0.0
7								0.7	0.3	0.2	0.0	0.0	0.0	0.0

$$= \frac{\text{winner's frequency}}{\text{sum of losers' frq.}} \times \text{loser's frq.}$$

$$= \frac{\text{column total}}{\text{sum of row totals}} \times \text{row total}$$

$$= \frac{\text{row total} \times \text{column total}}{\text{sum of row totals}},$$

which, of course, is analogous to the usual formula for determining the expected frequency for each cell of a standard contingency table.

Summary

From tables giving the distributions of game scores, a wealth of concepts in probability and statistics can be illustrated. Among those used in this paper were the addition rule for non–mutually exclusive events, conditional probability and expectation, the law of total probability, the common measures of central tendency, hypothesis testing, and the chi-square goodness-of-fit test. A few follow-up suggestions follow.

1. Form tables like tables 3, 4, and 5 for, say, baseball scores. Is the probability of winning certain when eight runs or more are scored? Distinguish between conditional and unconditional probability.

2. Form a table like table 5 for losing. Is it the complement of table 5?

3. Form a table of probabilities of winning up to and including certain numbers of goals, runs, or points. What are the complementary probabilities?

4. Find the mean, median, and modal game scores. How does the model game score compare with the comparison of the modal winning score to the modal losing score?

5. Form a table like table 6. Are the average winning scores strictly increasing?

6. Form a table like table 7 and compare successive differences. Do overtime games significantly change the number of ties?

7. Form distributions for each winning or losing score and compare the observed and expected frequencies.

BIBLIOGRAPHY

Ercolani, Benny, and Jeff Boyle. *NHL Data, 1984–85 Season*. Montreal, Canada: National Hockey League Communications Department, 1985.

Mosteller, Frederick. "Collegiate Football Scores." In *Statistics by Example—Exploring Data*, Set 7. Reading, Mass.: Addison-Wesley Publishing Co., 1973a.

———. "Collegiate Football Scores." In *Statistics by Example—Weighing Chances*, Set 11. Reading, Mass.: Addison-Wesley Publishing Co., 1973b.

Seymour, Dale. "We Can Dream, Can't We?" *Mathematics Teacher* 77 (October 1984):496–98.

"Sports Monday." *New York Times*, 15 April 1985. ✊

LEAST SQUARES AND THE 3:40-MINUTE MILE

Can we predict when, if ever, a 3:40 mile will be run?

By CLETUS O. OAKLEY
Haverford College
Haverford, PA 19041
and JUSTINE C. BAKER
University of Pennsylvania
Philadelphia, PA 19174

ONE of the main objectives in all the sciences is to be able to estimate or predict the values of one variable from those of another variable. Often the data, perhaps coming from observations, appear as sets of ordered pairs (x_i, y_i) where there may be several y's for a given x. The graph of such a set of points is usually called a *scatter diagram*.

In many cases the first approximation to the problem of estimating extrapolated values of y is to fit a straight line to the data, if the scatter diagram seems to warrant it. If the assumption is that, ideally, the data should lead to a straight line but, because of errors of various kinds, the known points of the scatter diagram do not fall on a straight line, then the most probable straight line is that produced by the immortal Gauss's method of least squares. Although the idea is well known, a few remarks might be in order.

Let the equation of the line be $y = a + bx$. From this equation, for a given x we compute the *theoretical* value of y, say y_T. The square of the difference between y_T and y_O, the *observed* value of y, is $(y_T - y_O)^2$; and to get the line of best fit, we must determine the a and b that make $\Sigma(y_T - y_O)^2$ a minimum. Where n is the number of ordered pairs (x, y), the elementary problem in calculus of minimizing this sum leads to the *normal equations* for a and b:

$$\sum y = na + b\sum x$$
$$\sum xy = a\sum x + b\sum x^2$$

The simultaneous solution for a and b gives us our desired line, $y = a + bx$.

The following application of least squares may be of interest to mathematicians and track buffs alike. In the 1930s, mile runners cracked the 4:10 record and were hot on the trail of the much talked-about four-minute mile. Table 1 shows how the world record for the one-mile run has

TABLE 1

EVOLUTION OF THE WORLD RECORD FOR THE ONE-MILE RUN

Time	Runner	Year
4:56	Charles Lawes, Britain	1864
4:36.5	Richard Webster, Britain	1865
4:29	William Chinnery, Britain	1868
4:28.8	W. C. Gibbs, Britain	1868
4:26	Walter Slade, Britain	1874
4:24.5	Walter Slade, Britain	1875
4:23.2	Walter George, Britain	1880
4:21.4	Walter George, Britain	1882
4:19.4	Walter George, Britain	1882
4:18.4	Walter George, Britain	1884
4:18.2	Fred Bacon, Scotland	1894
4:17	Fred Bacon, Scotland	1895
4:15.6	Thomas Conneff, U.S.	1895
4:15.4	John Paul Jones, U.S.	1911
4:14.6	John Paul Jones, U.S.	1913
4:12.6	Norman Taber, U.S.	1915
4:10.4	Paavo Nurmi, Finland	1923
4:09.2	Jules Ladoumegue, France	1931
4:07.6	Jack Lovelock, New Zealand	1933
4:06.8	Glen Cunningham, U.S.	1934
4:06.4	Sydney Wooderson, Britain	1937
4:06.2	Gunder Haegg, Sweden	1942
4:06.2	Arne Andersson, Sweden	1942
4:04.6	Gunder Haegg, Sweden	1942
4:02.6	Arne Andersson, Sweden	1943
4:01.6	Arne Andersson, Sweden	1944
4:01.4	Gunder Haegg, Sweden	1945
3:59.4	Roger Bannister, Britain	1954
3:58	John Landy, Australia	1954
3:57.2	Derek Ibbotson, Britain	1957
3:54.5	Herb Elliott, Australia	1958
3:54.4	Peter Snell, New Zealand	1962
3:54.1	Peter Snell, New Zealand	1964
3:53.6	Michel Jazy, France	1965
3:51.3	Jim Ryun, U.S.	1966
3:51.1	Jim Ryun, U.S.	1967
3:51	Filbert Bayi, Tanzania	1975
3:49.4	John Walker, New Zealand	1975

The *World Almanac and Book of Facts*, 1975 edition. Newspaper Enterprise Association, New York, 1974.

been lowered in the past 111 years. It is reproduced here by permission of the *World Almanac and Book of Facts* (1974, p. 865). We have inserted the figures for 1975.

In 1937, when the record stood at 4:06.4, we thought an attractive exercise for students in an elementary statistics class would be to compute the least-squares line for the world records up to that year and from it estimate when the four-minute mile might occur. In the equation $y = a + bx$, x was the deviation, in years, from 1895—the chosen origin with time 4:17. The time y was reduced to minutes, and the least-squares line had the equation

$$y = 4.339\ 075\ 64 - 0.006\ 449\ 59x.$$

For $y = 4.00$, x turned out to be ap-

proximately 53, corresponding to the year 1948, six years before Roger Bannister ran it in 3:59.4.

Then, in 1954, the year of Bannister's world-acclaimed accomplishment, the question arose as to when a new record run of, say, 3:50 could be expected; and once again our students computed another least-squares line using all the known data from 1864 to 1954. This line suggested that the 3:50 mile might come sometime around 1978—in fact, it came in 1975 with Bayi's record of 3:50 and Walker's subsequent time of 3:49.4.

Now we have a rash of speculations about the year of the 3:40 mile. The least-squares line in figure 1 suggests the year 2001—another kind of space odyssey.

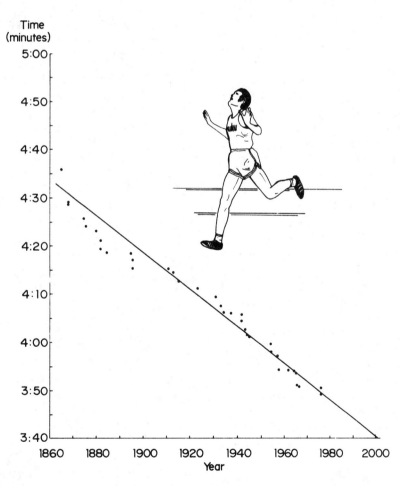

Fig. 1

Several remarks seem desirable. First, our figure shows only one line because the three lines are almost coincident. Second, our prediction of the year 2001 for the 3:40 mile agrees with the opinion of track and field experts, as suggested in an article by James O. Dunaway in the *New York Times* of 17 August 1975. Third, it is safe to say that in the future the records will be leveling off and that some curve other than a straight line would give better predictions. What about the three- or the two-minute mile? There must be an asymptote!

APPLICATIONS

USING DATA ANALYSIS IN PRECALCULUS TO MODEL COOLING

By GLORIA BARRETT, DOT DOYLE, and DAN TEAGUE

The first two recommendations of the National Council of Teachers of Mathematics in *An Agenda for Action* (1980) encourage teachers to make problem solving the focus of school mathematics and to broaden the definition of basic skills in mathematics to encompass more than computational facility. Although many teachers agree with these recommendations and are attempting to implement them, they frequently lack good resources with problem-solving activities. Now, as in 1980 when the *Agenda* was written, most textbooks emphasize computational skills with only a smattering of word problems. Even the application problems generally require students to do no more than translate a carefully stated word problem into an algebraic statement and then perform the algebraic manipulations necessary to obtain a solution. Rarely does a student need to select and use skills in "unexpected, unplanned settings," "formulate key questions," or "seek out appropriate data" as are suggested in the *Agenda*. Consequently, a large percentage of our students are given the impression that there is always a rule to be followed when solving a mathematics problem. In this article we shall modify a fairly traditional precalculus problem to address some of the concerns in the *Agenda*.

Gloria Barrett, Dot Doyle, and Dan Teague teach at the North Carolina School of Science and Mathematics in Durham, NC 27705. Barrett and Teague have worked with the summer institutes sponsored by the Woodrow Wilson Fellowship Foundation. Doyle is the director of the school's outreach program for in-service teachers.

Pose the Problem

The problem that follows is similar to one included in many precalculus textbooks in a chapter on exponential and logarithmic functions.

When a cup of hot tea is left in a room to cool, the temperature of the tea is an exponential function of time. As a matter of fact, the temperature T of the tea is given by

$$T = ae^{bt} + c,$$

where t represents the number of minutes from the first temperature measurement. The difference between the initial temperature and the temperature of the environment is represented by a, whereas b and c can be determined. You are given that the tea is originally 120°F and the temperature of the room is 70°F. Also, at $t = 15$ the temperature of the tea is 98°F. At what time will the tea be 77°F?

What does this problem require of the students? Essentially they only need to substitute the given numbers into a stated model and then solve a simple equation. Although the situation deals with a real-world experience, one questions whether the solution is really problem solving. It is possible to present this problem in a different way so that students are required to use a variety of skills. Consider the following restatement of the problem.

A curious student sees a pitcher of hot tea on a table, with steam rising into the air. Someone is apparently planning to make iced tea, and the student wonders how long it will take to cool to a certain temperature. Suppose the tea were placed in a refrigerator. What will the temperature be an hour from now? Does the liquid cool at the same rate throughout the cooling process?

A major difference between the two statements of the cooling problem is that in the second problem students are asked several questions about a real-world phenomenon, but they are not presented with a mathematical relationship, nor are they provided with any numbers. Instead, they must experiment for themselves and gather the data needed to determine a function that models the relationship among the temperature of the liquid, the temperature of the environment, and the elapsed time. Determining a model and its associated parameters requires that students use data-analysis techniques for fitting a curve to a set of data. A calculator is essential for finding a solution to this problem. The use of a computer is helpful, though not required, since it reduces data manipulation. After the student determines a satisfactory model, it can be used to analyze the observed phenomenon and answer the questions posed in the problem.

Model the Problem

A data set is given in table 1 to illustrate the process involved in solving this problem. To gather these data a liquid with an initial temperature of 124°F was placed in a refrigerator, and the temperature was recorded at the times indicated. It is, however, preferable for students to collect such data for themselves, thus allowing them to observe the cooling phenomenon firsthand.

A good way to begin working toward an understanding of the cooling phenomenon is to look at the graph. The graph in figure 1 displays time on the horizontal axis and temperature on the vertical axis. What function might model these data? Does the graph seem to behave like a quadratic, or an exponential, or a reciprocal-power func-

TABLE 1	
Original Data	
Time (min.)	Temp (°F)
0	124
5	118
10	114
16	109
20	106
35	97
50	89
65	82
85	74
128	64
144	62
178	59
208	55
244	51
299	50
331	49
391	47
Overnight	45

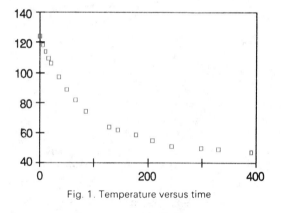

Fig. 1. Temperature versus time

tion? After a little thought, students usually recognize the horizontal asymptote and therefore reject the quadratic model. Typically, students are most familiar with functions that have a horizontal asymptote at the x-axis. They will probably assume, then, that this function has undergone a vertical shift. A model can more easily be determined if we modify our data by subtracting 45 degrees from each temperature. The new ordered pairs are listed in table 2, and the graph is shown in figure 2. We have merely made a vertical shift of the data, so we have not changed the basic shape of the graph.

TABLE 2	
Transformed Data	
Time	Temp — 45°
0	79
5	73
10	69
16	64
20	61
35	52
50	44
65	37
85	29
128	19
144	17
178	14
208	10
244	6
299	5
331	4
391	2

TABLE 3	
Reexpressed Data	
Time	ln (Temp — 45°)
0	4.3694
5	4.2905
10	4.2341
16	4.1589
20	4.1109
35	3.9512
50	3.7842
65	3.6109
85	3.3673
128	2.9444
144	2.8332
178	2.6391
208	2.3026
244	1.7918
299	1.6094
331	1.3863
391	0.6931

Fig. 2. (Temp. — 45°) versus time

Transform the Data

Since it is difficult to write directly an equation to model a reciprocal power or an exponential data set, we need to transform the data so that the reexpressed data are linear. The mathematics of linear functions can then be used to fit a line through the transformed data set. Once this task is accomplished, we "undo" the transformation and change the variables back to their original state.

How should we reexpress these data if they are exponential? We seek a function g such that applying g to the y-values of the data set results in ordered pairs that are linear. A student's knowledge of inverse functions will help him or her realize that if the data set is exponential, taking the logarithm of the y-values will result in linear data, since a logarithm will undo the operation of exponentiation. That is, if

$$y = Ae^{mx},$$

then

$$\ln y = \ln A + mx,$$

which is a linear function with ordered pairs $(x, \ln y)$. The computer or calculator is used to reexpress the y-values from table 2 by computing their natural logarithm; table 3 displays the new data set. The graph of the ordered pairs (x, y_l), called a semilog graph, is shown in figure 3. These points

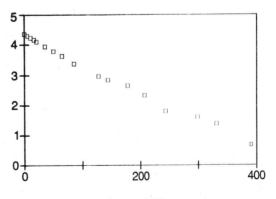

Fig. 3. ln (Temp — 45°) versus time

appear to lie along a line, so students can proceed to fit a line through the transformed data.

Fit a Line

To obtain an equation of a line through the reexpressed data (x, y_l), students can use either the method of least squares or the median-median (resistant) line. The method of least squares is tedious without the use of a computer; *Minitab* (Minitab 1985) and *Advanced Mathematics #744* (MECC 1981) are among the software packages that can be used for least-squares analysis. The calculations required for the median-median line are simple ones that do not require a computer. The process involves dividing the ordered pairs into three equal groups based on increasing x-values and then finding the median x-value and the median y_l-value for each third. These three points are called *summary points*. The line through the two outermost summary points is determined, and then this line is shifted one-third of the distance toward the middle summary point (Landwehr 1987).

In our example, the summary points are $P_1(13, 4.1965)$, $P_2(85, 3.3673)$, and $P_3(271.5, 1.7006)$. They are graphed with the transformed data set in figure 4. The line through P_1 and P_3 is

$$y_l = -0.00966x + 4.322,$$

the dashed line in figure 5. It is then necessary to slide the line one-third of the distance toward P_2. Since the point P_4 (85, 3.5009) lies on the line, the vertical distance from P_2 to P_4 is 0.1336, and we shift the line down $0.1336/3 = 0.045$. The equation of the median-median line is

$$y_l = -0.00966x + 4.277,$$

the solid line in figure 5.

Recall that $y_l = \ln(y - 45)$. In terms of the original variables, the equation is

$$\ln(y - 45) = -0.00966x + 4.277,$$

or

$$y = e^{-0.00966x + 4.277} + 45,$$

or

$$y = 72.02e^{-0.00966x} + 45.$$

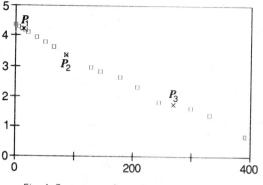

Fig. 4. Summary points with transformed data

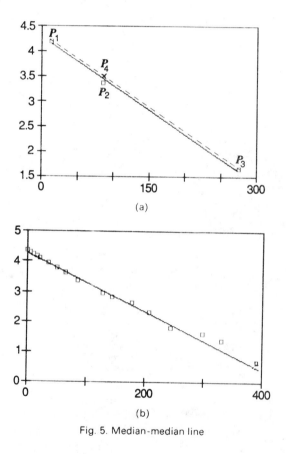

Fig. 5. Median-median line

Examine the Solution

Considering the phenomenon we are attempting to model, this function seems appropriate. It is a decreasing exponential function (the coefficient of x is negative) with initial temperature 117.02°F and eventual temperature 45°F. A graph of the exponential model superimposed on the orig-

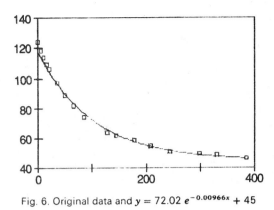

Fig. 6. Original data and $y = 72.02\, e^{-0.00966x} + 45$

inal data set is shown in figure 6; a good fit seems to be evident. The student is now ready to answer a variety of questions, including those posed in the statement of the problem.

Those with access to a computer who want to investigate this problem even further may find it interesting to examine the residuals associated with the model. A residual is the difference between the data value and the model value at a given x-value. (*Data Analysis* [NCSSM 1987] will calculate and graph residuals.) The residual plot shown in figure 7 seems to indicate a cyclical pattern. Students may speculate that these variations reflect compressor cycles of the refrigerator or the periods when the door was held open.

Finally, some students may question whether a reciprocal power function of the form $y = A/x^p$ would provide a better model

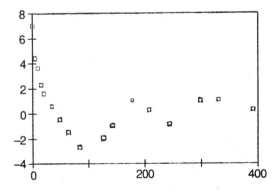

Fig. 7. Residuals for original data and exponential function

for this phenomenon. If a data set can be modeled by such a function, the ordered pairs (ln x, ln y) should be linear. Students can perform this log-log reexpression and plot the resulting ordered pairs to verify that this transformation does not produce a linear data set. The exponential, therefore, is the better model.

Conclusion

The open-ended statement of the cooling problem addresses a number of the recommendations made in *An Agenda for Action* that are not addressed by the more traditional problem. The student is encouraged to perform the experiment and to gather appropriate data. Each student then has a different set of ordered pairs to analyze, yet the modeling process is the same for each. Using the graph, students ask themselves questions, reexpress data, and conclude that an exponential function is an appropriate model. The ability to write the equation of a line and a thorough understanding of inverse functions are essential skills to produce a solution. Finally, the problem calls for extensive work with the calculator or computer and a sustained effort. Because this approach more closely models real-world problem solving, students find both the problem and the solution more interesting.

BIBLIOGRAPHY

Landwehr, James M., and Ann E. Watkins. *Exploring Data*. Palo Alto, Calif.: Dale Seymour Publications, 1987.

Minitab. *Minitab*. State College, Pa.: Minitab, 1985.

Minnesota Educational Computing Consortium (MECC). *Advanced Mathematics #744*. St. Paul, Minn.: MECC, 1981.

National Council of Teachers of Mathematics. *An Agenda for Action: Recommendations for School Mathematics of the 1980s*. Reston, Va.: The Council, 1980.

North Carolina School of Science and Mathematics (NCSSM) Mathematics Department. *Data Analysis, a Data Analysis Program*. Durham, N.C.: NCSSM, 1987. (The material in this article, along with other units, has been published by the NCTM in the booklet entitled *Data Analysis* from the series Contemporary Topics in Mathematics.)

——— *Introduction to College Mathematics*. Durham, N.C.: NCSSM, 1987. (The preparation of this document was supported in part by a grant from the Carnegie Corporation of New York.) ●

THE BARBER QUEUE

Have you ever waited in line for something?
Mathematics can help students analyze this problem.

By JOLLY MATHERS
Students and Professor
Mathematical Modeling for Teachers' Class
Seattle Pacific College
Seattle, WA 98119

EVERYBODY gets involved in waiting lines—lines in cafeterias, supermarkets, banks, toll booths, service stations, the doctor's office, restrooms, and many other places. If you are waiting for a service, you probably don't want to wait very long, and if you are the one providing the service, you probably don't want to make the people being served wait very long because they will become disgruntled and go somewhere else with their business. Since waiting lines are a common occurrence, it is important that people providing services understand more about them, in order to assure their customers satisfaction with service delivery. The purpose of this article is to explore the theory of waiting lines by considering a simple example and by simulating the waiting line with a computer.

The theory of waiting lines is called *queuing theory,* and a waiting line is called a *queue.* The literature on queuing theory is extensive and is growing rapidly. In colleges, queuing theory is generally taught in courses in operations research or mathematical modeling. The elementary aspects of the theory can be understood by secondary school mathematics students, and projects involving the collection and analysis of data involving queuing are easily introduced and enjoyed by students.

In order to study a queue, one needs to know three things about it. First, *the arrival scheme*—how or at what time do persons or objects arrive at the service port(s)? Do they come at random, by appointment, or by some other procedure? Second, *the queue discipline*—what is the procedure for selecting the one to get serviced next from those waiting? Is it first come–first served, a random selection, last come–first served, or otherwise? Third, *the service scheme*—how long does it take to get serviced? The arrival scheme, the queue discipline, and the service scheme completely determine the queue.

In order to illustrate these ideas, let us model the queue at a one-chair barbershop. On this first attempt at studying the queuing problem, let us make the following assumptions about the barber queue:

1. Arrival scheme—n customers come at random between 9:00 A.M. and 5:00 P.M.

2. Queue discipline—first come–first served.

3. Service scheme—one person served at a time, with each haircut taking twenty-five minutes. On completing a haircut, the barber will begin cutting the next customer's hair with no loss of time, provided, of course, there is a waiting customer. Any person arriving at or before 5:00 P.M. gets a haircut, even if the barber has to remain past 5:00 P.M.

With this information we can proceed to simulate a typical day's operation at the barbershop.

The first thing we need to determine is the arrival time of the n customers. This may be done by picking n times at random in the time interval 9:00 A.M. to 5:00 P.M. In order to keep the arithmetic simple, let us pick arrival times to the nearest minute. Picking n arrival times for the customers can then be approximated by picking n numbers, each of which is an integer in the interval [0,480]. Letting A_1 denote the arrival time of the earliest customer, A_2 the arrival time of the second customer, and so on, we will have n numbers $A_1, A_2, \ldots, A_n$ satisfying $A_1 \leq A_2 \leq \cdots \leq A_n$.

After the arrival times have been determined, the next step is to determine the actual starting times for the haircuts. Letting S_i be the time the ith person starts getting a haircut, we have the relationships $S_1 = A_1$ and $S_i = \max (A_i, S_{i-1} + 25)$, $i = 2, 3, \ldots, n$. For example, of the 10th customer arrives at 326 (2:26 P.M.) and the 9th customer's haircut begins at 283 (1:43 P.M.), the 10th customer would begin his haircut at 326 = max(326, 283 + 25), or 2:26 P.M. As a second example, suppose the 13th customer arrives at 445 (4:25 P.M.) and the 12th customer's haircut begins at 430 (4:10 P.M.). The 13th customer's haircut will begin at 455 = max(445, 430 + 25), or 4:35 P.M.

We now have two ordered sets of numbers, one set giving arrival times and the other set giving the times the haircuts begin. In order to determine the waiting time W_i for the ith customer, we need only subtract the arrival time from the time service starts, that is, $W_i = S_i - A_i$. The total waiting time W for all customers is then found by summing the individual waiting times; the formula is $W = \sum_{i=1}^{n} W_i$. The average waiting time A is found by the formula $A = W/n$.

The longest time T any one individual has to wait is given by the formula $T = \max_{i} \{W_i\}$. The longest waiting line L is given by the formula $L = [T/25] + 1$, where $[T/25]$ is the greatest integer in $T/25$.

The BASIC program to simulate the model is seen in figure 1. The program allows one to select the number of customers to be serviced during the day. The output of the program is the average waiting time, the longest waiting time, and the longest waiting line. If one simulates the case of more than twenty-five customers coming during the day, one needs to change line 210 of the program appropriately.

When the program was run twenty times with $n = 15$, thus simulating twenty days' experience at the barbershop, additional information (table 1) was obtained.

TABLE 1
THE 20-DAY RECORD OF A BARBERSHOP SERVING 15 CUSTOMERS A DAY

Average Waiting Time	Longest Individual Waiting Time	Longest Waiting Line
14.5333	42	2
18.2	44	2
19.8	75	4
12.9333	52	3
8.73333	22	1
25.4	64	3
16.3333	50	3
15.8667	50	3
18.8	42	2
39.0667	93	4
21.0667	59	3
28.2667	75	4
7.33333	29	2
28.6667	53	3
8.6	35	2
35.1333	82	4
7.06667	38	2
39.8	95	4
21.4667	55	3
13.4	44	2

To get a better idea of the averages of and variations in the numbers obtained in table 1, a program to determine the means and standard deviations was developed. The listing, along with the output using twenty average waiting time numbers, is given in figure 2.

From this analysis we can expect that the average waiting time will be around twenty minutes and that most (approximately 68%) of the people will be waiting between ten and thirty minutes (within one standard deviation of 20). When the program was run using the longest individual waiting times from table 1, it was found that the average of the numbers was 54.95 and the standard deviation was 20.2185. The average and standard deviation of the lengths of the longest waiting line were 2.8 and 0.894427, respectively. The figures for the longest waiting line would indicate that the barber should provide four chairs for people to use while they are waiting to get into the barber chair.

```
100  ! THIS PROGRAM SIMULATES THE QUEUE AT A ONE-CHAIR
110  ! BARBERSHOP.  DATA INPUT IS NUMBER OF CUSTOMERS
120  ! PER DAY.  OUTPUT IS AVERAGE WAITING TIME, LONGEST
130  ! WAITING TIME AND LONGEST WAITING LINE.
200        RANDOMIZE
210        DIM A(25), S(25), W(25)
220        INPUT "NUMBER OF CUSTOMERS PER DAY";N
300  ! STEPS 310-330 DETERMINE ARRIVAL TIMES
310        FOR I = 1 TO N
320        LET A(I) = INT(480*RND(0)+ .5)
330        NEXT I
340  ! STEPS 350-420 ORDER THE ARRIVAL TIMES
350        FOR I = 1 TO N
360        FOR J = 1 TO N
370        IF A(I) >= A(J) THEN GOTO 410
380        LET Q = A(J)
390        LET A(J) = A(I)
400        LET A(I) = Q
410        NEXT J
420        NEXT I
500  ! STEPS 510-570 DETERMINE START OF SERVICE TIMES
510        LET S(1) = A(1)
520        FOR I = 2 TO N
530        IF S(I - 1) + 25 >= A(I) GOTO 560
540        LET S(I) = A(I)
550        GOTO 570
560        LET S(I) = S(I - 1) + 25
570        NEXT I
600  ! STEPS 610-630 DETERMINE WAITING TIMES
610        FOR I = 1 TO N
620        LET W(I) = S(I) - A(I)
630        NEXT I
700  ! STEPS 720-770 DETERMINE TOTAL WAITING TIME OF ALL
710  ! CUSTOMERS AND LONGEST INDIVIDUAL WAITING TIME
720        LET T = 0
730        FOR I = 2 TO N
740        LET W = W + W(I)
750        IF W(I) < T GOTO 770
760        LET T = W(I)
770        NEXT I
800  ! STEPS 820-830 DETERMINE AVERAGE WAITING TIME AND
810  ! LONGEST WAITING LINE
820        LET A = W/N
830        LET L = INT(T/25) + 1
900  ! STEPS 910-930 PRINT OUT RESULTS
910        PRINT "THE AVERAGE WAITING TIME IS";A
920        PRINT "THE LONGEST INDIVIDUAL WAITING TIME IS";T
930        PRINT "THE LONGEST WAITING LINE IS";L
940  END

NUMBER OF CUSTOMERS PER DAY? 15
THE AVERAGE WAITING TIME IS 18.8
THE LONGEST INDIVIDUAL WAITING TIME IS 42
THE LONGEST WAITING LINE IS 2
```

Fig. 1

```
100 ! PROGRAM TO DETERMINE MEANS
110 ! AND STANDARD DEVIATIONS,
120 ! INPUT IS NO. OF ITEMS TO BE
130 ! ANALYZED AND THE DATA,
140 ! OUTPUT IS ARITHMETIC MEAN
150 ! AND STANDARD DEVIATION
200 ! STEPS 220-300 INPUT DATA
201 ! AND DETERMINE SUMS AND
202 ! SUMS OF SQUARES OF DATA
220    INPUT "HOW MANY NUMBERS?";N
230    INPUT "FIRST NUMBER";X
240    LET S = S + X
250    LET T = T + X*X
260    FOR I = 2 TO N
270    INPUT "NEXT NUMBER";X
280    LET S = S + X
290    LET T = T + X*X
300    NEXT I
400 ! STEPS 410-420 CALCULATE
401 ! MEAN AND STANDARD DEVIATION
410    LET A = S/N
420    LET D = SQR((T-S*S/N)/(N-1))
500 ! PRINT OUT RESULTS
510    PRINT "THE MEAN IS";A
520    PRINT "THE ST. DEV. IS";D
600 END
```

```
HOW MANY NUMBERS? 20
FIRST NUMBER 14.5333
NEXT NUMBER 18.2
NEXT NUMBER 19.8
NEXT NUMBER 12.9333
NEXT NUMBER 8.73333
NEXT NUMBER 25.4
NEXT NUMBER 16.3333
NEXT NUMBER 15.8667
NEXT NUMBER 18.8
NEXT NUMBER 39.0667
NEXT NUMBER 21.0667
NEXT NUMBER 28.26667
NEXT NUMBER 7.33333
NEXT NUMBER 28.6667
NEXT NUMBER 8.6
NEXT NUMBER 35.1333
NEXT NUMBER 7.06667
NEXT NUMBER 39.8
NEXT NUMBER 21.4667
NEXT NUMBER 13.4
THE MEAN IS 20.0233
THE ST. DEV. IS 10.0098
```

Fig. 2

The program can also be used to generate data for barbershops with a daily number of customers other than fifteen. Table 2 shows the average of three hundred days' experience in the barber queue for each number of customers per day.

TABLE 2
AVERAGE WAITING TIMES FOR 300 DAYS
EXPERIENCE IN A BARBER QUEUE OF n CUSTOMERS
$(10 \leq n \leq 25)$

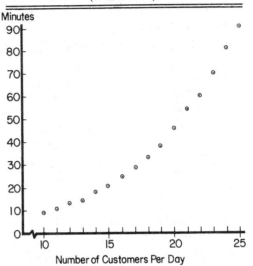

The graph represents a discrete exponential function. Students can obtain a similar graph by plotting the averages of data obtained from several runs of the program, although the random nature of the arrivals will not provide a perfect exponential on any given number of finite sets of data.

This model of the one-chair barbershop gives students some understanding of the modeling process and the major ideas involved in queuing. After using this model the teacher may take the opportunity to discuss some of the theory and practice of mathematical modeling, emphasizing that after as much information as possible is gleaned from this model a more sophisticated model can be constructed, which incorporates more of the real-life situation. Other aspects of queues in barbershops that might be considered include the following:

1. The length of time needed to cut hair is not constant, but varies according to some distribution, perhaps a Poisson distribution.

2. The barber speeds up the haircuts if more people are waiting in line.
3. The barber takes appointments as well as walk-ins.
4. The number of customers varies from day to day.
5. If the waiting line is too long, the customer does not join the queue.
6. More customers come in during certain periods of the day.

Persons desiring to explore queuing further may go in many different directions. Study of the two-chair barbershop, the *n*-chair barbershop, and the limiting infinite-chair barbershop provides opportunity to introduce many ideas from mathematics. Service facilities that open or close service ports according to the number of individuals or objects waiting to be served also provide many interesting occasions for using the computer as a simulation device.

A short bibliography of books where one may get information about mathematical modeling or queuing theory follows. The two operations research books are among the most widely used operations research books in the United States. They contain voluminous information about queueing and other modeling situations and are written at a level understandable to most teachers of secondary school mathematics. Saaty's book, *Thinking with Models,* is a compendium of modeling theory and examples of mathematical models, most of which would be of interest to secondary school teachers and students. The book by Maki and Thompson contains much information on queuing and, in general, attempts to present mathematical modeling from a rigorous point of view. Almost any book on operations research will contain a section on queuing.

BIBLIOGRAPHY

Hillier, Frederick S., and Gerald J. Lieberman. *Introduction to Operations Research,* 2d ed. San Francisco: Holden-Day, 1974.

Maki, Daniel, and Maynard Thompson. *Mathematical Models and Applications.* Englewood Cliffs, N. J.: Prentice-Hall, 1973.

Saaty, Thomas L. *Thinking with Models.* AAAS Study Guides on Contemporary Problems, No. 9. Washington, D.C.: American Association for the Advancement of Science, 1975.

Wagner, Harvey M. *Principles of Operations Research.* Englewood Cliffs, N.J.: Prentice-Hall, 1975.

Game Theory: An Application of Probability

By ROBERT E. RECTOR, Indiana State University, Terre Haute, IN 47809

In searching for topics to include in a summer honors seminar for high school students, we have found game theory to be a most appropriate area of study. The directors of the seminar determined that the program of study for these academically talented high school students should include topics that are unfamiliar, interesting, challenging (but understandable), and adaptable to applications. The theory of games meets these criteria and has proved to be a successful segment of the program. We would recommend it highly as a final topic in a unit on probability or as a topic for a mathematics club. Matrix notation

---

Morra provides an excellent introduction to game theory.

---

and matrix operations provide a model for analyzing certain situations involving conflict. Probability theory can be used to determine the best strategies for the players.

The ancient game of morra provides an excellent introduction to game theory. In one version of morra, each of two players, say R and C, simultaneously extends one or two fingers from a closed fist. If the sum of the number of fingers shown is even, then C pays R that amount in dollars. If the sum is odd, then R pays C that amount. Several questions arise immediately. Does the game favor either player? If so, which player has the advantage? What is the best strategy for each player? How can it be determined?

Many people conclude that this game is fair and that each player should extend one finger one-half the time. Actually, using only the concepts of probability, mathemat-

ical expectation, and elementary algebra, we can show that the game favors the odd-sum player (player C) and that if player C plays wisely, he or she will win an average of 8 1/3 cents a game over an extended period of play.

The even-odd morra game is representative of games that are two-person, finite, zero-sum, and strictly competitive. That is, the game involves two competitors; a finite number of moves or courses of action are available to each player; the amount lost by one player is equal to the amount won by the other (zero-sum); and each player plays wisely, rationally, and selfishly—cooperation is never advantageous (strictly competitive).

Any game having the properties just described can be modeled by an $m \times n$ matrix called a *payoff matrix*. The m rows of the matrix contain the payoffs associated with the m moves or courses of action available to player R, and the n columns contain the payoffs associated with the n moves available to player C. In particular, each entry a_{ij} in a payoff matrix represents the payoff to R when player R selects move i and player C selects move j. We define a_{ij} as positive if C pays R and negative (a negative payoff to R) if R pays C. If R and C tie or break even, then $a_{ij} = 0$.

For example, the possible moves and resulting payoffs for the even-odd morra game can be displayed as shown in figure 1. The

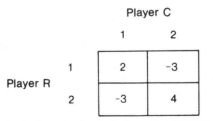

Fig. 1. Moves and payoffs for even-odd morra

numbers outside the cells denote the moves (extend one finger or two fingers) available to each player. The numbers within the cells denote the associated payoffs for each combination of moves by the players. Thus, the payoff matrix is

$$\mathbf{A} = \begin{bmatrix} 2 & -3 \\ -3 & 4 \end{bmatrix}.$$

If a player uses the same move in every game, then the selection of moves is called a *pure strategy*. If a player selects from the available moves in some varying, unpredictable (random) fashion, then the set of moves is called a *mixed strategy*. Any selection of a finite number of moves is called a *strategy*. It is possible to represent each strategy available to a player as a probability distribution on the set of moves in that strategy. In a game represented by an $m \times n$ matrix, a strategy for player R can be written as a row probability vector,

$$\mathbf{P} = [p_1 \quad p_2 \quad \cdots \quad p_m],$$

where each p_i for $i = 1, 2, \ldots, m$ denotes the probability that player R selects move i. Note that $p_i \geq 0$ for $i = 1, 2, \ldots, m$ and $\sum p_i = 1$. Each strategy for C can be represented by a column probability vector,

$$\mathbf{Q} = \begin{bmatrix} q_1 \\ q_2 \\ \vdots \\ q_n \end{bmatrix},$$

where each q_j for $j = 1, 2, \ldots, n$ denotes the probability that player C selects move j. Similarly, $q_j \geq 0$ for $j = 1, 2, \ldots, n$ and $\sum q_j = 1$. If some entry in a strategy $\mathbf{P}$ (or $\mathbf{Q}$) is 1, then all other entries must be 0 and $\mathbf{P}$ (or $\mathbf{Q}$) is a pure strategy.

The objective of game theory is to determine the best, or optimal, strategy for a given game. An *optimal strategy* can be defined as one that either maximizes the gains of a player or minimizes the losses, if a loss is unavoidable, regardless of the strategy adopted by the opponent. In 1928 John von Neumann, the founder of modern game theory, proved the remarkable theorem that at least one optimal strategy exists for each

player in any finite, zero-sum, two-person game.

Now let us analyze the even-odd morra game described previously. An examination of the payoff matrix for this game suggests that each player should select from the available moves (extend one finger or two fingers) in some varying manner. That is, the optimal strategies for R and C will be mixed strategies. The optimal strategy for R can be represented by the row probability vector

$$\mathbf{P}^* = [p_1^* \quad p_2^*],$$

where p_1^* and p_2^* denote the probabilities (in effect the percentage of time) R should extend one finger and two fingers, respec-

At least one optimal strategy exists for each player.

tively, to maximize his or her gains (or minimize his or her losses). Similarly, the optimal strategy for C can be denoted by the column probability vector

$$\mathbf{Q}^* = \begin{bmatrix} q_1^* \\ q_2^* \end{bmatrix}.$$

Our goal is to find the values p_1^*, p_2^*, q_1^*, and q_2^*.

We begin by considering the expected value of the game for various mixtures of moves. In general, the expected payoff to a player for a matrix game can be found by computing the mathematical expectation. Suppose a game has payoff matrix $\mathbf{A}$ and strategies $\mathbf{P}$ and $\mathbf{Q}$ (expressed in matrix form), as follows,

$$\mathbf{A} = \begin{bmatrix} a_{11} & a_{12} \\ a_{21} & a_{22} \end{bmatrix},$$
$$\mathbf{P} = [p_1 \quad p_2],$$
$$\mathbf{Q} = \begin{bmatrix} q_1 \\ q_2 \end{bmatrix},$$

where $p_1 + p_2 = 1$ and $q_1 + q_2 = 1$. The payoff a_{11} will occur only if R selects move 1 and C selects move 1. Hence, the probability that payoff a_{11} occurs is $p_1 q_1$. Likewise, the probabilities of payoffs a_{12}, a_{21}, and a_{22}

are p_1q_2, p_2q_1, and p_2q_2, respectively. The expected value of the game, denoted by $E(\mathbf{P}, \mathbf{Q})$ when R uses strategy $\mathbf{P}$ and C uses strategy $\mathbf{Q}$, is

$$E(\mathbf{P}, \mathbf{Q}) = p_1q_1a_{11} + p_1q_2a_{12} + p_2q_1a_{21}$$
$$+ p_2q_2a_{22}.$$

Note that the right side of this expression is precisely the lone entry in the matrix product $\mathbf{PAQ}$.

From the convention we adopted, it is clear that when $E(\mathbf{P}, \mathbf{Q}) > 0$, the game is favorable to R and when $E(\mathbf{P}, \mathbf{Q}) < 0$, the game is favorable to C, in the amount $|E(\mathbf{P}, \mathbf{Q})|$, on the average, for each game played. If $E(\mathbf{P}, \mathbf{Q}) = 0$, then neither player has the advantage and the game is said to be *fair*.

Example: Find the expectation of R (the expected payoff of C to R) in the even-odd morra game if R extends each of one and two fingers one-half the time and C extends one finger one-third of the time and two fingers two-thirds of the time.

Solution:

$$\mathbf{PAQ} = \begin{bmatrix} \frac{1}{2} & \frac{1}{2} \end{bmatrix} \cdot \begin{bmatrix} 2 & -3 \\ -3 & 4 \end{bmatrix} \cdot \begin{bmatrix} \frac{1}{3} \\ \frac{2}{3} \end{bmatrix}$$

$$= \begin{bmatrix} \frac{1}{6} \end{bmatrix}$$

$$\therefore E(\mathbf{P}, \mathbf{Q}) = \frac{1}{6}$$

In this example, it is clear that for the strategies assumed, the morra game favors player R. In this case, R can expect to win an average of 1/6 of a dollar a game provided the game is played a large number of times. However, are these the best strategies for players R and C? The goal of game theory is to find optimal strategies. To investigate this question, we can without loss of generality focus again on player R.

To find the optimal strategy $\mathbf{P^*}$ for player R in the even-odd morra game, we must find the strategy that assures R as large an expectation as possible regardless of the strategy adopted by C. That is, the optimal strategy for R can be found by de-

termining the maximum of all minimum expectations $E(\mathbf{P}, \mathbf{Q})$ for the set of *all* possible strategies $\mathbf{Q}$ available to C. This task is greatly simplified by the fact that this maximum expectation is always attained when $\mathbf{Q}$ is one of C's pure strategies. A proof of this assertion is given by Owen (1982). Thus to find the maximum expectation for R, we need look only at C's pure strategies,

$$\mathbf{Q}_1 = \begin{bmatrix} 1 \\ 0 \end{bmatrix} \quad \text{and} \quad \mathbf{Q}_2 = \begin{bmatrix} 0 \\ 1 \end{bmatrix}.$$

To find the optimal strategy $\mathbf{P^*}$ for R, let x denote the probability that R chooses move 1 (extends one finger). Then $1 - x$ is the probability that R selects move 2. Now, if C chooses the first pure strategy described earlier, the expected payoff, E, to player R is found by computing the product $\mathbf{PAQ}_1$. Thus

$$\mathbf{PAQ}_1 = \begin{bmatrix} x & 1-x \end{bmatrix} \cdot \begin{bmatrix} 2 & -3 \\ -3 & 4 \end{bmatrix} \cdot \begin{bmatrix} 1 \\ 0 \end{bmatrix}$$
$$= [5x - 3];$$
$$\therefore E = 5x - 3.$$

Similarly, if C selects the second pure strategy,

$$\mathbf{PAQ}_2 = \begin{bmatrix} x & 1-x \end{bmatrix} \cdot \begin{bmatrix} 2 & -3 \\ -3 & 4 \end{bmatrix} \cdot \begin{bmatrix} 0 \\ 1 \end{bmatrix}$$
$$= [-7x + 4];$$
$$\therefore E = -7x + 4.$$

The graphs of the two lines representing the expected payoffs to R as x varies from 0 to 1 are given in figure 2.

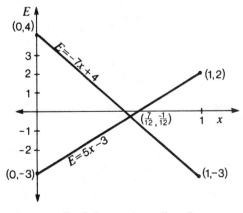

Fig. 2. Expected payoffs to R

The optimal strategy for R is the maximum of the minimum expectations (the best of the worst). An examination of the graph reveals that the minimum expectations (the smallest amounts that can be won) are represented by the points of the lines $E = 5x - 3$ and $E = -7x + 4$, which are below the point of intersection. Graphically, therefore, it is apparent that the optimal strategy for R (the maximum of the minimum values of E) occurs where the two lines intersect. The abscissa of the point of intersection is p_1^*, the probability that R should select move 1. The ordinate is E^*, the expected value of the game when the optimal strategies are employed. To find the coordinate of the point of intersection, we set the two expressions representing the expectations equal to each other and solve for x. Hence,

$$5x - 3 = -7x + 4.$$

Therefore,

$$x = \frac{7}{12}; \qquad 1 - x = \frac{5}{12}.$$

Substituting 7/12 for x in either equation for E yields

$$E^* = \frac{-1}{12}.$$

Since $p_1^* = x$ and $p_2^* = 1 - x$, the optimal strategy for R is

$$\mathbf{P}^* = \begin{bmatrix} \dfrac{7}{12} & \dfrac{5}{12} \end{bmatrix}.$$

In a similar manner it can be shown that the optimal strategy for C is

$$\mathbf{Q}^* = \begin{bmatrix} \dfrac{7}{12} \\[2mm] \dfrac{5}{12} \end{bmatrix},$$

and again $E^* = \frac{-1}{12}$. Thus, $\frac{7}{12}$ of the time C should extend one finger, and $\frac{5}{12}$ of the time, two fingers. If C adopts this strategy and if the game is played a large number of times, C will win an average of $\frac{1}{12}$ of a dollar (8 1/3 cents) a game regardless of the strategy adopted by R. This is a powerful, nonintuitive statement. Students are urged to verify

this assertion by proving that if

$$\mathbf{Q} = \begin{bmatrix} \dfrac{7}{12} \\[2mm] \dfrac{5}{12} \end{bmatrix}, \qquad \mathbf{A} = \begin{bmatrix} 2 & -3 \\ -3 & 4 \end{bmatrix},$$

and $\mathbf{P}$ is *any* arbitrary strategy $[x \quad 1 - x]$, then $E^* = \frac{-1}{12}$. Similarly, if R selects his or her optimal strategy, he or she will lose 1/12 of a dollar a game in the long run. Only if *both* players deviate from their opti-

Some results are not intuitive.

mal strategies can player C win more or player R lose more than this amount. Also, students can check these assertions by playing the game. A dodecahedron die, with seven faces labeled "1" and five faces labeled "2," is an excellent device to enable a student to implement either of the strategies

$$\mathbf{P}^* = \begin{bmatrix} \dfrac{7}{12} & \dfrac{5}{12} \end{bmatrix} \quad \text{or} \quad \mathbf{Q}^* = \begin{bmatrix} \dfrac{7}{12} \\[2mm] \dfrac{5}{12} \end{bmatrix}$$

in a random manner.

Optimal strategies for any nonstrictly determined 2×2 matrix game can be found by using the techniques given for the even-odd morra game. Let the payoff matrix be denoted by

$$\mathbf{A} = \begin{bmatrix} a_{11} & a_{12} \\ a_{21} & a_{22} \end{bmatrix}.$$

The individual components of the optimal strategies

$$\mathbf{P}^* = [p_1^* \quad p_2^*]$$

and

$$\mathbf{Q}^* = \begin{bmatrix} q_1^* \\ q_2^* \end{bmatrix}$$

are given by the following formulas:

$$p_1^* = \frac{a_{22} - a_{21}}{a_{11} + a_{22} - a_{12} - a_{21}}$$

$$p_2^* = \frac{a_{11} - a_{12}}{a_{11} + a_{22} - a_{12} - a_{21}}$$

$$q_1^* = \frac{a_{22} - a_{12}}{a_{11} + a_{22} - a_{12} - a_{21}}$$

$$q_2^* = \frac{a_{11} - a_{21}}{a_{11} + a_{22} - a_{12} - a_{21}}$$

In another version of morra, called *matching morra,* each of two players, R and C, simultaneously extends zero or two fingers. If a match occurs, R wins the sum in dollars of the number of fingers shown. If no match occurs, then C pays R the sum. The payoff matrix for this game is

$$\mathbf{A} = \begin{bmatrix} 0 & -2 \\ -2 & 4 \end{bmatrix}.$$

Using the formulas given previously, show that the game again favors player C. Also, find the optimal strategy for each player and show that if C selects his or her optimal strategy, he or she will win an average of 50 cents a game in the long run regardless of the strategy adopted by R.

Although the formulas given here apply only to mixed-strategy matrix games of size 2 × 2, techniques have been developed to reduce some special game matrices of higher order to 2 × 2. Also, methods have been developed to solve the special cases of m × 2 games and 2 × n games. Additionally, in 1951, Dantzig proved that every two-person, zero-sum game is equivalent to a linear-programming problem and its dual. This finding allowed for the easy calculation of the optimal strategies for any m × n matrix game using the simplex method. The simplex method is a computational procedure for solving linear-programming problems. A simple introduction to these concepts and procedures can be found in most books on finite mathematics, including those by Rector and Zwick (1979) and Anton and Kolman (1982).

BIBLIOGRAPHY

Andree, Josephine P., ed. *Theory of Games.* Lines from the O. U. Mathematics Letter, vol. 2. Norman, Okla.: Mu Alpha Theta, 1971. (Available from NCTM)

Anton, Howard, and Bernard Kolman. *Applied Finite Mathematics.* 3d ed., New York: Academic Press, 1982.

Dantzig, George B. "A Proof of the Equivalence of the Programming Problem and the Game Problem." In *Activity Analysis of Production and Allocation,* Cowles Commission for Research in Economics, Monograph No. 13. New York: John Wiley & Sons, 1951.

Luce, R. Duncan, and Howard Riaffa. *Games and Decisions.* New York: John Wiley & Sons, 1957.

Owen, Guillermo. *Game Theory.* 2d ed. New York: Academic Press, 1982.

Rector, Robert E., and Earl J. Zwick. *Finite Mathematics and Its Applications.* Boston: Houghton Mifflin Co., 1979.

von Neumann, John, and Oskar Morgenstein. *Theory of Games and Economic Behavior.* Princeton, N.J.: Princeton University Press, 1953. ☙

ANNOTATED BIBLIOGRAPHY

Readers interested in learning more about applications in mathematics should consult the following sources. Some have been referenced in the introductions to the chapters.

Consortium of Mathematics and Its Applications (COMAP). 60 Lowell Street, Arlington, MA 02174.

COMAP publishes a newsletter, *Consortium*, containing applications of mathematics appropriate for precollege mathematics instruction. Modules on applications can be purchased for a nominal amount. A more advanced journal, *UMAP*, is devoted to applications of mathematics for college-level mathematics instruction.

Eves, Howard. *Great Moments in Mathematics*. 2 vols. Washington, D.C.: Mathematical Association of America, 1983.

These two books provide extremely readable accounts of the historical development of mathematics. Both books have historical applications as well as exercises and references for additional reading on each topic considered.

Kline, Morris. *Mathematical Thought from Ancient to Modern Times*. New York: Oxford University Press, 1972.

This three-volume series is a rich source of information about the problems that were instrumental in the development of mathematics. The chapters have extensive references for additional reading, though the books have no exercises.

Kline, Morris, ed. *Mathematics: An Introduction to Its Spirit and Use*. San Francisco: W. H. Freeman & Co., 1979.

This book contains a series of readings from *Scientific American* on mathematics and is an excellent source for information on mathematics and its applications. Many articles discuss problems and solutions in historical papers.

National Council of Teachers of Mathematics. *Applications in School Mathematics*. 1979 Yearbook of the National Council of Teachers of Mathematics, edited by Sidney Sharron. Reston, Va.: The Council, 1979.

This yearbook has articles on the classroom use of applications and gives many examples with suggestions on how they can be used in teaching and learning mathematics.

———. *Historical Topics for the Mathematics Classroom*. Thirty-first Yearbook of the National Council of Teachers of Mathematics. 2d ed. Reston, Va.: The Council, 1989.

This is an excellent single-volume reference on most mathematics taught in secondary schools. (Statistics is not included.) The index makes it easy to find a particular reference. Although there are no exercises and the mathematical problems are often not solved, the historical problems that are solved are well suited to classroom use.

Resnikoff, H. J., and R. O. Wells, Jr. *Mathematics in Civilization*. New York: Dover Publications, 1984.

This one-volume survey text on the historical development of mathematics offers a sampling of historical problems with solutions and exercises.

Steen, Lynn Arthur, ed. *Mathematics Today: Twelve Informal Essays*. New York: Springer-Verlag New York, 1978.

This book is a very readable overview of current applications of and research in mathematics.

INDEX A

Application Area

335

INDEX B

Mathematical Topic

Trigonometry and Elementary Anaysis

Calculus